Analyzing Energy Crises and the Impact of Country Policies on the World

Merve Suna Ozel Ozcan
Kirikkale University, Turkey

IGI Global
PUBLISHER of TIMELY KNOWLEDGE

A volume in the Advances in Public Policy and Administration (APPA) Book Series

Published in the United States of America by
IGI Global
Engineering Science Reference (an imprint of IGI Global)
701 E. Chocolate Avenue
Hershey PA, USA 17033
Tel: 717-533-8845
Fax: 717-533-8661
E-mail: cust@igi-global.com
Web site: http://www.igi-global.com

Library of Congress Cataloging-in-Publication Data

Names: Özel Özcan, Merve, 1988- editor.
Title: Analyzing energy crises and the impact of country polices on the world / edited by Merve Özel Özcan.
Other titles: Corrected title: Analyzing energy crises and the impact of country policies on the world
Description: Hershey, PA : Engineering Science Reference, [2024] | Includes bibliographical references and index. | Summary: "The impact of energy crises can be mitigated or exacerbated by the policies implemented by different countries. This book aims to analyze the various types of energy crises worldwide and examine the impact of country policies on energy crises from the past to the present"-- Provided by publisher.
Identifiers: LCCN 2023038630 (print) | LCCN 2023038631 (ebook) | ISBN 9798369304402 (hardcover) | ISBN 9798369304419 (paperback) | ISBN 9798369304426 (ebook)
Subjects: LCSH: Energy policy. | Petroleum products--Prices. | Petroleum reserves--Political aspects. | Petroleum industry and trade--Political aspects. | Energy consumption.
Classification: LCC HD9502.A2 A568 2024 (print) | LCC HD9502.A2 (ebook) | DDC 333.79--dc23/eng/20230905
LC record available at https://lccn.loc.gov/2023038630
LC ebook record available at https://lccn.loc.gov/2023038631

This book is published in the IGI Global book series Advances in Public Policy and Administration (APPA) (ISSN: 2475-6644; eISSN: 2475-6652)

British Cataloguing in Publication Data
A Cataloguing in Publication record for this book is available from the British Library.

Advances in Public Policy and Administration (APPA) Book Series

ISSN:2475-6644
EISSN:2475-6652

Mission

Proper management of the public sphere is necessary in order to maintain order in modern society. Research developments in the field of public policy and administration can assist in uncovering the latest tools, practices, and methodologies for governing societies around the world.

The **Advances in Public Policy and Administration (APPA) Book Series** aims to publish scholarly publications focused on topics pertaining to the governance of the public domain. APPA's focus on timely topics relating to government, public funding, politics, public safety, policy, and law enforcement is particularly relevant to academicians, government officials, and upper-level students seeking the most up-to-date research in their field.

Coverage

- Government
- Law Enforcement
- Political Economy
- Politics
- Public Administration
- Public Funding
- Public Policy
- Resource allocation
- Urban Planning

IGI Global is currently accepting manuscripts for publication within this series. To submit a proposal for a volume in this series, please contact our Acquisition Editors at Acquisitions@igi-global.com or visit: http://www.igi-global.com/publish/.

The Advances in Public Policy and Administration (APPA) Book Series (ISSN 2475-6644) is published by IGI Global, 701 E. Chocolate Avenue, Hershey, PA 17033-1240, USA, www.igi-global.com. This series is composed of titles available for purchase individually; each title is edited to be contextually exclusive from any other title within the series. For pricing and ordering information please visit http://www.igi-global.com/book-series/advances-public-policy-administration/97862. Postmaster: Send all address changes to above address.

Titles in this Series

For a list of additional titles in this series, please visit: http://www.igi-global.com/book-series/advances-public-policy-administration/97862

Using Crises and Disasters as Opportunities for Innovation and Improvement
Saeed Siyal (School of Economics and Management, Beijing University of Chemical Technology, China)
Information Science Reference • copyright 2024 • 323pp • H/C (ISBN: 9781668495223) • US $240.00 (our price)

Cognitive Governance and the Historical Distortion of the Norm of Modern Development A Theory of Political Asymmetry
Renny Rueda (American University in the Emirates, UAE)
Information Science Reference • copyright 2024 • 254pp • H/C (ISBN: 9781668497944) • US $215.00 (our price)

Financial Evaluation and Risk Management of Infrastructure Projects
Kleopatra Petroutsatou (Aristotle University of Thessaloniki, Greece) and Constantin Zopounidis (Technical University of Crete, Greece & Audencia Business School, France)
Information Science Reference • copyright 2024 • 248pp • H/C (ISBN: 9781668477861) • US $225.00 (our price)

Policies, Practices, and Protocols for International Commercial Arbitration
Basheer Ahmed Mohammed Khan (Supreme Court of India Bar Association, India) and Kaushal Kishore (Supreme Court of India Bar Association, New Delhi, India)
Information Science Reference • copyright 2023 • 271pp • H/C (ISBN: 9781668440407) • US $225.00 (our price)

Governmental Power Market-Ing in the VU-CHAOS World
Kittisak Jermsittiparsert (University of City Island, Cyprus) Srirath Gohwong (Universitas Muhammadiyah Sidenreng Rappang, Indonesia) Shayut Pavapanunkul (Universitas Muhammadiyah Sidenreng Rappang, Indonesia) and Nasaran Mahittichatkul (Universitas Muhammadiyah Sidenreng Rappang, Indonesia)
Information Science Reference • copyright 2023 • 296pp • H/C (ISBN: 9781668472804) • US $205.00 (our price)

Historical and Political Analysis on Power Balances and Deglobalization
Emily Brynn Stacey (Rose State College, USA)
Information Science Reference • copyright 2023 • 253pp • H/C (ISBN: 9781668456330) • US $205.00 (our price)

Juvenile Justice in African and Western Criminal Justice Systems
Simeon Peter Sungi (United States International University-Africa, Kenya) George Rugaimukamu Kakoti (Tennessee State University, USA) and Deneil D. Christian (Tennessee State University, USA)
Information Science Reference • copyright 2024 • 300pp • H/C (ISBN: 9781668493434) • US $215.00 (our price)

IGI Global
PUBLISHER of TIMELY KNOWLEDGE

701 East Chocolate Avenue, Hershey, PA 17033, USA
Tel: 717-533-8845 x100 • Fax: 717-533-8661
E-Mail: cust@igi-global.com • www.igi-global.com

Table of Contents

Detailed Table of Contents

In the last two decades, the world has been under the influence of various crises experienced by countries trying to meet the increasing energy demand, especially after the Second World War, using exhaustible resources. In addition to the relations, conflicts, and disagreements between countries, regions, and economic cooperation, the fact that global warming is becoming a climate crisis more and more every day has forced the energy market to seek different quests. This study blends critical theoretical information, such as how and to what extent renewable energy sources can be used based on sustainable economic conditions and how much potential they can offer, with practical examples and suggestions. This study will likely provide guiding implications for decision-makers in the economies of countries that shape the world energy market in the future and will present some innovative ideas for future studies in this field.

Chapter 4
Navigating Investment Risks in the Renewable Energy Market of Developing Countries: Efficiency vs. Effectiveness.. 54
Aida Guliyeva, Azerbaijan State University of Economy, Azerbaijan
Ulviyya Rzayeva, Azerbaijan State University of Economics, Azerbaijan
Aslan Azimzadeh, Azerbaijan State University of Economy, Azerbaijan

The chapter deals with investment risks in the energy markets. Two important aspects are compared: efficiency and effectiveness. Efficiency is related to the optimal use of resources, both financial and human, to achieve goals. Efficiency is assessed by the achievement of the final goals and expected results. Investment risk management in the energy sector of developing countries requires a balance between efficiency and effectiveness. The chapter gives unexpected results in the management of investment risks in the renewable energy market in developing countries, which may be interesting and meaningful for discussion and further research. An accurate assessment of investment risks in alternative energy and fossil energy depends on specific conditions, regional characteristics, and other factors. However, in the long term, there are arguments in favor of the fact that investment risks in alternative energy may be higher than the risks of investments in fossil energy.

Chapter 5
Oil Prices and Spain's Interest Rates: Did the Link Change After EU Accession?.............................. 82
Rebeca Jiménez-Rodríguez, University of Salamanca, Spain
Marcelo Sanchez, European Central Bank, Germany

This chapter studies the impact of oil shocks on Spain's short-term interest rates. In so doing, it investigates whether the connection between these two variables changed after 1986 – a period marked by both Spain's EU accession and the move to interest rates as the monetary policy instrument. For the period after 1986, we find that, in response to oil shocks, real short-term interest rates tended to rise, while nominal interest rates increased only gradually. Oil prices impacted interest rates in periods of high oil prices, such as that around the 1990 spike and in some instances since 1999. The increase in interest rates after an oil price shock contributed to reducing inflation, while also making the economic slowdown more marked. The main results are not robust to starting the estimation in 1970, implying that monetary policy became more restrictive in reaction to oil price changes after EU accession.

Chapter 6
EU's Energy Policy and Assessing Europe's Spiraling Energy Security Crises 101
Mukesh Shankar Bharti, Amity University, India

the Soviet era, they were energy peripheries of the Union. Post dissolution, these nations reaped the rents generated from hydrocarbons which translated to economic development in the region. However, Kyrgyzstan and Tajikistan are hydrocarbon energy poor and do not dominate the geopolitics of Central Asia. However, it is critical to note that the ecology of Central Asia was massively impacted by Soviet projects in the regions, for instance the nuclear waste in Kazakhstan or the drying up of the Aral Sea and the Belt and Road Initiative projects since 2013. Nations have announced their net-zero targets and doled out renewable energy projects. This chapter will compare the renewable energy policies of Central Asian countries.

The continuation of the worsening climate crisis and the severe environmental degradation caused by fossil fuels is not sustainable for the world. It is important for major energy suppliers and importing countries to turn to renewable energy to meet the intense demand for energy and for future generations. In addition, governments are turning to renewable energy sources and increasing their investments in order to reduce foreign dependency in an economic and political context. Therefore, renewable energy strategies offer new opportunities for competitive strategies and cooperation in the world. This study evaluates the current renewable energy studies and investments of the Turkish Republics. In addition, policy recommendations will be made within the framework of the possible economic/political effects of these resources, which will create potential in the long run for the countries.

The aim of this chapter is to shed light on the industry-politics nexus in resource-rich Algeria with emphasis on the connection between hydrocarbon processing industry and the economic-political goals of the Algerian state. The chapter involves a historical and political inquiry by focusing on the change in economic and technological capacity of the industry over the years, drawing attention to the relevant developments in domestic and foreign policy, as well as their reflections in Algeria's energy policy. The development of the Algerian hydrocarbon industry within a period of 70 years is investigated in terms of anti-colonialism, nationalism, and rentier relations between the state and interest groups (i.e., elites, foreign states, and international companies).

Efficient energy utilization should contribute to poverty alleviation in developing countries. A society that successfully shifted from non-modern sources of energy consumption to modern ones is said to witness more significant development. In developing countries such as Nigeria, inefficient modern energy use

Preface

As we find ourselves at the crossroads of history and progress, the world is increasingly shaped by the energy we generate and consume. It is a powerful force that drives our industries, powers our homes, and fuels our aspirations. From the modest beginnings of oil's industrial applications in the 19th century to the intricate web of international relations that it weaves today, the journey of energy has been truly transformative. In the 20th century, energy's indispensable role in global security and geopolitics became ever more apparent, giving rise to a fundamental question: How do we secure and sustain our energy future in the face of an uncertain world?The concept of energy crises, with their profound economic, social, and political repercussions, has gripped nations, regions, and the entire globe. Energy, or the lack thereof, can be a catalyst for stability or strife, cooperation or conflict. In this edited reference book, "Analyzing Energy Crises and the Impact of Country Policies on the World," we delve into the multifaceted dynamics of energy crises and explore the critical role of national policies in shaping the energy landscape. Our journey takes us through the historical tapestry of energy crises, offering insights into their root causes and historical context.

As editor, my aim is twofold. First, I seek to offer a comprehensive analysis of the different manifestations of energy crises worldwide, spanning from past episodes to the challenges of the present day. Second, I endeavor to provide a roadmap for policymakers, energy industry stakeholders, academics, researchers, and students, guiding them in crafting strategies to mitigate the impacts of energy crises and foster a more sustainable and secure global energy system. The importance of these objectives cannot be overstated, as the decisions we make today will influence the well-being of generations to come.

The reference book's structure is designed to systematically address complex issues related to energy. We explore the historical background of energy crises and the evolution of concerns regarding energy security. We categorize energy crises into various types, including supply-side and demand-side issues, and examine their environmental impacts. The role of geopolitics in fueling or alleviating energy crises is examined closely, illuminating the global dynamics at play. We investigate the impact of national policies on energy crises, an area where strategic decisions can either ameliorate or exacerbate the challenges we face. This reference book also delves into the economic and social impacts of energy crises on both producing and consuming countries, further underscoring the far-reaching consequences of energy shortages and disruptions. Looking forward, we ponder the future of energy and energy policies, contemplating the opportunities and uncertainties that lie ahead.

To illustrate these concepts, we present case studies from diverse countries and regions, each facing its unique energy challenges. From the resource-rich Middle East to the energy powerhouse of Russia, the complexities of energy in Africa, and the surging demand in China, we cover a range of geographic areas, examining the interplay of local policies and global trends. Central Asia, the Far East, India, and the European Union are also spotlighted, demonstrating the intricate mosaic of energy landscapes that shape our world.

In Chapter 1, Dr. Emine Erden Kaya and Dr. Şeyma Eşki Çaylak provide a critical examination of the recent energy crises, with a particular focus on how they have been exacerbated by global events such as the Covid-19 pandemic and the Russia-Ukraine conflict. It highlights the disruptive effects on the supply-demand balance and the resulting impact on the world economy. The chapter also explores how the world's growing population, urbanization, and industrialization have intensified energy demand, especially in regions like the European Union (EU). We delve into how countries, including EU member states, have responded to the current energy crisis with new measures and policies. The comparative analysis of historical perspectives and present-day actions sheds light on how crises influence energy policies and encourage the evaluation of alternative energy sources and technologies. In examining generated energy policies, we aim to present potential solutions for a more secure and sustainable energy future.

In Chapter 2, Assoc. Prof. Dr. Emre Çıtak focuses on the foundational framework for exploring energy and energy policies.It comprehensively covers the meaning of energy, the importance of energy resources, their types and usage, the factors that influence energy policies, energy-related sectors, energy security, and the role of energy security in government policies. Additionally, we delve into the root causes of energy crises, the principles of energy management, and the realm of energy diplomacy. The chapter's aim is to provide readers with a multidimensional understanding of the world of energy in the context of today's developments.

In Chapter 3, Dr. Selçuk Efe Küçükkambak embarks on a journey through the shifting landscape of energy over the last two decades, marked by increasing energy demand and the imperative to transition away from exhaustible resources. The interplay of international relations, regional conflicts, and the escalating climate crisis is explored. This chapter integrates critical theoretical insights into the potential of renewable energy sources under sustainable economic conditions and offers practical examples and suggestions. The study is expected to provide guidance for decision-makers shaping the future of the world energy market and inspire innovative ideas for further research.

In Chapter 4, Lecturer Aslan Azimzadeh, Aida Guliyeva, and Ulviyya Rzayeva delve into the delicate balance of investment risk management in the energy sector, comparing efficiency and effectiveness. It investigates the optimal use of resources, both financial and human, in achieving energy goals, taking into account the final outcomes and expected results. The chapter discusses unexpected results in the management of investment risks in renewable energy markets in developing countries, opening the door to further research and discussion. It emphasizes the importance of context-specific assessments for investment risks in alternative energy and fossil energy.

In Chapter 5, Prof. Rebeca Jiménez-Rodríguez and Marcelo Sanchez investigate the relationship between oil shocks and Spain's short-term interest rates, with a focus on the period after 1986, marked by Spain's EU accession and the shift to interest rates as the monetary policy instrument. The findings reveal the impact of oil price fluctuations on real short-term interest rates and nominal interest rates, especially in times of high oil prices. The chapter underscores how adjustments in interest rates following oil shocks impact inflation and economic slowdown, providing critical insights into the connection between energy and monetary policy.

In Chapter 6, Dr. Mukesh Bharti offers an in-depth analysis of the energy crisis in Europe, highlighting the ongoing challenges that have emerged in recent years. It delves into the EU's efforts to reduce dependence on fossil fuels, particularly from Russia, and explores the reasons behind the limited success in these endeavors. This chapter employs a qualitative approach to decipher empirical data on the EU's energy security policy and its interactions with Russia. It aims to answer critical questions about the EU's measures in response to the energy crisis in Europe and their implications.

In Chapter 7, Researcher Ejazul Haq Ateed examines the far-reaching implications of the Russia-Ukraine war on the global energy crisis, with a focus on the disruptions and uncertainties it has generated in energy flows worldwide. The chapter addresses the vulnerability of crucial energy infrastructure, resulting in reduced natural gas and energy supplies to European nations heavily reliant on Russian exports. It discusses the subsequent fluctuations in energy prices and heightened market volatility, which have spurred nations to seek alternative energy sources and prioritize energy security. This chapter underscores the importance of proactive measures, international cooperation, and resilience building in addressing the challenges of the global energy crisis.

In Chapter 8, Dr. Mohamad Zreik provides a comprehensive analysis of China's energy dilemma, considering its historical and geopolitical context. China's status as the world's largest energy consumer and the challenges posed by rapid industrial growth and fossil fuel dependency are thoroughly examined. The chapter explores China's strategies to diversify its energy supply, increase the use of renewable energy, and enhance energy efficiency, both domestically and in global energy governance. This study sheds light on the implications of China's energy policies for its economy, social stability, environment, and foreign relations. It concludes by offering insights into the future of China's energy plans, with an emphasis on promoting a sustainable and secure global energy system.

In Chapter 9, Ayushi Saini and Rajoli Siddharth Jayaprakash delve into the geopolitical interests and energy dynamics of Central Asian nations, which have been historically shaped by their abundant hydrocarbon resources. The post-Soviet era brought economic development driven by hydrocarbon rents, but it also left a significant environmental footprint in the region. This chapter compares the renewable energy policies of Central Asian countries, taking into account their net-zero targets and renewable energy projects. It offers valuable insights into the future of renewable energy in a region that has been historically defined by its hydrocarbon wealth.

In Chapter 10, Dr. Baybarshan Kazancı, Dr. Selin Dinçer, and Researcher Osman Furkan Arslan address the urgent needs for a transition to renewable energy sources to mitigate the climate crisis and reduce environmental degradation caused by fossil fuels. It examines how governments and major energy suppliers are increasing investments in renewable energy to reduce foreign dependency in economic and political contexts. The chapter evaluates the current state of renewable energy initiatives in the Turkish Republics and offers policy recommendations that consider the potential long-term economic and political effects of these resources.

In Chapter 11, Assoc. Prof. Dr. Mürsel Bayram and Researcher Assistant Mustafa Kurt delve into the complex relationship between Algeria's hydrocarbon processing industry and the economic-political goals of the Algerian state. It explores the historical and political context of the industry's development over seventy years, with an emphasis on its anti-colonialist and nationalist roots. The chapter sheds light on how the evolution of the hydrocarbon industry has impacted domestic and foreign policies, reflecting Algeria's energy policy. It offers a historical and political inquiry into the intricate nexus of industry and politics in a resource-rich nation.

In Chapter 12, Dr. Yusuf Abubakar investigates the connection between efficient energy utilization and poverty alleviation in developing countries, with a focus on the shift from non-modern to modern sources of energy consumption. It explores how improving modern energy usage can enhance society's well-being, the physical environment, and production. The chapter aims to establish the relationship between modern energy efficiency, health improvement, wealth, environmental protection, wealth, and increased production wealth. It tests the hypothesis that higher modern energy utilization leads to lower poverty levels in society and offers insights into how efficient energy utilization can alleviate poverty

In the final chapter, Lecturer Lütfi Tututş explores the transformative role of liquefied natural gas (LNG) in Qatar's economic rise in the 21st century. It traces the history of LNG development in Qatar and its impact on the nation's industrial and economic transformation. The chapter highlights Qatar's ability to leverage LNG trade to generate revenues and invest in various sectors, from infrastructure to industry, health, culture, and education. Qatar's journey to becoming one of the world's leading welfare nations is examined. This chapter underscores the central role of LNG trade in Qatar's remarkable economic ascent.

The intended audience for this reference book encompasses governments, international organizations, academics, researchers, energy policymakers, and students alike. It is our hope that this comprehensive analysis will serve as a valuable resource for those seeking a deeper understanding of energy crises and the pivotal role of country policies in addressing them.

In a world where the energy we consume is not only the lifeblood of our societies but a potential source of global contention, the need for a thoughtful and informed discourse on energy crises and their solutions has never been more pressing. I invite you to embark on this journey with us, as we navigate the intricate terrain of energy, politics, and policy, striving for a brighter and more secure energy future for all.

Merve Suna Ozel Ozcan
Kirikkale University, Turkey

Introduction

Energy is a mighty tool that can be leveraged for foreign policy control and dominance. It plays a pivotal role in expanding a state's power capacities, enabling development, progress, and empowerment. Energy power is critical, with technology's increasing importance. In the realist approach, energy security is linked to national power. Controlling and owning energy resources is a situation that can attract attention and make a state's territory stand out in the international arena. This natural substance has a historical dimension and has been transformed into an element of power, exemplified by the Russian Federation. However, British Royal Navy Secretary Winston Churchill played a crucial role in transforming energy into power. He switched the fuel consumption of the navy's warships from coal to oil, even though it meant relying on unsafe Iranian oil instead of reliable Welsh coal. This decision made energy security an essential aspect of national security. Churchill also emphasized the importance of diversity in energy supply.

Classification of energy is essential. The significance of energy in the lives of individuals and nations has increased considerably at international level due to industrialization. In the new world created by industrialization in the 18th century, there was a need for new energy sources and, therefore, exploration initiatives. As the world progressed, the demand for energy resources has become increasingly evident. For instance, during the Industrial Revolution, the energy requirements of developing countries skyrocketed. Throughout this process, new energy sources were discovered and categorized as either renewable or non-renewable. Fossil fuels are non-renewable, while renewable energy sources can be replenished. Oil, a non-renewable energy source, was formed from the remnants of ancient marine plants and animals that lived millions of years ago. Energy resources prodcued from residues are called fossil energy resources (EIA, 2023). People's need for energy resources increased during the Industrial Revolution, and new energy sources were discovered. These sources are classified as renewable or non-renewable. Fossil fuels like oil are non-renewable energy sources from ancient marine plants and animals. States have been facing challenges in accessing non-renewable energy resources, which has put them in a difficult situation. As a result, energy security has emerged as a crucial concept, given the security threats that states have been dealing with in the context of energy (Özel Özcan et al., 2022a). Generally, there are two main categories of energy security: short-term and long-term. The short term pertains to managing sudden supply fluctuations, while the long term involves harmonizing sustainable economic development and clean energy consumption. Essentially, energy security entails uninterrupted energy provision at a reasonable cost (IEA, 2019).

Energy security, as defined by the World Energy Council, involves ensuring a reliable energy supply for current and future demands, withstanding sudden shocks, quick recovery, effective management of resources, and reliable energy infrastructure (World Energy Council, 2020). According to the Asia Pacific Energy Research Center, energy security can be analyzed using the "4A approach", which groups availability into three categories: existence, accessibility, and affordability. In addition to these factors, the availability of clean energy is also a critical consideration. While affordability remains a concern, it is essential to ensure that energy is accessible and sustainable for all (APERC (Asia Pacific Energy Research Centre, 2007).

During the Cold War, energy crisis emerged as a security problem whose impact was worldwide. Although many European countries realized the reality of foreign energy dependence in the 1950s and 1960s, they did not consider it a problem. As a result, the EU's energy policies were also influenced by this situation, and during these years, more focus was placed on energy policies at the national level. The 1973 Oil Crisis marked a significant shift in international energy security. Prior to this, there were nationalization efforts to control energy supply. However, the growing oil demand caused multiple crises in the Middle East during the early Cold War years. The region's importance attracts many. During the first Arab-Israeli War in 1948, a crisis delayed the approval of the Trans Arabian Pipeline Project by a year—the project aimed to transport oil from Saudi Arabia to the Mediterranean. Iraq's oil production decreased during the war, halving its revenues (Issawi, 1978).

During the early 1970s, the Persian Gulf witnessed a significant rise in security and military concerns. The formation of Organization of Petroleum Exporting Countries (OPEC)in 1960 aimed to increase oil prices, led the region to take measures to avert crises and capitalize on the circumstances. The energy crisis of 1973 was a significant event caused by the ideological divide between the East and West during the bipolar era. Arab nations utilized their energy resources as a tool in foreign policy after Western nations, notably the United States, supported Israel in the Arab-Israeli Wars. The OPEC curbed oil production, resulting in current account deficits and payment crises in nations that imported oil. The outcome of the 1973 Oil Crisis was an array of negative consequences, including high prices, economic stagnation, and protective measures implemented by various countries. As a result, the International Energy Agency (IEA) was established in 1974 through the efforts of the Organization for Economic Co-operation and Development (OECD) members (Jones,2012; Arı, 2017).

Table 1. Example cases and problems about energy security

Actor and Crisis Levels	Cases
Global Crises	Crisis of 1973, Iran-Iraq War (1980-1988), Gulf War (1990-1991), etc.
Companies/International Actors	Exxon Mobile, Gazprom, etc.
Tools of Foreign Policy	Crises and Russia's stopping/reducing energy exports
Problem of Energy Storage	2020 China Example overbought limited storage
Different policies for different Energy needs	USA- Oil- EU-Natural gas
Instability in Energy Market Price	The energy-oriented nature and fragility of the Russian economy
Natural Disasters, natural events	Hurricanes Katrina and Rita etc.

Source: Özel Özcan, 2020

This crisis caused much chaos but was not the only energy crisis. Another crisis occurred in 1979 when the Islamic Revolution, led by Ayatollah Khomeini, took place in Iran. As a result, oil prices surged again, causing significant economic turmoil. However, these revenues were not distributed in different ways, leading to the rise of opposition movements. The control of oil reserves has been a significant factor in numerous conflicts since the latter half of the 20th century. This has resulted in energy security becoming a crucial consideration in global affairs. Furthermore, the energy issue is vital for international markets (Özel Özcan et al., 2022b).

Therefore, oil control has been central in various wars since the second half of the 20th century. Energy security has become a key concept in the international arena. However, the balance between supply and demand creates dependence on market forces. The earthquake and tsunami that hit Japan in 2011 caused the collapse of the electrical system, leading to chronic electricity problems in countries such as China and India. Table I provides us with real-life examples of energy crises experienced worldwide. These instances, especially those that began in the Middle East, demonstrate the intricate relationship between global events, energy markets, and geopolitics. They emphasize the significant role that energy resources can play in shaping international relations and the importance of protecting energy security by implementing various energy policies. The lessons we learn from these crises are crucial in ensuring a stable, sustainable, and secure global energy future for future generations.

Table I contains examples of energy crises experienced internationally. The examples of these energy crises, especially those that started in the Middle East, show the interconnectedness of global events, geopolitics, and energy markets. This highlights the potential for energy security, various energy policies, and geopolitical actors to use energy resources as a tool in international relations. In this book, we address the international energy crisis by examining different dimensions of energy. This study highlights actions taken to combat the crisis locally, nationally, and globally.

The Covid-19 pandemic has brought about a new energy crisis, distinct from previous ones. Unlike other crises that specific actors caused, this crisis has highlighted the need for a broader perspective on energy security. The Middle East has relied heavily on its vast oil reserves since the 20th century, but the current situation has revealed that this cannot be taken for granted. Big or small crises create a ripple effect that impacts the entire system. As a result, the energy sector has become a target for various actors seeking to exploit any security gaps, as seen in the sanctions imposed on Russia.

Furthermore, the energy crisis in the 21st century has significantly impacted the relationship between Russia and Ukraine. Since the 2000s, Russia has implemented policies focused on its energy resources and has become a significant energy exporter. At the Summit meeting, the parties aimed to address issues such as improving energy efficiency, ensuring energy supply security and upgrading pipelines and energy routes. Positive energy relationships were established, but the EU heavily relied on Russia's cheap gas. This issue made energy a critical factor in Russia-EU relations, but good relations supported the EU's environmental goals. Even during the Covid-19 period, the issue of renewable energy, seen as an alternative to Russian energy, is also at the forefront for the EU. However, the rupture in EU energy policies emerged with the sanctions applied completely mixedly after February 2022. In response to Russia's announcement of a "special military operation" against Ukraine, the European Council President, Charles Michel, held an extraordinary meeting with EU member states. Following the meeting, Michel declared that the EU would stand with the Ukrainian people, and Russia would face heavy sanctions. As we approach the end of 2023, it is worth noting that the sanctions remain in place (European Commission, 2022).

Hence, the most important example is the energy crisis between Russia and the EU. The effects of the problem are global. In this process, the EU diversifies its energy supply, increasing energy saving and efficiency, as well as energy security. However, at the same time, Russia aims to gain prestige in the international system by supporting directly or indirectly affected countries to maintain its influence on the EU in the energy field. Energy independence of the European Union is a prerequisite for becoming a more influential actor in the international system. However, the most critical problem is that although renewable and sustainable energy transition is the EU's top priority energy policy, since it does not have reserves in terms of fossil resources, it is long-term. It is also developing new collaborations and partnerships to reduce dependence on Russian fossil energy resources. Russia carries its energy abroad through new partnerships with the East to bypass EU sanctions (Conte, 2023).

Conclusion

Energy plays a critical role in a state's power capacities, enabling development, progress, and empowerment. Energy security is linked to national power, and controlling and owning energy resources is a situation that can make a state's territory stand out in the international arena. The significance of energy has increased considerably due to industrialization and the demand for energy resources. Energy security is a crucial concept, given the security threats that states have been dealing with in the context of energy. It entails uninterrupted energy provision at a reasonable cost, and there are two main categories of energy security: short-term and long-term. The short term pertains to managing sudden supply fluctuations, while the long term involves harmonizing sustainable economic development and clean energy consumption. The World Energy Council defines energy security as ensuring a reliable energy supply for current and future demands, withstanding sudden shocks, quick recovery, effective management of resources, and reliable energy infrastructure.

Energy security entails uninterrupted energy provision at a reasonable cost. During the Cold War, the energy crisis emerged as a security problem that affected the global arena. The 1973 Oil Crisis marked a significant shift in international energy security. Arab nations utilized their energy resources as a tool in foreign policy after Western nations, notably the United States, supported Israel during the Yom Kippur War. During the crisis, Arab nations utilized their energy resources as a tool in foreign policy, resulting in high oil prices, economic stagnation, and protective measures implemented by various countries. OPEC curbed oil production, resulting in current account deficits and payment crises in nations that imported oil.

There have been many changes and innovations in the international arena since the Cold War era. These changes have also impacted the energy sector globally, resulting in different elements and crisis effects compared to the 1973 energy crisis. Today, all actors are vulnerable to rapid energy crises due to the inherent fragility of energy security. However, energy crises can also provide an opportunity to create new alternatives, as explored in all chapters of this book. It is important to remember that each crisis changes the actor and system effects of the next crisis. At this point, The Covid-19 pandemic has exposed the vulnerabilities of the energy sector, highlighting the need for a wider perspective on energy security. The region's heavy reliance on oil reserves cannot be taken for granted, as any crisis creates a ripple effect that impacts the entire system. For instance, the energy crisis between Russia and the EU has global effects. While the EU is diversifying its energy supply, increasing efficiency and security, Russia aims to maintain its influence by supporting affected countries. To become more influential, the

EU needs energy independence, but renewable energy transition is long-term. The EU is developing new partnerships, while Russia seeks Eastern partners to bypass EU sanctions.

REFERENCES

APERC. (2007). *A quest for energy security in the 21st century: resources and constraints.* Inst. of Energy Economics.

Arı, T. (2017). *Geçmişten Günümüze Ortadoğu Cilt-1.* Alfa Akademi Basın Yayın.

Conte, N. (2023). *Who's Still Buying Russian Fossil Fuels in 2023?* Retrieved from: https://www.visualcapitalist.com/whos-still-buying-russian-fossil-fuels-in-2023/

EIA. (2023). *What is energy? Sources of energy.* Retrieved from: https://www.eia.gov/energyexplained/what-is-energy/sources-of-energy.php

Issawi, C. (1978). The 1973 Oil Crisis and After. *Journal of Post Kenyesian Economics, 1*(2), 3-26.

Jones, T.C. (2012). America, Oil, and War in the Middle East. The Journal of American History, 99(1), 208–218.

Özel Özcan, M. S. (2020). Enerji Kaynağı Mücadelesi ve Enerji Güvenliği. In Uluslararası Güvenlik: Gelenekselden Güncele Bir Gündem Analizi. Ankara: Orion Yayınevi.

Özel Özcan, M. S., & Öten, C. (2022a). Enerji Kriz Girdabı Kavramsallaştırması Bağlamında Orta Doğu'da Petrol Krizleri. *Bölgesel Araştırmalar Dergisi, 6*(1), 174–208.

Özel Özcan, M. S., & Öten, C. (2022b). Turkish Energy Policy and Energy Security. Turkey In A Changıng World Order Economıcs, Polıtıcs And Foreıgn Polıcy. IJOPEC Publication Limited.

Yergin, D. (2006). Ensuring Security. *Foreign Affairs, 85*(2), 69–82. doi:10.2307/20031912

Yergin, D. (2011). *The Quest: Energy, Security, and the Remaking of the Modern World.* The Penguin Press.

Chapter 1
Global Energy Crises:
Measures Taken and Policies Adopted in the Recent History

Emine Erden Kaya
Amasya University, Turkey

Şeyma Eşki Çaylak
https://orcid.org/0000-0002-3690-041X
Muş Alparslan University, Turkey

ABSTRACT

Recent events like the COVID-19 pandemic and the Russia-Ukraine conflict have disrupted the supply-demand balance and triggered a new energy crisis, impacting the world economy. The rapid increase in the world's population, coupled with industrialization and urbanization, has exacerbated energy demand issues, affecting countries worldwide, especially the EU. As a result of these developments, countries have been prompted to take new energy measures and formulate policies to address the energy crisis. This study examines historical perspectives and conducts a comparative analysis of energy crises from the past to the present, focusing on the current energy crisis and the measures taken by various countries, including the EU member states. The study aims to explore how crises shape energy policies, how countries evaluate "opportunity windows" for new/alternative energy sources and technologies in response to crises, and how they present potential alternative energy sources for the future through the discussion of adopted energy policies.

INTRODUCTION

Today, it is realized again that the peoples of the world, who are more connected to each other with the effect of globalization and experience a "time-space compression," actually form a "risk society." In this context, Ulrick Beck's conceptualization of the 'risk society,' which connects the idea that global dangers impact large populations with the random, unconscious, and uncontrolled experiences of modernization, appears to be a valid concept. This concept reminds us that the world's societies now have

DOI: 10.4018/979-8-3693-0440-2.ch001

more invisible boundaries and exemplifies how any regional crisis can quickly create a global impact. Because risks are uncertain and unpredictable, it is difficult to take precautions against risks. As seen during the pandemic, these risks emerge within a specific geography, yet they can easily disseminate worldwide and affect everyone. When the effects of these crisis examples are examined, it also facilitates the understanding of globalization's roles in the military, political, economic and sociological dimensions of nation-states. With the 2022 Russia-Ukraine war, the world has faced a new crisis that will likely start a new era after the Cold War, or even be called the post-Cold War era. In addition, this war started while the effects of the COVID-19 epidemic on the world economies and the period of struggle continued. With the effect of the China-USA trade war that occupied the global economy before and after the pandemic, this new crisis disrupted the balance of supply and demand, climate crises and the existing balances in all countries trying to repair their disrupted supply chains.

The continuous increase in the world population, the acceleration of industrialization and urbanization have a parallel impact on the need for energy, resulting in a continuous increase in energy demand and consumption. On the other hand, when we examine the world in general, it is observed that the most energy consumption is in the EU countries. At the same time, the fact that the EU member states lack sufficient resources to meet the increasing energy needs leaves it with a difficult struggle in the energy field. Another reason for this problem is that the EU countries, find themselves in an externally dependent position concerning energy resources. As a consequence of all these developments, the "new great energy crisis", which corresponds to various dimensions of globalization, especially the economy, has rapidly affected the whole world, especially Europe. This situation has also necessitated the formulation of new policies and the implementation of new measures. European countries, relying on Russia for energy supply, initially imposed sanctions on Russia with a united approach during this process. In return, they faced energy shortages and hiked prices. While the Russia-Ukraine war continues, the fears regarding the rapidly rising gas and oil prices as well as supply security, also affect the global energy markets to a great extent. The new energy crisis has deepened due to the rapid increase in the prices of all energy sources, ranging from natural gas to coal.

This historical process has also led European countries to seek new alternative sources for the following few reasons; (1) the decrease in energy supply from Russia, which has been going on for many years or even coming to an end, (2) the decrease in the energy provided by hydroelectric power plants due to drought. However, since it is not easy to quickly replace the long-standing Russian supply, EU countries had to implement restrictions and measures on energy consumption, especially in the winter months. On the other hand, the EU countries reviewed their energy policies with suggestions such as the ceiling price application for Russian gas while taking precautions, especially for energy supply security. After the Russia-Ukraine War, however, the energy supply security of the EU's energy policies has yet to be overcome due to the following difficulties; (1) the creation of the European energy market, (2) increasing energy efficiency to contribute to reducing energy demand, and (3) the main challenge in policies that continue to develop in the axis of research, innovation, and competitiveness. The reason for the failure of the EU's policies is that the EU's countries are still heavily dependent on Russia in the short term and their energy supply is unstable. On the other hand, in the historical process, one of the first solutions to overcome energy crises has been renewable energy sources. In this context, renewable energy targets have been determined to be used in industry, buildings, transportation, district heating, and cooling sectors. However, these energy sources are considered as a long-term solution. Considering their reliability, diversity, and costs, as well as their mitigating effects on the climate crisis, renewable energy sources are considered to be essential alternatives in solving energy crises. Another important contribution and return of the discovery and expansion of alternative energy sources is that it will make countries independent in many fields such as energy, finance, and communication, and will protect them from the dangers of the global risk society as a stakeholder. Emphasizing renewable energy investments is in line with a common consensus, given the potential future crises and countries' aspirations for independence. To serve these purposes, different policies and plans continue to be developed in many countries, especially in the EU member states.

This new energy crisis, which we have seen recently, reminds us of the power balance wars and crises in the historical background, especially in the 20th century, with the use of fossil fuels. It also reminds us of the policies that such crises do not happen again in the field of energy or that existing problems are aimed at solving crises between countries and limiting their negative effects on climate change. As it is evident, energy crises have a determining and guiding effect on domestic and foreign policies as well as energy policies. Although the energy crises have negative socio-economic effects that last for many years, the crises also have positive effects such as the search and use of alternative sources against the energy source that has a supply problem. For example, efforts to overcome the wood crisis, known as the first resource crisis, brought about the use of an alternative resource such as coal. The use of coal in the 1600s led to the emergence and spread of modern technologies. Crises maintain this characteristic even today. The emphasis on renewable energy investments as one of the ways out of the energy crisis in recent history serves as an indicator of this situation. In this regard, while the crises indeed bring about negative effects, it's feasible to assess the policies formulated during these periods of crisis that foster the emergence and utilization of novel energy sources and technologies, presenting a "window of opportunity" that arises alongside these crises.

In this study, it is essential to examine the measures and policies developed by various countries, especially the member states of the EU, regarding the energy crises from the past to the present to the new energy crises. In this context, the study aims to analyze energy crises experienced in the 20th and 21st centuries in terms of their causes and effects, evaluate the measures taken to avoid the crises or to prevent new crises, and assess the policies formulated for a solution, using a historical perspective and comparative analysis method. The questions of the study include what types of energy have emerged in the globalization process and how their importance has increased, what the energy supply types are and how they are shared, what are the reasons for energy crises, and with which policies these crises are tried to be addressed. Alongside these research questions, it is important to understand and convey the issue to examine the new energy crisis after the Russia-Ukraine war, as well as the global effects of this crisis, which are not confined to the region, and to analyze various findings. In this context, the study aims to discuss how the crises shape energy policies and how countries evaluate the "window of opportunity" opened by crises such as turning to new/alternative energy sources and technologies and presenting alternative energy sources of the future to address the crises in line with the formulated energy policies.

CONCEPTS OF ENERGY AND ENERGY SOURCES

According to the Energy Information Administration (EIA), the concept of energy is defined as the "ability to do work" (EIA, 2022). Another meaning of the concept of energy is "energy means the ability to do useful work" (Islam, 2017). With modernization, energy has become an important need in every aspect of human life. People have used energy in many areas such as vehicles, cooking, storing food in freezers, lighting living spaces, and producing various products. Some of the different forms of energy can be counted as "heat, light, motion, electrical, chemical and gravitational." These energy forms can be grouped into two categories (a) potential or stored energy and (b) kinetic or working energy. On the other hand, many different energy sources are categorized into two categories renewable energy sources and non-renewable energy sources. These two energy sources can be both the primary energy source to produce the necessary energy such as heat, and they are used to produce secondary energy sources such as electricity and hydrogen (EIA, 2022).

Today, non-renewable energy sources such as petroleum, hydrocarbon gas liquids, natural gas, coal and nuclear energy are used in many countries around the world, especially for daily work. On the other hand, the main renewable energy sources are solar energy from the sun, geothermal energy from the heat inside the earth, wind energy, biomass from plants and hydropower from flowing water (EIA, 2022). Non-renewable fossil fuels and nuclear energy sources, once consumed, are gone forever without being renewed. However, renewable energy sources are almost unlimited when considering energy sources such as the sun, wind, ocean waves, and geothermal (Holzman, 2006).

Renewable energy has been the main source of energy for most of human history. However, this situation began to change in the early 1800s. In the early 1900s, fossil fuels became the main energy source. At the same time, due to the political, economic and social effects of non-renewable resources on the world, especially after the 1980s, incentives and efforts for the use of renewable energy sources have begun to increase. Today, many countries are still working to increase the use of renewable energy as a way to help reduce and avoid carbon dioxide emissions (EIA, 2022). However, the Industrial Revolution stands out as a crucial turning point in this context. In particular, while people used only renewable energy sources before the Industrial Revolution, they have become increasingly dependent on fossil fuels

Figure 1. Energy consumption by source between 1965-2022 in the world
Sources: Our World in Data, "Energy consumption by source, World," 2023, https://ourworldindata.org/grapher/energy-consumption-by-source-and-country?stackMode=absolute

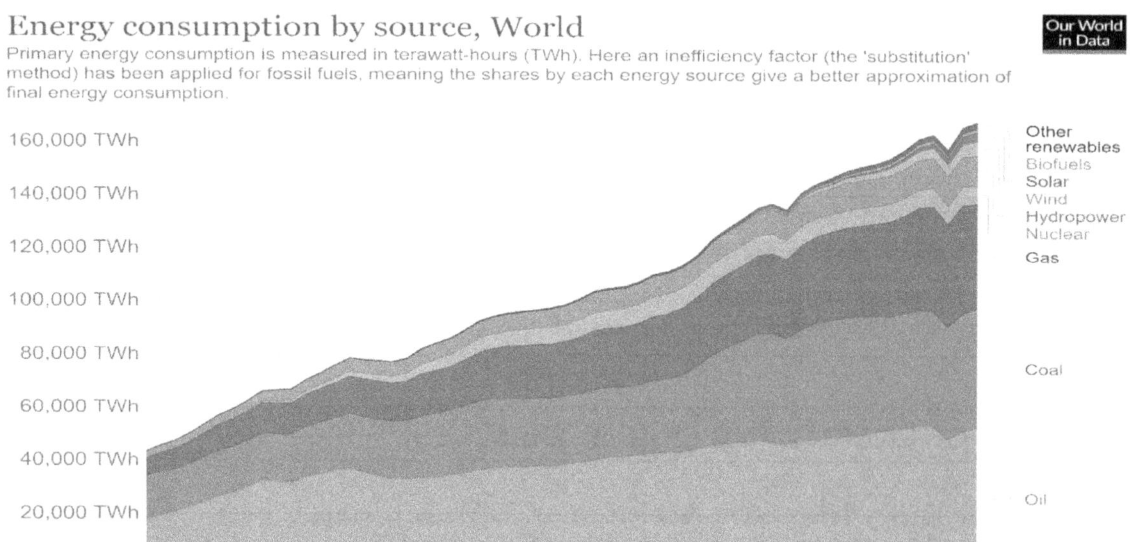

in the last 150 years. Today, despite technological developments, the use of renewable energy sources still has a very small share in the global energy landscape (Öztürk et al., 2013).

In the 20th century, energy has been a driving force that has enabled unprecedented levels of economic growth, prosperity and globalization. During this period, various primary energy sources, particularly traditional biomass, coal, oil and natural gas, gained considerable popularity (Simmons et al., 2014). These energy sources also constitute the areas of highest energy consumption (*Figure* 1).

ENERGY CRISES IN RECENT HISTORY

Today, energy crises continue to have a deep impact on the political, social and economic policies of many countries and the quality of life of people globally. The need for energy is constantly increasing day by day in all areas of life. "Growth in demand, challenges to energy supplies, security of our energy supply in some cases, and the environmental impacts of energy utilization" can be identified as a few important reasons or drivers for the ongoing energy crises. These areas are also closely related to technology and politics (Schlachter, 2010: 34). However, today's energy crises are significantly broader, more effective, and more complex than previous ones when compared to recent energy crises. For example, the energy crises of the 1970s were often oil-related, and the tasks of policymakers were relatively simple. These tasks were to reduce dependence on oil and oil imports. On the contrary, today's energy crises have many different dimensions such as natural gas, oil, coal, electricity, food security and climate (World Energy Outlook, 2022).

In contemporary history, the most important energy crises of the 20th century, with the increasing dependence and need for oil, originated from the Middle East. Due to the oil, the international importance of the region has increased over time and the countries rich in oil resources, which have realized this, have instrumentalized this trump card in the political crises. In the early 1970s, after the British government announced that it would end its long-standing imperial presence in the region, the US presence in the Middle East became even stronger. However, in the process, this situation also increased the concern that it would create a large power vacuum (Jones, 2012). Until the 1970s, US dominance in the Middle East was based on (a) international oil companies' control over the region's vast oil reserves and (b) alliances between conservative Arab regimes and the US government. However, this situation started to change after Richard Nixon became President in January 1969 (Schneider, 1975). On the other hand, in 1960, major oil-producing countries established the Organization of Petroleum Exporting Countries (OPEC) to raise prices. The organization achieved little in the early years but later became very strong, especially in the 1970s, as major producers began to nationalize the operations of oil companies (Jones, 2012). This situation has been an important development in preventing a power vacuum in the region.

The first significant energy crisis of the 1970s occurred in 1973 due to the Arab-Israeli War. Previously, after the June 1967 war, Israel had occupied the Golan Heights, the Sinai Peninsula, and the western bank of the Jordan River. After these developments, Arab nationalism increased, posing a threat to the continued existence of conservative Arab regimes that traditionally had been allies of the US. This situation also changed the balance in the control of oil reserves, imports and exports. Nations beyond the confines of the US and Britain, often labelled as "newcomers," boldly initiated a challenge against the unassailable dominance of the Middle East oil industry, a supremacy that had been firmly clutched by the seven largest multinational corporations[1] throughout the 1950s.

Another important development in the period was that the US supported Israel for a long time and the oil producers in the region were greatly disturbed by this situation. To force Israel to surrender the occupied territories, Egypt and Syria launched a joint offensive on Yom Kippur on October 6, 1973 (Juliet et al., 2017). During the war, the US aid to the Israeli army caused the Gulf oil producers to react more (Jones, 2012). Shortly after, the Organization of the Arab Petroleum Exporting Countries (OAPEC, made up of Arab members of OPEC plus Egypt and Syria) declared that they would no longer ship oil to countries that support Israel. In the aftermath of these developments, on October 15, 1973, a period of crisis began when OPEC declared an oil embargo against the US for providing support to Israel in the Yom Kippur War (Bolsen, 2011). On the other hand, at the OAPEC meeting held in Kuwait on October 17, it was announced that the oil price increased by 70 percent above the 1 October level (Wariavwalla, 1975). In response, a decision was made to gradually reduce oil production by 5% each month until Arab countries and Israel withdrew from the occupied territories, once again as a form of retribution against the US (Juliet et al., 2017). The decrease in oil production was directly reflected in the prices and oil prices increased continuously throughout the 1970s. The US economy was badly affected by this situation. Gas had become both expensive and scarce. Seeing queues at gas stations had now become commonplace. At the same time, in some cities, police had to be stationed at gas stations to prevent violence (Smith et al., 2003).

In 1978 and 1979, sparked by the overthrow of the Shah in Iran, the second energy crisis unfurled as a consequence of the disruption in the global oil supply (Bolsen, 2011). Under the new regime, oil exports resumed inconsistently. However, it was at a much lower volume than before (Smith et al., 2003). After this revolution, oil prices again increased significantly. After the 1973 energy crisis, an economic transformation process called the economic crisis, started in Europe as well as the US. In this process, the momentum of regular expansion in the industrialized countries of the North was disrupted. High inflation and increases in unemployment, the slowdown in productivity growth and increases in domestic and external deficits were other problems. All these negative developments continued in an aggravated manner after the second oil shock in 1979-1980 (Caffentzis, 1980).

Another energy crisis occurred in 1980 during the Iraq-Iran War. During the war, the two oil-rich countries stopped their oil production. At the same time, the parties attacked each other's oil refineries (Özel & Öten, 2022). Simultaneously, Iran stopped its oil exports and Iraq's exports decreased by 70 percent. Once again oil shortages emerged, leading to long queues forming at gas stations (Smith et al., 2003). The next energy crisis of the 1980s took place in 1986. The underlying cause of this crisis was Saudi Arabia's decision to initiate a gradual reduction in oil production beginning in 1982. This strategic move was rooted in the necessity for key facets of oil production to undergo a period of strategic rest. This situation was also reflected in the prices. This was the result of the price war initiated by Saudi Arabia. In the process, oil prices dropped significantly and producers faced significant challenges (Özel & Öten, 2022).

The first energy crisis of the 1990s started with the invasion of Kuwait by Iraq on August 2, 1990, which triggered the first Persian Gulf War (Hamilton, 2011). Saddam Hussein claimed that Kuwait was a province of Iraq and that Kuwait was smuggling Iraqi oil. After the invasion, Kuwait's oil production stopped completely and Iraq's oil production decreased. Furthermore, while oil prices were 20.7 dollars per barrel in January 1990, they increased to 32.5 in September of the same year. Indeed, the cessation of oil production greatly affected the global energy markets (Özel & Öten, 2022). Another energy crisis of the 1990s occurred in 1997-1998 due to the East Asian Crisis (Hamilton, 2011). With this crisis, oil demands and imports from countries decreased significantly in 1998. At the same time, the increase in oil production in exporting countries caused significant decreases in prices.

The next energy crisis began in the first months of 2000 due to OPEC's decision to cut production and raise prices. Moreover, in the 2000s, the 9/11 terrorist attacks in the US and the launch of the global war on terror in response ushered in a new era (Smith et al., 2003). On March 20, 2003, the US initiated a military intervention in Iraq based on allegations of collaborating with al-Qaeda in the execution of the Twin Tower attack, alongside Iraq's purported possession of weapons of mass destruction. However, it was also claimed that this intervention was made to control Iraq's oil. In this process, Iraq's oil production decreased and oil prices experienced a considerable increase. In 2008, yet another energy crisis was experienced due to increasing demand and stagnant supply, and as a result of this crisis, oil prices rose again. It is evident, that the cause of the crisis is the failure of oil-producing countries to increase production and the increase in global oil consumption demand (Hamilton, 2011). In the historical process, the 2008 global crisis has deeply affected all governments and changed almost all balances (Öztürk et al., 2013). The Arab Spring process, which started in the Middle East in 2011, caused another energy crisis, and oil prices increased again due to countries with reduced oil production (Özel & Öten, 2022).

Recently, with the outbreak of the COVID-19 pandemic, a new energy crisis has been experienced in the world, especially in 2020. The closure of the country's borders weakened economic ties and led to a decrease in oil consumption. This process resulted in decreased oil prices and oil production. The effects of the crisis continued to be felt in 2021 and 2022. Even now, as the global economy continues to recover from the COVID-19 pandemic slowly, energy prices and availability threaten to destabilize the economy. The pandemic has caused a historic drop in energy demand and prices, but recovery in demand is now straining fossil fuel markets for oil gas and even coal. Prices continue to rise as demand chases fuel supply, which has not yet rebounded from the pandemic slump (Gilbert et al., 2021)

Figure 2. Evolution of key regional natural gas prices, June 2021-October 2022
Source: IEA, Evolution of key regional natural gas prices, June 2021-October 2022, IEA, Paris https://www.iea.org/data-and-statistics/charts/evolution-of-key-regional-natural-gas -prices-june-2021-october-2022, IEA. License: CC BY 4.0

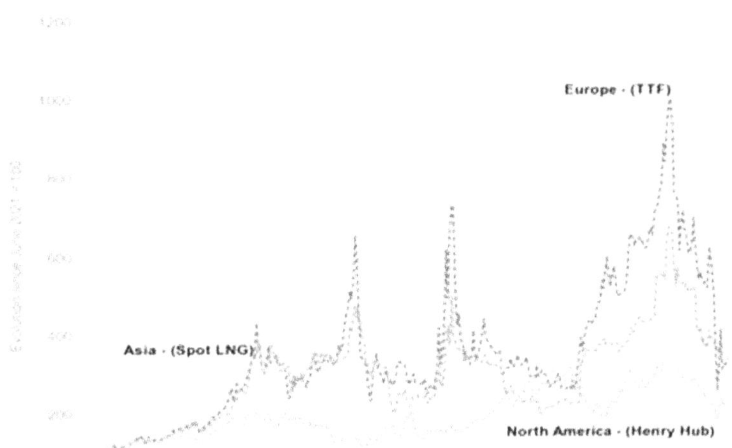

Global supply crises in the past have typically been limited to oil, but rapidly changing natural gas markets are also in a significant crisis. A growing and more flexible liquefied natural gas (LNG) market has enabled global competition for gas supply (Gilbert et al., 2021) The latest energy crisis experienced by the world started after Russia invaded Ukraine in February 2022. The price of natural gas (*Figure*: 2) increased considerably and electricity prices were also affected by this situation. On the other hand, oil prices reached their highest level since 2008. High energy prices caused high inflation (IEA, Global Energy Crisis).

In the face of the fragilities in the West-Russia relations, the political developments in Ukraine and Russia's recognition of the independence of the separatist groups in the Donbas region on February 21, 2022, the tension between all parties has escalated. In the same period, the Russian Parliament authorised the government to use the army, causing a new Cold War to begin between Russia and the West. Russia soon entered Ukraine on February 24, 2022, and carried out air and missile attacks on previously determined targets, thus the hot war started (Battır & Yiğittepe, 2023). The war led to an increase in the ongoing global energy crisis during the COVID-19 period. However, the fact that the measures and sanctions taken are not sufficient, indicates that the crisis will continue for a long time. Having entered an energy impasse, the EU's dependence on imports in energy supply caused it to reorganize its energy policies (Kesici, 2022). In addition, the flow of natural gas from Russia to European countries that imposed sanctions on Russia due to the Ukraine war has decreased significantly. Russia has reduced natural gas by 80 percent compared to the pre-war period, and the energy costs of European countries have increased with the contraction in supply volume. As a result, rapidly increasing natural gas and electricity prices starting from the first months of 2022 have affected the whole world, especially Europe (Rusya-Ukrayna Savaşı..., 2023). Decreasing Russian gas imports have been largely offset by LNG and source country diversification. The USA stands out in the EU's increasing LNG demand. In March 2022, the Biden administration and the European Commission agreed to increase US-EU gas trade by at least 50 billion cubic meters per year by 2030 (Guzman and Majkut, 2023).

It can be said that there is a mutual dependence between Russia and Europe. The reason is that the Kremlin depends on revenue from Europe, and Europe depends on Russian energy. However, according to general evaluations, imposing harsher sanctions on Russia means taking the risk of serious blows to the energy supply (McBride, 2022). The fact that global economies are now more interconnected than in previous years further highlights the effects of the crises. For this reason, it can be claimed that the world is experiencing the "first global energy crisis" in real terms. High energy bills have increased extreme poverty and retarded progress towards universal and affordable energy access. Even in developed economies, rising prices have affected vulnerable households and caused significant economic, social and political pressures (IEA, Global Energy Crisis).

SOLUTIONS TO THE ENERGY CRISIS

The measures taken to prevent or address energy crises are directly linked to the underlying causes. These crises are typically caused by a combination of factors, including population growth, deteriorating infrastructure, excessive consumption, energy wastage, natural disasters, global pandemics, and major accidents. The COVID-19 pandemic is a prime example where sudden lockdowns resulted in a significant drop in energy demand, leading to reduced investments and supply capacity. Following the reopening of economies, a new global energy crisis occurred in 2021 due to increased energy demands, inadequate infrastructure, and inconsistent energy policies. The pandemic-induced decline in energy demand quickly reversed with economic resurgence, yet energy production struggled to keep up with the surge in demand, causing challenges in the supply of fossil fuels like coal, oil, and natural gas. Additionally, climate change impacts have also posed issues for energy infrastructure, including transmission lines, storage facilities, refineries, and power grids. For instance, the state of Texas experienced power outages during freezing temperatures, while China faced restrictions in coal supply due to mine flooding incidents. Moreover, geopolitical tensions and disagreements over pricing between energy-producing and consuming countries have further destabilized energy policies. For example, Russia's reduction in natural gas shipments to Europe resulted in soaring gas prices in the region in 2022 (Yıldızoğlu, 2022). To tackle these global energy crises and their far-reaching economic, social, and environmental consequences, policymakers are implementing various measures and formulating comprehensive energy policies. These efforts are crucial to address the challenges posed by energy demand and supply dynamics and to build a more sustainable and resilient energy future for the world.

Measures

Energy measures are both permanent and temporary precautions implemented in response to an energy crisis. These precautions are tailored to the specific type of energy crisis and can vary from one country to another. In the shadow of this, certain European countries like Spain and Portugal have imposed limitations on local gas-based electricity prices, whereas France has restricted electricity price increases. Germany has also taken significant energy conservation steps, including lowering heating temperatures to 19 degrees Celsius in public buildings and offices, and down to 12 degrees Celsius in areas with high activity. Meanwhile, the UK has implemented an energy price cap approach due to widespread bankruptcies in the energy distribution sector (Aktan, 2022). Additionally, the EU Commission has been proactive in addressing the energy crisis by implementing measures that encompass reducing natural gas consumption, optimizing gas storage, accelerating investments in renewable energy sources, and diversifying energy supply away from Russia. Furthermore, international organizations such as the World Bank, and the International Monetary Fund (IMF) etc. have stepped in to support developing countries in alleviating the impact of the energy crisis, providing financial aid and technical assistance (Euronews, 2022).

As indicated by the measures adopted by various countries, the primary strategies to address the recent global energy crisis include public awareness campaigns that promote energy conservation and efficient energy utilization, along with an emphasis on increasing the adoption of renewable energy sources (EU Gas Demand Measures, 2022). In essence, proposed solutions to tackle energy crises involve *reducing electricity demand, promoting the usage of renewable resources, encouraging public transportation, and addressing energy leakages.* Employing solar energy for electricity conservation, complemented by initiatives like powering off unnecessary lights and appliances, are targeted measures to curb electricity demand. Renewable sources, particularly solar energy, represent vital avenues for overcoming the challenges of the energy crisis due to their efficiency in conserving energy. Another effective approach to cope with the crisis is to curtail fuel consumption in the transportation sector. Implementing measures to decrease private transportation usage while providing the public with a convenient mass transit system are practices aimed at conserving fuel (Coldwell Solar, 2023).

Generally, measures taken to address the energy crisis can be broadly categorized into short-term and long-term approaches. Short-term measures involve taking temporary actions aimed at mitigating the immediate impacts of the crisis. Examples include mandatory reductions in electricity demand and obligatory contributions from fossil fuel companies. These measures seek to safeguard consumers and businesses without disrupting energy markets or hindering competition. On the other hand, long-term measures are more permanent solutions designed to prevent the recurrence and exacerbation of the energy crisis. Initiatives like diversifying energy sources, developing domestic and renewable energy resources, and enhancing energy efficiency fall under this category. The primary objectives of these long-term measures are to ensure energy supply security and promote environmental sustainability.

The effectiveness and sufficiency of both short-term and long-term measures to address the global energy crisis are subjects of debate. However, it is widely acknowledged that ensuring international cooperation and coordination is crucial for resolving the crisis. Moreover, evaluating the impact of measures taken to mitigate the adverse economic, social, and environmental consequences of the energy crisis emphasizes the importance of adopting a sustainable energy policy. In essence, there is a strong interrelationship between the measures implemented and the energy policies devised to tackle the energy crisis. Energy policies establish an essential framework for determining appropriate measures, with the primary objectives encompassing the attainment of balance between energy supply and demand, the enhancement of energy efficiency, the assurance of energy security, and the mitigation of environmental impacts. Aligned with these objectives, the measures to be taken against the energy crisis encompass determining which resources and technologies will be prioritized, as well as which sectors and consumers will be supported or obligated. In this regard, energy measures serve as effective tools contributing to the implementation and achievement of energy policies and their targets. For instance, a measure focused on developing domestic and renewable energy sources contributes to the achievement of energy policy goals, such as reducing energy dependency and promoting environmental sustainability. Moreover, there is a feedback mechanism between energy policies and measures. As a result, energy policies can be updated or revised based on the outcomes of implemented measures. Conversely, energy measures can reveal the effectiveness or shortcomings of energy policies. For example, the implementation of a price cap on electricity may inadvertently disrupt the functioning of the electricity market or hinder competition. In such cases, there may be a need for new energy policies, such as restructuring the electricity market, to address these challenges.

Energy Policies

The measures taken in response to the recent energy crisis exemplify the scope of energy policies. As a result, energy policies generally entail making decisions and implementing measures to achieve energy conservation, promoting efficient energy consumption, and ensuring energy supply security. Furthermore, these policies aim to increase the utilization of renewable resources and offer cost-effective alternative energy sources that meet society's desired quantity and quality. Energy policy can be defined as the formulation of regulations, their implementation, and the establishment of future objectives within the energy sector. It involves a set of rules and strategies that take into account technological and economic factors to strike a balance between energy supply and demand, enhance energy efficiency, ensure energy security, and minimize environmental impacts. Energy policy plays a significant role in shaping a country's or region's regulations and strategies concerning energy resources, production, consumption, distribution, and pricing, all aimed at harmonizing these elements (MMO Report, 2022).

Energy policies vary in terms of characteristics, resources, needs, and goals of each country or region. For instance, the EU's energy policy aims to enhance competitiveness, ensure energy supply security, increase the share of natural gas and renewable energy sources, while maintaining the proportion of coal in total energy consumption, and protect the environment (EU Presidency, 2023). In Türkiye, the energy policy has several key objectives, including reducing energy dependency, increasing the share of domestic and renewable energy sources, and contributing to regional and global energy security (Republic of Turkey Ministry of Foreign Affairs, 2023). Measures and policies taken to address the global energy crisis vary from country to country, but they generally focus on improving energy efficiency, regulating energy markets, fostering cooperation, and diversifying as well as increasing the utilization of renewable energy sources.

It is asserted that a comprehensive energy policy comprises three main dimensions: economic, technological, and institutional. The economic dimension of energy is regarded as a concrete indicator of industrialization and growth strategies. Within this dimension, various factors such as energy pricing, consumption, sustainability, and resource allocation come into effect. While the technology dimension of energy is related to the management of energy resources and the institutional structure, the institutional dimension is related to the relations, roles, responsibilities and authorities among the stakeholders of the energy sector. Drawing upon these three dimensions of energy policy, various instruments are utilized, including pricing, taxation, privatization, nationalization, prohibitions, and quota applications. In light of the instruments employed and the areas of focus, energy policies can be categorized into energy price policy, alternative energy development policy, and energy conservation policy (Çetinkaya, 2019). The effectiveness of energy investments, the existence of a competitive market, and the consideration of both economic costs and benefits, as well as social benefits and costs of applications, are crucial determinants of the energy price policy. Energy conservation policy encompasses a comprehensive set of practices aimed at reducing consumption through energy conservation, extending energy storage durations, and enhancing energy production and consumption efficiency. Finally, the policy for developing alternative energy sources entails research and development activities geared towards finding energy sources that can serve as substitutes for fossil fuels in achieving both short and long-term objectives (Saygın, 2006).

Energy crises, particularly in the regions where these crises occur, play a significant role in shaping energy policies. Throughout history, it has been observed that energy crises, especially those related to oil, electricity, and natural gas, have influenced the formulation of energy policies over time. Since the second half of the 20th century, oil has become one of the most crucial energy sources worldwide, extensively used in sectors such as transportation, industry, agriculture, and heating, exerting a significant impact on the global economy and politics. The Middle East stands out as the region with the highest oil production and export. Political and military conflicts in the Middle East have affected oil supply and prices, leading to oil crises in 1973, 1979, and 1990 (Pekmezci, 2020). Policies formulated in response to oil crises have varied depending on the interests, objectives, and capacities of countries involved in oil production, consumption, or mediation. Countries that produce oil have implemented policies such as establishing the Organization of the Petroleum Exporting Countries (OPEC), nationalizing oil resources, and diversifying oil revenues in response to the oil crisis (Hariciye, 2020). On the other hand, countries that consume oil have formulated policies to increase energy efficiency and conservation, switch to renewable energy sources, and diversify their oil supply.

Historically, electricity has been another significant area where energy crises occur, given its usage in various fields, such as lighting, communication, entertainment, and healthcare. Notable energy crises related to electricity include the 2000-2001 California electricity crisis, the 2004 Argentina energy crisis, and the 2008 Central Asia energy crisis. These electricity crises have emerged due to factors such as increasing electricity demand alongside reduced production, resulting in rising electricity prices, power outages, and economic losses. In response to the causes and consequences of electricity crises, various policies have been implemented, encompassing assistance for electricity and natural gas bills, tax reductions, price caps, energy efficiency measures, and diversification of renewable energy sources (Damar, 2022).

Recent energy crises have occurred in the natural gas sector due to the political tensions that originated between Russia and Ukraine in 2006 and escalated into a war in 2022. The first major natural gas crisis occurred in 2006, triggered by the political tensions between Russia and Ukraine during the 2004 Ukrainian presidential elections. Subsequent natural gas crises took place in 2009, 2014, and 2022. The common denominator of these crises is that they revolve around Russia's actions of limiting, increasing prices, or threatening to cut off natural gas supply to Ukraine (Kalkışım, 2019).

The international community has made various initiatives to address this crisis. Some of these include the Minsk Agreements, which provide a roadmap for a peaceful resolution of the crisis, and platforms like the Normandy Format, created to support and implement these agreements. In this crisis, the role of the US has been to provide military and economic support to Ukraine, exert pressure on Russia through sanctions, and call for dialogue to prevent the escalation of the crisis. Türkiye's role, on the other hand, has been supporting Ukraine's territorial integrity and sovereignty by cooperating in areas such as military training and arms sales. Additionally, Türkiye has attempted to mediate for a peaceful resolution of the crisis. The effectiveness of these solutions in addressing the crisis depends on the willingness of the parties involved and the international community's stance (T.C. Dışişleri Bakanlığı, 2023).

Solutions proposed for the Russia-Ukraine energy crisis vary at both regional and global levels, but some general possible solutions are as follows: The cessation of the Russia-Ukraine war and, consequently, Russian sanctions. This situation, dependent on the political will of the parties and the stance of the international community, may help lower prices in energy markets and enhance supply security. Another solution is the diversification of energy resources, which is a strategy aimed at reducing the EU's dependence on Russia. In this context, investments in renewable energy, increased energy efficiency, and a reduction in carbon emissions are targeted. Additionally, solutions such as reducing energy consumption and saving have been suggested. The effectiveness of these solutions is related to the size, duration, and dynamics of the energy crisis (İnat, 2022).

EU countries, which rely on Ukraine as a key transit route for Russian natural gas imports, have been heavily impacted by these crises. Approximately one-fourth of all energy used in the EU is derived from natural gas, making many EU nations highly dependent on external sources for their gas supply. Consequently, these countries have been the most affected by the recent energy crisis. In response to the repercussions of these crises, the EU has pursued a more effective energy policy concerning natural gas. For example, the energy crisis caused by the Russia-Ukraine war has disrupted gas supply in EU countries, leading to the declaration of an "energy emergency" and the implementation of a "gas emergency plan." This plan is a crucial tool aimed at securing gas supply by incorporating measures and actions to mitigate the impact of gas supply disruptions and address the ongoing energy crisis (EU Secure Gas Supplies, 2023).

Amid the possibility of Russia cutting off or reducing natural gas flow to Europe through Ukraine, the EU and the US are developing joint policies to address this crisis and safeguard the energy security of the EU. These policies involve sourcing additional supply from the global liquefied natural gas (LNG) market, increasing resource diversification, advancing and promoting the use of renewable energy sources, and lifting sanctions on Iran. These policies aim to decrease Europe's energy dependence on Russia and mitigate the risk of an energy crisis. However, there may be challenges and obstacles encountered in this process. For instance, the completion of Russia's new natural gas pipeline project, Nord Stream 2, could potentially increase Europe's reliance on Russian gas. Additionally, price fluctuations in the LNG market may elevate Europe's energy costs. Therefore, the effectiveness and sustainability of the policies developed in response to the crisis will depend on the dynamics of regional energy markets (Kesici, 2022).

The EU's efforts to formulate energy policy date back to the post-World War II period. Throughout history, different periods have been identified regarding the development of energy policies. The first period spans from the establishment of the European Community to the first oil crisis in 1973. The second period covers the years from 1973 to the Single European Act in 1987. The third period extends from 1987 to the beginning of the New Energy Policy in the 2000s, and finally, the developments from the beginning of the 2000s until the present are evaluated as the fourth period.

After World War II, addressing the energy needs became a significant concern during the reconstruction of Europe. As a result, European leaders focused on formulating energy policies and initiated efforts to develop a cooperative action plan. In the initial phase, known as the first period, coal was the most important energy source. The conducted efforts during this time aimed at controlling coal production and usage, utilizing existing resources to meet energy needs, exploring nuclear energy production, and preparing plans related to energy sources (Dursun, 2011).

The second phase of energy policy development was marked by the occurrence of the 1973 and 1979 oil crises, which led to problems such as energy supply insecurity, price instability, and balance of payments deficits. In response to these issues, policies were formulated to address them, including reducing the share of oil in electricity production, promoting the use of coal and nuclear energy, and decreasing dependency on imported oil by taking energy conservation measures. Furthermore, the importance of developing an effective energy policy was emphasized, leading to the adoption of the "International Energy Program" in 1974. This program aimed to create an effective energy policy for member countries, taking into account issues such as energy security, conservation, conscious energy use, economic development, and environmental protection. The third period of energy policy is characterized by the reorganization of previously established policies through changes made in foundational agreements. In these restructuring endeavours, paramount issues include establishing an internal energy market, ensuring energy supply security, and promoting environmentally conscious energy utilization.

In the fourth period, which is considered the most recent, the EU's energy policy has focused on various issues such as the global natural gas crisis, climate change, energy supply security, competitiveness, and renewable alternative energy sources. These policies aim to foster collaboration and unity among member states in the energy sector, unite energy markets, boost the utilization of renewable energy sources, enhance energy efficiency, and decrease greenhouse gas emissions (Kavaz, 2018).

Energy crises play a significant role in guiding and shaping energy policies. For example, during the oil crises of the 1970s, it became evident that the EU faced challenges with energy supply security. As a response, the EU countries aimed to establish common energy policies to ensure energy security (Kaya, 2012). Crises have compelled countries to adopt policies focused on enhancing energy efficiency and investing in renewable energy sources, as they escalate energy costs and negatively impact economic growth, industrial production, and competitiveness. Furthermore, the imbalances created by crises in energy markets have prompted countries to regulate energy prices, ensure market transparency, and implement measures to protect consumers. Despite the adverse effects of energy crises, it is important to acknowledge the positive outcomes of measures taken to prevent or mitigate their consequences and the policies developed in response. For instance, the electricity crisis in the US in the 2000s led to positive developments in the country's energy policy, such as market reforms, strengthening consumer rights, and the emergence of new energy sources and technologies. These advancements resulted from countries capitalizing on the opportunity windows presented by crises and transforming them into advantages.

After the windows of opportunity opened by crises, one area that has been effectively leveraged is "renewable energy sources." The negative impacts of energy crises on the fossil fuel sector, including depletion and environmental damage, have driven countries to explore alternative energy sources. These sources offer renewable, economically viable, and environmentally friendly alternatives to fossil fuels. Among them are solar, wind, hydroelectric, geothermal, biomass, wave, and nuclear energy. Emphasizing the significance of these energy types, they contribute to reducing the dependency on energy, fostering economic development, ensuring energy security, preserving the environment, and addressing climate change challenges. Consequently, these aspects are integral parts of renewable energy policies and action plans.

Many countries have included the goal of increasing the share and diversity of renewable energy sources in their fundamental energy policy objectives. For instance, the US aims to make substantial reductions in greenhouse gas emissions through the Clean Energy and Security Act and has implemented tax incentives to encourage the adoption of renewable energy sources. In China, where a significant portion of energy production relies on coal, the "Law on Prevention and Control of Air Pollution" was enacted in 2000 to support renewable energy sources. This law focuses on establishing renewable energy targets and reducing carbon emissions. China's efforts have made it the world's largest producer of solar energy equipment and wind turbines. Similarly, in Germany, the "Renewable Energy Sources Act" was introduced in 2000 to promote the use of renewables, improve energy efficiency, and lower greenhouse gas emissions. Various measures were implemented within the framework of these objectives, and as a result, Germany is often considered to have the world's best legislation and incentive system for renewable energy sources (Başol, 2022). Türkiye is also among the countries directing their energy policies towards renewable energy sources. In Türkiye's renewable energy policies, key documents include the Electricity Market Law, the Law on the Use of Renewable Energy Resources for Electricity Generation, the National Action Plan, and the Regulation on Renewable Energy Resource Areas. These policy documents aim to increase and promote the utilization of renewable energy sources. They encompass incentives such as domestic contribution for renewables, non-licensed electricity generation, tax reductions, customs exemptions, and land allocation (Ministry of Energy and Natural Resources of the Republic of Türkiye, 2023).

In line with the formulated energy policies, it is observed that the future alternative energy sources to address crises are renewable, economically viable, and environmentally friendly, such as solar, wind, hydroelectric, geothermal, biomass, wave, and nuclear energy. In this context, countries have given considerable importance to "renewable energy sources" in their energy policies to ensure sustainable growth and development.

CONCLUSION

With globalization, countries in the international system have become more interconnected and borders have become invisible. At this point, the rapid development of technology has made energy the most basic need. Today, energy plays a dominant role in basic areas such as shelter, nutrition, health, communication, transportation, education and defence. Even the shortest power outage can negatively affect human life.

Examining recent history reveals a clear escalation in reliance on non-renewable energy sources, which in turn has intensified power struggles and geopolitical conflicts on the global stage. Particularly the recent energy crises stemming from oil confronted great powers with the countries possessing substantial oil reserves in the Middle East. However, the countries of the world, which have more interconnected economic systems than before, have been significantly affected by these energy crises, even if the crisis region is small. These developments have led the countries of the world to cooperate and avoid tensions to prevent global energy crises, take precautions and find solutions. In this process, the importance of renewable energy sources has increased significantly. The diverse array of renewable energy sources, coupled with their significant long-term cost advantages and their role in mitigating the climate crisis, is driving a growing shift towards these energy sources with each passing day. Renewable energy sources are very important in terms of reducing the increasing energy dependence between countries and preventing energy crises.

Throughout history, energy policies have been shaped by the type, timing, and countries affected by energy crises. The causes and adverse consequences of these crises have played a crucial role in determining the direction of energy policies. The solutions presented in energy policies include measures and regulations aimed at preventing crises or addressing their impacts. Energy policies share common and fundamental objectives, such as ensuring energy security, enhancing energy independence, safeguarding the environment, and fostering economic development. In pursuit of these objectives, countries have placed significant emphasis on exploring alternative energy sources, with the promotion and utilization of renewable energy sources becoming central to their energy policies. Consequently, diversifying renewable energy sources and promoting their widespread adoption in various sectors are considered fundamental pillars for economic growth and development. To this end, setting targets, formulating strategies, and creating action plans are essential to encourage, support, and expand the use of renewable energy sources in the future. These policies need to be adaptable to different sectors and energy sources. For example, in the electricity sector, policies may encompass aspects such as purchase guarantees, pricing mechanisms, incentives, and grid integration for electricity generated from renewable sources. Similarly, in the heating and cooling sectors, policies can focus on installation procedures, efficiency enhancements, cost management, and subsidies for renewable heating systems. In the transportation sector, specific policies can be designed to address the production, consumption, quality, and taxation of biofuels. Ultimately, all regulations and efforts in the realm of renewable energy are pivotal in contributing to sustainable growth and development for countries.

REFERENCES

Aktan, S. (2022, 25 August). Avrupa ülkeleri enerji krizinden nasıl etkileniyor; hangi önlemleri aldılar? *Euronews*. Retrieved from https://tr.euronews.com/2022/08/25/avrupa-ulkeleri-enerji-krizinden-nasil-etkileniyor-hangi-onlemleri-aldilar

Başol, F. (2021). *Yenilenebilir Enerji Kaynaklarının Avantaj, Risk ve Tehlikeleri. Çankaya Üniversitesi Fen Bilimleri Enstitüsü*. Yayımlanmamış Yüksek Lisans Tezi.

Battır, O., & Yiğittepe, L. (2023). Rusya-Ukrayna Savaşında Yaptırımlar ve Enerji Güvenliği; Karşılıklı Ekonomik Bağımlılıklar Perspektifinden Bir Değerlendirme. *Yönetim ve Ekonomi Dergisi*, *30*(3), 549–573. doi:10.18657/yonveek.1222200

Bolsen, T. (2011). The Construction of News: Energy Crises, Advocacy Messages, and Frames toward Conservation. *The International Journal of Press/Politics*, *16*(2), 143–162. doi:10.1177/1940161210392782

Caffentzis, G. (1980). The Work/Energy Crisis and the Apocalypse. In In Letters of Blood and Fire: Work, Machines, and the Crisis of Capitalism. PM Press.

Çetinkaya, B. (2019). *Erken Cumhuriyet Dönemi Enerji Politikaları. Karabük Üniversitesi Sosyal Bilimler Enstitüsü.* Yayımlanmamış Yüksek Lisans Tezi.

Damar, N. B. (2022). Elektrik Enerjisinde Uygulanan Politikalar Elektrik Hizmetinde Krizi Kapıya Getirmektedir. *Makine Mühendisleri Odası*, *731*, 89–104.

Dışişleri Bakanlığı, T. C. (2023). *Türkiye'nin Uluslararası Enerji Stratejisi.* https://www.mfa.gov.tr/turkiye_nin-enerji-stratejisi.tr.mfa

Dışişleri Bakanlığı, T. C. (2023). *No: 56, 12 Şubat 2015, Ukrayna Krizi'ne Çözüm Bulunmasına Yönelik 12 Şubat Tarihli Minsk Anlaşması Hk.* https://www.mfa.gov.tr/no_-56_-12-subat-2015_-ukrayna-krizi_ne-cozum-bulunmasina-yonelik-12-subat-tarihli-minsk-anlasmasi-hk_.tr.mfa

Dursun, S. (2011). Avrupa Birliği'nin Enerji Politikası ve Türkiye. *Ankara Üniversitesi Avrupa Toplulukları Araştırma ve Uygulama Merkezi Araştırma Dizisi*, 36.

Energy Information Administration (EIA). (2022, December 22). *What is Energy?* Retrieved from https://www.eia.gov/energyexplained/what-is-energy/

Energy Information Administration (EIA). (2022, June 28). *What is Energy? Sources of Energy*. Retrieved from https://www.eia.gov/energyexplained/what-is-energy/sources-of-energy.php

European Commission. (2023). *Secure Gas Supplies*. Retrieved from https://energy.ec.europa.eu/topics/energy-security/secure-gas-supplies_en

Gilbert, A., Bazilian, M. D., Gross, S. (2022). *The Emerging Global Natural Gas Market and the Energy Crisis of 2021–2022.* Brookings Report.

Guzman, L. P., & Majkut, J. (2023, January 17). *U.S. LNG remapping energy security.* Retrieved from https://features.csis.org/us-lng-remapping-energy-security/

Hamilton, J. D. (2011). Historical Oil Shocks. In R. Parker & R. Whaples (Eds.), Routledge Handbook of Major Events in Economic History. Routledge.

Hariciye. (2020). *1973 Petrol Krizi: Etkileri ve Sonuçları.* Retrieved from https://medium.com/hariciye/1973-petrol-krizi-etkileri-ve-sonu%C3%A7lar%C4%B1-7ec1d90ad4a1

Holzman, S. L. (2006). *A Need for Change: The Looming Energy Crisis.* Army War College. Retrieved from http://www.dtic.mil/dtic/tr/fulltext/u2/a461433.pdf

İnat, K. (2022). Rusya-Ukrayna Savaşı'nın Avrupa Enerji Politikalarına Etkisi. *Kriter*, *7*(73). Retrieved from https://www.iea.org/data-and-statistics/charts/evolution-of-key-regional-natural-gas-prices-june-2021-october-2022

International Energy Agency (IEA). (n.d.). *Global Energy Crisis*. IEA. Retrieved from https://www.iea.org/topics/global-energy-crisis

Islam, M. S. (2017). Alternative Energy Sources for Energy Crisis: Rethinking the Global and Bangladesh Perspectives. *Journal of Technology Innovations in Renewable Energy*, *6*(1), 18–31. doi:10.6000/1929-6002.2017.06.01.3

Jones, T. C. (2012). America, Oil, and War in the Middle East. *The Journal of American History*, *99*(1), 208–218. doi:10.1093/jahist/jas045

Juliet, E. C., Jessica, T. F., Kristy, E. H. M., & Eric, R. A. N. S. (2017). *The Politics of Energy Crises*. Oxford University Press.

Kakışım, C. (2019). Enerji Krizlerinin Etkisiyle Şekillenen Avrupa Birliği'nin Enerji Politikası. *Gümüşhane Üniversitesi Sosyal Bilimler Enstitüsü Elektronik Dergisi*, *10*(2), 460–472.

Kavaz, İ. (2018). Küresel Piyasalar Kapsamında AB'nin Son Dönem Enerji Politikaları. *SETA Perspektif*, *185*, 1–8.

Kaya, İ. S. (2012). Uluslararası Enerji Politikalarına Bir Bakış: Türkiye Örneği. *TBB Dergisi*, *102*, 269–288.

Kesici, G. E. (2022). Rusya-Ukrayna Savaşı'nın AB'nin Enerji Politikalarına Yansıması. *EURO Politika*, *15*, 46–54.

Makine Mühendisleri Odası. (2022). Türkiye'nin Enerji Görünümü. *MMO Yayınları*, 731.

McBride, J. (2022, February 22). R*ussia's Energy Role in Europe: What's at Stake With the Ukraine Crisis | Council on Foreign Relations*. Retrieved from https://www.cfr.org/in-brief/russias-energy-role-europe-whats-stake-ukraine-crisis

Our World in Data. (2023). *Energy Consumption by Source, World*. Retrieved from https://ourworldindata.org/grapher/energy-consumption-by-source-and-country?stackMode=absolute

Özel Özcan, M. S., & Öten, C. (2022). Enerji Kriz Girdabı Kavramsallaştırması Bağlamında Orta Doğu'da Petrol Krizleri. *Bölgesel Araştırmalar Dergisi*, *6*(1), 174–208.

Özturk, S., Sözdemir, A., & Ülger, O. (2013). The Real Crisis Waiting for the World: Oil Problem and Energy Security. *International Journal of Energy Economics and Policy*, *3*(4), 74–79.

Pekmezci, Z. (2020). *Nükleer Santrallere Karşı Yerel Halkın Bakışı: Sinop İli Örneği. Ondokuz Mayıs Üniversitesi Lisansüstü Eğitim Enstitüsü*. Yayımlanmamış Yüksek Lisans Tezi.

Rusya-UkraynaS. K. E. N. E. (2023, March 14). Retrieved from https://www.trthaber.com/haber/dunya/rusya-ukrayna-savasi-kuresel-ekonomiyi-nasil-etkiledi-752972.html

Saygın, H. (2006). Küresel Enerji Politikaları ve Türkiye. *Türk Harb-İş Dergisi*, (219), 26–31.

Schlachter, A. (2010). Worldwide Energy Crisis: Energy Trends in Brazil. *Revista Mexicana de Física*, *56*(2), 34–39.

Schneider, S. A. (1975). The Tiger Starts to Roar: The Origins of The Energy Crisis. *Berkeley Journal of Sociology*, *20*, 13–54.

Simmons, R. A., Coyle, E. D., & Chapman, B. (2014). Global Energy Policy Perspectives. In R. A. Simmons & E. D. Coyle (Eds.), *Understanding the Global Energy Crisis* (pp. 27–72). Purdue University Press.

Smith, E. R., Carlisle, J., & Michaud, K. (2003). *Trust During an Energy Crisis.* UC Berkeley: University of California Energy Institute. Retrieved from https://escholarship.org/uc/item/3v30p0wh

Solar, C. (2023). *Causes, Effects and Solutions to the Global Energy Crisis.* Retrieved from https://coldwellsolar.com/commercial-solar-blog/causes-effects-and-solutions-to-the-global-energy-crisis/

T.C. Dışişleri Bakanlığı AB Başkanlığı. (2023). *Fasıl 15: Enerji.* https://www.ab.gov.tr/fasil-15-enerji_80.html

T.C. Enerji ve Tabi Kaynaklar Bakanlığı. (2023). *Yenilenebilir Enerji Çalışmaları.* https://enerji.gov.tr/enerji-isleri-genel-mudurlugu-yenilenebilir-enerji

Wariavwalla, B. (1975). The Energy Crisis, the Developing World and Strategy. *Adelphi Papers, 115*(115), 32–37. doi:10.1080/05679327508448397

World Energy Outlook. (2022). *International Energy Agency.* Retrieved from https://iea.blob.core.windows.net/assets/830fe099-5530-48f2-a7c1-11f35d510983/WorldEnergyOutlook2022.pdf

Yıldızoğlu, E. (2022, 16 August). Enerji Krizinin Bu Sefer Küresel Olması Dünyayı Nasıl Değiştiriyor? *BBC News*. Retrieved from https://www.bbc.com/turkce/articles/cp6kpy4g4r6o

KEY TERMS AND DEFINITIONS

Alternative Energy Sources: They are renewable, environmentally friendly and economical energy sources that can be used instead of fossil fuels. Alternative energy sources include various types such as solar energy, wind energy, hydroelectric energy, geothermal energy and biomass energy.

Energy: It is defined as the “ability to do work” or “ability to useful work”.

Energy Crisis: This term refers to a shortage or interruption in the provision of energy resources. Growth in demand, difficulties in energy supply, security of energy supply and environmental effects of energy use are among the causes of the most important energy crisis.

Energy Efficiency: It means reducing the amount of energy needed to provide a product or service to better use energy resources, lower energy costs, protect the environment, and increase energy supply security.

Energy Measures: These are the measures taken to use energy effectively and efficiently, to prevent energy waste, to reduce energy costs and to protect the environment.

Energy Policy: It is the set of rules and strategies that determine the energy resources, production, consumption, distribution and pricing of a country or a region.

Energy Supply Security: It means the continuous, sufficient, and affordable supply of energy resources necessary for the economic and social development of a country.

Fossil Resources: Fossil resources are natural energy resources such as coal, oil and natural gas, which are formed by the dissolution of living organisms that died millions of years ago in an oxygen-free environment.

Non-Renewable Sources: Non-renewable energy is a source of energy that will eventually run out. Most sources of non-renewable energy are fossil fuels, such as coal, gas, and oil. Non-renewable energy sources are used in many countries around the world, especially for doing work. They also have a lot of disadvantages due to their negative impact on the environment and their limited supply which is constantly depleted.

Renewable Energy Sources: It is a type of energy that is obtained from inexhaustible sources in nature, offers unlimited use because it constantly renews itself, does not harm the environment, reduces greenhouse gas emissions, increases energy supply security and provides economic benefits. Solar energy, wind energy, hydroelectric energy, geothermal energy, wave energy and tidal energy are among the renewable energy sources.

ENDNOTE

1 Seven Sisters: Exxon, Royal Dutch Shell, Mobil, Texaco, Gulf, Standard Oil of California, and British Petroleum

Chapter 2
From Concept to Policy:
Discussing Energy Politics and Energy Crises

Emre Çıtak
Hitit University, Turkey

ABSTRACT

In this study, a detailed framework regarding energy and energy policies will be drawn in line with the general framework of the book. The meaning of energy; the importance, types, and usage of energy resources; the factors in the formation of energy policies; energy-related sectors; energy security; the place of energy security in government policies; the causes of energy crises; energy management; and energy diplomacy will be introduced, and a comprehensive discussion will take place. Thus, in the light of today's developments, the world of energy will be presented to the reader in different dimensions.

INTRODUCTION

The gradual increase in the need for energy resources in the continuation of social life and economic development has brought the importance of energy policies both in general government policies and in international relations. While traditional energy policies are handled in the context of accessing and transferring energy resources, it is expected that new energy policies will be formed with dimensions such as resource supply, security, infrastructure development, control of commercial dynamics, sustainability, efficiency and environmental awareness. While the success in the preparation and implementation of energy policies can bring serious gains to the states, otherwise they may face problems in case of energy crises. Therefore, approaches such as energy management and energy diplomacy are becoming more and more popular.

Intense relations are observed between the actors such as states and multinational companies in the energy field, sometimes through cooperation and sometimes through conflict. Undoubtedly, the reason for this situation is that traditional energy sources are exhaustible, they are only found in some parts of the world and their profitability is quite high. The conflict of individual policies and interests thus paves

DOI: 10.4018/979-8-3693-0440-2.ch002

the way for the formation of crises. It is inevitable that the crises arising from energy conflicts will have global and long-term effects.

The increasing value of energy resources, usage areas and trade brings the social, national, regional and international dimensions of the issue to the fore. Continuation of energy flow, price stability, smooth trade, and development of relevant technologies and systems are very important. It is very important to evaluate energy, especially in terms of continuity, cost and sustainability. In this regard, while energy security and energy policies are handled in a more serious framework, problems occurring in energy-related processes and practices can cause crises on a global scale. For this reason, it will be very useful to develop a common understanding in order to seize the opportunities in the field of energy and to combat the problems.

In this study, a detailed framework regarding energy and energy policies will be drawn in line with the general framework of the book. The meaning of energy, the importance, types and usage of energy resources, the factors in the formation of energy policies, energy-related sectors, energy security, the place of energy security in government policies, the causes of energy crises, energy management and energy diplomacy will be introduced and a comprehensive discussion will take place. Thus, in the light of today's developments, the world of energy will be presented to the reader in different dimensions. After focusing specifically on energy security and energy crises, the study will come to end with a discussion on the understanding of global energy governance.

1. CONCEPTUAL APPROACH TO ENERGY

1.1. Energy

Dealing with the conceptual dimension of energy can be both easy and difficult. It is possible to define energy simply as "the ability to do work" and to encounter this definition in almost every source. The definition is correct, but it does not provide an understanding of all aspects of energy. This is where the difficult part of the subject begins. Energy is a concept that appeals to different disciplines and can take on different identities when viewed from any field such as physics, chemistry, biology, economics, health or physical education. For this reason, the aforementioned general definition creates an upper framework and together with the supporting terms, it becomes clear what energy really is. Energy should be taken from the aspect of political, economic, and social value that humanity needs to sustain its daily life. Beyond the basic definition, the comprehensive nature of energy emerges when it is considered from the perspectives of fields such as economics, sociology, politics, international relations, history, technology, environmental science, geology, business, security, and engineering, etc., and this is what this study aims to achieve.

The state of being able to perform work is a useful definition for drawing the general framework of energy. Energy can even be expressed in the context of the concept of "power". Before the word energy became widespread, the term "power" filled its place and is still used as an equivalent in some fields today. Power is seen as the most important factor and trigger necessary to accomplish a task. It is also possible to think of power as a measure of energy and can be used to measure the rate of doing work. The energy expended, produced, or transferred per unit time in the performance of a task can be defined as power (McElroy, 2010, pp. 78-79). When talking about energy or power, the key word is "work". Work refers to the physical or mental effort to get a result or produce a desired output (Priest, 2004, pp. 1-2).

Energy, in this context, is the capacity to do work or produce work (Goldemberg, 2012, p. 2). However, in addition to work, heat, and radiation can also be added to this definition. Thus, energy can also be expressed as a property of matter that can be converted into work, heat, or radiation (Walker, 1996, p. 8). Energy can create change to produce useful work, the necessary heat or radiation, and produces light, heat, motion, sound, and growth. Various units are used to measure energy. Watt (Symbol: W) and Watt hours/ kilowatt hours (Symbol: Wh/ Symbol: kWh) are the most commonly used. Other units such as Joule (Symbol: J), Electron Volt (Symbol: eV) and Calorie (Symbol: cal) are used (Krischer and Schönleber, 2015, pp. 3-4). There are also units of measurement used to measure energy resources, such as tons of oil equivalent. Energy exists in many forms. However, the general classification is made in the context of potential energy and kinetic energy. Potential energy refers to the energy of an object due to its position and state, while kinetic energy refers to the energy of an object in motion. Mechanical energy, heat energy, radiant energy, electrical energy, nuclear energy, chemical energy, sound energy, gravitational energy, and elastic energy are listed as other types of energy.

The determiner of energy crises, which should be mentioned about energy and which forms the core of this study, is energy resources. An energy source is a common definition used for all resources that provide usable energy. These resources produce the energy needed after various processes they are subjected to. In other words, they are substances that provide the ability to do work. Energy sources are divided into two renewable and non-renewable. Renewable energy sources are recognized as solar, water, wind, geothermal, and biomass. These resources are also called clean, green, inexhaustible or sustainable resources. Non-renewable sources are listed as fossils such as coal, oil, natural gas, and nuclear. These resources are also referred to as exhaustible or conventional resources. Nonrenewable energy sources are finite in nature, yet renewable ones recur themselves. Although it is known that energy resources such as oil, coal, and natural gas have been used in every field for a long time, it should be noted that there are also new energy resources that are becoming more well-known and whose benefits of use are increasing (Wiser, 2000; Casper, 2007, pp. 29-62; Ngo and Natowitz, 2009). The starting point of the energy policies that form the basis of this study is oil and natural gas, also known as hydrocarbon resources. Since the use of these two commodities for energy purposes, they have increasingly become a matter of economy, politics, security, and diplomacy. Although renewable energy sources are mentioned more frequently today, it should be said that international energy relations are still shaped by oil and natural gas, and in this direction, they are the determinants of cooperation-conflict situations (Claes, 2013; Simmons, Coyle and Champman, 2014, pp. 27-72) Currently, a significant concentration of the resources used for needs such as fuel, heat and electricity are fossil resources; however, the increase in costs, environmental concerns, the danger of depletion, and the desire to pursue independent policies lead countries to abandon fossil fuels and turn to renewable energy sources (Narayan, 2006; Rathore and Panwar, 2022, pp. 1-14).

Energy production refers to the process required to make the type of energy that various sources have available for the energy needed by humanity ready for end-use. For example, it is possible to consider the conversion of the chemical energy of coal or the kinetic energy of wind into electrical energy as energy production, or the fuels produced after the distillation of crude oil are also examples of energy production. Many sources and production methods can be utilized. Production plans are made by taking into account their pros and cons, their availability, and the cost of obtaining them (Demirel, 2012, p.175). When we talk about energy production, the concepts of primary and secondary energy first come to mind. This classification is based on the way the resource is formed. Primary energy sources are resources obtained directly from nature. They are obtained by underground extraction or capture methods. Renewable and non-renewable energy sources fall into this category. For example, while it is necessary to dig underground to reach oil, it is necessary to install systems that can capture the wind to benefit from wind energy. These resources can be transformed as well as directly used. This is where secondary energy comes into play. These are the resources resulting from the conversion of primary energy sources, i.e. natural resources, using various systems and facilities. They are also called energy carriers. Electricity, hydrogen, and secondary fuels are in this group.

When discussing energy resources, it is beneficial to consider Yulia Selivanova's thoughts. According to Selivanova energy is drawing a different path from any other commodity because of some reason. Firstly, energy has been more useful to the economic and social development of modern life. Secondly, hydrocarbon resources are distributed unevenly and unequally throughout the world. Thirdly, energy trade is often linked to the fixed infrastructure necessary for the transportation of hydrocarbons and electricity. Pipelines and transmission grids require substantial investments of high specificity, that is, such transportation networks can be used only for the transportation of specified energy products (2010, p. 49).

Energy-related issues have many aspects. Resources, reserves and production, transportation, systems, trade relations, usage areas and related sectors are important areas. Through all of these, national, regional and international policies emerge and energy, which is vital for human and social life, becomes a political issue.

1.2. Importance and Function of Energy

All existence is based on energy, and energy transformation. It is not possible to imagine a world and life without a varieties of energy. Every event in life or our environment is related to energy in one way or another. From the movement of our bodies to the growth of trees and plants, from the operation of our cars to the formation of wind, from preparing a cup of hot tea to heating our homes, everything is related to energy. From fields such as chemistry, biology, physics, earth sciences, mechanics, and cosmology, the role of energy in the formation, building blocks, and continuity of the universe, our world, and all living things is better understood. Just imagining a world without electricity or gasoline for a few seconds can explain the importance of energy better than volumes of books. Even more fundamentally, what if we consider that the sun, which is at the origin of almost all energy sources, as well as many other things, has lost its power? One can only speak of a planet where life cannot be sustained. The function of energy can be grasped more clearly when one considers for a moment the scale of the crisis that can occur when energy production runs out or when production cannot meet the need.

Energy is at the heart of economic development for all countries. It drives every step of us and powers factories, government, and office buildings. It heats homes and keeps food cold and fresh. Every stage of daily life is somehow related to energy. The direction of the relationship can be expressed as humanity becoming more and more energy-dependent. Such a value attribution also causes energy to become a difficult subject and its centrality refers to its complexity. Energy is the source of wealth and competition, the basis of political debate and technological innovation, and at the heart of an epochal challenge to our global environment (Pascual and Elkind, 2009, p.1). Energy is directly related to civilization, social development, economic development, and technological innovation. There is a deep history of energy, from the efficient use of energy with the invention of fire or the wheel to primitive water or windmills. As humanity's needs and activities such as heating, nutrition, cooking, transportation, communication, and production have increased, the importance and demand for energy have also increased. The emergence and development of steam engines was a turning point in the history of both humanity and energy.

These coal-fired engines have entered many aspects of life, from factories to trains. In the following period, electricity generation activities started, and for this purpose, water power plants were put to work alongside steam engines. The historical background of the subject is the introduction of petroleum and then natural gas as energy sources, the establishment of nuclear reactors and the increasing interest in renewable energy sources and investment in this context (Smil, 1994, pp. 93-148, 223-292). Following the developments in almost all fields from the half of the eighteenth century until almost the end of the twentieth century, oil and petroleum products had a great impact. During this period, the presence of oil has been a driving factor in wars, social developments, economic dynamics, and technological development. This is why this period is also called the age of oil (Salameh, 2018, p.235).

Today's world order is based on energy. From nutrition to technological research, the stability and order of almost every field depends on the continuity of energy production, supply and utilization. Energy enables more production, relationships, and convenience, which in turn require more energy production. In other words, the world's energy needs are in a constant upward trend. In this context, the energy sector is growing every day. There is a huge energy system made up of governments, international energy companies, buyers, suppliers, engineers, policy experts, the transportation sector, legislation, energy technology, investments, resources, production facilities, security companies, communication lines, and academic studies. This system in turn supports other fields, sectors, and systems - in short, all the dynamics on which the modern world is built.

Energy has been becoming a factor that increasingly affects all aspects of life, and its deficiency can create problems from industry to healthcare, from education to transportation. It is seen that political, economic, and social problems are experienced in countries that have difficulties in commercializing energy resources or cannot access sufficient energy resources. Therefore, access to energy, effective usage, and related security are very important to national interests (Jefferson, 2013; Koulori and Mouraviev, 2019). In the next section, energy policy, energy security, and energy crisis issues will be discussed in the context of the importance of energy.

2. POLITICS ON ENERGY

2.1. Energy-Policy and Energy-Politics

The increasing importance of energy leads countries to take firm steps in this sense. What is meant by firm steps is the preparation of plans, strategies, and roadmaps that set the direction of energy-related activities, namely the formulation of energy policies. Today, countries base their economies, development, and social progress on energy. Energy is increasingly involved in foreign and security policies and is one of their main determinants. In addition, the energy sector is the main supporter of many sectors. For these reasons, a comprehensive, coherent energy policy that is in line with national realities and the dynamics of the international arena is seen as a serious necessity.

Considering that all energy relations, activities, and markets are a system, energy policy represents the will to maintain this system in the right way. Economic growth, energy security, and environmental sensitivity are the basic building blocks of energy policy (Simpson and McNamara, 2011). Topics such as sustainability, diversity, security, cooperation, continuity, flexibility, market foresight, and stakeholders come to the forefront of energy policymaking. The country's current energy production and consumption data, forecasts of near and far-term needs, market fluctuations, developments in the energy sector, international events that may closely affect energy security and the market, the status of existing agreements, and technological developments in the field are also taken into account. The targets set for the short, medium, and long term form the basis of energy policy. In similar way, Andreas Goldthau alleges markets, security, sustainability, and development as the four deeply intertwined aspects of global energy policies (2013, pp. 3-5).

Energy politics refers to a concept related to international relations. Energy-politics deals with the activities and relations carried out by states, international organizations, or large corporations on energy in the international arena. Trade relations, agreements, partnerships, and projects that emerge based on the energy market constitute the essence of energy politics. The relevant actors and groups, led by states, operate in the field by taking into account the international and regional situation, the struggle over energy resources, the balance of supply and demand, prices in the market, environmental impacts, and the behavior of the main actors. The fact that overall energy production and consumption are largely based on the traditional sources of fossil fuels and nuclear energy also affects the energy policies of the countries that have these resources and those that do not, and their roles and strategies in international energy policies. Likewise, since the energy needs of developed, developing and underdeveloped countries are not at the same level, there are serious differences in the energy policies put forward (Hughes and Lipscy, 2013, pp. 449-469). Despite the differences, no country can separate its foreign and security policies from its energy policies, making special investments in this field and developing complex networks of relations.

In her book, Brenda Shaffer discusses the politics and energy nexus in several topics. She alleges such key findings that (1) politics and energy are inextricably linked. International politics and energy trends are inseparable, and energy security is a key component of states' foreign and domestic security strategies, (2) the international system's structure is impacted by energy consumption because of the interdependence that oil use brings about. Since oil is a commodity that is traded internationally, the demand of each nation influences the price and supply of oil for all customers, (3) increased internationalization of internal political developments in oil producing and important transit states is a result of tight oil market conditions. Local political unrest in an oil exporter or significant transit state can have global repercussions when the global oil markets are tight, (4) an additional connection between a state's internal and foreign policies is made through energy. The domestic energy consumption habits and policies of a state are becoming a topic of interest and concern in international politics due to the effects of hydrocarbon use on climate change, energy pricing, and worries about the availability of energy supply, (5) energy provides yet another link between a state's domestic and foreign affairs. Due to the impacts of hydrocarbon use on climate change, the cost of energy, and concerns about the supply of energy, a state's domestic energy consumption habits and policies are becoming a matter of attention and concern in international politics, (6) due to its tremendous susceptibility to political influence, natural gas is now at the center of energy security strategies. Actually, compared to the oil market, the gas market is much more susceptible to political interference. Increased worldwide natural gas consumption and booming cross-border natural gas trade present increased opportunities for politics to influence the dynamics of the energy supply, (7) the gas supply between suppliers and consumers is often stable and less susceptible to political and security ebbs and flows when there is interdependence between them in the supply relationship. The degree to which a supplier and a consumer are dependent on one another and the degree to which each side has access to alternative supply or market options, including transportation infrastructure, appear to determine whether the relationships are dependent or interdependent, (8) energy export projects that involve multiple states, lengthy, and costly are now very normal. This is a direct outcome of the tendency toward oil exportation from troubled regions, (9) the energy trade's physical security is vulnerable. Energy infrastructure has also become an attractive target for terrorist groups and a focus in civil conflicts, (10) states that rely on imported energy should increase their energy storage capacity to improve energy security. While not requiring the assistance of other states, doing so is useful in preventing crisis scenarios. Despite this, only a few states have enough energy storage and (11) the danger of climate change could be the impetus for a significant long-term shift in the world's reliance on fossil fuels. The issue of climate change is being seen as directly affecting human and international security rather than just quality of life and the environment (2009, pp 3-6).

As the areas of use of energy increase and the importance of having energy becomes more apparent, the political dimension of the issue becomes more prominent. One of the foundations of this politicization is international relations, and these relations are shaped by interdependence. Some countries rely heavily on international energy trade, i.e. energy dependence. Producing countries need energy demand to monetize their natural wealth and create wealth that, if managed effectively, can contribute to social welfare. Producers therefore seek to set higher prices as long as these prices do not lead to a reduction in demand. Consumer countries, on the other hand, rely on continuity of supply, or at least systematically functioning energy markets, to ensure adequate energy supplies for their economies. They also seek to limit the degree to which their economies are dependent on energy production and imports by seeking to develop policies to increase efficiency and reduce energy intensity, thereby protecting themselves from the ups and downs of the global energy market. In this context, it is necessary to say that there are differences between the political approaches of reserve-holder states and importing states. Since states in these groups will have different interests, motivations, needs, and expectations, it is possible to make sense of differences in policies. However, the question of whether and how producer and consumer countries can engage in a productive dialogue to contribute to mutually beneficial developments in their energy practices needs to be discussed (Pascual and Elkind, 2009, p.4).

Environmental responsibility, environmental benefits, or environmental safety are becoming more and more important topics in energy policies. In addition to the search for the most cost-effective and safe ways to obtain and trade energy, it is also one of the points given attention to producing environmentally friendly solutions. The energy-environment relationship constitutes a situation that is taken seriously in both national and international policies (Hodgson, 2010; Bradshaw, 2013). Undoubtedly, environmental awareness often falls behind the national interests of states. Many sensitivities are ignored when it comes to access to energy sources or energy security. For this reason, initiatives related to environmental problems in the international arena fail or cannot reach the desired effect level. It should be said that the solution at this point is to create a balance between energy security- energy interests and the environment (Lovaas, 2009; Fay and Golomb, 2002).

Energy efficiency is one of the most important focal points in both energy policies and energy security. Because energy efficiency strategies suggest a more logical and efficient use of energy resources. For this, both the taking of savings-oriented measures and the production of technology for efficiency constitute the basic approaches (Roy et al., 2013, pp. 283-286). Nowadays, when energy production is highly dependent on fossil resources, energy efficiency, and energy saving are becoming increasingly important. Getting maximum efficiency from limited resources constitutes one of the foundations of policies. In this regard, while it is necessary to use technologies and methods that will minimize the loss in the extraction, processing, transportation, and conversion of energy resources, it will be useful to draw attention to the necessity of awareness-raising activities regarding the conservation and efficient use of energy.

On the basis of renewable energy, it stands as a very strong alternative for the solution of energy crises and energy security problems. Because there is a general perception that the advantages they have over traditional energy sources can remove energy from being an issue of conflict in the international arena. Although many countries meet a significant part of their energy needs from sources such as solar, wind and wave power, it is not easy to say that renewable energy is used at a sufficient level. However, with renewable energy, it has become possible to reconsider energy-related issues such as efficiency, accessibility, dependency, profitability, cost, environmental awareness, and conflicts of interest. Of course, while making these discussions, it should not be ignored that there are myths and exaggerations as well as facts or strong potentials (Mallon, 2006).

While developing energy-related technologies and systems, states are especially sensitive about efficiency, reliability, vulnerability and safety. It should be noted that technology investments are very important at this point in creating energy policies (Sovacool, Sidortsov and Jones, 2014, pp. 168-170). While an important pillar of national energy policies is based on technology and system development, opportunities for international cooperation on the same issues also appear.

2.2. Energy Security

It is possible to search for the roots of energy security in the way energy resources affect the development, economy, and industry of countries. Therefore, accessing energy resources and using them beneficially has become a main concern. Securing the supply of energy resources has been seen as the main goal of both exporting and importing states. While more energy was required to carry out the struggle during the First and Second World Wars, it was very difficult to reach hydrocarbon resources due to the conflict environment. However, energy security fully came to the fore in 1973. Although energy resources have been extremely important since the first periods of their use until today, in October 1973, the Organization of Arab Petroleum Exporting Countries (OAPEC) decided to impose an embargo on countries that supported Israel in the Yom Kippur War. In just a few months, oil prices have nearly quadrupled. Even though the embargo was partially lifted in March, prices continued to remain high. During this process, it was realized that energy resources could be a political weapon or a tool of oppression. At the same time, it has been observed that an increase in energy resource prices or a problem in its supply for any reason may create problems at the global level (Lynch, 2018; Kester, 2018).

Jonathan Elkind states that the understanding of energy security is based on four elements: availability, reliability, affordability, and environmental sustainability. The table he prepared in his work availability includes the physical endowment of producer countries, the ability of producers, transit countries, and consumers to agree on terms of trade, technological solutions for production, transportation, conversion, storage, and distribution, capital investment, viable legal and regulatory structures, and compliance with environmental and other regulatory requirements. Reliability contains a robust, diversified energy value chain, adequate reserve capacity for the entire value chain, short- and long-term protection from terrorist attacks, extreme weather, and political interruptions, and adequate information about the functioning of the global energy market. Affordability covers low price volatility, transparent pricing, realistic expectations for future prices, prices that reflect full costs, as a matter of short-term incremental cost and over the full lifecycle. Sustainability refers to low emissions of greenhouse gas and other pollutants, minimal contribution to local, regional, or global threats to environmental quality, and protection of energy systems from the impacts of a changing climate (2009, pp. 121-130). Bert Kruyt et al. adopt energy security in four dimensions availability (elements related to geological existence), accessibility (geopolitical elements), affordability (economical elements), and acceptability (environmental and societal elements) (2009, p. 2167).

Benjamin Sovacool and Ishani Mukherjee outline energy security as (1) availability, (2) affordability, (3) technology development and efficiency, (4) environmental sustainability, and (5) regulation and governance. They explain availability saving sufficient supplies of energy, being energy independent, promoting a diversified collection of different energy technologies, harnessing domestically available fuels and energy resources and ensuring prudent reserve to production ratios; affordability as producing energy services at the lowest cost, having predictable prices for energy fuels and services, and enabling equitable access to energy services; technology development and efficiency as producing energy services at the lowest cost, having predictable prices for energy fuels and services, and enabling equitable access to energy services, capacity to adapt and respond to the challenges from disruptions, researching and developing new and innovative energy technologies, making proper investments in infrastructure and maintenance, delivering high quality and reliable energy services; environmental and social sustainability as minimizing deforestation and land degradation, possessing sufficient quantity and suitable quality of water, minimizing ambient and indoor pollution, mitigating GHG emissions associated with climate change, adapting to climate change; regulation and governance as having stable, transparent, and participatory modes of energy policymaking, competitive markets, promoting trade of energy technology and fuels, enhancing social and community knowledge about education and energy issues (2011, p. 5345).

While Daniel Yergin states that energy security is traditionally the availability of sufficient supplies at affordable prices for developed states, he says that it is based on the understanding of the continuation of the demand for energy resources that make a significant contribution to the economies of exporting states. On the other hand, the main concerns of developing countries are based on price stability/fluctuation. Thus, while the traditional approach prioritizes the healthy and reasonable continuation of energy resource trade, with a broader perspective, he suggests that factors such as developments in global trade, supply-chain vulnerabilities, terrorism and the integration of new economies into the world market should be taken into account (2006, pp.70-71). Gal Luft and Anne Korin state that the combination of the factors that come from states or non-state actors and cause disruptions in the energy field should be evaluated within the scope of energy security, while they allege that the perception of energy security varies from society to society. At this point, it is argued that the general perception towards energy and security and the need in this direction are decisive. Countries are exposed to a number of energy security challenges that determine their behavior and national priorities in the international arena (2009, pp. 1-5).

Meghan O'Sullivan argues that energy security means having access to affordable energy without having to unduly distort one's political, security, diplomatic, or military arrangements. She also presents a different approach by adding the question "Is a country really energy safe when obtaining adequate energy resources depends on a particular expensive, high-risk, and limiting stance in the world?" (2013, p. 31). With another approach, Micheal Klein draws the basic lines of energy security as petroleum insufficiency, intensified competition for the available supply, shift in the center of gravity of world oil production, and the militarization of energy security. In this context, the amount of energy resources, the impact of the change in producer-consumer-transit countries, the struggle to dominate resources and the instability caused by armed conflicts stand out as determining factors (2009, pp. 40-49). According to Brenda Schaffer, three primary factors are frequently considered to make up energy security: supply reliability, cost-effectiveness, and environmental friendliness. Diversifying energy sources and providers, storing fuel, building redundant infrastructure, and encouraging flexibility in fuel use are all ways to attain energy security (2009, pp. 91-92). Sovacool, Sidortsov and Jones define energy security with a broader approach as equitably providing available, affordable, reliable, environmentally benign, proactively governed, and socially acceptable energy services to end users (2014, p.11).

According to Johannes Kester, the initial worry over the political security of supply soon gave way to a range of issues involving market externalities, political and military interference, environmental effects, affordability, health, and system resilience. The idea of energy security is still growing, reflecting the wide range of issues and reference points that accompany the advancement of energy technology in our daily lives. Contextualization is necessary since the conversation that followed revealed the hollow and polysemic nature of energy security. A commonplace understanding of energy security results from such a developing conceptualization on two fronts. First, it propagates a naive binary concept of security derived from the two main theoretical interpretations of energy security (neo-liberalism and geopolitics). Both of these just observe and reflect the normative logic and power dynamics behind the current energy markets; neither offers a genuine reflection of the more comprehensive (ethical) security theories and issues surrounding energy security. Second, in order to address newly discovered flaws, it continuously adds new referent objects. As a result, energy security will never be achieved since there will always be a subsequent flaw (2018, pp. 29-30).

Koulouri and Mouraviev allege that the transformation in energy security in the new period is realized in the light of change at the (1) cognitive level, (2) the emergence of many actors in this field, (3) experts bringing different perspectives and (4) practices carried out around the world. According to them, energy security is evaluated in different dimensions beyond access to oil. Firstly, in this context, a common set of principles has emerged depending on the interests of the actors. These include diversification (of sources, suppliers and routes), efficiency (in meeting the demand and in supply chains), sustainability (economic and environmental), system resilience and emergency response capacity underpinned and facilitated by technological innovation and reliable energy markets. Secondly, in light of the dynamic and complex nature of the issues surrounding energy security, actors like the IEA, the World Bank, the EU, the World Energy Council, ministries of energy, and environmental groups are tasked with redefining energy security and developing mitigation and response strategies. Thirdly, special experts have also been identified to provide input to academic institutions and research groups in the areas of energy policy, renewable energy technologies, natural resource management, and environmental sustainability. The goal is to improve our comprehension of what energy security is, how to best address related concerns, and how to assess the efficacy of suggested solutions. The rapidly expanding number of pertinent studies and publications in recent years, as well as the involvement of experts by governments to guide policy design and execution, reflect the growing interest in the field of energy security and many other disciplines. Lastly, the use of measures in the form of legislative and regulatory actions to solve the issues related to energy security that have surfaced in countries all over the world. Furthermore, a lot of countries have passed legislation to support renewable energy based on both quantity and price (2019, pp. 16-17).

An increasing approach to energy security is the belief that many problems can be solved with the increasing use of renewable energy sources. It is known that many conflicts and concerns in the field arise from the distribution and sharing, transportation, and use of fossil resources. Considering the environmental, economic, and political burden of all these processes, it is inevitable that renewable energy will bring into question what is known about issues such as availability, efficiency, sustainability, and affordability (Valentine, 2011; Johansson, 2013). Domestic violence, the regional conflicts it creates, and the intervention of great powers in the crisis are among the reasons that affect energy security. It should not be ignored that all these situations arise from the sharing of the areas with the current controversial energy source. Possessing hydrocarbon energy resources can be a matter of conflict both by the powers within the state and by the actors in the international arena (Klare, 2009). It seems that as the usage areas of renewable energy and related technology develop, a positive future can be built to ensure energy security. However, it should not be forgotten that the promotion of renewable energy as a substitute for traditional energy sources in an effort to improve energy security is another problem. Renewable energy sources are hampered by problems like intermittency and high operating costs, despite the fact that they are often more sustainable than traditional energy sources and may lessen the demand for energy imports (Ang, Choong and Ng, 2015, p.1090).

The international energy market, like other markets, is susceptible to any war or unrest that would cause interruption, disruption, or turmoil. Throughout history, political conflicts and serious violent situations, especially where energy resources are extracted or trade routes, have led to a pessimistic atmosphere in the markets, disruption of price stability, and interruption of resource flows. Of course, market security is shaped in this context by ensuring the balance of supply and demand and determining a price that buyers and sellers can tolerate (Moran and Russell, 2009, pp. 1-5). For energy security, each state creates its strategies and policies and takes measures, including military ones. Such different approaches also expand the boundaries of the concept when defining it. Changing approaches and definitions towards energy security lead to the redesign of energy security within national policy and national security (Flaherty and Filho, 2013, pp. 14-16).

Consequently, energy security is multidimensional, stressing a variety of issues like resource availability and accessibility, policy design and implementation, economic and environmental sustainability, and proper technology and systems. Nowadays, energy security needs to be considered multifacetedly with its political, economic, commercial, military, social and cultural dimensions. In addition, the different interests and expectations of the actors in the field differentiate the definitions of energy security and diversify the policies. In this regard, it should be taken into consideration that the strategies, understanding, or practices to ensure energy security are extremely variable, flexible, and dynamic (Chester, 2010, 889-891; Ang, Choong, and Ng, 2015; Mouraviev and Koulouri, 2019, pp. 259-260). The discourse of sustainable energy security comes to the fore in discussions ranging from the basis of maintaining oil supply to the multidimensional understanding that has survived to the present day. An understanding that will be put forward in the context of all factors, actors, and future plans (concerns, developments, systems, needs) will be the approach that will provide security.

2.3. Energy Crisis

Energy crisis refers to negative situations that occur in any energy-related field and can bring serious consequences. Problems in energy supply, production, transmission for any reason, or price fluctuations that cause global effects can create a crisis in the energy market. While these crises may be short-lived, they can also leave an impact for many years. Energy crises are an important topic in energy policies and provide no benefit to any actor in the energy world. Crises affect exporting and importing countries, energy companies, and societies directly and indirectly. The need for energy is increasing worldwide and it is clear that the energy demands of developed and developing countries will follow such a course in the coming years. The fact that energy resources are not evenly distributed geographically and the depletion of reserves of hydrocarbon resources will mean that a serious problem will arise in the face of this demand (Chatuverdi, 2017).

The most important international energy crisis, which also gave its name to the concept, was experienced in 1973 as mentioned above. With this crisis, it has emerged that energy can be used as a tool in conflicts between states and thus can create an atmosphere that can affect the entire international system (Yergin, 2006). In the period from 1973 to the present, developments that led to the energy crisis have occurred under the influence of national, regional, or international situations and conditions. It is necessary to state that the world has experienced energy crises of various degrees during the times of the Iranian revolution, the Iran-Iraq War, the Gulf War between 1990 and 1991, the 2003 Iraq War, international crisis periods when oil prices peaked, and the Covid-19 pandemic (Coyle et al., 2014; Carlisle et al., 2017). Political unrests, conflicts, and economic crises in the international arena can pave the way for crises with their direct and indirect reflections on energy relations. Today, the international energy market is so intertwined and built on delicate balances that any international problem can lead to international energy crises. Thus, it is not impossible to see new crises in the coming years.

According to Cutler Cleveland and Christopher G. Morris energy crisis a general term for economic, political, and social distresses in a society, resulting from a severe shortage of available energy resources (2006, p. 144). It should be noted that energy constitutes a crisis domestically as well as internationally. Depending on the sources of supply and demand, the political aspect of energy becomes salient in times of crisis. When unstable energy markets raise prices and hinder long-term investment planning in times of volatility, politicians hear the protests of their constituents. Energy management has become more important for today's societies. The fact that every aspect of modern life relies on energy consumption in some way means that any problem is likely to be met with a serious public backlash. For example, transportation systems are heavily dependent on energy, so a disruption in oil markets can lead to disruption, increased service costs, and, in the longer term, to a standstill. Access to energy is critical for sustaining growth, especially in developing countries, to keep people employed and keep pace with a rapidly growing population. As populations become more educated and demanding, unfulfilled hopes for greater prosperity can put severe pressure on political regimes (Pascual and Zambetakis, 2009, p.9).

It is well-known that states can use energy as a foreign policy card, tool, or weapon. The goal here is to get policy priorities or put pressure on others to take a step back on issues they're uncomfortable with. While most supplier states can resort to pressure such as cutting off energy flow or terminating contracts, importing or transit states can also show their soft power over energy from time to time (O'Sullivan, 2013, pp. 37-39). In this way, the politicization of energy relations can bring crises and even escalate to the level of military confrontation. It is quite possible that any intervention that have potential to affect the general course of the energy market could lead to a widespread crisis in this context. In this context, it should be noted that the use of commercial relations on energy resources as an element of political pressure has a crisis-promising aspect.

Many suggestions can be offered to prevent energy crises. Increasing cooperation and understanding between actors, increasing the use of renewable energy instead of fossil resources, introducing modern approaches to energy security, developing environmentally compatible systems, and preventing energy waste are the points that should be highlighted in this context (Hodgson, 2010; Jefferson, 2013; Dark et al., 2014; Carlisle, 2017).

IN LIEU OF CONCLUSION: ENERGY DIPLOMACY AND GLOBAL ENERGY GOVERNANCE

Energy policies are traditionally formed within the scope of states' own needs and interests and are seen as a dimension of foreign policy. Therefore, it is quite natural for energy policies to be competitive and crisis-producing. In addition, energy policies may lead to losses for some, deficiencies in combating threats to global energy security, and insufficient initiatives on sustainability. For this reason, the idea of global energy management, which aims to bring all stakeholders together to carry out energy-related processes and to create a common understanding of the struggle against problems, comes to the fore.

Global energy governance is based on the idea that energy should be jointly managed on a global basis so that the approach to energy is more comprehensive, systematic, and peaceful. Many aspects of energy around the world, such as resources, sectors, technology, agreements, pricing, transmission lines, security threats, etc., can be addressed at the international level for the benefit of all. Thus, it is aimed to ensure cooperation in the field of energy and to establish a stable environment (Florini and Sovacool, 2009; Goldthau, Hoxtell and Witte, 2010; Kottari, 2016).

According to Ann Florini, although there isn't a widely accepted global energy agency or organization, some intergovernmental bodies and nongovernmental groups exist to address global energy issues; including large multilateral organizations such as the IEA, the Energy Charter Treaty, and the International Energy Forum; a variety of small-scale, public-private partnerships and multi-stakeholder processes; bodies that focus on a specific energy source, such as the International Atomic Energy Agency; funders such as the multilateral development banks that include energy projects in their loan portfolios; and various business organizations, advocacy groups, and research institutions. A number of other institutions are also concerned with energy, including the G-8, the European Union (EU), and the Asia-Pacific Economic Cooperation (APEC) (2009, pp. 157-158). In the process that has come to the present, there has been a general perception that some issues concern the entire globe, that the outputs have a global impact and that they should be handled with general participation. Of course, the debates on globalization have been decisive in this regard. Issues such as climate change, global security threats and famine have aspects that concern everyone in the world. Energy can also be considered in this context. The role of energy in sustaining modern life, in international trade and in meeting basic human needs requires that issues such as energy supply, investment, price, technology, and the impact of environmental conditions should be addressed with global energy management (Kottari, 2016, pp. 126-129).

Energy diplomacy is not a new term. Relations over energy resources and trade have kept states, international organizations, and private companies involved in an intense chain of negotiations. According to Andreas Goldthau, energy diplomacy generally refers to the way countries use state power to give energy companies a competitive advantage in bidding for resources. Consumer countries strengthen their supply position by diplomatically supporting energy contracts, while producer countries use diplomacy to increase their access to markets or reserves. Besides, the term refers to use of foreign policy tools to get clean access to energy supplies and to promote cooperation in the energy sector (2010, pp. 25-28).

Van de Graff and Colgan draw attention to some cleavages in the table they prepared for global energy management. They underline that there are differences between importing, exporting and transit countries in terms of energy security, between developed and developing countries in development and environment and between multinational companies, states and international civil society in terms of management approach. They state that international security causes more serious differences of opinion (2016, p. 8).

Leonardo Baccani et al. in their study on global energy governance, stated that producer and consumer countries have different approaches to such cooperation in line with their interests, that the general policies of the states towards international organizations are decisive at this point, and that cooperation tendencies are higher when there are projects such as pipeline construction in which the regional states need to act jointly (2013, pp. 212-213). Aleh Cherp et al. state that three global energy challenges - ensuring access to modern forms of energy for all people, ensuring energy security for every nation, and minimizing the climate impacts of energy systems - must be addressed urgently and simultaneously. In their view, this requires an unprecedented transformation of national energy systems, guided by internationally shared energy goals that focus on these challenges. To them in one way, global energy governance aimed at addressing these challenges must command long-term commitment, determination, focus and resources, with a high level of integration of energy policies across scales of governance, supply and demand aspects of energy systems and energy technologies. And in another way, the complexity of energy challenges requires flexibility, innovation, openness and diversity, as well as the broad participation of different actors. Nations, energy industries and communities will need to find unique solutions that work for them. No panacea, whether technological or institutional, is likely to succeed (2011, pp. 75-76).

Although it may seem like a social or national problem at first glance, energy is a global issue and energy security is an area of global concern. It is clear that the continuity, efficiency and sustainability of energy flow will benefit all stakeholders, from individuals to energy companies, from exporting states to international energy-related organizations. For this reason, despite all kinds of disagreements and conflicts of interest, the development of a common understanding of energy is the most important criterion in preventing new energy crises.

REFERENCES

Ang, B. W., Choong, W. L., & Ng, T. S. (2015). Energy security: Definitions, dimensions and indexes. *Renewable & Sustainable Energy Reviews*, *42*, 1077–1093. doi:10.1016/j.rser.2014.10.064

Baccani, L. (2013). Global energy governance: Trade, infrastructure, and the diffusion of international organization. *International Interactions*, *39*(2), 192–216. doi:10.1080/03050629.2013.768512

Bradshaw, M. (2013). Sustainability, climate change, and transition in global energy. In A. Goldthau (Ed.), *The handbook of global energy policy* (pp. 48–64). Wiley-Blackwell. doi:10.1002/9781118326275.ch3

Carlisle, J. E. (2017). *The politics of energy crises*. Oxford University Press.

Casper, J. K. (2007). *Natural resources-energy: Powering the past, present, and future*. Chelsea House Publishers.

Chatuverdi, A. K. (2017). Geopolitics of energy. In A. Shukla & A. Sharma (Eds.), *Energy security and sustainability* (pp. 363–398). CRC Press.

Cherp, A., Jewell, J., & Goldthau, A. (2011). Governing global energy: Systems, transitions, complexity. *Global Policy*, *2*(1), 75–88. doi:10.1111/j.1758-5899.2010.00059.x

Chester, L. (2010). Conceptualising energy security and making explicit its polysemic nature. *Energy Policy*, *38*(2), 887–895. doi:10.1016/j.enpol.2009.10.039

Claes, D. H. (2013). Cooperation and conflict in oil and gas markets. In A. Goldthau (Ed.), *The handbook of global energy policy* (pp. 176–189). Wiley-Blackwell. doi:10.1002/9781118326275.ch11

Cleveland, C., & Morris, C. G. (2006). *Dictionary of energy*. Elsevier.

Dark, M. (2014). Taking emerging renewable technologies to market. In E. D. Coyle & R. A. Simmons (Eds.), *Understanding the global energy crisis* (pp. 193–213). Purdue University Press.

Demirel, Y. (2012). *Energy: Production, conversion, storage, conservation, and coupling*. Springer. doi:10.1007/978-1-4471-2372-9

Elkind, J. (2009). Energy security: Call for a broader agenda. In C. Pascual & J. Elkind (Eds.), *Energy security: Economics, politics, strategies and implications* (pp. 119–148). Brookings Institution Press.

Fay, J. A., & Golomb, D. S. (2002). *Energy and the environment*. Oxford University Press.

Flaherty, C., & Filho, W. L. (2013). Energy security as a subset of national security. In W. L. Filho & V. Voudouris (Eds.), *Global energy policy and security* (pp. 11–26). Springer. doi:10.1007/978-1-4471-5286-6_2

Florini, A. (2009). Global governance and energy. In C. Pascual & J. Elkind (Eds.), *Energy security: Economics, politics, strategies and implications* (pp. 149–181). Brookings Institution Press.

Florini, A., & Sovacool, B. J. (2009). Who governs energy? The challenges facing global energy governance. *Energy Policy, 37*(12), 5239–5248. doi:10.1016/j.enpol.2009.07.039

Goldemberg, J. (2012). *Energy: What everyone needs to know*. Oxford University Press. doi:10.1093/wentk/9780199812905.001.0001

Goldthau, A. (2010). Energy diplomacy in trade and investment of oil and gas. In A. Goldthau & J. M. Witte (Eds.), *Global energy governance: The new rules of the game* (pp. 25–48). Brookings Institution Press.

Goldthau, A. (2013). Introduction: Key dimensions of global energy policy. In A. Goldthau (Ed.), *The handbook of global energy policy* (pp. 1–11). Wiley-Blackwell. doi:10.1002/9781118326275.ch0

Goldthau, A., Hoxtell, W., & Witte, J. M. (2010). Global energy governance: The way forward. In A. Goldthau & J. M. Witte (Eds.), *Global energy governance: The new rules of the game* (pp. 341–356). Brookings Institution Press.

Hodgson, P. E. (2010). *Energy, environment and climate change*. Imperial Collage Press. doi:10.1142/p651

Hughes, L., & Lipscy, P. Y. (2013). The politics of energy. *Annual Review of Political Science, 16*(1), 449–469. doi:10.1146/annurev-polisci-072211-143240

Jefferson, M. (2013). Challenges to global energy policy and supply security. In W. L. Filho & V. Voudouris (Eds.), *Global energy policy and security* (pp. 27–44). Springer. doi:10.1007/978-1-4471-5286-6_3

Johansson, B. (2013). Security aspect of future renewable energy systems- A short overview. *Energy, 61*, 598–605. doi:10.1016/j.energy.2013.09.023

Kester, J. (2018). *The politics of energy security: Critical security studies, new materialism and governmentality*. Routledge. doi:10.4324/9781315177892

Klare, M. T. (2009). Petroleum anxiety and the militarization of energy security. In D. Moran & J. A. Russell (Eds.), *Energy security and global politics: The militarization of resource management* (pp. 39–61). Routledge.

Klare, M. T. (2009). There will be blood: Political violanece, regional warfare, and the risk of great-power conflict over contested energy resources. In G. Luft & A. Korin (Eds.), *Energy security challenges for the 21st century: A reference handbook* (pp. 44–65). Praeger Security International.

Kottari, M. (2016). A new era for global energy governance? The environmental imperatives and the EU perspective. *Politikon: IAPSS Political Science Journal*, *29*, 124–139. doi:10.22151/politikon.29.7

Koulouri, A., & Mouraviev, N. (2019). Energy security through the lens of renewable energy resources and resource efficiency. In N. Mouraviev & A. Koulouri (Eds.), *Energy security: Policy challenges and solutions for resource efficiency* (pp. 9–36). Palgrave Macmillan. doi:10.1007/978-3-030-01033-1_2

Krischer, K., & Schönleber, K. (2015). *Physics of energy conversion*. De Grutyer. doi:10.1515/9781501510632

Kuyt, B. (2009). Indicators for energy security. *Energy Policy*, *37*(6), 2166–2181. doi:10.1016/j.enpol.2009.02.006

Lovaas, D. (2009). Balancing energy security and the environment. In G. Luft & A. Korin (Eds.), *Energy security challenges for the 21st century: A reference handbook* (pp. 318–334). Praeger Security International.

Luft, G., & Korin, A. (2009). Energy security: In the eyes of the beholder. In G. Luft & A. Korin (Eds.), *Energy security challenges for the 21st century: A reference handbook* (pp. 1–17). Praeger Security International.

Lynch, M. (2018). New energy and the geopolitics of the future. In J. I. Considine & K.-W. Paik (Eds.), *Handbook of energy politics* (pp. 276–287). Edward Elgar. doi:10.4337/9781784712303.00022

Mallon, K. (2006). Myhts, pitfalls and oversights. In K. Mallon (Ed.), *Renewable energy policy and politics: A handbook for decision-making* (pp. 5–34). Earthscan.

McElroy, M. B. (2010). *Energy: Perspectives*. Oxford University Press.

Moran, D., & Russell, J. A. (2009). Introduction: The militarization of energy security. In D. Moran & J. A. Russell (Eds.), *Energy security and global politics: The militarization of resource management* (pp. 1–18). Routledge.

Mouraviev, N., & Koulouri, A. (2019). Renewable energy and resource efficiency: Governance is key. In N. Mouraviev & A. Koulouri (Eds.), *Energy security: Policy challenges and solutions for resource efficiency* (pp. 255–262). Palgrave Macmillan. doi:10.1007/978-3-030-01033-1_10

Narayan, R. (2006). Rationale, drivers, standards, and technology or biobased materials. In P. Fornasiero & M. Graziani (Eds.), *Renewable resources and renewable energy: A global challange* (pp. 3–18). CRC Press. doi:10.1201/9781420020861.pt1

Ngo, C., & Natowitz, J. (2009). *Our energy future: Resources, alternatives, and the environment*. Wiley. doi:10.1002/9780470473795

O'Sullivan, M. L. (2013). The entanglement of energy, grand strategy, and international security. In A. Goldthau (Ed.), *The handbook of global energy policy* (pp. 30–47). Wiley-Blackwell. doi:10.1002/9781118326275.ch2

Pascual, C., & Elkind, J. (2009). Introduction. In C. Pascual & J. Elkind (Eds.), *Energy security: Economics, politics, strategies and implications* (pp. 1–8). Brookings Institution Press.

Pascual, C., & Zambetakis, E. (2009). The geopolitics of energy: From security to survival. In C. Pascual & J. Elkind (Eds.), *Energy security: Economics, politics, strategies and implications* (pp. 9–35). Brookings Institution Press.

Priest, J. (2004). Mechanical energy. In C. Cleveland (Ed.), *Encyclopedia of energy* (Vol. 4, pp. 1–9). Elsevier. doi:10.1016/B0-12-176480-X/00078-4

Rathore, N. S., & Panwar, N. L. (2022). *Fundamentals of renewable energy*. CRC Press.

Roy, J. (2013). Energy efficiency: Technology, behavior, and development. In A. Goldthau (Ed.), *The handbook of global energy policy* (pp. 282–301). Wiley-Blackwell. doi:10.1002/9781118326275.ch17

Salameh, M. G. (2018). Will there ever be a post-oil era? In J. I. Considine & K.-W. Paik (Eds.), *Handbook of energy politics* (pp. 235–247). Edward Elgar. doi:10.4337/9781784712303.00020

Selivanova, Y. (2010). Managing the patchwork of agreements in trade and investment. In A. Goldthau & J. M. Witte (Eds.), *Global energy governance: The new rules of the game* (pp. 49–72). Brookings Institution Press.

Shaffer, B. (2009). *Energy politics*. University of Pennsylvania Press. doi:10.9783/9780812204520

Simmons, R. A., Coyle, E. D., & Chapman, B. (2014). Global energy policy perspectives. In E. D. Coyle & R. A. Simmons (Eds.), *Understanding the Global Energy Crisis* (pp. 27–72). Purdue University Press.

Simpson, J., & McNamara, K. (2011). *Elements of energy Policy*. International Energy Agency.

Smil, V. (1994). *Energy in world history*. Westview Press.

Sovacool, B. K., & Mukherjee, I. (2011). Conceptualizing and measuring energy security: A synthesized approach. *Energy*, *36*(8), 5343–5355. doi:10.1016/j.energy.2011.06.043

Sovacool, B. K., Sidortsov, R. V., & Jones, B. R. (2014). *Energy security, equality and justice*. Routledge.

Valentine, S. C. (2011). Emerging symbiosis: Renewable energy and energy security. *Renewable & Sustainable Energy Reviews*, *15*(9), 4572–4578. doi:10.1016/j.rser.2011.07.095

Van de Graff, T., & Colgan, J. (2016). Global energy governance: A review and research agenda. *Palgrave Communications*, *2*(1), 1–12. doi:10.1057/palcomms.2015.47

Walker, M. (1996). *Chapter II: Concept of Energy*. Centre Daily Times.

Wiser, W. H. (2000). *Energy resources: Occurrence, production, conversion, use*. Springer. doi:10.1007/978-1-4612-1226-3

Yergin, D. (2006). Ensuring energy security. *Foreign Affairs*, *85*(2), 69–82. doi:10.2307/20031912

ENDNOTE

1 Assoc. Prof., Hitit University, Turkiye, emrecitak@hitit.edu.tr, ORCID: 0000-0002-8704-6495.

Chapter 3
Environmental Solutions and Alternative Policies to Energy Crises on the Basis of Renewable Energy Production and the Global Renewable Energy Market

Selçuk Efe Efe Küçükkambak
https://orcid.org/0000-0001-6633-1492
Aydın Adnan Menderes University, Turkey

ABSTRACT

In the last two decades, the world has been under the influence of various crises experienced by countries trying to meet the increasing energy demand, especially after the Second World War, using exhaustible resources. In addition to the relations, conflicts, and disagreements between countries, regions, and economic cooperation, the fact that global warming is becoming a climate crisis more and more every day has forced the energy market to seek different quests. This study blends critical theoretical information, such as how and to what extent renewable energy sources can be used based on sustainable economic conditions and how much potential they can offer, with practical examples and suggestions. This study will likely provide guiding implications for decision-makers in the economies of countries that shape the world energy market in the future and will present some innovative ideas for future studies in this field.

INTRODUCTION

Energy, in terms of both the economic system, the individual, and the mass order, is a phenomenon that is on the agenda in many aspects of today's world, mainly due to its various critical features such as being an exhaustible resource, substitutability, supply costs, and sustainable qualities. In order to create a

DOI: 10.4018/979-8-3693-0440-2.ch003

sustainable world order, renewable energy sources and sustainable energy policies, which have become a concept that all societies should emphasize, provide efficient production and consumption of conventional energy sources and minimize the harmful effects of fossil fuel-based energies on the environment; has brought the transition to clean and inexhaustible energy sources on the agenda. Following the industrial revolution, especially after the Second World War, Western countries' rapid economic growth and increasing energy demand gained tremendous momentum, especially with the end of the Cold War (Chandler, 2018). Although the concept of "*Global Warming,*" which came to the fore in the 2000s, is hesitantly followed by many developed and developing countries, it seems that global warming, ignited by the uncontrolled release of high carbon released by countries while producing energy into the atmosphere, will cause severe problems for the world shortly (Stiglitz, 2011). The problems of global warming and environmental pollution as a result of the fact that a significant part of the world's energy demand is met from fossil fuels today, and various projections that fossil fuels may be depleted in the not-too-distant future have led to the widespread use of renewable energy studies (Bhattacharyya et al., 2021).

Renewable energy, which can be obtained from the sun, wind, water, and hydrogen, is obtained from the existing energy flow in continuously ongoing natural processes (Mohtasham, 2015). However, since resources such as coal, oil, and other fuels obtained from petroleum and natural gas can be depleted in time, or there are various speculations about how long they can last, it is among the non-renewable and unsustainable energy resources. Considering that more than half of the world's energy demand is obtained by using fossil fuels today, it is possible to say that renewable energy sources can play an essential role in reducing the dependence on fossil fuels such as coal, oil, and natural gas and promise potential for the future (York, 2012; Overland et al., 2022).

The interest in renewable energy sources is familiar. The share of electricity produced using lower carbon emission technologies in the total electricity production in the world was 21.5% in 1975, while this rate increased to 39% in 2020 (Statista, 2023). Of course, this rate increased due to the policies aimed at overcoming the climate crisis among countries, especially the Kyoto Protocol, and energy supply and consumption became more massive and politicized. In addition, while the share of solar energy, which was zero percent in the nineties, reached 4% in 2020, the percentage of wind energy increased to 6.7% (Reanin, 2023).

At the end of 2019, the COVID-19 epidemic, which was first seen in China and then in other world countries, and the economic fluctuations after it, and the military war process between Russia and Ukraine in 2022, brought the issue of creating "*strategic reserves*" against possible shocks. In the post-Cold War period, incredibly underdeveloped or developing countries, energy importers whose energy consumption needs are increasing and relatively poor, need more financial resources to create strategic reserves (Chandler, 2018). Therefore, the vulnerabilities of these countries against external shocks still need to cross the critical threshold.

The energy crisis is not a shallow crisis that can only be taken lightly with the exhaustion of fossil resources or the uncontrolled and extraordinary release of greenhouse gases into the atmosphere. Especially after the epidemic, the war environment that broke out in Europe, and the global energy crisis experienced by Western countries, in addition to being global, increased the transportation and production costs of food products and the prices of consumer products at the end of the chain (Schramm et al., 2022).

Not staying away from the studies in the world in these fields depends on both the workforce trained in these subjects and the intensification of research on these subjects in universities. This research aims to approach the global market for the production, supply, and sale of environmentally friendly and renewable energy sources and to approach the global market with an innovative and up-to-date perspective by focusing on producing ecologically friendly solutions to the energy crises that may arise in the future in various ways, and to offer multiple solutions to the sector by considering the current situation in depth.

BACKGROUND

Eight billion people live together today, home to humanity for centuries. Although the world has faced rapid population increases from time to time, it has experienced sharp decreases in various periods; today, the population growth rate is at a level that will bring many problems. The world population, which increased by 82.3 million in 2020, is growing by approximately one person every three seconds today (Worldmeter, 2023). According to a projection updated by the United Nations Population Fund (UNFPA), the world population is estimated to reach eight and a half billion people in about seven years, 9.7 billion people in 2050, and 10.4 billion people in 2100 (UNFPA, 2023). Although this forecasting model predicts a future population increase, the population growth rate is thought to decrease gradually. The population growth rate, which has declined since the 1970s, fell below 1% annually for the first time in 2020. The United Nations (UN) highlights that due to this population increase, various injustices may be experienced in humanity's access to limited resources (World Social Report, 2020).

The history of humanity has passed various tests in accessing scarce resources many times. One of the most recent crises, which has left its mark on these problematic exams even today, was experienced in the 70s (Erfle et al., 1989). As a result of the embargo imposed by the Union of Arab Petroleum Exporting Countries (OAPEC), oil exports to the United States (USA) and European countries stopped in 1973, and as a result, the rising oil prices shook the stock markets of many countries deeply, causing the world markets to enter a global economic crisis (Erfle & McMillan, 1990). Moreover, it has caused the effects of this crisis to last for many years. While the situation's impact was still fresh, this time, six years later, with Iran's transition to the Islamic Republic after the revolutionary movement, oil production in the country decreased (Stern, 2007). Oil prices have started to rise again in world markets, which have not yet recovered from the effects of the previous crisis. Moreover, after the Iran-Iraq war that broke out in 1980, the contraction in oil supply accelerated, and oil prices peaked (Karsh, 2014).

Two consecutive oil crises have pushed countries dependent on foreign energy and poor in underground resources to turn to more efficient energy sources. This situation has also led to the acceleration of field explorations to find new oil resources outside traditional oil exploration regions. The developments have led to a decrease in the income of Saudi Arabia. Oil prices started to decline after the reaction of the Saudi Arabian Government, which preferred to increase oil production to tolerate this situation (Stern, 2007). However, this stagnant process did not last long, and after a few years of calm, oil prices re-activated due to Saddam Hussein's invasion of Kuwait (Mylroie, 2019). The imbalance in oil supply first led to various speculative news and uncertainties in the market, and over time, it caused oil prices to increase again.

The last oil crisis in the '90s emerged due to the troublesome process of Asian countries, which achieved rapid economic growth (Fesharaki et al., 1991). Economic problems in Thailand, Indonesia, the Philippines, South Korea, and Malaysia have grown uncontrollably and narrowed the oil demand. However, in the same period, as OPEC reduced production, oil prices entered a decreasing trend instead of increasing, and oil prices rapidly depreciated and decreased by approximately 60%.

The September 11 terrorist attack on the World Trade Center Towers in the USA shook the whole world deeply in the early 2000s, and the US war with Iraq two years later was the first energy crisis of the millennium (Fan & Xu, 2011; Makinen, 2002). Although Russia has made many efforts since the late 90s to ensure supply security, the fact that the US economy has just come out of the recession period, oil production in Iraq was prevented during the war between Iraq and the USA, and in 2004, the USA was facing the Atlantic Ocean. After "Hurricane Katrina" devastated the East Coast, when US companies had difficulty extracting oil from the Gulf of Mexico, oil prices saw $70 for the first time in history (Blair & Rezek, 2008; Cashell & Labonte, 2005). The millennium era, which started painfully regarding energy supply, has not yet healed these wounds. Still, in 2008, the US sanctions threats against Iran, the depreciation of the US dollar, the rapid increase in the energy demand of China and India, the cold winter scenarios, and Algeria, Pakistan, and Kenya. The geopolitical tension in the world has almost skyrocketed the oil price. So much so that prices reached $147 per barrel in June 2008 (Macrotrends, 2023). Then, the 2008 global crisis broke out. In December 2008, oil fell to $ 36, the fastest decline in history (Investing, 2023). The price of crude oil, which started to rise after the global economic crisis, rose to $128 per barrel in 2012 (Investing, 2023). The excess supply in the oil market as a result of the fact that the US oil production doubled in 7 years to 10 million barrels a day in 2014, and OPEC members under the leadership of Saudi Arabia did not reduce their production, drove crude oil prices from 115 dollars to below 30 dollars in June 2014 (Investing, 2023; Venn, 2016). Many energy companies in the USA went bankrupt. OPEC decided to cut 1.8 million barrels a day, but the US became the largest oil producer (Venn, 2016).

While a significant part of the world is still struggling with poverty and experiencing many economic shortcomings, a large part is trying to meet its scarce resources with endless energy needs and is facing energy crises. So, how sustainable is this situation? In other words, how long will we be able to turn the key to our car and start the engine on the way to work in the morning? When our children go to the bedroom to study, will they be able to press the light switch and continue to operate the lamp? Considering the extraordinary seasonal conditions due to global warming, how ready are European Union member countries for a harsh 2030 winter? How can developed countries tolerate this if oil is drawn from oil wells, while the water wells we use for garden irrigation may decrease or completely withdraw water over time due to drought? Unfortunately, it is challenging to answer all these questions clearly; it may even be impossible for some. The Massachusetts Institute of Technology (MIT) estimates that worldwide energy demand will triple today's market by 2050 (Qi et al., 2016). Moreover, while the consumption demand is increasing daily due to the electricity produced with natural gas, the supply has become increasingly problematic. With the power cuts in the USA, Europe, and Russia in recent years, regular power cuts in China, India, and other developing countries have reached alarming proportions.

Demand for alternative energy sources is becoming more critical day by day due to the unfavorable economic conditions seen after the coronavirus epidemic since 2020 and the energy embargoes imposed by Russia on countries that support Ukraine or take actions against Russia after the military war between Russia and Ukraine in the recent period. So, it would be helpful to look at the current energy crises of the last few years, alternative solutions for possible energy crises in the future, and the world renewable energy market.

THE MAIN FOCUS OF THE CHAPTER

In this part of the book, the causes and effects of the crisis are discussed in depth by going down to the foundations of the latest and current energy crisis observed worldwide, especially after 2020. In the following stage, against the possibility of similar problems to be seen in the modern world system in the future, environmental and society-oriented, renewable energy-based solution policies were examined with their theoretical basis. Finally, the current stage of renewable energy worldwide was inquired in detail according to its types, and its potential is discussed.

An Up-To-Date Look at the World's Energy Crises

From the beginning of 2020 until May 2023, the modern world fought with all its might against the largest epidemic it has ever seen. While countries and nations cooperated on many issues, governments and international institutions mobilized to get through this process with the least possible damage to the economic activity of different sectors, which came to a standstill during the epidemic process. However, the long duration of the epidemic also caused other problems. In the same period, since the population in the world was many times higher than the epidemics so far, the mobility of people, vehicles, trade, goods, and services was high; the epidemic process was prolonged despite many restrictive measures and vaccines produced over time. This situation shook the country's economies over time, and one by one, governments began to announce inflation figures that they had not yet experienced throughout their history. This situation was reflected in many resources used in energy production, especially oil and natural gas. So much so that the barrel price of Brent Oil, which was $ 19.45 on January four, 2020, increased almost continuously for about two years and broke the record by rising to $ 139.13 during the day on January three, 2022 (Bloomberg, 2023). Towards the end of the epidemic, this time, the war between Russia and Ukraine broke out. The world is in this process.

The war between Russia and Ukraine, which started in February 2022 while still experiencing an epidemic and related economic pains, has deeply engulfed the world from East to West, from North to South. When the energy crisis combined with the food crisis, the financial problems in the European continent started to deepen (Moloney, 2023). The tension between Russia and Western countries due to the Russia-Ukraine war has further exacerbated the current energy crisis. Particularly concerned about energy security, EU member states tried to take steps to diversify their energy resources and reduce their dependence on Russia. In this period, natural gas flow from Russia to European countries that imposed sanctions on Russia due to the Ukraine war decreased significantly (Rabbi et al., 2022). In this process, Russia reduced natural gas by 80 percent compared to the pre-war period (Wolowiec, 2022). With the shrinkage of the supply volume, the energy costs of European countries have increased, and many countries have prepared public service ads with the content of saving measures. In the same period, the rapidly growing natural gas and electricity prices since the first months of 2022 affected the whole world, especially Europe. As the effects of the epidemic began to wane, natural gas prices, which were 25 euros per megawatt hour in August 2021, reached an all-time high in August 2022, reaching 342.8 euros per megawatt hour (Tradingeconomics, 2023; Uribe et al., 2022).

While the economic, health, and energy developments in the last three years have been like this, what could be the thing that deepens the experiences? It would be insufficient to give a single answer to this question. Russia transports a significant part of its natural gas to EU member states through pipelines passing through different geographies. As a matter of fact, until recently, 40% of the natural gas used by EU member states was supplied by Russia (Horton & Palumbo, 2022). For this reason, Russia has a crucial role in meeting the energy needs of the EU and has a significant say both in its region and the global arena with its oil and natural gas reserves. The current energy crisis between the EU and Russia is not the first. Russia has often used the cold winter conditions as an excuse to overshadow political reasons and restrict the gas flow to Europe. Today, the energy supply to Europe from Russia has become quite problematic due to realistic reasons such as natural gas flow to Europe through Ukraine, the continuation of conflicts between Russia and Ukraine, and retaliation against European countries that have imposed sanctions against Russia.

As in the past, Russia continues to use its energy resources as an element of sanction and power against EU countries. Ukraine, which has differences between the eastern and western parts regarding Russian and Ukrainian bias, is strategically critical for Europe and Russia. Due to the recent nuclear power plant threat and the possibility of sabotage against the natural pipeline, Europe has been on edge for almost a year because the developments are threatening the energy supply security of EU countries in the simplest terms. The EU's dependence on Russian natural gas and oil leads EU countries to alternative energy sources and routes.

Interpreting this situation in Europe as only an embargo on Russia would limit his perspective considerably. Therefore, consider the issue more broadly. The gas money that Ukraine refuses to pay Russia due to its economic conditions should be regarded as another obstacle to gas flow. Because of the instability in Ukraine in the past, the energy flow to EU countries has been adversely affected. Russia's geopolitically strong position in the region is quite contrary to the interests of EU member states. However, Ukraine's close relations with Eurasia, supported militarily and economically by the EU, are wanted to be prevented by the same countries. This is precisely why Ukraine, on the line of contention, is also the center of energy crises. Moreover, this process will likely occur in the winter of 2023, as no concrete and finalized steps toward peace have yet been taken between the EU and Russia. Well, this crisis will be neither the first nor the last. However, isn't there a way to overcome these crises so that the industry does not stop and basic needs are not disrupted? For example, according to Oxford Analytica (2022), Germany met much of its electricity in the sector with liquefied natural gas (LNG), while Denmark switched its electricity to more efficient production (Kirkegaard et al., 2023). However, countries in the continent's inner parts are not so lucky. Renewable energy is the most hot topic for these countries nowadays. The renewable energy issue, which will become the essential way to overcome such crises more efficiently, is a candidate to be the way out and even the savior of many countries in the future.

The energy crisis that Europe has been experiencing for the last two years, Due to various reasons, such as not taking concrete steps at the desk, and tensions in bilateral relations with many countries rich in energy resources, continues to deepen. Although the demand decreased relatively and the supply was gradually reduced when the global pandemic made itself felt most intensely, there was a heavy imbalance between supply and demand in the post-pandemic economic recovery process. In this process, the pool was insufficient in the face of the rising market, and as a result, the energy prices obtained by using fossil fuels in the current situation reached record levels. In addition to the rise in oil prices, Rotterdam coal, whose price was below $40 in April and May 2020, rose to $233.05 as of October 1, 2021 (Investing, 2023). Undoubtedly, natural gas is the energy source unit in which the sharpest price rise is experienced. In the Netherlands, futures, considered an indicator, natural gas prices, which decreased to 3.50 euros per megawatt-hour in May 2020, increased to 93.80 euros as of October 1, 2021 (Investing, 2023). Rising prices, in this way, adversely affected the income levels and economic conditions of households and individuals, as well as the recovery efforts of industry and economies after the epidemic.

Many factors cause the supply-demand imbalance, the basis of the rise in natural gas prices. For example, Europe, which is foreign-dependent in natural gas, mainly uses imported gas for electricity generation in industry and residences (Khatiwada et al., 2022). Due to curfews and measures to prevent people from being together within the scope of various measures implemented during the pandemic, the demand for natural gas fell considerably in 2020, especially in the industrial field. However, as the pandemic became effective for a long time and countries gradually brought up conditions such as working in shifts, working with fewer employees, and working remotely, industrial production regained momentum in many European countries by the end of 2020. Especially in the first months of 2021, natural gas demand increased sharply due to the need for heating. Due to the water shortage caused by the extraordinary drought that Europe experienced in the winter of 2021, production in many hydroelectric power plants has come to a partial or complete halt. In the winter months, which are relatively rainless, mild, and unsuitable for the season, electricity generation from wind also decreased. Therefore, natural gas consumption increased with more emphasis on electricity generation from natural gas power plants to meet the increasing demand. For example, this is why natural gas consumption across Europe in the first quarter of 2021 was 7.6 percent higher than in the previous year (Erias & Iglesias, 2022).

Although it was initially thought to have emerged only for global warming, the issue of "*Green Transformation*" has been brought to the agenda much more frequently today, especially to meet the increasing consumption demand after the pandemic and to tolerate somehow the crisis that occurred after the embargoes applied after the war between Russia and Ukraine (Scoones et al., 2015; Tian et al., 2022; Cheba et al., 2023). Many European Union member countries have taken significant steps in green transformation (Cheba et al., 2022). For example, Germany has made considerable progress towards zero carbon targets by reducing its coal consumption.

However, the world needs to take faster steps towards green transformation, that is, the transition to renewable energy sources, the spread of carbon-neutral energy sources, and the reduction of carbon emissions. For example, although the use of coal in Europe has decreased, renewable and environmentally friendly energy types still need to completely replace it, so the need in between is met by using more natural gas. According to the "*World Energy Statistical Outlook*" (2020) data published by British Petroleum (BP), China still meets 57.6 percent of its total energy consumption with coal and 19.7 percent with oil. The share of renewable energy is only 4.7 percent. On the other hand, although Germany has increased the share of renewable energy to 16.1 percent and the percentage of coal to 17.5 percent, it still needs 24.3 percent natural gas and 35.6 percent oil to meet its needs.

Accepting that the long-term solution lies in renewable energy sources to eliminate the current crises, take precautions against new crises, and show that lessons have been learned from these crises is the first and priority stage for green transformation. As the share of clean and renewable energy sources in the total consumption of countries increases, the need for fossil fuels will gradually decrease. Thus, market energy prices will have a more stable and predictable structure. Green transformation is not just about leaving a more livable world to future generations by protecting the environment. At the same time, it is also related to economic stability and even closely related to the issue of national sovereignty. For example, the fact that it can replace the oil and natural gas it has to buy in European countries with the renewable energy types that you produce in its own country because the amount of reserves is not sufficient in European countries also means a declaration of economic independence and strengthens the country's position in the geopolitical balances.

Although the current energy crisis is quite deep in Europe, it affects the whole world. For this reason, short-term measures to be taken by European countries can only provide a temporary solution and save the day. In the long run, the green transformation seems to be the only solution for a more sustainable energy structure, stronger economies, a more livable environment, and an order in which economic welfare is less affected by geopolitical struggles for Europeans and other countries.

The need for renewable energy in the world is urgent, but the initiatives have just started and are progressing slowly. So what can be done? Which renewable energy sources can be used?

Environmentalist Solution Policies for Energy Crisis and Overview of the World Renewable Energy Market

The use of renewable energy resources has become a necessity rather than a necessity to meet the high demand for energy of the world's current dense population in terms of industry. Renewable energy sources' distribution, availability, storability, and efficiency vary considerably. Therefore, it is crucial to handle alternatives to using renewable energy sources flexibly. This title discusses some renewable and carbon-neutral energy sources, which can be environmentally friendly alternative solutions to current or future energy crises.

The Concept of Renewable Energy

The most important handicap of the transition of the world countries to renewable energy today is various physical and technical conditions. These conditions can be summarized as follows (Kaltschmitt et al., 2007);

- Productivity,
- Usage rate,
- Technical usability,

Efficiency is the ratio of the total amount of energy obtained from any carbon-neutral energy source to the total energy input. It may vary depending on the operating conditions of the facility and some variable factors related to the source. The utilization rate is the ratio of the total output of the total energy produced in a given period (for example, a year) to the total energy input. On the other hand, technical availability defines the part of a facility in which it is usable for its intended purpose. It thus provides a calculation that considers the periods when the facility is unavailable due to malfunctions.

It is renewable energy, produced by releasing zero carbon on earth and renews itself in the natural cycle of the world throughout human history; inexhaustible, environmentally friendly, and clean energy type. These can be listed as various types of energy, such as solar energy, wind energy, energy obtained from waves in the ocean or seas, large ocean or strait currents, hydroelectric energy, and geothermal energy. These energies are fed from the earth, planets, or various atmospheric motions. Solar radiation coming to the earth is weakened in the atmosphere and is partially converted into other forms of energy. Among all carbonless energy sources, solar energy has a share of more than 99.9% of all energy converted worldwide (Kaltschmitt et al., 2007).

- **Solar Energy:** Solar energy is the only planet that provides energy. It is an inexhaustible, easily convertible, relatively more widespread, and zero-carbon energy source worldwide (Duffie & Beckman, 2013). One of the most important reasons why so much emphasis is placed on solar energy worldwide is that it is an inexhaustible and clean energy source, which can be obtained without using water, without any environmental damage, and is relatively easy to transform (Kabir et al., 2018). One of the main reasons solar energy is in such high demand worldwide is the expectation for this energy. It is known that if the world today has sufficient infrastructure for converting energy from the sun, it has the potential to meet all the world's energy needs (Foster et al., 2009). However, this clean energy source has such high potential and needs to be addressed today. Considering the possible positive contributions that the progress in solar energy technology can make to problems such as energy security, climate change, unemployment, and fuel transportation, it can be said that it is a clean energy source that should be considered as a solution alternative to future energy crises (Solangi et al., 2011). In this context, for developing and disseminating solar energy technologies, countries should establish incentives and discount systems for using this renewable energy system, with some efforts such as decision-makers and politicians in the energy field and various investment supports such as research financing.

- **Wind Energy:** Movement between air masses occurs due to solar radiation in the atmosphere, the direction of the earth around its axis, and the sun, such as global hot and cold water currents on the earth's surface. About 2.5% of the total solar radiation coming to the outer layer of the atmosphere causes atmospheric motion and results in a theoretical full wind power of about 4.3 1015 W (Blanco,2009). The energy found in moving air masses, which can be converted into mechanical and electrical energy by windmills, is a secondary form of solar energy and is considered among the clean powers. More than 100 countries, especially China, the USA, and Germany, are trying to increase their wind farm-installed power capacities at a rapid pace (European Wind Energy Association, 2009). Wind turbines occupy less space in terms of their vertical orientation. This renewable energy application, a preferable alternative for habitat protection, can even be placed in areas with agricultural areas. Moreover, it ensures that even high and rough areas unsuitable for settlement are transformed into valuable areas for clean energy production. It is an excellent advantage that these power plants can be easily installed in the middle of the seas. According to the 2021 year-end figures of the International Renewable Energy Agency (IRENA), China, the USA, and Germany are the leading countries in the world regarding the total megawatt (MW) installed power capacity of wind power plants. India, Spain, the United Kingdom, Brazil, France, Canada, and Sweden follow these countries. Accordingly, the total WPP usage worldwide is 328 thousand 973 MW in China, 132 thousand 738 MW in the USA, 63 thousand 760 MW in Germany, 40 thousand 067 MW in India, and 14 thousand 304 MW in Canada. Among the most prominent countries in terms of watts (W) per capita, Denmark takes the first place with 1,218 W. The following three countries are Sweden 1,200W, Ireland 910W, and Norway 881W.
- **Geothermal Energy:** Geothermal energy is the energy found in liquid form in the lower layer of the earth and can be used as a heat source. Today, 27% of the total electricity production in the Philippines, 7% in the State of California, 60% of El Salvador's energy needs, and 92% of the total heat energy (city heating) needed in Iceland are met by geothermal resources (IEA, 2023). According to International Energy Agency (2023) reports and International Renewable Energy Agency (2023) reports, the top 5 countries in the world in geothermal electricity production are the USA, Indonesia, Philippines, Turkey, and Kenya. The top 5 countries in geothermal heat and spa applications worldwide are China, USA, Sweden, Turkey, and Japan. As of 2020, geothermal electricity production in 29 countries is over 16.000 MW (95.000 GWh/year) electricity installed power, and the target of the world countries for 2050 is 250,000 MWe established power electricity production. 200,000 MWe of this is expected from EGS/HDR (Enhanced et al./Hot Dry Rock). The non-electrical use of geothermal in the world is approximately 108,000 MWt as of 2020,

equivalent to roughly 14 million residential heating. Despite all these figures, only 6.5% of the world's geothermal potential is utilized (GEA, Geothermal Energy Association, USA).

- **Hydroelectric Energy:** Hydroelectric energy is a renewable energy source like wind and solar (Sims, 1991). With hydraulic energy, benefits are obtained in various fields, such as modern agriculture, irrigation, tourism, and sports activities (Bagher et al., 2015). However, the most important of all is the generation of electricity. Today, kinetic energy is obtained from water power thanks to water turbines. The first hydroelectric power plant was established in America in 1882 (Pandey & Karki, 2016). Today, 90% of the electricity in Norway comes from hydroelectric energy (Energifaktonorge, 2023). According to Zhang et al. (2017), in 2016, the world's largest hydroelectric power plant was established in China. It is known that this power plant has a production capacity of 22,400 MW. It produces 80 to 100 terawatt-hours annually, powering 70 million to 80 million households. In the world, 90% of the total national electricity production in 24 countries and 50% in 63 countries is obtained from hydroelectric power plants (Pandey & Karki, 2016).

SOLUTIONS AND RECOMMENDATIONS

The world was familiar with many things it struggled with until the end of 2019. While the global climate crisis came before many of the things emphasized in the energy crises, the issue of fossil energy resources, which was thought to be depleted, came second. However, in 2020, when the world is alone with the biggest epidemic of the modern age and the economic crisis, community managers begin to see the problems from a different and realistic perspective. Managers and energy policymakers must make basic energy policy choices in the coming years by evaluating various vital issues together. The world is currently highly dependent on fossil fuel consumption, which, unfortunately, is constantly increasing. Although the possibility of discouraging people from this addiction in a short time seems like a utopia at this stage, it is possible to turn it into a vision. The preference for natural gas instead of coal for both electricity generation and heating purposes in fossil fuels in the last two decades, or the use of oil to a lesser extent, is a first but small step in this direction. However, with this change, since natural gas releases less carbon dioxide per unit of energy than coal, this has helped limit greenhouse gas emissions into the atmosphere. However, the political events experienced caused a different concern in the EU and other countries regarding the increasing dependence on this special fuel. Initially, a possible alternative route was considered to be a return to reliance on coal. Indeed, coal is abundantly available in many developed countries, including the USA, Australia, many EU countries, Canada, Russia, and developing countries such as China, South Africa, and Turkey. However, this includes a one-way approach. Fossil fuel imports and exports between countries will likely be interrupted due to political or political reasons.

Moreover, it is only possible to stop global climate change if fossil fuels or energy production based on the combustion of carbon are abandoned. Therefore, new solution alternatives must be found. In this direction, many developing countries are looking for alternative channels. Among these, a program is to produce energy directly or indirectly from all sources derived from the sun, biomass, wind, thermal, hydroelectricity, and sea and ocean waves using advanced technological methods or large ocean currents. All these energy sources can also be called "*carbon neutral*" sources.

Moreover, the energy and tidal energy produced by the controlled removal of groundwater to the ground should be considered a renewable and sustainable energy source, as it is among the carbon-neutral sources and is so large that it is almost inexhaustible. However, more than this approach is needed for the move toward sustainability. Other processes necessary to achieve sustainability require initiatives such as more efficient electricity generation by reducing energy needs and improving energy use efficiency. The planet's fossil fuel and mineral reserves are limited and uncertain. Therefore, the exploitation of coal, oil, gas, and uranium is not sustainable in the long run. Renewable energy from naturally occurring energy flows is inexhaustible and has no long-term harmful environmental effects. Therefore, over time, the basis of the energy supply system and possibly the only means by which electricity is produced will be built on renewable energies.

FUTURE RESEARCH DIRECTIONS

In the last 20 years, developed countries, especially the European Union, have been trying to take concrete steps to use renewable energy sources more in daily life. For example, at the "*World Sustainable Development Summit*" held in Johannesburg, South Africa, in 2002, the "*Johannesburg Summit Statement*," which includes national, regional, and global targets to support technologies for the use of renewable energy sources and to increase the use of these resources significantly, was adopted by the EU, published under his leadership. In addition, the EU continues its efforts to implement the "*Kyoto Protocol*," which envisages reducing greenhouse gas emissions in the fight against climate change. If these targets are realized, a total decrease of more than 500 million tons in carbon dioxide emissions will be achieved annually. However, the extent to which the actions and measures taken by the EU to promote the use of renewable energy resources will be successful in achieving its goals will be determined by the political will of the member states.

One of the essential points emphasized in this part of the book is to keep the concept of sustainability at the forefront for businesses operating in the energy sector, policy-making institutions on managing energy supply and demand, and research to be conducted on the manageability of energy from a macro perspective. Because the focus of energy crises is dominated by the idea that fossil fuels, which constitute 80% of power in the world order, are no longer sustainable, undoubtedly, the first and most crucial issue that should be focused on in studies investigating what kind of contributions renewable energy sources will provide in the future in terms of the solution of energy crises should be the determination of how and how a transition should be made from which traditional energy source to a renewable energy source. An interdisciplinary approach is needed for this. Because during the process, from determining the necessary energy to consuming energy, knowledge and effort from many fields of expertise are required. For example, the resolution of energy needs is a type of needs analysis based on field research and requires a situation analysis to reveal the current situation. This should be a task for marketers and marketing researchers to conduct. Then, issues such as the energy source's type, efficiency, and cost come into play, in which case economists' opinions are needed. The cost of energy production comes into play by economists through various statistical models for the future and time series analysis. At another stage, energy distribution and its strategic suitability should be examined. In this process, while the distribution unit of marketing, production management, and engineering knowledge is required, economists also have a job in matters such as choosing the factory's location. The most important branch of science that can support the previous disciplines in almost all aspects, from generation to energy consumption, before it becomes a crisis, is undoubtedly politics. It should not be forgotten that renewable energy sources are an environmentally friendly, relational, and versatile solution alternative that promises to traditional energy sources by responding to both energy shortages, energy crises, and environmental pollution problems. Renewable energy is essential to countries' political, ecological, and social sustainability.

CONCLUSION

In this book chapter, renewable energy sources have been presented as an alternative solution to the energy crises experienced around the world, drawing attention to the future potential of renewable energy, which still occupies a tiny place in the total energy supply, and why and how much more important the rate of use in energy production has become. The basic principles of how to prevent energy crises from a social point of view, thanks to renewable energy systems, are discussed.

The issue of implementing solutions and policies for renewable energy resources is a current issue that should be taken into consideration not only on a global scale or a country basis but also by local governments and even companies. Local governments should also be actively involved in the policies to be implemented in energy production and saving because almost every geographical region has its renewable resources. The important thing is to recognize and transform these resources. Local governments' involvement in using these resources will provide a significant advantage in terms of efficiency. In planning cities, location selection for buildings such as hospitals and shopping malls with high energy consumption should be made correctly. Areas that will strain infrastructure facilities and increase energy consumption should not be allowed. In addition, public transportation should be provided through rail systems and electric vehicles instead of vehicles running on fossil fuel resources. Traffic density should be reduced by encouraging the use of environmentally friendly means of transportation and opening bicycle and pedestrian paths. Of course, it should not be forgotten that to achieve these, local governments must be allowed to employ a sufficient number of engineers, architects, urban planners, technicians, and technicians. In addition, an architectural order that will benefit more from solar energy should be implemented in cities. Municipalities should primarily invest in renewable energy facilities that meet their needs, and regulations that encourage energy production should be made in laws and legislation. Energy cooperatives should be established under the leadership of municipalities. The importance of public management in energy production should be increased.

The most critical features of renewable energy sources are that they help protect the environment by reducing carbon dioxide emissions, contribute to the reduction of foreign dependency on energy, and increase employment because they are domestic sources. They receive widespread and strong support from the public. In other words, renewable energy sources have all the features of accessibility, availability, and acceptability.

Compared to the groundbreaking developments in information technologies, today's world needs to catch up in energy generation and distribution technology. One of the most important reasons for this situation is that the renovation work in energy systems takes decades. In this process, the differences in politics and political views between countries affected the development of information technologies. They negatively affected the spread of fair and egalitarian order. However, the expectations are that it aims to accelerate the painful experiences, economic and social wear and tear, and the use and prevalence of revolutionary renewable energy sources. It should also be noted that the diversity of renewable energy, the variety of its distribution among geographies, and its variable nature create a suitable space for maintaining the obtained power quality and optimizing energy flows.

The energy source's prevalence, flexibility, and controllability will also greatly benefit the current and future generations. Undoubtedly, another reason for such severe and optimistic predictions for renewable energy resources is the expectation that the economic life of the distribution network in countries rich in fossil energy resources is 50 years and that the distribution network in most countries will be changed within a few years. This expectation is that there is an excellent opportunity in these countries to introduce innovative technologies and renewable energy sources instead of replacing them with similar energy distribution systems.

Traditionally, energy within the economic system has been run on the principle that whenever the consumer demands energy, it must be met immediately from dispatchable production. As renewable energy production begins to be integrated into daily life more and more, as the technological integration of traditional energy production facilities to transfer the energy produced by modern and renewable energy sources over time, this situation should be made more flexible and sustainable without being passed on to the consumer. Of course, such innovations should not proceed unilaterally. Adopting new technologies also necessitates changing the mindset or "culture" of policymakers and political engineers.

REFERENCES

Bagher, A. M., Vahid, M., Mohsen, M., & Parvin, D. (2015). Hydroelectric energy advantages and disadvantages. *American Journal of Energy Science*, *2*(2), 17–20.

Bhattacharyya, S. S., Leite, F. F. G. D., Adeyemi, M. A., Sarker, A. J., Cambareri, G. S., Faverin, C., Tieri, M. P., Castillo-Zacarías, C., Melchor-Martínez, E. M., Iqbal, H. M. N., & Parra-Saldívar, R. (2021). A paradigm shift to CO2 sequestration to manage global warming–With the emphasis on developing countries. *The Science of the Total Environment*, *790*, 148169. doi:10.1016/j.scitotenv.2021.148169 PMID:34380249

Blanco, M. I. (2009). The economics of wind energy. *Renewable & Sustainable Energy Reviews*, *13*(6-7), 1372–1382. doi:10.1016/j.rser.2008.09.004

Chandler, W. (2018). *Energy and environment in the transition economies: between cold war and global warming*. Routledge. doi:10.4324/9780429500817

Cheba, K., Bąk, I., & Pietrzak, M. B. (2023). Conditions of the green transformation. The case of the European Union. *Technological and Economic Development of Economy*, *29*(2), 438–467. doi:10.3846/tede.2022.17993

Cheba, K., Bąk, I., Szopik-Depczyńska, K., & Ioppolo, G. (2022). Directions of green transformation of the European Union countries. *Ecological Indicators*, *136*, 108601. doi:10.1016/j.ecolind.2022.108601

Duffie, J. A., & Beckman, W. A. (2013). *Solar engineering of thermal processes*. John Wiley & Sons. doi:10.1002/9781118671603

Energifaktonorge. (2023). Retrieved from: https://energifaktanorge.no/en/norsk-energiforsyning/kraft-produksjon

Erfle, S., & McMillan, H. (1990). Media, political pressure, and the firm: The case of petroleum pricing in the late 1970s. *The Quarterly Journal of Economics*, *105*(1), 115–134. doi:10.2307/2937821

Erfle, S., McMillan, H., & Grofman, B. (1989). Testing the regulatory threat hypothesis: Media coverage of the energy crisis and petroleum pricing in the late 1970s. *American Politics Quarterly*, *17*(2), 132–152. doi:10.1177/1532673X8901700202

Erias, A. F., & Iglesias, E. M. (2022). The daily price and income elasticity of natural gas demand in Europe. *Energy Reports*, *8*, 14595–14605. doi:10.1016/j.egyr.2022.10.404

European Wind Energy Association. (2009). *The economics of wind energy*. EWEA.

Fan, Y., & Xu, J. H. (2011). What has driven oil prices since 2000? A structural change perspective. *Energy Economics*, *33*(6), 1082–1094. doi:10.1016/j.eneco.2011.05.017

Fesharaki, F., Isaak, D., & Yamaguchi, N. (1991, May). The Asia-Pacific petroleum market: Critical issues for the 1990s. *Natural Resources Forum*, *15*(2), 140–153. doi:10.1111/j.1477-8947.1991.tb00125.x

Foster, R., Ghassemi, M., & Cota, A. (2009). *Solar energy: renewable energy and the environment*. CRC press. doi:10.1201/9781420075670

Horton, J., Palumbo, D., & Bowler, T. (2022). *Russia sanctions: Can the world cope without its oil and gas*. BBC News.

IEA. (2023) Retrieved from: https://www.iea.org/reports/renewable-energy-essentials-geothermal

IRENA. (2021) Retrieved from: https://www.irena.org/publications/2021/Aug/Renewable-energy-statistics-2021

Kabir, E., Kumar, P., Kumar, S., Adelodun, A. A., & Kim, K. H. (2018). Solar energy: Potential and future prospects. *Renewable & Sustainable Energy Reviews*, *82*, 894–900. doi:10.1016/j.rser.2017.09.094

Kaltschmitt, M., Streicher, W., & Wiese, A. (Eds.). (2007). *Renewable energy: technology, economics and environment*. Springer Science & Business Media.

Karsh, E. (2014). The Iran–Iraq War 1980–1988. Bloomsbury Publishing.

Khatiwada, D., Vasudevan, R. A., & Santos, B. H. (2022). Decarbonization of natural gas systems in the EU–costs, barriers, and constraints of hydrogen production with a case study in Portugal. *Renewable & Sustainable Energy Reviews*, *168*, 112775. doi:10.1016/j.rser.2022.112775

Kirkegaard, J. K., Rudolph, D., Nyborg, S., & Cronin, T. (2023). The landrush of wind energy, its socio-material workings, and its political consequences: On the entanglement of land and wind assemblages in Denmark. Environment and Planning C. *Politics and Space*, *41*(3), 548–566. doi:10.1177/23996544221143657

Makinen, G. (2002). The economic effects of 9/11: A retrospective assessment. Congressional Research Service (CRS).

Mohtasham, J. (2015). Renewable energies. *Energy Procedia*, *74*, 1289–1297. doi:10.1016/j.egypro.2015.07.774

Moloney, N. (2023). *EU securities and financial markets regulation*. Oxford University Press.

Mylroie, L. (2019). Saddam Hussein's invasion of Kuwait: A premeditated act. In *The Iraqi Aggression Against Kuwait* (pp. 39–50). Routledge. doi:10.4324/9780429312007-3

Overland, I., Juraev, J., & Vakulchuk, R. (2022). Are renewable energy sources more evenly distributed than fossil fuels? *Renewable Energy*, *200*, 379–386. doi:10.1016/j.renene.2022.09.046

Oxford Analytica. (2022). *Germany may struggle to fill new LNG import capacity.* Emerald Expert Briefings.

Pandey, B., & Karki, A. (2016). *Hydroelectric energy: renewable energy and the environment.* CRC Press. doi:10.1201/9781315374840

Qi, T., Winchester, N., Karplus, V. J., Zhang, D., & Zhang, X. (2016). An analysis of China's climate policy using the China-in-Global Energy Model. *Economic Modelling*, *52*, 650–660. doi:10.1016/j.econmod.2015.09.036

Rabbi, M. F., Popp, J., Máté, D., & Kovács, S. (2022). Energy security and energy transition to achieve carbon neutrality. *Energies*, *15*(21), 8126. doi:10.3390/en15218126

ReportW. S. (2020). Retrieved from: https://desapublications.un.org/file/558/download

Schramm, L., Krotz, U., & De Witte, B. (2022). Building 'Next Generation'after the pandemic: The implementation and implications of the EU Covid Recovery Plan. *Journal of Common Market Studies*, *60*(S1), 114–124. doi:10.1111/jcms.13375

Scoones, I., Leach, M., & Newell, P. (2015). *The politics of green transformations.* Taylor & Francis. doi:10.4324/9781315747378-1

Sims, G. P. (1991). Hydroelectric energy. *Energy Policy*, *19*(8), 776–786. doi:10.1016/0301-4215(91)90047-R

Solangi, K. H., Islam, M. R., Saidur, R., Rahim, N. A., & Fayaz, H. (2011). A review on global solar energy policy. *Renewable & Sustainable Energy Reviews*, *15*(4), 2149–2163. doi:10.1016/j.rser.2011.01.007

Stern, R. (2007). The Iranian petroleum crisis and United States national security. *Proceedings of the National Academy of Sciences of the United States of America*, *104*(1), 377–382. doi:10.1073/pnas.0603903104 PMID:17190820

Stiglitz, J. E. (2011). A new agenda for global warming. In *The Economists' Voice: Top Economists Take On Today's Problems* (pp. 22–27). Columbia University Press. doi:10.7312/columbia/9780231143653.003.0003

Sulich, A., & Zema, T. (2023, June). The green energy transition in Germany: a bibliometric study. In Forum Scientiae Oeconomia (Vol. 11, No. 2). Academic Press.

Tian, C., Li, X., Xiao, L., & Zhu, B. (2022). Exploring the impact of green credit policy on green transformation of heavy polluting industries. *Journal of Cleaner Production*, *335*, 130257. doi:10.1016/j.jclepro.2021.130257

Uribe, J. M., Mosquera-López, S., & Arenas, O. J. (2022). Assessing the relationship between electricity and natural gas prices in European markets in times of distress. *Energy Policy*, *166*, 113018. doi:10.1016/j.enpol.2022.113018

Venn, F. (2016). *The oil crisis.* Routledge. doi:10.4324/9781315840819

Wołowiec, T., Kolosok, S., Vasylieva, T., Artyukhov, A., Skowron, Ł., Dluhopolskyi, O., & Sergiienko, L. (2022). Sustainable governance, energy security, and energy losses of Europe in turbulent times. *Energies*, *15*(23), 8857. doi:10.3390/en15238857

York, R. (2012). Do alternative energy sources displace fossil fuels? *Nature Climate Change*, *2*(6), 441–443. doi:10.1038/nclimate1451

Zhang, D., Wang, J., Lin, Y., Si, Y., Huang, C., Yang, J., Huang, B., & Li, W. (2017). Present situation and future prospect of renewable energy in China. *Renewable & Sustainable Energy Reviews*, *76*, 865–871. doi:10.1016/j.rser.2017.03.023

ADDITIONAL READING

Afridi, Y. S., Ahmad, K., & Hassan, L. (2022). Artificial intelligence based prognostic maintenance of renewable energy systems: A review of techniques, challenges, and future research directions. *International Journal of Energy Research*, *46*(15), 21619–21642. doi:10.1002/er.7100

Al-Shetwi, A. Q. (2022). Sustainable development of renewable energy integrated power sector: Trends, environmental impacts, and recent challenges. *The Science of the Total Environment*, *822*, 153645. doi:10.1016/j.scitotenv.2022.153645 PMID:35124039

Chang, R. D., Zuo, J., Zhao, Z. Y., Zillante, G., Gan, X. L., & Soebarto, V. (2017). Evolving theories of sustainability and firms: History, future directions and implications for renewable energy research. *Renewable & Sustainable Energy Reviews*, *72*, 48–56. doi:10.1016/j.rser.2017.01.029

Jurasz, J., Canales, F. A., Kies, A., Guezgouz, M., & Beluco, A. (2020). A review on the complementarity of renewable energy sources: Concept, metrics, application and future research directions. *Solar Energy*, *195*, 703–724. doi:10.1016/j.solener.2019.11.087

Khanra, S., Kaur, P., Joseph, R. P., Malik, A., & Dhir, A. (2022). A resource-based view of green innovation as a strategic firm resource: Present status and future directions. *Business Strategy and the Environment*, *31*(4), 1395–1413. doi:10.1002/bse.2961

Ng, J. H., Ng, H. K., & Gan, S. (2010). Recent trends in policies, socioeconomy, and future directions of the biodiesel industry. *Clean Technologies and Environmental Policy*, *12*(3), 213–238. doi:10.100710098-009-0235-2

Osmani, A., Zhang, J., Gonela, V., & Awudu, I. (2013). Electricity generation from renewables in the United States: Resource potential, current usage, technical status, challenges, strategies, policies, and future directions. *Renewable & Sustainable Energy Reviews*, *24*, 454–472. doi:10.1016/j.rser.2013.03.011

Panwar, N. L., Kaushik, S. C., & Kothari, S. (2011). Role of renewable energy sources in environmental protection: A review. *Renewable & Sustainable Energy Reviews*, *15*(3), 1513–1524. doi:10.1016/j.rser.2010.11.037

KEY TERMS AND DEFINITIONS

Alternative Energy Sources: Are new types of energy that can replace fossil fuels.

Carbon Emission: Refers to releasing carbon formed in nature into the atmosphere.

Carbonless Energy Resources: Is a clean energy source that does not contain any carbon in its content and does not release carbon due to its use.

Energy Crisis: Is a temporary bottleneck process in supplying any natural resource used in energy production or produced energy.

Energy Policies: Are high-level, equitable management strategies on energy resources, production, distribution, consumption, and sustainability.

Environmentalist Energy Policies: Are energy policies that focus on environmental protection and minimize carbon emissions throughout the process from energy supply to consumption.

Fossil Fuels: Are energy sources formed from the decomposition of living remains (animal and plant remains) under the ground for millions of years and contain a high amount of carbon in their content.

Global Warming: Is the cooling of the upper part of the atmosphere, namely the stratosphere, and the warming of the lower troposphere, as a result of the greenhouse effect caused by the gases given to the atmosphere by humans.

Renewable Energy: Can be obtained from natural sources such as sun, wind, rain, tides, hot or cold water currents, waves, and geothermal heat. It does not contain carbon in its source, production, or consumption and can be obtained from naturally renewable sources.

Sustainable Energy Policies: Cover implementing policies mainly based on renewable energy, energy efficiency, and energy demand management.

Chapter 4
Navigating Investment Risks in the Renewable Energy Market of Developing Countries: Efficiency vs. Effectiveness

Aida Guliyeva
Azerbaijan State University of Economy, Azerbaijan

Ulviyya Rzayeva
Azerbaijan State University of Economics, Azerbaijan

Aslan Azimzadeh
https://orcid.org/0000-0003-1441-440X
Azerbaijan State University of Economy, Azerbaijan

ABSTRACT

The chapter deals with investment risks in the energy markets. Two important aspects are compared: efficiency and effectiveness. Efficiency is related to the optimal use of resources, both financial and human, to achieve goals. Efficiency is assessed by the achievement of the final goals and expected results. Investment risk management in the energy sector of developing countries requires a balance between efficiency and effectiveness. The chapter gives unexpected results in the management of investment risks in the renewable energy market in developing countries, which may be interesting and meaningful for discussion and further research. An accurate assessment of investment risks in alternative energy and fossil energy depends on specific conditions, regional characteristics, and other factors. However, in the long term, there are arguments in favor of the fact that investment risks in alternative energy may be higher than the risks of investments in fossil energy.

DOI: 10.4018/979-8-3693-0440-2.ch004

INTRODUCTION

Nowadays the energy problems formed by the deepening structural crisis faced by the countries of the world make the use of alternative energy sources even more urgent. On the other hand, the main direction that levels the sustainable development of countries is investments. For this reason, the systematic analysis of certain aspects of investment risk management in the direction of fossil and alternative energy, which are the main directions of natural energy, maintains its importance. In general, it should be noted that in the context of the future of renewable energy, there is a need to analyze the rationality of investment in renewable energy by the countries of the world, as well as the determination of the main goals of progressive development in this direction. Within the framework of the mentioned improvement paths, the analysis of the return on investment in residual energy and the return on investment in renewable energy should be carried out in the framework of long-term analyses. The abundance of financial resources in developed countries means that these countries do not face serious financial problems related to renewable energy.

The paper analyzes the energy market of developing countries such as Turkey, Brazil, China, India, and Egypt, which is important for understanding the current state and prospects for the development of the energy industry in these countries. Each of these countries has its own unique characteristics due to the diversity of economic, social, geographical, and political conditions. It is important to keep these differences in mind when analyzing energy markets.

In the case of Turkey, this country has a strategic geographic position, which makes it an important transit point for energy resources. Türkiye is heavily dependent on energy imports, including oil and natural gas. In recent years, she has paid great attention to the development of renewable energy sources such as solar and wind energy (Kiliç, 2006).

Brazil has vast natural resources, including hydropower and biomass. Water resources play an important role in the country's energy, and it is also actively developing renewable energy sources such as solar and wind energy, as well as bioenergy (Lazaro et al., 2022).

China is the world's largest energy consumer. It relies heavily on coal, which makes up a large part of its energy mix. However, China is also actively investing in renewable energy sources, especially wind and solar energy, to reduce its dependence on coal and reduce greenhouse gas emissions (Yang et al., 2022).

India is also facing rapid growth in energy consumption due to economic development. It is actively developing renewable energy sources, especially solar and wind energy, to meet its growing energy needs and reduce its environmental impact (Gulagi et al., 2022).

Egypt has significant oil and gas reserves but is also looking to develop renewable energy sources, including solar and wind energy, to diversify its energy mix and improve energy security (Moussa & Gurguis, 2023).

Renewable energy sources are playing an increasingly important role in the energy industry in developing countries, and investors are increasingly evaluating opportunities in this area. However, developing countries may be at increased risk due to political instability, regulatory changes, financial problems, and other factors.

The results of this study may provide new examples and insights into how investment risk management can be effectively adapted to the specific conditions of developing countries and the renewable energy market. This can help investors, entrepreneurs, and regulators make more informed decisions and develop strategies for successful investments in this area.

BACKGROUND

Developing countries have a variety of economic, social, geographic, and political conditions that significantly affect the energy market. When analyzing the energy markets of these countries, it is necessary to take into account all these unique features in order to develop adequate strategies and solutions for sustainable energy development and energy risk management.

Studying the energy market of developing countries and their prospects in the field of renewable energy sources provides important information for decision-making in the energy sector, and can also serve as a starting point for further research and development aimed at the sustainable and efficient use of energy resources in these countries.

Analysis of the energy market in developing countries such as Turkey, Brazil, China, India and Egypt is of great importance for understanding the current state and forecasting the prospects for the development of the energy industry in these countries. Each of these countries has its own unique characteristics and features that strongly influence the energy market and must be taken into account in the analysis.

The main purpose of the authors' selection of the mentioned countries for the research work is that these countries, which are the leading developing countries of the world, are countries that have a serious energy demand due to the structure of their economy and the number of their population.

Within the framework of modern challenges in the world economy, the change of the geo-economic and geo-political conjuncture had a certain negative impact on the market of traditional energy carriers. In such a case, the issue of consumption of renewable energy has come up again. In the mentioned countries, serious reforms have been carried out in the production of renewable energy in recent years and certain positive results have been achieved. There are a number of factors that characterize the development of these countries in the mentioned direction, the most important of which is the geographical factor.

Some countries have developed solar energy due to their hot climates, hydro energy in some countries due to abundant rivers, and biofuel energy in some countries as a result of more ripening of sugar cane, which is the main raw material of biofuel. Of course, there are other factors here. It is for this reason that positive impulses are observed within the framework of renewable energy in the countries in question, so the researchers wanted to study the current state of renewable energy in these countries. For this reason, it may be very relevant to take a look at the current state of renewable energy in the countries in question.

Türkiye

The development period of renewable energy in Türkiye began in the mid-2000s with the increase of works related to hydropower plants. At the same time, it should be noted that despite the important share of hydropower plants in renewable energy here, the use of solar energy has been steadily increasing in recent years. In addition, wind turbines are currently installed in windy regions in Türkiye, and electricity is produced in many provinces under the influence of wind.

If we look at the table and the figure, we can see that within the time period from 2015 to the first 10 months of 2020, the increase in hydro energy was 5700, the increase in wind energy was 6809, the increase in solar energy was 8810, the increase of geothermal energy was 1062, and the increase of biomass energy was 1874 MW. At the same time, the total indicator increased by 24256 MW during the mentioned years.

As a whole, an increasing trend regarding alternative energy is being observed in Türkiye. Thus, the electricity installed on the basis of renewable energy sources, which was 31.6 GW in 2015, increased by

Figure 1. Development of renewable energy in Türkiye (MW)
Source: Prepared by authors based on IDBT energy outlook 2022, December (IDBT energy outlook, 2022)

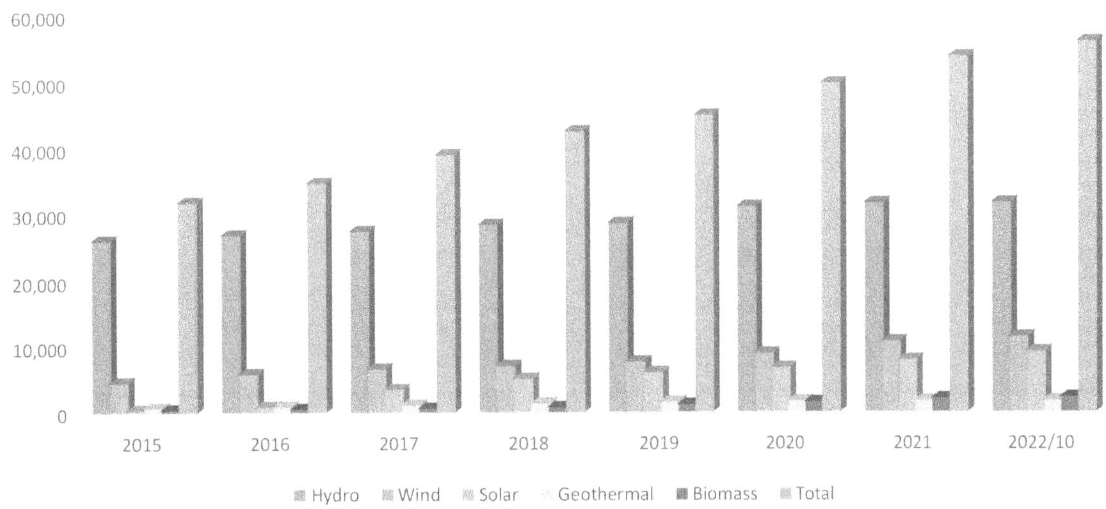

Table 1. Development of renewable energy in Türkiye, MW

Source	2015	2016	2017	2018	2019	2020	2021	2022/10
Hydro	25.868	26.682	27.273	28.291	28.503	30.985	31.493	31.568
Wind	4.498	5.751	6.516	7.005	7.591	8.832	10.607	11.307
Solar	310	833	3.421	5.063	5.995	6.667	7.816	9.120
Geothermal	624	821	1.064	1.283	1.515	1.613	1.676	1.686
Biomass	345	467	575	739	1.163	1.485	2.035	2.219
Total	31.645	34.554	38.849	42.381	44.767	49.582	53.627	55.901

Source: IDBT energy outlook 2022, December (IDBT energy outlook, 2022)

an average of 8.7% annually and reached the level of 55.9 GW by October 2022. At the same time, the share of renewable energy sources in the total installed electricity, which was 43.3% in 2015, increased to 54.1% by October 2022 (IDBT energy outlook, 2022)

Now let's take a look at the current situation by analyzing other important indicators related to renewable energy in Türkiye.

When we look at the table, we see that there is significant volatility in hydroelectricity consumption between 2011 and 2021. So, as a result of this volatility, the indicators of 2011 and 2021 became the same. However, the situation in renewable energy consumption is somewhat different. During the mentioned 10 years, renewable energy consumption increased 10.17 times. This characterizes the observation of positive trends in renewable energy consumption in Türkiye.

It should be noted that from 2011 to 2021, renewable energy production in Türkiye increased 10.81 times. If we look at solar capacity and wind capacity, we can see that both are increasing. So, if the solar capacity was less than 0.05 GW in 2011, this indicator was 7.8 GW in 2021. If we take the indicator of

Table 2. Hydroelectric and renewable energy consumption in Türkiye, MW

Sources	2011	2012	2013	2014	2015	2016	2017	2018	2019	2020	2021
Hydroelectricity consumption (Exajoules (input-equivalent))	0.52	0.57	0.58	0.40	0.65	0.65	0.56	0.57	0.84	0.74	0.52
Renewables consumption (Exajoules (input-equivalent))	0.06	0.08	0.11	0.12	0.17	0.24	0.29	0.38	0.43	0.50	0.61

Source: BP Statistical Review of World Energy, 2022 (BP Statistical Review of World Energy, 2022)

Table 3. Renewable energy generation, solar and wind capacity in Türkiye, MW

Sources	2011	2012	2013	2014	2015	2016	2017	2018	2019	2020	2021
Renewable energy generation (Terawatt-hours)	5.8	7.4	9.8	12.0	16.5	23.8	29.9	38.8	44.6	51.5	62.7
Solar capacity Installed photovoltaic (PV) power. GW	Less than 0.05	Less than 0.05	Less than 0.05	Less than 0.05	0.2	0.8	3.4	5.1	6.0	6.7	7.8
Wind capacity Installed wind turbine capacity. GW	1.7	2.3	2.8	3.6	4.5	5.8	6.5	7.0	7.6	8.8	10.6

Source: BP Statistical Review of World Energy, 2022 (BP Statistical Review of World Energy, 2022)

2011 in the simplest form as 0.049 GW, then in 2021 this indicator can be analyzed as having increased 159.2 times. On the other hand, an increase in wind capacity is observed. The wind capacity, which was 1.7 GW in 2011, was 10.6 GW in 2021, which means an increase of 6.24 times. All these factors show that renewable energy in Türkiye is currently experiencing a period of sustainable development in its advanced format. At the same time, these increases determine the high potential for developing renewable energy in Türkiye.

Brazil

Brazil is the most energy-consuming country in Latin America. As a country, both traditional and renewable energy sources are used. The location of the Amazon River, the most abundant river in the world, in Brazil, makes the country one of the world leaders in hydropower. Of course, it is very important to analyze the indicators of different renewable energy sources here.

The power connected to hydro sources increased from 80,703 MW in 2010, to 91,650 MW in 2015, and to 109,092 MW in 2019. The installed capacity of wind power in Brazil was 927 MW in 2010, 7,633 MW in 2015, and 15,364 MW in 2019. At the same time, Brazil's geographic location makes it a favorable location for solar energy. So, in 2010, the installed capacity of solar energy increased to 2 MW, in 2015 to 27 MW, and in 2019 to 2485 MW. Brazil is one of the world leaders in biomass energy. Thus,

Figure 2. Brazil's electricity generation by source
Source: U.S. Energy Information Administration (U.S. Energy Information Administration, n.d.)

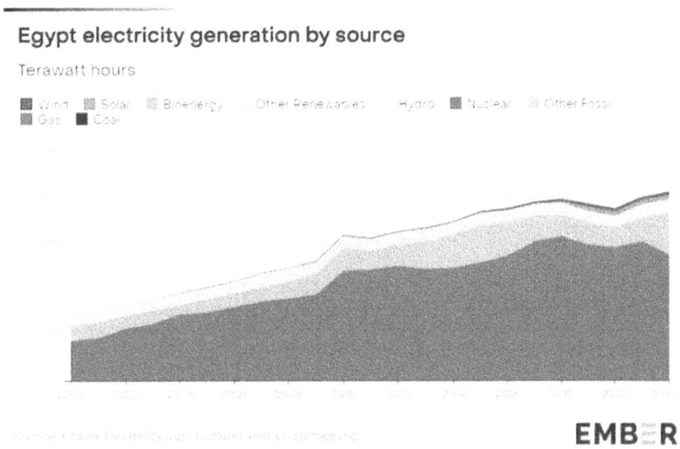

Table 4. Hydroelectric and renewable energy consumption in Brazil, MW

Sources	2011	2012	2013	2014	2015	2016	2017	2018	2019	2020	2021
Hydroelectricity consumption (Exajoules (input-equivalent))	4.25	4.10	3.84	3.64	3.49	3.67	3.55	3.70	3.78	3.75	3.42
Renewables consumption (Exajoules (input-equivalent))	0.93	0.96	1.12	1.30	1.55	1.61	1.75	1.96	2.16	2.19	2.39

Source: BP Statistical Review of World Energy, 2022 (BP Statistical Review of World Energy, 2022)

in 2019, Brazil had a result of 14,922 MW, accounting for 12.1 percent of the world's total biomass installed capacity of 124,026 MW (Durukan & Yilmaz, 2021).

As can be clearly seen, hydropower is the leader in Brazil's total energy. In 2020, hydro energy accounted for 66 percent of the total electricity demand, wind, and solar energy for 11 percent, biomass energy for 8 percent, fossil fuel energy for 12 percent, and nuclear energy for 2 percent. This shows that there is a wide range of renewable energy activities in Brazil.

In another interesting indicator, we observe a decrease in hydroelectricity consumption in Brazil. Thus, from 2011 to 2021, the consumption of hydroelectricity decreased by 1.24 times. However, an increase in the total consumption of renewable energy is observed. Compared to 2011, renewable energy consumption in 2021 has increased 2.57 times.

We see the growth of renewable energy production in Brazil, which acts as a very important indicator. In 2011, the production of renewable energy in Brazil was 35.3 terawatt-hours, and in 2021, this indicator was 144.0 terawatt-hours, which is 4.08 times more than in 2011. At the same time, Brazil ranks 5th in the world in terms of renewable energy production in 2021 (Figure 3).

Brazil's solar capacity appears to be less than 0.05 GW as of 2015. In 2021, this indicator was 13.1 GW, which is 267.35 times more than the first indicator below 0.05 GW, and 0.049 GW. We are also

Table 5. Renewable energy generation, solar and wind capacity in Brazil, MW

Sources	2011	2012	2013	2014	2015	2016	2017	2018	2019	2020	2021
Renewable energy generation (Terawatt-hours)	35.3	40.8	47.6	59.3	71.6	84.9	96.1	106.3	117.6	126.5	144.0
Solar capacity Installed photovoltaic (PV) power. GW	Less than 0.05	Less than 0.05	Less than 0.05	Less than 0.05	Less than 0.05	0.1	1.2	2.4	4.6	7.9	13.1
Wind capacity Installed wind turbine capacity. GW	1.4	1.9	2.2	4.9	7.6	10.1	12.3	14.8	15.4	17.2	21.2

Source: BP Statistical Review of World Energy, 2022 (BP Statistical Review of World Energy, 2022)

Figure 3. Top 5 renewable energy producing countries in 2021
Source: Prepared by the authors using BP Statistical Review of World Energy 2022 indicators (BP Statistical Review of World Energy, 2022)

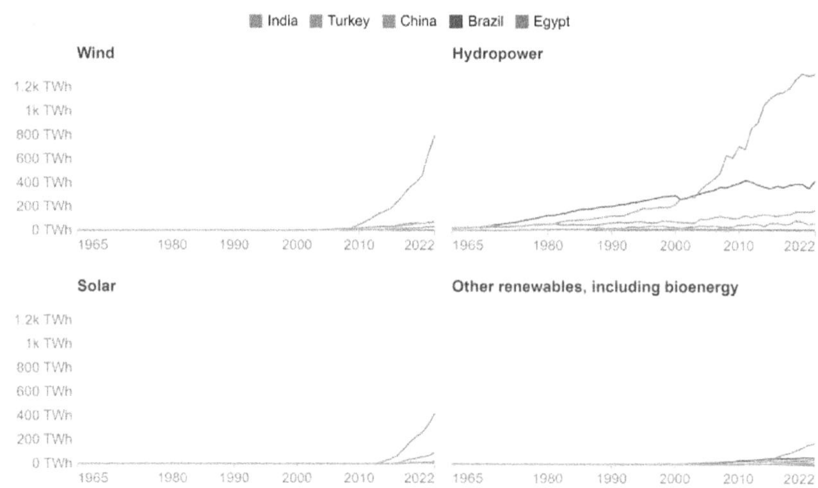

seeing steady growth in wind capacity. Thus, the wind capacity, which was 1.4 GW in 2011, was 21.2 GW in 2021, which is 19.8 times more than the comparison year. It should be noted that Brazil is the leading country in Latin America in the field of renewable energy within the framework of the indicators we have analyzed as a whole. Another important indicator is related to the consumption and production of biofuels. Brazil's richness in the components that make up the production of biofuels energy characterizes its high potential in this energy production.

So, today, sugar cane is used for the production of biofuel, and Brazil is the world leader in sugar cane production (Figure 4).

It should be noted that biogasoline and biodiesel are considered the two main types of biofuel today, so we included these types of fuel in our analysis. In terms of biofuel consumption, 235 thousand barrels of oil were consumed per day in 2011, and in 2021, this indicator equaled 412 thousand barrels of

Figure 4. Countries that are leaders in sugar cane production
Source: Our World in Data (Our World in Data, n.d.)

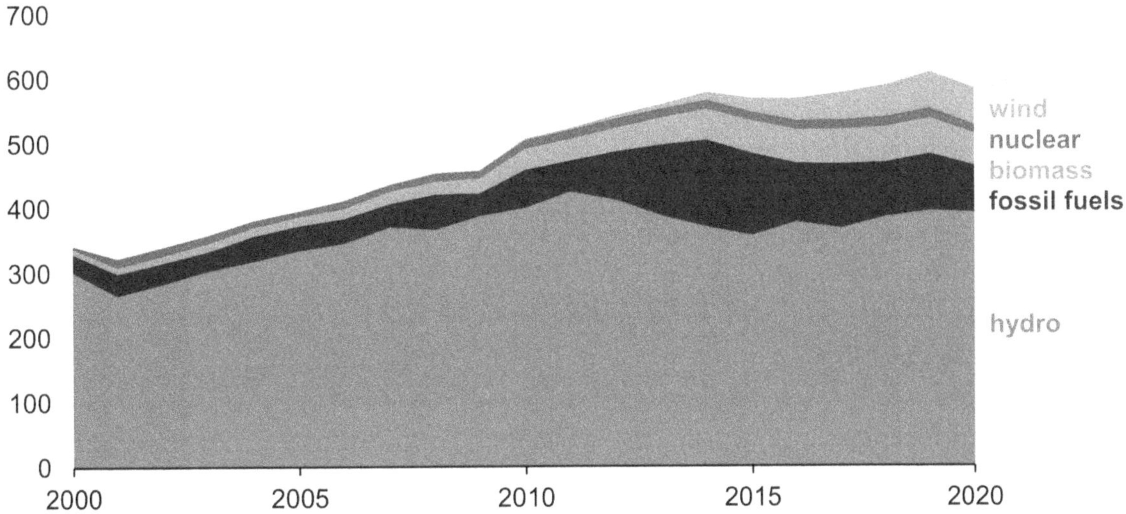

Figure 5. Consumption of biofuel and its main types, biogasoline and biodiesel, in Brazil, thousand barrels of oil equivalent per day
Source: Prepared by the authors using BP Statistical Review of World Energy 2022 indicators (BP Statistical Review of World Energy, 2022)

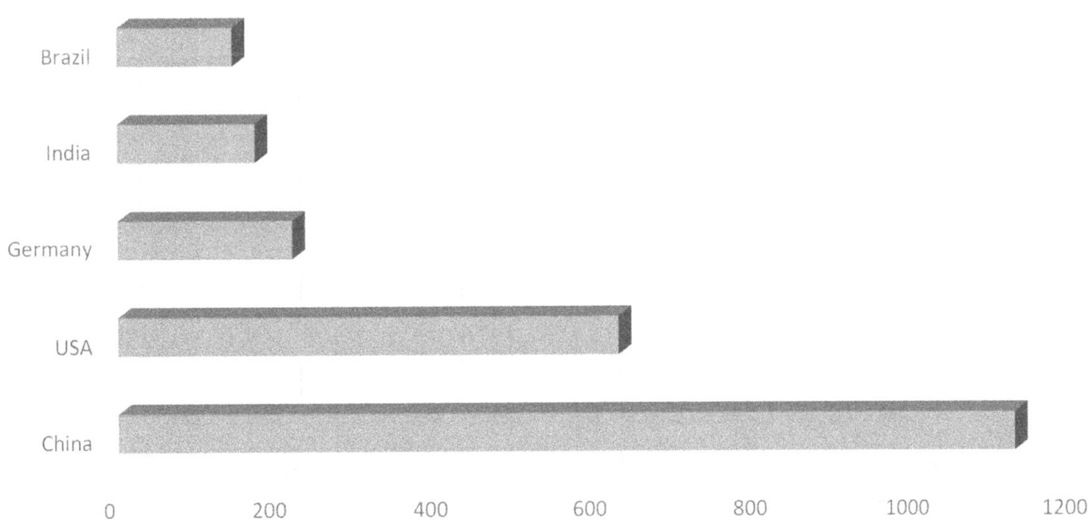

oil consumption, which is actually 1.75 times more than in 2011. At the same time, the consumption of biogasoline increased by 1.58 times, and the consumption of biodiesel by 2.66 times.

Finally, in order to analyze renewable energy in Brazil in a fundamental way, it is necessary to look at the production of biofuels.

Table 6. Consumption of biofuel and its main types, biogasoline and biodiesel, in Brazil, thousand barrels of oil equivalent per day

Sources	2011	2012	2013	2014	2015	2016	2017	2018	2019	2020	2021
Biofuels consumption.	235	222	261	288	341	310	326	378	420	390	412
Biogasoline consumption	197	181	218	238	283	254	236	300	333	295	311
Biodiesel consumption	38	40	43	50	58	56	63	79	87	95	101

Source: BP Statistical Review of World Energy, 2022 ((BP Statistical Review of World Energy, 2022)

Figure 6. Production of biofuel and its main types, biogasoline and biodiesel, in Brazil, thousand barrels of oil equivalent per day

Source: Prepared by the authors using BP Statistical Review of World Energy 2022 indicators (BP Statistical Review of World Energy, 2022

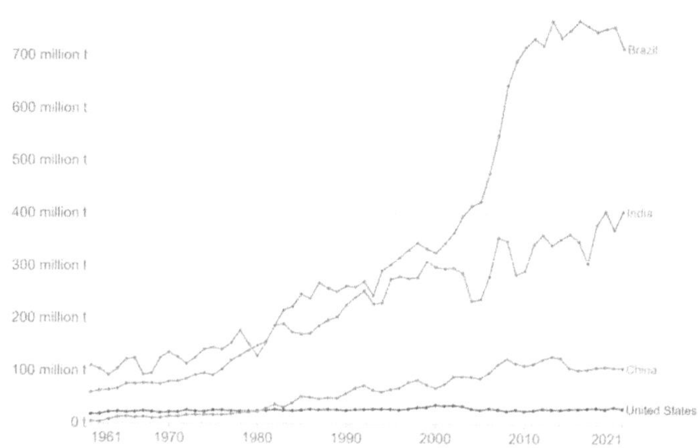

Table 7. Production of biofuel and its main types, biogasoline and biodiesel, in Brazil, thousand barrels of oil equivalent per day

Sources	2011	2012	2013	2014	2015	2016	2017	2018	2019	2020	2021
Biofuels production	251	257	299	315	338	317	320	384	411	394	376
Biogasoline production	212	217	256	264	280	261	256	305	324	299	276
Biodiesel production	39	40	43	50	58	56	63	79	87	95	100

Source: BP Statistical Review of World Energy, 2022 (BP Statistical Review of World Energy, 2022)

Analyzing the production of biofuels in Brazil, we see that although the production is increasing, a certain decrease is observed after 2020, which is related to the crisis of the COVID-19 pandemic and the transportation and logistics caused by it, as well as the production chain. But as a whole, in 2011, biofuel production was 251 thousand oil barrels equivalent per day, by 2021 this indicator is 376 thousand oil barrels equivalent per day, which is 1.5 times more than in 2011. At the same time, compared to 2011, in 2021, biogasoline is 1.3 times more, and biodiesel is 2.56 times more. Another important issue here is that biomass production in 2021 is less than consumption, which shows that Brazil is still unable to meet its biofuel consumption through domestic resources. The decrease caused by the pandemic is one of the main factors that caused this.

China

If we analyze the installed renewable energy capacities in China, we will see that there is a certain increase in installed hydro, solar and wind energy capacities in all three directions. So, if in 2010, the installed hydropower capacity in China was 216 GW, in 2020 this indicator is 370 GW. This is 1.71 times more than in 2010. On the other hand, in 2010, the installed wind power in China was 30 GW, and in 2020, tis indicator was 282 GW, which is 9.4 times more than in 2010. Finally, if we look at solar energy, we will see that in 2010 there was no installed solar energy capacity in China. In 2011, this indicator was 2 GW, and in 2020 it was 253 GW. This is 126.5 times more than in 2011 (Figure 7).

At the same time, it should be noted that in 2020, renewable energy accounted for 27 percent of China's total energy production. The share of hydro energy in the total energy production in this direction was 18 percent, the share of wind energy was 6 percent, and the share of solar energy was 3 percent. (Figure 8)

It is observed that the consumption of renewable energy is at a high level in China along with the production. China is the world leader in renewable energy consumption in 2021, especially in hydro-electricity consumption, which, as we mentioned, is also due to China's large population. The analysis in the mentioned direction is in the following form.

When we look at the table, we see a very high rate of growth. In fact, between 2011 and 2021, hydro-power consumption increased by 44.24 percent, and renewable energy consumption increased by 89.75 percent, which really shows that there is a huge demand for renewable energy in China. At the same time, it should be noted that China is also the world leader in renewable energy production (Figure 3).

Figure 7. Installed renewable energy capacities in China, GW
Source: Energy Brainpool (n.d.)

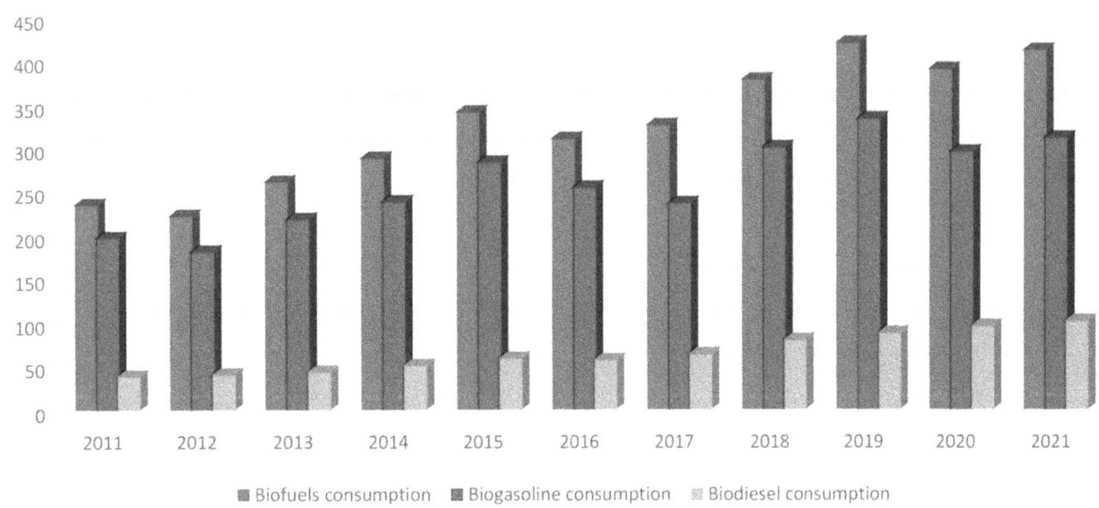

Figure 8. Shares of different generation technologies in the Chinese electricity mix in 2020
Source: Energy Brainpool (n.d.)

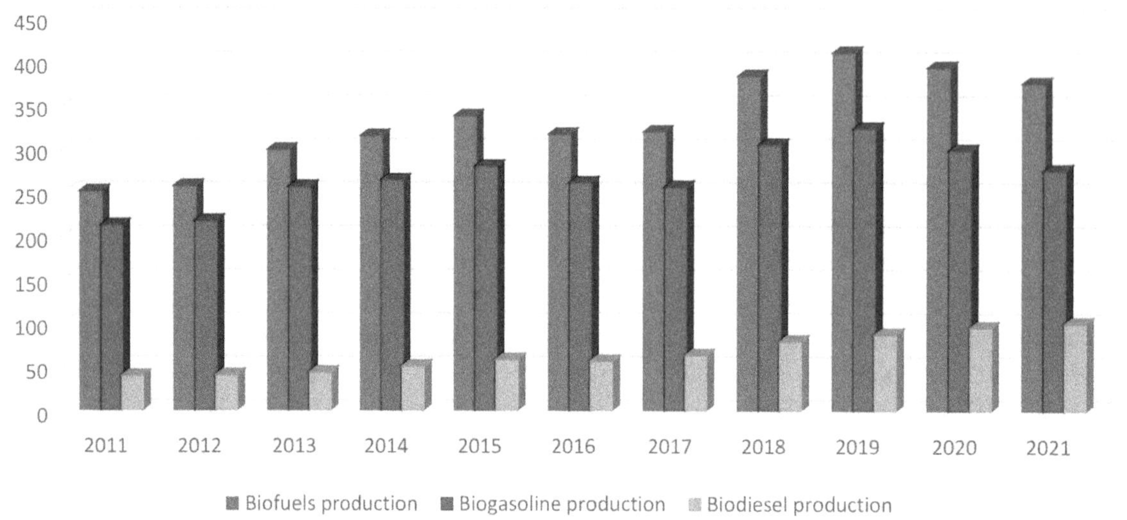

Table 8. Hydroelectric and renewable energy consumption in China

Sources	2011	2012	2013	2014	2015	2016	2017	2018	2019	2020	2021
Hydroelectricity consumption (Exajoules (input-equivalent))	6.83	8.52	8.92	10.33	10.80	11.11	11.16	11.42	12.08	12.50	12.25
Renewables consumption (Exajoules (input-equivalent))	1.16	1.49	1.99	2.45	2.90	3.78	5.06	6.37	7.38	8.52	11.32

Source: BP Statistical Review of World Energy, 2022 (BP Statistical Review of World Energy, 2022)

Table 9. Renewable energy generation, solar and wind capacity in China, MW

Sources	2011	2012	2013	2014	2015	2016	2017	2018	2019	2020	2021
Renewable energy generation (Terawatt-hours)	104.3	136.8	183.8	229.5	279.1	369.5	502.0	636.4	742.0	836.2	1152.5
Solar capacity Installed photovoltaic (PV) power. GW	3.1	6.7	17.7	28.4	43.5	77.8	130.8	175.0	204.6	253.4	306.4
Wind capacity Installed wind turbine capacity. GW	46.4	61.6	76.7	96.8	131.0	148.5	164.4	184.7	209.6	282.1	329.0

Source: BP Statistical Review of World Energy, 2022 (BP Statistical Review of World Energy, 2022)

Table 10. Production and consumption of biofuel in China, thousand barrels of oil equivalent per day

Sources	2011	2012	2013	2014	2015	2016	2017	2018	2019	2020	2021
Biofuels production	36	38	42	47	40	39	47	45	55	58	64
Biofuels consumption	35	42	57	60	42	46	42	55	49	38	48

Source: BP Statistical Review of World Energy, 2022 (BP Statistical Review of World Energy, 2022)

China is the world leader in 2021 for all three indicators shown in Table 9. First, if we look at the production of renewable energy, we will see that in 2011, this production was 104.3 terawatt-hours, and in 2021 it was 1152.5 terawatt-hours, which is 90.95 percent more than the indicator of 2011. On the other hand, if we look at the solar capacity, we will see that the 306.4 GW indicator achieved in 2021 is 98.99 percent more than the 3.1 GW indicator of 2011. At the same time, in 2011, the wind capacity in China was 46.4 GW, and in 2021, this indicator was 329.0 GW, which means an increase of 85.9 percent in 10 years.

Another important indicator is related to biofuel. China has left behind many countries in this direction, but it has not yet reached the production volume of Brazil, the USA, and Indonesia. When we analyzed Brazil, we also analyzed the volume of biogasoline and biodiesel production, which is the main direction of biofuel. However, the available statistics do not contain information about the production volume of these two types of biofuels in China. This may be due to the low production volume. If we look at Table 10, we can see that China produced 43.75 percent more biofuels in 2021 than in 2011. This allows us to say that there is development in the field of biofuels. But this development is below China's biofuel production potential. Because China is one of the world leaders in the production of the main raw materials of biofuel (Figure 4).

India

India is developing at a very high pace in the field of renewable energy during the last year. The geographical position of the country gives it a great potential for the production of renewable energy. On the other hand, the rapid growth of the population in India, as well as in China, creates the basis for the increase in consumption and demand in the field of renewable energy.

Figure 9. Cumulative installed power capacity mix in India in 2021
Source: Mercom India Solar Project Tracker (n.d.)

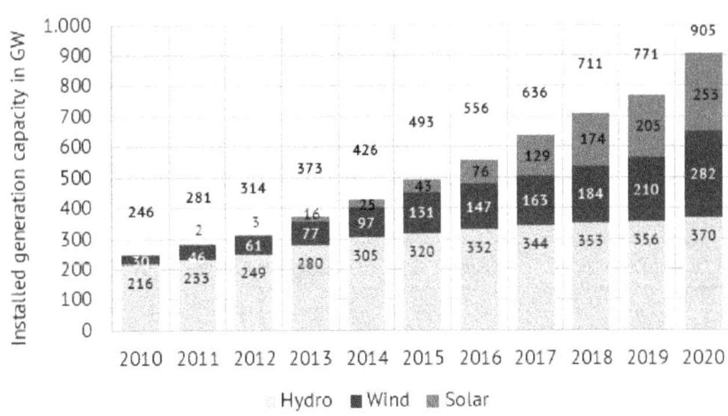

Table 11. Hydroelectric and renewable energy consumption in India, GW

Sources	2011	2012	2013	2014	2015	2016	2017	2018	2019	2020	2021
Hydroelectricity consumption (Exajoules (input-equivalent))	1.31	1.14	1.29	1.36	1.29	1.24	1.30	1.33	1.54	1.55	1.51
Renewables consumption (Exajoules (input-equivalent))	0.49	0.56	0.63	0.71	0.78	0.88	1.05	1.31	1.48	1.58	1.79

Source: BP Statistical Review of World Energy, 2022 (2022)

Table 12. Renewable energy generation, solar, and wind capacity in India, GW

Sources	2011	2012	2013	2014	2015	2016	2017	2018	2019	2020	2021
Renewable energy generation (Terawatt-hours)	41.9	49.5	55.9	63.0	69.9	79.8	99.1	123.9	141.1	152.0	171.9
Solar capacity Installed photovoltaic (PV) power. GW	0.6	1.0	1.4	3.4	5.4	9.7	17.9	27.1	34.9	39.0	49.3
Wind capacity Installed wind turbine capacity. GW	16.2	17.3	18.4	22.5	25.1	28.7	32.8	35.3	37.5	38.6	40.1

Source: BP Statistical Review of World Energy, 2022

If we look at the cumulative installed capacity mix in India for 2021, we see that renewable energy accounts for 38.41 percent of the total installed capacity. Among renewable energy, solar energy is 12.4 percent, large hydro energy is 11.8 percent, and wind energy is 10.2 percent. In fact, all three sources of energy are distributed proportionally. Due to the country's climate, solar and wind energy, and hydro energy due to abundant water rivers, have been developed sustainably.

India's hydroelectricity and total renewable energy consumption are increasing. Thus, the consumption of hydroelectricity in 2021 is 1.15 times more than the consumption of hydroelectricity in 2011. But one thing to note is the volatility in this consumption. This may be the result of certain climate changes, including changes in the country's energy policy. On the other hand, a non-volatile increase in renewable energy consumption is observed. Thus, renewable energy consumption in 2021 is 3.65 times more than renewable energy consumption in 2011.

It should be noted that there is development in all three directions shown in Table 12. First, if we look at renewable energy production, we can see that in 2011, renewable energy production was 41.9 terawatt-hours, and in 2021, renewable energy production was 171.9 terawatt-hours, which is 3.59 times compared to 2011. there are more. With this indicator, India is among the top 5 countries for renewable energy production in 2021 (Figure 3). When we look at solar and wind capacity, we see that solar ca-

Table 13. Production and consumption of biofuel in India, thousand barrels of oil equivalent per day

Sources	2011	2012	2013	2014	2015	2016	2017	2018	2019	2020	2021
Biofuels production	5	5	5	5	10	12	11	19	21	23	37
Biofuels consumption	20	19	19	22	23	28	25	33	37	36	43

Source: BP Statistical Review of World Energy, 2022

pacity was 0.6 GW in 2011, and 49.3 GW in 2021, which means an increase of 82.17 times in 10 years. Within the framework of wind capacity, the indicator which was 16.2 GW in 2011 has increased to the level of 40.1 GW in 2021, which means an increase of 2.48 times compared to the comparison year of 2011. In terms of both solar capacity and wind capacity, India is among the top 5 countries in the world (BP Statistical Review of World Energy, 2022).

The current situation in biofuels in India is somewhat similar to that in China. Thus, India shows high results in the production of sugarcane, which is the main raw material of biofuel (Figure 4). However, current biofuel production is below potential. Biofuel production in India was 5 thousand oil-equivalent barrels per day in 2011, and in 2021 this indicator was 37 thousand oil-equivalent barrels per day, which is a 7.4 times increase compared to 2011. Looking at biofuel consumption, we see that in 2011, biofuel consumption was 20 thousand oil-equivalent barrels per day, and in 2021, this indicator was 43 thousand oil-equivalent barrels per day, which means an increase of 2.15 times compared to 2011. Population growth in India may cause biofuel consumption to be higher than biofuel production. At the same time, it should be noted that the production of biogasoline and biodiesel, which is the main direction of biofuel, in India, as well as in China, is at a very low level, so it is not possible to analyze the mentioned indicators as in Brazil.

Egypt

Located at the crossing point of the world's longest river, the Nile, Egypt can have great potential in hydropower production. Therefore, renewable energy production in Egypt is a very important direction to explore. In recent years, positive trends regarding renewable energy have been observed in Egypt. If we look at Figure 10, we can see that renewable energy has been developing in Egypt for the past 22 years. However, this development does not seem to be such a fast and sustainable development. Because in the mentioned time period, we have seen that countries with less potential than Egypt observed more sustainable development trends. The first place here is hydropower due to the Nile River, the second place is solar power, and the third place is wind power. However, no development has been observed in Egypt regarding biofuels.

Although Egypt has a significant production volume of sugarcane, the main raw material of biofuel. One of the prominent factors here may be the expensiveness of the infrastructure that ensures the purchase of biofuel from sugarcane. However, in the context of Egypt's climate, the said production is far below the potential. We can analyze the issue more clearly by looking at other instructions.

The factors we have mentioned justify themselves in a certain sense. So, from 2011 to 2021, the consumption of hydroelectricity in Egypt has not actually changed. However, an increase in renewable

Table 14. Hydroelectric and renewable energy consumption in Egypt, GW

Sources	2011	2012	2013	2014	2015	2016	2017	2018	2019	2020	2021
Hydroelectricity consumption (Exajoules (input-equivalent))	0.13	0.13	0.13	0.13	0.13	0.13	0.12	0.12	0.13	0.14	0.14
Renewables consumption (Exajoules (input-equivalent))	0.02	0.02	0.02	0.1	0.02	0.03	0.03	0.03	0.06	0.09	0.10

Source: BP Statistical Review of World Energy, 2022

Figure 10. Electricity generation by source in Egypt
Source: Ember Climate (n.d.)

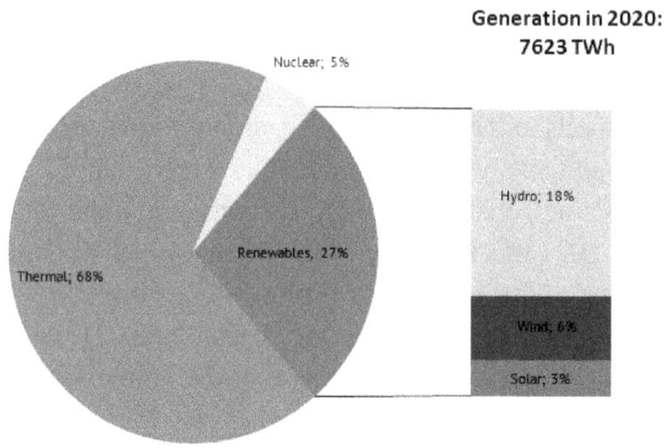

Table 15. Renewable energy generation, solar, and wind capacity in Egypt, GW

Sources	2011	2012	2013	2014	2015	2016	2017	2018	2019	2020	2021
Renewable energy generation (Terawatt-hours)	1.7	1.8	1.6	1.2	1.9	2.6	2.7	3.5	6.5	9.7	10.5
Solar capacity Installed photovoltaic (PV) power. GW	Less than 0.05	Less than 0.05	Less than 0.05	Less than 0.05	Less than 0.05	Less than 0.05	0.2	0.7	1.6	1.7	1.7
Wind capacity Installed wind turbine capacity. GW	0.6	0.6	0.6	0.6	0.8	0.8	0.8	1.1	1.1	1.4	1.6

Source: BP Statistical Review of World Energy, 2022

Figure 11. Renewable energy by source in Brazil, China, Egypt, India, and Türkiye
Source: Our World in Data (n.d.)

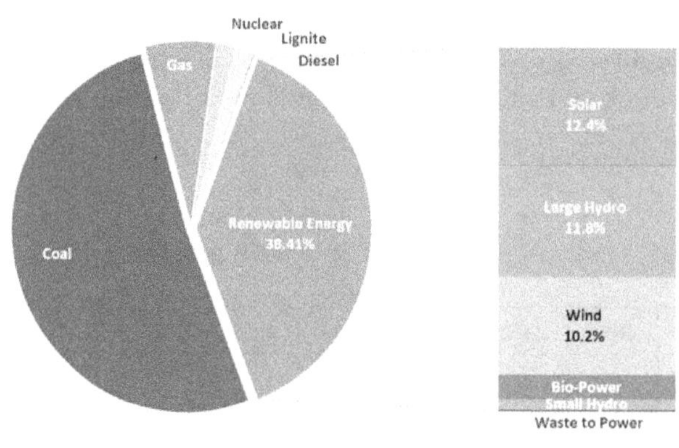

energy consumption is observed. Thus, renewable energy consumption in Egypt increased 5 times from 2011 to 2021.

When we look at Table 15, we see that the production of renewable energy in Egypt was 1.7 terawatt-hours in 2011, and in 2021 this indicator was 10.5 terawatt-hours, which means an increase of 6.18 times. The situation in solar capacity was a little different. As of 2016, solar capacity was less than 0.05 GW. In 2021, the solar capacity was 1.7 GW. If we take 0.049 GW abstractly in 2011, then from 2011 to 2021 we can see a 34.69 times increase in solar capacity. If the wind capacity was 0.6 GW in 2011, this indicator was 1.6 GW in 2021, which means an increase of 2.67 times compared to 2011. Although there is an increase in the indicators, we see that this increase is not sufficiently developed within the existing potential of Egypt. When we look at the comparative analysis of the countries we have studied, we can come to certain conclusions. However, it should be noted that the numbers may be reflected in different forms in different data sources. We used this method because it is quite difficult to find indicators.

When we look at Figure 11, we see that hydropower is the highest indicator for the mentioned countries. This shows that the potential of renewable energy in the future is higher in the field of hydropower. At the same time, we can analyze that wind energy is in the second place, solar energy is in the third place, and bioenergy is in the fourth place in the production of renewable energy in the mentioned countries.

MAIN FOCUS OF THE CHAPTER

Fossil energy performance and alternative energy investment risk management refer to the process of assessing and managing the risks associated with investments in energy projects based on fossil and alternative energy sources (Wu et al., 2022).

Fossil energy includes non-renewable resources such as oil, natural gas, and coal. These fossil energy sources have their own risks associated with price volatility, geopolitical factors, environmental impacts, and limited reserves. Risk management in this area requires analysis and action to mitigate such risks (Soeiro & Dias, 2020).

On the other hand, alternative energy such as solar, wind, hydro, and other renewable energy sources are cleaner and more efficient alternatives to fossil energy sources. However, investments in alternative energy also carry their own risks that need to be managed (Maqbool, 2018).

Investment risk management in the context of fossil energy performance and alternative energy efficiency includes the need to analyze and assess the risks associated with both fossil energy sources and alternative sources, taking into account the analysis of price volatility, political risk, environmental factors, technical risks and other factors that may affect the effectiveness and efficiency of energy projects (Kul et al., 2020).

To manage risks, it is recommended to diversify the portfolio of investments in energy projects, including both fossil energy and alternative sources. Diversity helps reduce dependence on a single resource or technology and mitigate possible risks.

Note that financial instruments such as insurance, derivatives, and other market risk instruments can be used to manage financial risks in investments in energy projects. (Taghizadeh-Hesary & Yoshino, 2020). For example, using futures or options on energy resources can help mitigate the risks associated with price fluctuations (Egli et al., 2018).

Expertise also needs to be taken into account: it is important to seek advice from experts in energy and finance for risk management advice. Experts will be able to provide risk analysis, advice on management strategies, and support in making decisions related to investments in energy projects (Apak et al., 2011).

The Efficiency of Fossil Energy vs. the Effectiveness of Renewable Energy

Some countries currently export large amounts of fossil fuels as part of their economic model and have some of the highest levels of energy intensity in the world (Suna et al., 2022). The number of countries and people whose respective national incomes and livelihoods depend on fossil energy sources is significant and will continue to be so over the period covered by our projection (until 2050). Despite widespread household electrification in terms of physical access, aging infrastructure, a lack of supply diversity and rising tariffs contribute to a poor quality of electricity supply and, according to some, energy poverty. The situation is particularly serious during the cold winter months and disproportionately affects the poor and the rural population. As a result, some consumers have returned to using local sources of solid fuel for cooking and heating, while others have returned to using electricity from off-grid diesel generators (Sharma et al., 2018).

Energy efficiency is defined as the ratio between the volume of energy consumption and the output of products (energy services) produced using this energy. Improving energy efficiency means using either less energy to produce the same output, or the same amount of energy to produce more output. For example, the term can be used at the micro level to express the energy efficiency of a sector, such as the iron and steel industry, but also at the product level, such as when referring to the energy efficiency of applications or the energy efficiency of electricity generation, particularly from coal, gas (De la Cruz-Lovera, 2017).

Most countries have developed national energy efficiency action plans but have made limited progress in their implementation. Improvement in the energy performance of buildings has been slow despite steady progress in energy efficiency in home appliances in North America and the European Union. There is much-untapped potential around the world to improve industrial energy productivity (Hepbasli, 2008). With the exception of the member countries of the European Union, the fuel efficiency of vehicles is not progressing. Global supply-side efficiency gains are driven primarily by investments in high-efficiency combined cycle gas turbines and the use of less efficient coal-fired power plants (Eguchi, 2022).

Fossil fuels dominate the global energy mix and underpin modern energy access and economic development (Tong et al., 2019). The long-standing dependence on fossil fuels is ignored in discussions about energy effectiveness and renewable energy, which slows down the process of achieving goals. The share of fossil energy sources in the countries is just over 80%. Even under a 2°C climate change scenario, fossil fuels will still account for 40% of the energy mix in 2050 (Ahlborg, 2017).

Energy effectiveness is a policy enabler on many fronts: reducing the amount of energy required to produce goods in an economy through the use of capital, labor, and other material resources, it increases energy productivity. Since the release of the McKinsey report, it has been recognized as one of the most affordable means to meet global goals and targets, but there is still room for improvement in the implementation of energy effectiveness measures (Peñasco & Díaz Anadón, 2023). Energy intensity is commonly used to measure energy effectiveness, although the two are not equivalent and energy intensity alone does not take into account differences in economic structure, resource endowments, levels of activity, or climatic factors that drive energy use. Energy intensity indicates how much energy is needed to produce a unit of output in an economy. A lower ratio indicates that less energy is used to produce a unit of output. This indicator is usually used at the macroeconomic level and is defined in the context of energy rather than output (Luciani, 2022). For example, high energy intensity in a country may be a direct result of the extraction and export of energy-intensive minerals in cold climates (for example, Canada, Sweden, or the Russian Federation), while low energy intensity may be the result of a high level of development of service industries (for example, Switzerland). In none of these cases does the energy intensity indicator provide insight into the underlying performance of the economy, historical development paths and improvements in energy effectiveness, or opportunities for further improvements in energy effectiveness.

The energy industry has succeeded in improving the quality of life around the world, especially in advanced economies, and even in developing countries. Today, the energy business is a commodity business, whose participants make a profit by increasing production and sales. Currently, decisions about the future are shaped by the existing infrastructure, in particular the physical, regulatory, political, and organizational infrastructure of the energy sector, due to the existing expectation that today's structures will continue into the future. However, energy services for consumers are inadequate. Globally, there is evidence of problems with the affordability of heating services, the reliability of aging systems, and future needs for resilience (Nieto et al., 2020). Achieving true sustainability requires rethinking the energy industry as a complex service industry. Such reformatting would encourage innovation, investment, and energy effectiveness. A genuine transformation of the energy system will require a creative shift in policy and regulation, but in many countries, the current political, regulatory, and industrial infrastructure is not yet ready for such a transformation.

Methodology and Data

This paper considers the main criteria for evaluating the efficiency of the use of non-renewable energy sources in the global fuel and energy balance. The proposed system of criteria is complex, takes into account the costs of creating a production base for the energy sector, and allows you to evaluate the efficiency of the use of non-renewable energy sources. Evaluation of the above criteria in accordance with the above methodology is the basis for the development of a predictive model that takes into account the efficiency of non-renewable energy and the effectiveness of alternative energy.

Fossil Energy Efficiency Index

The presented methodology for determining the percentage of energy efficiency uses the average and the method of effects (Lapillonne, 2020). We assume that there are energy performance index data for each of the various sectors that consume energy. This aggregate index is determined in accordance with the following methodology.

Assuming that the value of I_t refers to year t, then the ratio $\frac{I_t}{I_{t-1}}$ can be interpreted as the ratio of energy consumption in year t to the energy consumption that would occur in year t if the consumption level corresponded to the level in year $t-1$.

$$\frac{I_t}{I_{t-1}} = \frac{\sum_i EC_{i,t}}{\sum_i A_{i,t} \cdot UC_{i,t-1}} \tag{1}$$

where i is the sector, $A_{i,t}$ is an activity variable of sector i in year t; $UC_{i,t}$ is unit consumption in sector i in year t.

This formula can be generalized by noting that for sector i it takes the form:

$$\frac{I_t}{I_{t-1}} = \frac{UC_t}{UC_{t-1}} \tag{2}$$

For a particular sector, the energy efficiency index can be viewed as an indicator of specific energy consumption.

Equation (2) can be written as follows:

$$UC_{t-1} = \frac{I_{t-1}}{I_t} \cdot UC_t.$$

Replacing UC_{t-1} with its value in (1) leads to:

$$\frac{I_t}{I_{t-1}} = \frac{\sum_i EC_{i,t}}{\sum_i A_{i,t} \cdot UC_t \cdot \frac{I_{t-1}}{I_t}},$$

or

$$\frac{I_t}{I_{t-1}} = \frac{\sum_i EC_{i,t}}{\sum_i EC_{i,t} \cdot \frac{I_{i,t-1}}{I_{i,t}}}.$$

Inverted, this gives:

$$\frac{I_{t-1}}{I_t} = \frac{\sum_i EC_{i,t} \cdot \frac{I_{i,t-1}}{I_{i,t}}}{\sum_i EC_{i,t}},$$

or

$$\frac{I_{t-1}}{I_t} = \sum_i ec_{i,t} \cdot \frac{I_{i,t-1}}{I_{i,t}},$$

where $ec_{i,t}$ is share of sector i in total energy consumption in year t.

This last formula shows that $\frac{I_{t-1}}{I_t}$ is the average of the industry ratio $\frac{I_{i,t-1}}{I_{i,t}}$ weighted by each sector's share of total energy consumption.

Alternative energy Effectiveness Index

Another purpose of this article is to present analytical calculations of alternative energy effectiveness. The calculations are based on the most common methods used to calculate the share of renewable energy in energy consumption in the European Union (Camacho Ballesta, et al., 2022). In addition, this article also provides additional methodological information about the content of renewable energy in electrical capacity (%) and the share of RES in electricity generation (%), which are important for understanding the calculation of different types of shares of renewable energy sources.

In practice, the calculation of the effectiveness of alternative energy must be predictive, that is, take into account the future time (in our model, as already mentioned, the period under consideration covers the time until 2050). So, the formula for evaluating the effectiveness of alternative energy is as follows:

$$E = K \cdot \frac{A^2}{T},$$

where E is effectiveness, K is amount of renewable energy in electricity generation (IRENASTAT, 2022), A is acceptance rate (Wisevoter, 2022), T is the predicted time (Yazdani et al., 2020).

Data and Calculations

Table 16 lists the variables used in the analytical model, their names and meaning. The data sources are the independent research company Enerdata, which specializes in the analysis and forecasting of problems in the field of energy and climate.

It is important to note that the efficiency of using fossil energy depends on many factors, including the technologies chosen, operating conditions, infrastructure and energy policy. It must also be taken into account that even with high efficiency in the use of fossil resources, they are still non-regenerative and have negative environmental impacts, including greenhouse gas emissions and other environmental problems. Therefore, the rational use of renewable energy sources is also an important aspect in ensuring sustainability and reducing the negative impact on the environment.

Table 17 shows the Effectiveness of using alternative energy.

It must be taken into account that each energy market has its own unique characteristics, and investors need to carefully assess and analyze risks before making investment decisions. While alternative energy sources have their own characteristics and risks, they also represent important opportunities for sustainable energy development in the future.

RESEARCH RESULTS

The process of decarbonization of the electricity sector is proceeding at a rapid pace. Although developing countries' investments in renewable energy fall far short of meeting the electricity needs of people and industry, they remain part of growing efforts to use alternatives to fossil fuels.

As the calculations show, in the short term, investments in alternative energy sources in developing countries are not justified from an economic point of view. Significant infrastructure costs represent a

Table 16. Efficiency of fossil energy

Years	Primary Fossil Energy (MW)	Primary Alternative Energy (MW)	Final Consumption of Energy (MW)	Efficiency of Total Energy (x100%)
1990	88551,17004	6641,516301	8734,469205	1,003541272
1991	89040,97326	6807,195451	8788,081843	0,999194408
1992	89543,3475	6841,930679	8795,636771	1,003954752
1993	89891,35291	7240,91194	8883,556038	0,997591298
1994	91038,16381	7300,025351	8957,184922	1,003989677
1995	92867,79789	7695,473133	9182,242686	1,002477072
1996	95648,84543	7808,073938	9411,82332	1,001903796
1997	96528,39637	7990,452397	9509,855797	1,005107526
1998	97084,36616	8074,881731	9559,058558	1,011565846
1999	98804,34047	8171,69578	9772,775974	0,9918743
2000	101422,7503	8356,317698	10008,38917	0,996898389
2001	102714,2055	8162,420117	10089,83405	1,00633772
2002	104892,9853	8327,771003	10312,2672	0,991544048
2003	108906,6992	8339,079816	10678,50271	0,997872772
2004	114097,2824	8954,294318	11151,77764	1,001433941
2005	117781,7923	9297,213588	11468,11501	1,004335169
2006	120925,7364	9692,313065	11804,43706	1,00377633
2007	124586,467	9961,564026	12120,39981	0,994971682
2008	125365,8044	10621,5432	12258,19183	1,003615089
2009	122923,0171	10791,15204	12138,53782	1,002582268
2010	128522,7799	11581,33309	12815,69413	0,995236946
2011	131220,2973	12093,72933	13026,0219	1,004531525
2012	132467,5221	12881,98693	13189,85765	1,006086968
2013	134138,1032	13703,33342	13385,42415	1,004694904
2014	134986,0519	14363,05921	13559,15396	1,007359868
2015	135662,0312	14874,6858	13578,30516	1,009960095
2016	136589,0119	15718,87059	13700,93309	0,997655448
2017	138815,5651	16679,31917	14000,09296	0,998057924
2018	141977,1887	17728,92299	14352,94359	1,007362153
2019	142705,9363	18660,60587	14522,9271	1,015575394
2020	135819,2973	19852,34246	13965,64972	1,01353879
2021	143187,3491	20961,24123	14646,63539	0,996004475
2022	143498,2317	22421,29933	14951,19378	1,011523984

Data Source: International Energy Agency, 2023, https://www.iea.org/countries
All calculations made by authors

Table 17. Effectiveness of alternative energy

Years	RE Share of Electricity Capacity (%)	RE Share of Electricity Generation (%)	Effectiveness (x100%)
2000	21,4	18,32	0,713333
2001	21,78	17,81	0,726
2002	21,56	17,73	0,718667
2003	21,51	17,27	0,717
2004	21,7	17,68	0,723333
2005	21,91	17,82	0,730333
2006	21,93	17,98	0,731
2007	22,2	17,73	0,74
2008	22,78	18,46	0,759333
2009	23,49	19,22	0,783
2010	24,12	19,39	0,804
2011	25,05	19,71	0,835
2012	26,12	20,8	0,870667
2013	27,21	21,42	0,907
2014	28,21	22,22	0,940333
2015	29,52	22,66	0,984
2016	26,12	23,58	0,870667
2017	22,07	24,23	0,735667
2018	23,14	24,81	0,771333
2019	24,54	25,86	0,818
2020	26,56	27,67	0,885333
2021	28,31	0	0,943667
2022	20,2	0	0,673333

Data Source: International Renewable Energy Agency, 2023, https://www.irena.org/Data
All calculations made by authors

major obstacle to increasing the share of alternative energy. The desire to transition to alternative energy sources, such as solar, wind or geothermal energy, requires the creation of new systems and modernization of existing infrastructure. In addition, equipment costs must be taken into account. Installing alternative energy systems such as solar panels, wind turbines or geothermal plants requires a large investment. To integrate alternative energy into the grid, it is necessary to modernize the grid infrastructure. Ensuring the reliability of energy supplies from alternative sources may require energy storage and buffering infrastructure. Working with alternative energy systems requires specialized knowledge and skills. In some cases, investors face additional costs and delays due to regulatory and administrative procedures associated with obtaining permits and licenses.

To overcome these obstacles, it is critical to create incentives for investors and provide government support for alternative energy projects. This could include tax incentives, subsidies, guaranteed tariffs to reward alternative energy production, and simplified permitting procedures. It is also important to develop long-term strategies and development plans for the transition to more sustainable energy.

SOLUTIONS AND RECOMMENDATIONS

The article presents the results of a comparative analysis of the efficiency of various fossil energy sources and the effectiveness of alternative energy in terms of investment.

The performance and efficiency of various fossil and alternative energy sources were reviewed in terms of affordability and sustainability. Information has been provided on the abundance of fossil sources in some regions, making them relatively accessible. However, they are non-renewable resources and may become increasingly limited and less sustainable in the future. While alternative sources (solar, wind, hydropower, etc.) are based on renewable resources such as solar radiation, wind and water flows, which makes them more sustainable and long-term.

A comparative analysis of environmental impacts was also presented. Fossil sources are often accompanied by negative environmental impacts such as greenhouse gas emissions, air and water pollution, and the destruction of natural ecosystems. Alternative sources have a much smaller negative environmental footprint, do not emit greenhouse gases or other pollution, and have little or no impact on the climate and environment.

The main emphasis in the article is on the conversion efficiency. Fossil sources usually have a high efficiency in converting energy into electricity or other forms of energy. For example, gas and steam turbines are highly efficient in converting energy. Alternative sources may have different effectiveness depending on technology and conditions. For example, solar panels can have different effectiveness depending on the intensity of solar radiation and the angle of inclination, while wind turbines depend on wind speed.

Fossil sources may have relatively low investment costs for production and distribution, but may face price fluctuations in world markets.

The main finding of this study is that investment in alternative energy sources in developing countries is not economically viable in the near future. There can be many reasons for this. Among them, the main one is that significant investment in infrastructure may be one of the main obstacles to increasing the share of alternative energy. It is important to understand that the transition to alternative energy sources, such as solar, wind or geothermal energy, requires the creation of new systems and modernization of existing infrastructure. In this case, it is necessary to take into account the costs of equipment. Installing alternative energy systems such as solar panels, wind turbines or geothermal plants requires large capital investments. Integrating alternative energy into the grid requires upgrading the grid infrastructure. To ensure a stable supply of energy from alternative sources, energy storage and buffering infrastructure may be required. Working with alternative energy systems requires specialized knowledge and skills. In some cases, investors face additional costs and delays due to regulatory and administrative procedures associated with permits and licenses.

To overcome these obstacles, it is important to create incentives for investors and provide government support for alternative energy projects. This may include tax incentives, subsidies, guaranteed tariffs to reward alternative energy production, and simplified permitting procedures. It is also important to develop long-term strategies and development plans for the transition to more sustainable energy.

FUTURE RESEARCH DIRECTIONS

Future directions of research on the efficiency of fossil energy and the efficiency of alternative energy play an important role in the development of a sustainable energy system for the future. Including these areas in the article can provide readers with an idea of what technologies and innovations could impact the energy sector in the coming years.

Research and development of new technologies and improvements to existing ones can significantly affect the efficiency and effectiveness of both types of energy sources. A deeper understanding of the integration of various energy sources, such as hybrid hybrid systems, energy storage and smart grid management, will optimize power systems for efficiency and effectiveness.

Analyzing the behavior of energy consumers and their preferences for different energy sources will also help develop measures to encourage the use of alternative energy sources. Optimization of energy consumption and distribution can be facilitated by the development of intelligent energy network management systems (smart grids) and decentralized energy systems. Using computer models and systems analysis to assess the relationship and impact of various factors on the performance and efficiency of fossil and alternative energy.

Studies aimed at assessing the prospects and mechanisms for the transition to sustainable energy, including the analysis of economic, social and political aspects. The use of scientific research and innovative approaches will create a more sustainable and efficient energy system, which can have a global and positive effect on the environment and society.

CONCLUSION

The energy problem in the world economy is still ongoing. For this reason, renewable energy sources are in the center of attention of both developed and developing countries. Due to the diversity of the energy market of developing countries, we analyzed the energy market of countries such as Turkey, Brazil, China, India and Egypt, and the general situation of renewable energy in these countries. Due to the death of abundant rivers, we can analyze that in each of these countries, the specific weight of hydropower is actually high. Climate and geographical location act as the main direction characterizing the country's renewable energy potential. For biofuel, which is one of the main directions of renewable energy, the resource factor is equally important as the climate factor. Thus, the main raw material of biofuel is sugar cane, and the consumption and production of biofuel energy should be high in countries that are leaders in its production (Brazil, India, China). However, in this direction, we can see that only Brazil is developing more sustainably than China and India. At the same time the efficiency of fossil energy and the effectiveness of renewable energy, as well as the feasibility of investing in these types of energy, were studied in the research work. On the other hand, a comparative analysis of the return on investment in residual energy and the return on investment in renewable energy was made in the long-term analysis.

Investment risk management in the energy sector of developing countries is a complex and multifaceted process that requires a balance between efficiency and effectiveness. Features of the economic and political situation in developing countries, as well as market uncertainty, may affect decision-making and risk assessment. Developing countries may have more immediate needs, such as providing energy access to the population or infrastructure for economic growth, and these needs may take higher priority over investment in alternative energy sources. Investments in alternative energy sources often have a long payback period, which means investors will not see a quick return on their money. In developing countries where funds are needed to solve urgent problems, such a long payback period may not be acceptable.

The results obtained may stimulate interest in further research and risk analysis in the energy market of developing countries. The discovery of unexpected trends and connections could lead to new ideas and approaches to manage risk and ensure the sustainability of renewable energy investments.

REFERENCES

Ahlborg, H. (2017). Towards a conceptualization of power in energy transitions. *Environmental Innovation and Societal Transitions*, *25*, 122–141. doi:10.1016/j.eist.2017.01.004

Apak, S., Atay, E., & Tuncer, G. (2011). Financial risk management in the renewable energy sector: Comparative analysis between the European Union and Turkey. *Procedia: Social and Behavioral Sciences*, *24*, 935–945. doi:10.1016/j.sbspro.2011.09.013

Camacho Ballesta, J. A., da Silva Almeida, L., & Rodríguez, M. (2022). An analysis of the main driving factors of renewable energy consumption in the European Union. *Environmental Science and Pollution Research International*, *29*(23), 35110–35123. doi:10.100711356-022-18715-z PMID:35044609

De la Cruz-Lovera, C., Perea-Moreno, A.-J., De la Cruz-Fernández, J.-L., Alvarez-Bermejo, J. A., & Manzano-Agugliaro, F. (2017). Worldwide research on energy efficiency and sustainability in public buildings. *Sustainability (Basel)*, *9*(8), 1294. doi:10.3390u9081294

Durukan, A., & Yilmaz, M. (2021). Yenilenebilir Enerjinin Önemi Ve Latin Amerika Coğrafyasindaki Yeri: Brezilya Örneği. *Ankara Üniversitesi Dil ve Tarih-Coğrafya Fakültesi Dergisi*, *61*(1), 339–358. doi:10.33171/dtcfjournal.2021.61.1.13

Egli, F., Steffen, B., & Schmidt, T. (2018). A dynamic analysis of financing conditions for renewable energy technologies. *Nature Energy*, *3*(12), 1084–1092. doi:10.103841560-018-0277-y

Eguchi, S. (2022). CO2 Reduction potential from efficiency improvements in China's coal-fired thermal power generation: A combined approach of metafrontier DEA and LMDI. *Energies*, *15*(7), 2430. doi:10.3390/en15072430

Ember Climate. (n.d.). https://ember-climate.org/countries-and-regions/countries/egypt/

Energy Brainpool. (n.d.). https://blog.energybrainpool.com/en/chinas-energy-system-in-2020-record-expansion-of-renewables-despite-corona-pandemic/

Gulagi, A., Ram, M., Bogdanov, D., Sarin, S., Mensah, T. N. O., & Breyer, C. (2022). The role of renewables for rapid transitioning of the power sector across states in India. *Nature Communications*, *13*(1), 5499. doi:10.103841467-022-33048-8 PMID:36130937

Hepbasli, A. (2008). A key review on exergetic analysis and assessment of renewable energy resources for a sustainable future. *Renewable & Sustainable Energy Reviews*, *12*(3), 593–661. doi:10.1016/j.rser.2006.10.001

IDBT Energy Outlook. (2022). https://www.tskb.com.tr/uploads/file/enerji-gorunumu-final.pdf

International Energy Agency. (2023). https://www.iea.org/countries

International Renewable Energy Agency. (2023). https://www.irena.org/Data

IRENASTAT. (2022). https://pxweb.irena.org/pxweb/en/IRENASTAT/IRENASTAT__Power%20Capacity%20and%20Generation/RESHARE_2023_cycle1.px/table/tableViewLayout1/

Kiliç, A. M. (2006). Turkey's Main Energy Sources and Importance of Usage in Energy Sector. *Energy Exploration & Exploitation*, *24*(1-2), 1–17. doi:10.1260/014459806779388001

Kul, C., Zhang, L., & Solangi, Y. A. (2020). Assessing the renewable energy investment risk factors for sustainable development in Turkey. *Journal of Cleaner Production*, *276*, 124164. doi:10.1016/j.jclepro.2020.124164

Lapillonne, B. (2020). *Definition of energy efficiency index ODEX in ODYSSEE database*. Energy efficiency index. Retrieved from: https://www.odyssee-mure.eu/publications/other/odex-indicators-database-definition.html

Lazaro, L. L. B., Soares, R. S., Bermann, C., Collaço, F. M. A., Giatti, L. L., & Abram, S. (2022). Energy transition in Brazil: Is there a role for multilevel governance in a centralized energy regime? *Energy Research & Social Science*, *85*, 102404. doi:10.1016/j.erss.2021.102404

Luciani, G. (2022). Macroeconomics of the Energy Transition. In M. Hafner & G. Luciani (Eds.), *The Palgrave Handbook of international energy economics*. Palgrave Macmillan. doi:10.1007/978-3-030-86884-0_25

Maqbool, R. (2018). Efficiency and effectiveness of factors affecting renewable energy projects; an empirical perspective. *Energy*, *158*, 944–956. doi:10.1016/j.energy.2018.06.015

Mercom India Solar Project Tracker. (n.d.). https://www.mercomindia.com/solar-share-india-power-mix-q4-2021

Moussa, R. R., & Gurguis, M. N. (2023). Integrating renewable energy devices with streetscape elements to electrify the Egyptian roads. *Scientific Reports*, *13*(1), 6720. doi:10.103841598-023-32773-4 PMID:37185786

Nieto, J., Carpintero, Ó., Miguel, L. J., & de Blas, I. (2020). Macroeconomic modeling under energy constraints: Global low carbon transition scenarios. *Energy Policy*, *137*, 111090. doi:10.1016/j.enpol.2019.111090

Our World in Data. (n.d.). https://ourworldindata.org/grapher/modern-renewable-prod?facet=metric&country=EGY~IND~TUR~BRA~CHN

Our World in Data. (n.d.). https://ourworldindata.org/grapher/sugar-cane-production?tab=chart

Peñasco, C., & Díaz Anadón, L. (2023). Assessing the effectiveness of energy efficiency measures in the residential sector gas consumption through dynamic treatment effects: Evidence from England and Wales. *Energy Economics*, *117*, 106435. doi:10.1016/j.eneco.2022.106435

Sharma, A., Rajpurohit, B. S., & Singh, S. N. (2018). A review on economics of power quality: Impact, assessment and mitigation. *Renewable & Sustainable Energy Reviews*, *88*, 363–372. doi:10.1016/j.rser.2018.02.011

Soeiro, S., & Dias, M. F. (2020). Energy cooperatives in Southern European countries: Are they relevant for sustainability targets? *Energy Reports*, *6*, 448–453. doi:10.1016/j.egyr.2019.09.006

Statistical, B. P. Review of World Energy. (2022). https://www.bp.com/content/dam/bp/business-sites/en/global/corporate/pdfs/energy-economics/statistical-review/bp-stats-review-2022-full-report.pdf

Suna, M., Ozcan, O., & Öten, C. (2022). *Turkish Energy Policy and Energy Security*. IJOPEC Publication Limited.

Taghizadeh-Hesary, F., & Yoshino, N. (2020). Sustainable Solutions for Green Financing and Investment in Renewable Energy Projects. *Energies*, *13*(4), 788. doi:10.3390/en13040788

Tong, Zh., Xunpeng, Sh., Dayong, Zh., & Junji, X. (2019). Socio-economic development and electricity access in developing economies: A long-run model averaging approach. *Energy Policy*, *132*, 223–23. doi:10.1016/j.enpol.2019.05.031

U.S. Energy Information Administration. (n.d.). https://www.eia.gov/todayinenergy/detail.php?id=49436

Wisevoter. (2022). https://wisevoter.com/country-rankings/renewable-energy-by-country/#map

Wu, H., Carroll, J., & Denny, E. (2022). Harnessing citizen investment in community-based energy initiatives: A discrete choice experiment across ten European countries. *Energy Research & Social Science*, *89*, 102552. doi:10.1016/j.erss.2022.102552

Yang, Y., Wang, H., Löschel, A., & Zhou, P. (2022). Energy transition toward carbon-neutrality in China: Pathways, implications and uncertainties. *Front. Eng. Manag.*, *9*(3), 358–372. doi:10.100742524-022-0202-8

Yazdani, M., Torkayesh, A. E., Santibanez-Gonzalez, D. R., & Otaghsara, S. K. (2020). Evaluation of renewable energy resources using integrated Shannon Entropy—EDAS model. *Sustainable Operations and Computers*, *1*, 35–42. doi:10.1016/j.susoc.2020.12.002

KEY TERMS AND DEFINITIONS

Alternative Energy: Energy from natural and renewable sources, such as solar or wind.

Alternative Energy Risks: Factors and events that may adversely affect the development, production, distribution, or use of renewable energy sources such as solar, wind, hydropower, geothermal and biomass.

Energy Effectiveness: The degree to which energy is successful in producing a desired result.

Energy Efficiency: The use of less energy to perform the same task or produce the same result.

Fossil Energy: Sources, including oil, coal, and natural gas, are non-renewable resources that formed when prehistoric plants and animals died and were gradually buried by layers of rock.

Fossil Energy Risks: Factors and events that may adversely affect the extraction, production, transportation, or consumption of fossil energy sources such as oil, natural gas and coal.

Investment Risk in the Energy Sector: The possibility of loss of capital or return for investors who invest their money in energy projects or companies.

Investment Risk Management in the Energy Sector: A process and methodology aimed at identifying, analyzing, reducing, and controlling the risks associated with investing in energy projects or companies.

Chapter 5
Oil Prices and Spain's Interest Rates:
Did the Link Change After EU Accession?

Rebeca Jiménez-Rodríguez
https://orcid.org/0000-0002-7669-2467
University of Salamanca, Spain

Marcelo Sanchez
European Central Bank, Germany

ABSTRACT

This chapter studies the impact of oil shocks on Spain's short-term interest rates. In so doing, it investigates whether the connection between these two variables changed after 1986 – a period marked by both Spain's EU accession and the move to interest rates as the monetary policy instrument. For the period after 1986, we find that, in response to oil shocks, real short-term interest rates tended to rise, while nominal interest rates increased only gradually. Oil prices impacted interest rates in periods of high oil prices, such as that around the 1990 spike and in some instances since 1999. The increase in interest rates after an oil price shock contributed to reducing inflation, while also making the economic slowdown more marked. The main results are not robust to starting the estimation in 1970, implying that monetary policy became more restrictive in reaction to oil price changes after EU accession.

1. INTRODUCTION

There is a large literature on the macroeconomic consequences of oil price shocks, which largely focuses on the latter's impact on domestic prices and especially real output. Given that crude oil is a basic input to production, the theory normally predicts that supply-side consequences of oil price hikes include a contraction in overall economic activity and inflationary pressures. In addition, aggregate demand is expected to fall in oil importing countries, and go up in oil exporting countries. Existing empirical work has by and large confirmed the results found in the theoretical literature.[1] The initial studies for the US

DOI: 10.4018/979-8-3693-0440-2.ch005

identified a linear negative link between oil prices and real activity. It was eventually found that by the mid-1980s such linear relationship began to lose significance. Three leading non-linear approaches have been developed by Mork (1989), Lee et al. (1995), and Hamilton (1996) with the aim of re-establishing the negative relationship between increases in oil prices and real output developments.[2] Mork's (1989) study found that the real effects of oil price increases are different from those of decreases, with oil price decreases not having a statistically significant impact on US economic activity. Two other non-linear models were later developed in the literature, namely: the scaled specification (Lee et al., 1995), which takes the volatility of oil prices into account; and the net specification (Hamilton, 1996), which considers the amount by which oil prices have gone up over the last year.

The present paper is meant to extend the empirical work on oil price impacts by examining the case of macroeconomic developments in Spain, the fourth largest euro area economy. We shall focus on the behaviour of interest rates in the face of oil price shocks. In what represents another focus, we shall investigate whether the connection between Spain's interest rates and oil prices has changed since 1986, the year in which this country entered the European Union (EU) and started using interest rates as the monetary policy instrument. The institutional changes involved may have modified in a substantial and broad fashion the environment in which the Spanish economy had been operating, potentially affecting the way oil prices affected domestic interest rates.[3] The abandonment of previously dominant monetary intermediate targets (see e.g. Ayuso and Escrivá, 1998, and Camarero et al., 2002) may have had specific direct consequences on the link between short-term interest rates and oil shocks – a link that reflects the way monetary authority responds to the disturbances. While the monetary policy's regime change highlighted above is not the only structural transformation taking place in the Spanish economy between 1970 and the financial crisis of 2007, it is the most relevant to the present study.[4] The latest global financial crisis, which erupted in 2007, in retrospect would point to some exuberance in the period immediately leading to it; very importantly, the transmission mechanism of monetary policy has remained somewhat impaired ever since – a concern only compounded in recent years by the outbreak of the COVID-19 pandemic. In order for our study to establish the specific role of EU accession (with Spain's concomitant adoption of a new style of monetary policy), our estimation sample must leave out the period starting somewhat before the outbreak of the 2007 financial crisis. On top of the relevance that our study has for understanding historical transition between monetary policy regimes (in Spain and indirectly in other countries that have already graduated to some sort of inflation targeting approach), it is worth recalling that similar transition processes are currently underway or envisioned in a number of countries around the world (see e.g. Mæhle and King, 2022).

The approach to model estimation pursued here considers the linear and three leading non-linear methods described above. We use of two different identification schemes, a recursive one and one based on short-run restrictions drawing from Cushman and Zha (1997), and Kim and Roubini (2000). The latter approach is used here in a counterfactual monetary policy analysis comparing the period before and after Spain's EU accession.[5] Unlike most of the literature, which focuses on the effect of oil shocks on real output developments, we concentrate on short-term interest rates, although also exploring the latter's structural relationship with both inflation and economic activity. Our analysis combines impulse responses (including counterfactual experiments), variance decompositions and historical decompositions – the latter showing the contribution of oil prices to interest rate fluctuations over time.

The impact of oil prices on interest rates has received comparatively less research attention. One important exception is the debate between Bernanke et al. (1997) and Hamilton and Herrera (2004) about the relative role played by oil shocks and monetary policy in US business cycle fluctuations. The former study suggests that monetary policy could be used to undo any recessionary consequences of an oil price shock. The latter study emphasises that the size of the effect that Bernanke et al. (1997) attribute to oil shocks is substantially smaller than the one that results from choosing an optimal lag length. The present paper differs from these earlier contributions, which only study the US economy, by analysing the link between oil price shocks and monetary policy in the Spanish case.

The period under study covers a number of energy crisis episodes, including the 1990 spike in oil prices and some more subdued and protracted rises in the latter from 1999 and into the early 2000s. The most important energy shock has undoubtedly been the one arising in the mid-1970s – its detailed consequences on the Spanish macroeconomy being however obscured by how little we know about the specific workings of the country's approach to monetary targeting at the time. By analysing the consequences of Spain moving away from monetary targeting, the present study aims to fill the gap about the profession's understanding of this country's evolving connection between oil prices and interest rates. This has not been analysed in the relatively small number of studies covering the Spanish economy of the period. Our paper also differs from previous studies of macro impacts of oil prices in Spain in both scope and methodology. De Miguel et al. (2003) used an extended real business cycle model to analyse the real output impact of the shock, estimating that a one standard deviation shock to real oil prices (amounting to about a 20% hike) induced a fall in real output of some 0.5% in the short run. Barrell and Pomerantz (2004), using NiGEM international simulations as from 2005, computed the real output impact of an oil price shock in Spain, showing that this impact was rather modest over the first year and that it gained in strength over the following three years. Cuñado and Pérez de Gracia (2003), while focusing on other European economies in their impulse response analysis, reported some results for Spain. In particular, the negative correlation between oil prices and industrial production was found to drop somewhat after the mid-1980s. Álvarez et al. (2011) found that the inflationary effect of oil price changes in Spain was limited, even though crude oil price fluctuations were a major driver of inflation variability. They also reported that the direct inflationary effects had increased in 2000s – reflecting the higher expenditure share of households on refined oil products – even as indirect and second-round effects seemed to be losing importance. Also broadly sharing our interest in structural change, Gómez-Loscos et al. (2011) analysed the effect of oil price shocks on both GDP growth and inflation in Spain by using the Qu and Perron (2007) procedure to detect structural breaks in multivariate regressions. This empirical study found that oil price shocks had a decreasing influence on GDP growth and inflation from the mid-1970s to the mid-1980s, before the effects gained renewed strength after the mid-1980s.

Our extension of the existing empirical literature on the Spanish economy is meant to shed light on some neglected aspects of an interesting transition in the monetary policy strategy, which had to face world energy shocks of different magnitude and duration. Our econometric toolbox should be well equipped for the study of the implications of the institutional changes taking place in 1986. In particular, we shall be in a very good position to assess whether the behaviour of the Spanish macroeconomy were stable between 1970 and (sometime before) the 2007 financial crisis, or whether monetary policy became more responsive/restrictive in the face of oil price changes during the period since 1986.

The rest of the paper is organised as follows. Section 2 describes the methodology. Section 3 presents the empirical results. Section 4 concludes.

2. METHODOLOGY

The first step consists of estimating a reduced form as given by a vector autoregression model of order *p*, or simply, VAR(p). We can write this system as $y_t = Ax_t + \varepsilon t$ where yt is an n×1 vector of endogenous variables, xt is an np×1vector grouping all lagged terms of yt up to order p, A is an n×np rectangular matrix, and εt_is an n×1 vector of white noise processes with variance-covariance matrix Σ. The optimal lag length for the VAR is determined by using the likelihood ratio test.

We consider the following set of endogenous variables: real GDP, real effective exchange rate (REER), real oil price, real wage (CPI deflated), CPI inflation,6 and real short- and long-term interest rates. Oil prices and short-term interest rates are included since they are the main variables of interest of this study. The remaining variables in the model are added in order to capture the most important transmission channels of oil price shocks, including a variety of demand- and supply-side effects. These channels are allowed to operate via exchange rates, the labour market and domestic financial markets (as captured, in particular, in the relationship between short- and long-term interest rates). Of particular interest to the present paper is the impact of oil prices on interest rates via output and inflation. Fluctuations in the latter variables, which are normally seen as the goals of monetary policy, are thus expected to induce changes in the interest rate.

The data used are quarterly and run from 1970:1 through 2006:1. We justify the end of the estimation period as follows. Our interest in studying the potential structural transformation that occurred at the time of EU accession (which was associated with the switch to the interest rate as the monetary policy instrument) prompts us to exclude data from the period since the latest global financial crisis. While erupting in 2007, the latter was arguably pre-announced by some exuberance in the period immediately leading to it. From an econometric perspective, a short-lived – if severe – recession could be handled by adding a few impulse dummies to the VAR model. Unfortunately, the aftermath of the 2007 crisis involved a sustained impairment of the transmission mechanism of monetary policy – a condition that had not healed by the time the COVID-19 pandemic shocked the world in 2020. Therefore, we have been forced to cutting the estimation period as here detailed.

Turning to the variables included in our dataset, the measure of real oil prices that we have chosen is defined as the ratio of the price of an internationally traded variety of crude (UK Brent) in US dollars to the US Producer Price Index (both from IMF's *International Financial Statistics* - henceforth IFS).[7] Regarding Spanish data, real GDP and short-term interest rate data come from Datastream; CPI from the OECD's *Main Economic Indicators* (henceforth MEI); long-term interest rates from OECD's *Economic Outlook*; nominal (hourly) wages from IFS; and REER (based on CPI) from MEI.

Turning to the study of the stochastic properties of the series considered here, we assess their order of integration by means of unit root tests. Specifically, we perform the DFGLS and P_T tests of Elliott et al. (1996), and the $DFGLS_u$ and Q_T tests of Elliott (1999), as well as the Augmented Dickey-Fuller (ADF) test. Results of these formal tests are summarised in Table 1.[8] We shall use a model in which the vector of endogenous variables is given by the first log-differences of four variables (real GDP, REER, real oil price, and real wage), along with the levels of inflation, and short and long-term real interest rates. From Table 1, the growth rates of real GDP, real oil price, REER and the real wage appear to be stationary. In the absence of model misspecification, the remaining variables are the levels of real interest rates and inflation as this enhances economic interpretability.[9] In light of possible non-stationarity of inflation and the real interest rate measures, we have also estimated all models with these variables in first differences. The results are however not substantially affected compared to the ones reported in this paper.

Table 1. Unit-root tests

		Model with constant and trend					Model with constant					Model without constant	
		ADF	DFGLS	P_T	$DFGLS_U$	Q_T	ADF	DFGLS	P_T	$DFGLS_U$	Q_T	ADF	DFGLS
Real GDP	Levels	-2.98	-2.38	7.23	-2.79	2.17	0.08	1.85	222.5	0.42	41.33	2.76	2.76
	First Log-diff.	-3.37*	-3.38**	5.03**	-3.53**	1.58***	-3.46**	-2.46**	3.54**	-3.50***	1.51***	-2.08**	-2.08**
REER	Levels	-3.08	-2.08	8.05	-2.66	2.88*	-2.88*	-0.49	16.86	-2.69*	6.74	0.93	0.93
	First Log-diff.	-4.80***	-4.33***	0.77***	-4.90***	0.18***	-4.78***	-3.87***	0.53***	-4.79***	0.06***	-4.68***	-4.68***
CPI	Levels	-2.25	-1.74	1.88***	-2.26	2.12**	-3.86***	-0.47	6.34	-1.58	18.77	0.19	0.19
	First Log-diff.	-2.97	-1.08	36.74	-1.77	11.41	-0.81	-0.89	11.90	-0.85	22.15	-0.75	-0.75
Real wage	Levels	-2.23	0.39	247.7	-0.59	80.64	-5.13***	2.13	652.5	-2.66*	299.3	-6.82***	-6.82***
	First Log-diff.	-14.26***	-14.26***	1.53***	-14.03***	0.83***	-1.78	-0.88	34.95	-1.83	45.50	-1.77*	-1.77*
Real short-term interest rate	Levels	-1.30	-1.47	20.28	-1.47	10.48	-1.47	-1.44	5.90	-1.48	10.69	-1.40	-1.40
	First diff.	-6.73***	-2.40	24.53	-4.49***	2.14**	-6.71***	-1.14	16.27	-5.68***	0.01***	-6.74***	-6.74***
Real long-term interest rate	Levels	-1.29	-1.28	22.94	-1.34	11.57	-1.28	-1.26	6.60	-1.29	12.51	-1.22	-1.22
	First diff.	-5.67***	-2.26	40.73	-3.99***	1.96***	-5.68***	-1.03	25.43	-4.78***	0.16***	-5.70***	-5.70***
Real oil price	Levels	-2.02	-1.21	29.10	-1.58	11.29	-2.03	-0.02	29.23	-1.91	12.86	0.74	0.74
	First Log-diff.	-6.50***	-6.45***	0.06***	-6.43***	0.03***	-6.53***	-6.51***	0.01***	-6.52***	0.02***	-6.46***	-6.46***

The sample is 1970:1 -2006:1 for the variables in levels, and starts one quarter later for the variables in first differences. We use data-driven lag selection procedures for the Augmented Dickey-Fuller tests, taking 1.645 as the critical value used for significance of lagged terms and 8 as the maximum number of lags allowed in these procedures into account. The same number of lags is used in the other tests considered. We denote with one/two/three asterisks the rejection of the null hypothesis at a 10%/5%/1% critical level.

Critical levels used for ADF test are the following:

- In the model with constant and trend: -4.05 (1%), -3.45 (5%) and -3.15 (10%).
- In the model with constant: -3.50 (1%), -2.89 (5%) and –2.58 (10%).
- In the model without constant: -2.59 (1%), -1.94 (5%) and –1.62 (10%).

Critical levels used for DFGLS test are the following:

- In the model with constant and trend: -3.48 (1%), -2.89 (5%) and –2.57 (10%).
- In the model with constant: -2.58 (1%), -1.95 (5%) and –1.62 (10%).
- In the model without constant: -2.58 (1%), -1.95 (5%) and –1.62 (10%).

Critical levels used for P_T test are the following:

- In the model with constant and trend: 3.96 (1%), 5.62 (5%) and 6.89 (10%).
- In the model with constant: 1.99 (1%), 3.26 (5%) and 4.48 (10%).

Critical levels used for $DFGLS_U$ test are the following:

- In the model with constant and trend: -3.71 (1%), -3.17 (5%) and –2.91 (10%).
- In the model with constant: -3.28 (1%), -2.73 (5%) and –2.46 (10%).

Critical levels used for Q_T test are the following:

- In the model with constant and trend: 2.05 (1%), 2.85 (5%) and 3.44 (10%).
- In the model with constant: 3.06 (1%), 4.65 (5%) and 5.94 (10%).

Our baseline approach to identification of oil price shocks consists of a Cholesky decomposition in which the real oil price is put first in the recursive ordering for the variables in the system, being allowed to have an immediate impact on the remaining macroeconomic variables. As a robustness check, we also report in subsection 3.5 impulse response results from an alternative identification to one presented earlier, imposing short-run restrictions.

As mentioned earlier, we focus on the period since Spain's accession to EU membership in 1986. Given our focus on interest rates, the choice of 1986 appears to be a reasonable choice. Indeed, the existing literature suggests that, by then, a switch in the monetary policy regime was well underway, with the role of the interest rate as an instrument gaining importance at the expense of monetary intermediate targets. Along these lines, López (2002) estimates a Taylor rule for Spain over the period 1984-1998. We also report results from a "full sample" period starting in 1970. For both of our main sample periods (namely, 1986:1-2006:1 and 1970:2-2006:1), we aim at checking whether our results change when we shorten the estimation sample to the period before Spain joins the European Monetary Union (EMU) in 1999. However, depending on the optimal lag length for estimation over the period since 1986, we might not pursue such robustness check if the degrees of freedom were to become too small.[10]

In addition to linear vector autoregressions (VAR), we estimate three leading non-linear approaches, namely, Mork's (1989) asymmetric model, Lee et al.'s (1995) scaled model, and Hamilton's (1996) net oil model. Such non-linear models have proved useful to capture the macroeconomic effects of oil prices, often beating linear models in terms of stability when estimated over longer sample periods. The asymmetric specification allocates positive realisations of the rate of change in the oil price to variable o_t^+, and negative such realisations to o_t^-. In the scaled approach, the relevant oil variable - standing for "scaled oil price increases" - is $SOPI_t = \max\left(0, \hat{e}_t / \sqrt{\hat{h}_t}\right)$, where $\hat{e}_t$ and $\hat{h}_t$ are, respectively, the error and the conditional variance of the rate of change in oil prices from a AR(4)-GARCH(1,1) representation. Finally, the net oil model uses the "net oil price increase" variable, defined as the amount by which oil prices (in logs), p_t, exceed - if at all - the maximum value over the previous 4 periods (quarters); that is, $NOPI_t = \max\left(0, p_t - \max\left\{p_{t-1}, p_{t-2}, p_{t-3}, p_{t-4}\right\}\right)$.[11]

3. EMPIRICAL RESULTS

This section reports all the empirical results of this paper. These results are presented with a focus on the sample starting in 1986. Two alternative estimation samples – a full sample one and, in some cases, one covering the period 1970-1998 – are also discussed. The reason for not reporting estimations over 1986-1998 is that the optimal lag for the model estimated since 1986 is six, which would leave us with too small degrees of freedom if we were to shorten the end of the sample to 1998. Of course, this situation is rather unfortunate since it would be interesting to investigate whether joining the EMU has made a difference for Spain also in a sample starting in 1986.

More concretely, the next subsections include the following results. First, we report a number of preliminary tests for significance and model selection. Second, we describe our results for accumulated responses of real GDP growth, inflation and real short-term interest rates to oil price shocks. Third, we discuss our results for the corresponding variance decompositions. When describing our results, we focus on the approach (linear or non-linear) that performs best for each sample. Fourth, we report historical decompositions. Finally, we present results from an alternative model. The latter's reduced form is of the near-VAR type (with oil prices not being affected by lags of the remaining variables), while the identification approach used relies on short-run restrictions. This alternative modelling approach is used for robustness and counterfactual analysis.

3.1. Testing for Significance and Model Selection

In this subsection we investigate the significance of the relationship between oil prices and the other variables of the model. We test for the significance of the oil price variables under consideration for the VAR system as a whole, using the null hypothesis that all of the oil price coefficients are jointly zero in all equations of the system but its own equation (see Table 2). The likelihood ratio test is informative in that oil prices, in addition to their direct effect on real GDP and inflation, could well impact the latter two variables through the rest of the system. We find that the oil price variable in the linear model, as well as the positive changes in the asymmetric, scaled and net models, are all significant at the 5% level for the system for all three sample periods considered. Moreover, the negative changes in the asymmetric, scaled, and net models enter significantly in all models estimated for the period since 1986. In contrast, these negative changes are not significant in any of the two periods starting in 1970, except for the corresponding net specifications. The price decrease variable is subsequently eliminated from those non-linear specifications in which it is not significant.

For model selection purposes, we look at two selection criteria as given by the Akaike information criterion (AIC) and Schwarz Bayesian information criterion (BIC). Table 3 reports the AIC and BIC obtained from each econometric specification.[12] On the basis of these two criteria, we conclude that the linear model turns out to be the best-performing for the post-1986 period, while the scaled specification is the preferred model for the full sample and the period 1970-1998.[13] This means that, for the period since EU accession, oil price declines of a given size entail an impact on macroeconomic developments that is comparable to that induced by oil price increases of the same size. Interestingly, our model selection results for Spain stand in contrast with the literature for the US, which finds that the linear model breaks down in the mid-1980s and is thereafter outperformed by non-linear specifications.[14] We now turn to the description of the main results of the paper, concentrating on the preferred specifications for each sample.

Table 2. Likelihood ratio tests

	LINEAR	*ASYMMETRIC*		*SCALED OIL PRICE*		*NET OIL PRICE*	
	o_t	o_t^+	o_t^-	$SOPI_t$	$SOPD_t$	$NOPI_t$	$NOPD_t$
1986:1-2006:1	2.3E-008***	3.0E-016***	1.3E-015***	2.0E-014***	3.2E-016***	1.7E-011***	1.1E-016***
1970:2-2006:1	2.2E-005***	2.0E-08***	0.12225	1.5E-007***	0.19521	4.4E-007***	0.02136**
1970:2-1998:4	1.2E-007***	0.00028***	0.47977	0.00222***	0.65855	0.01061**	0.00672***

One/two/three asterisks mean a *p*-value less than 10%/5%/1%.

Table 3. Relative performance of the models

		Linear	*Asymmetric*	*Scaled*	*Net*
1986:1-2006:1	*AIC*	13.133	18.922	17.240	16.649
	BIC	22.031	30.509	28.828	28.237
1970:2-2006:1	*AIC*	18.846	18.301	18.042	24.797
	BIC	25.231	24.686	24.749	33.112
1970:2-1998:4	*AIC*	19.411	19.003	18.126	28.384
	BIC	26.843	23.958	23.081	34.828

The results for the periods 1970:2-2006:1 and 1970:2-1998:4 are based on a seven-variable VAR that excludes oil price decrease variables from all three non-linear models, namely, the asymmetric, scaled and net specifications, with one exception: the Spain's net model, where oil price decrease variable is found to be statistically significant for the system. For the period 1986:1-2006:1, the results are based on an eight-variable VAR that includes oil price decrease variables from all three non-linear models, namely, the asymmetric, scaled and net specifications.

3.2 Accumulated Impulse Responses

This subsection contains a discussion of the impact of oil price shocks on real GDP, inflation and short-term interest rates, with a focus on the preferred model. Table 4 reports accumulated responses to a 100% oil price shock for the best-performing models. The latter are given by the linear specification for the period since 1986 and the scaled approach for the full sample and the period 1970-1998. As described in section 2, the models used here include in the vector of endogenous variables the growth rates of three variables (real GDP, REER, and real wage) and the real oil price variable, along with the levels of inflation, and short and long-term real interest rates.

In line with Spain being a net oil importing economy, a qualitatively robust impulse response finding is that unexpected hikes in oil prices reduce real output and increase inflation. Focusing on the period since 1986, the impact of the oil shock on real GDP growth is an order of magnitude bigger than the inflationary pressures arising from the disturbance. For instance, after the second year the oil shock

Table 4. Accumulated responses in the baseline VAR model

	1986:1-2006:1			**1970:2-2006:1**			**1970:2-1998:4**		
Variables	**after 1 year**	**after 2 years**	**after 3 years**	**after 1 year**	**after 2 years**	**after 3 years**	**after 1 year**	**after 2 years**	**after 3 years**
Real GDP growth	-1.5	-4.2	-5.1	-2.9	-7.3	-6.4	-1.9	-5.9	-6.8
Inflation	1.0	1.9	1.1	1.5	0.9	2.2	0.3	2.8	5.8
Real short-term interest rate	0.7	-0.2	0.9	-1.1	-3.1	-7.5	0.0	-4.0	-7.6
Nominal short-term interest rate	1.7	1.7	2.0	0.4	-2.2	-5.3	0.3	-1.2	-1.8

The entries refer to the accumulated responses attributed to a 100% oil price shock.
The models used are: linear model for the period 1986:1-2006:1and scaled models for 1970:2-2006:1 and 1970:2-1998:4.
Identification is achieved by ordering the oil price variable first in the VAR system.

induces a reduction of 4.2% in real GDP while the inflationary effect is of only 1.9%. The impact on real GDP is larger in the full sample case in absolute terms. Since 1986, inflationary pressures appear to be larger than in the full sample case after two years, but they are relatively smaller at the end of both the first and third years. The finding that, as a result of an oil hike, Spanish economic activity contracts strongly is broadly consistent with the findings reported in Barrell and Pomerantz (2004) and De Miguel et al. (2006).[15]

Finally, we also report the short-term interest rate responses to the exogenous oil price hike. For the post-1986 period, the real short-term interest rate is found to increase after the first and third year, while it is below baseline at the end of the second year. The corresponding nominal rate is above the baseline by 170 basis points at the end of both the first and second years, then rising further to 200 basis points at the end of the third year. The results for the full sample and the period 1970-1998 stand in sharp contrast to the ones just described. We find that real short-term interest rates decline, except at the end of the first year for the period 1970-1998 for which no change is reported. Both in the full sample case and the period 1970-1998, nominal interest rates are found to increase after the first year but thereafter fall after the second and third years. We will investigate the behaviour of interest rates further in subsection 3.5, in which the identification of monetary policy shocks will allow us to draw monetary policy implications from impulse response results.

3.3. Variance Decompositions

Table 5 reports the variance decompositions of real GDP and inflation due to oil price shocks under the preferred specification for the period since 1986, the full sample and the period 1970-1998. The fraction of Spanish real output's forecast variance explained by oil prices is high, especially after the second and third years. These results happen to be very robust across estimation periods. The result that Spain's share of real output variability explained by oil prices tends to be rather high is consistent with De Miguel et al.'s (2006) finding that a higher share of the empirical real output variability is explained by their theoretical model to be associated with oil price shocks.

Turning to the share of inflation variability attributed to oil prices, it is lower than that of real output variability, especially in the two estimation periods starting in 1970. For the period since 1986, the share of inflation variability explained by oil prices at the end of the first year share is actually above the corresponding one for real GDP growth. Finally, the share of real short-term interest rate variability

Table 5. Forecast error variance decomposition

	1986:1-2006:1			1970:2-2006:1			1970:2-1998:4		
Variables	**after 1 year**	**after 2 years**	**after 3 years**	**after 1 year**	**after 2 years**	**after 3 years**	**after 1 year**	**after 2 years**	**after 3 years**
Real GDP growth	6.9	15.6	16.3	8.0	16.2	15.9	6.6	14.2	13.9
Inflation	9.1	10.2	10.8	4.4	5.2	5.2	2.0	2.5	2.6
Real short-term interest rate	10.5	9.6	9.4	3.0	3.6	5.8	1.8	3.1	3.8

The entries refer to the fraction of each variable's variance attributed to oil price shocks (in percentage).
The models used are: linear model for the period 1986:1-2006:1and scaled models for 1970:2-2006:1 and 1970:2-1998:4.
Identification is achieved by ordering the oil price variable first in the VAR system.

explained by oil prices is around 10% in the period since 1986. This value is found to lie well above that displayed over the entire sample and the period 1970-1998.

3.4. Historical Decompositions

Here, we perform historical decompositions showing the contribution of oil prices to short-term interest rates over time. Figure 1 assesses the role of oil prices in the determination of real interest rates for the period since 1986 (top panel) and for the full sample (lower panel). Figure 2 displays the corresponding historical decompositions for nominal interest rates. In all these Figures, we report the actual series and the contribution of oil price shocks to the forecast, both of them in percentage deviations from a 6-quarter-ahead base projection.[16]

Unexpected developments in oil prices appear to play a limited role in driving Spanish real short-term interest rates over time (see Figure 1). Using results since 1986, oil prices also appear to have contributed to movements in real rates in a muted way, with their impact being spread out over the entire estimation period. The contribution to a real interest rate hike is sizeable in one quarter (namely, 1991:1) at the end of the oil price spike following the 1990 Iraqi war. Another episode of higher oil prices where we observe an impact on real interest rate movements is in 1999-2001, with real rates reacting by moving down in 1999 and thereafter on the way up. When we look at full sample results, effects on real rates are visible in 1974-1975 and less so around 1990.

Oil price shocks are found to have exerted some influence on nominal short-term interest rates (see Figure 2). Our results for the sample starting in 1986 show that oil prices impacted interest rates in periods of high oil prices, such as that around the 1990 spike and more recently in 1999 and 2005-2006. The finding that oil shocks have driven nominal interest rates up in 1999 stands in contrast with the downward pressure on real interest rates displayed in Figure 1. This gap is explained by the rather quick and substantial inflationary effect taking place in that year. Employing full sample results, we detect an impact on nominal rates for 1974-1975, and to a smaller degree, around 1990. Overall, one rather robust – and surprising - result is that no perceptible change in interest rates (either real or nominal) is found during the major oil shock of the late 1970s and early 1980s.

3.5. Robustness and Counterfactuals

As a robustness check, here we report the impulse response results from an alternative VAR approach to one presented earlier. This alternative method relies on short-run restrictions for identification, while the reduced form of the model is estimated as a near-VAR system in which all lagged variables except oil prices are excluded from having any impact on the oil prices themselves. With regard to the short-run restrictions used, we draw from the identified VAR literature stemming from Cushman and Zha (1997), and Kim and Roubini (2000), while adapting it to the current environment. In doing so, we likewise combine a recursive block with some non-recursive exclusion contemporaneous restrictions. We set up a recursive block starting from oil prices which remain the most exogenous variable, followed by real GDP growth, inflation and real wage growth, in that order. We then postulate a monetary policy reaction function in which the real short-term interest rate is allowed to be immediately affected by all other variables but two: real output growth, which is assumed to be observable only with a lag,[17] and the real long-term interest rate which is rather allowed to be responsive to short-term rate fluctuations. Furthermore, the real long-term interest rate is allowed to react directly to all other variables except

Figure 1. Historical decompositions of real short-term interest rates

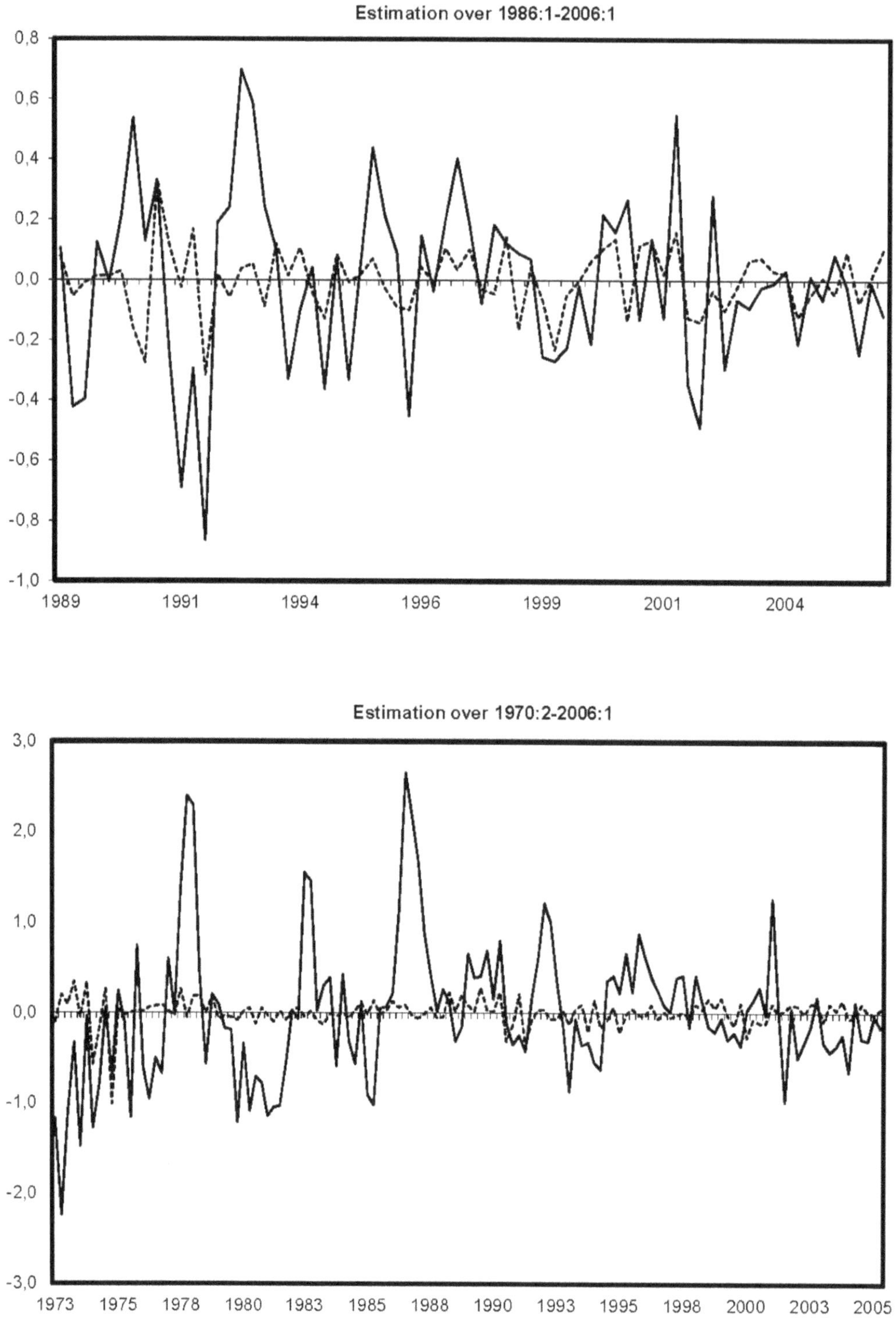

Figure 2. Historical decompositions of nominal short-term interest rates

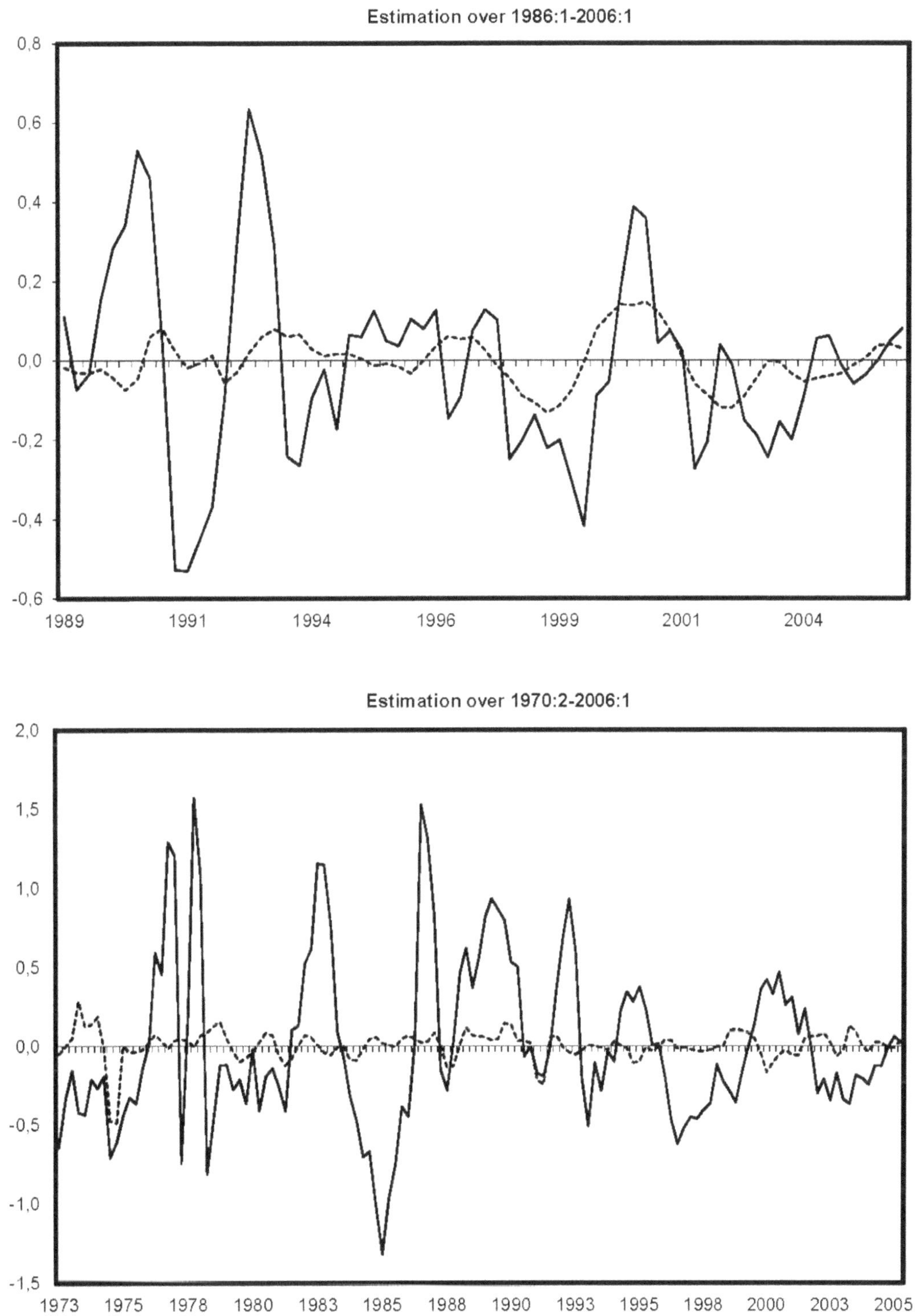

Table 6. Accumulated responses using short-run restrictions and counterfactuals

Variables	1986:1-2006:1			1970:2-2006:1		
	after 1 year	after 2 years	after 3 years	after 1 year	after 2 years	after 3 years
A) Short-run restrictions						
Real GDP growth	-1.6	-5.1	-6.8	-3.0	-8.5	-9.6
Inflation	1.1	2.4	1.9	1.6	1.3	2.9
Real short-term interest rate	0.7	-0.1	1.1	-1.1	-3.4	-9.0
Nominal short-term interest rate	1.8	2.3	3.0	0.5	-2.1	-6.1
B) Counterfactuals (unchanged real short-term interest rate)						
Real GDP growth	-1.3	-4.6	-6.4	-2.9	-9.2	-10.9
Inflation	1.6	2.9	2.2	1.5	1.0	0.8
Real short-term interest rate	0.0	0.0	0.0	0.0	0.0	0.0
Nominal short-term interest rate	1.6	2.9	2.2	1.5	1.0	0.8

The entries refer to the accumulated responses attributed to a 100% oil price shock.
The models used are: linear model for the period 1986:1-2006:1and scaled model for 1970:2-2006:1.
The near-VAR system used here does not allow for feedback to oil prices from lags of the remaining variables.
Identification is achieved by means of short-run restrictions in the VAR system. For details, see the main text.

REER, which can only exert a contemporaneous impact on the former via the real short-term interest rate. Finally, REER may respond immediately to all shocks in the model. In particular, this implies that we allow the short-term interest rate to interact contemporaneously with the exchange rate, as in the identification approaches of Smets (1997) and Smets and Wouters (1999).

By focusing on interest rates for the identification of monetary policy shocks, we deviate from the structural VAR literature cited in the previous paragraph, which attaches the role of the monetary policy instrument to money supply. While this is a point in common with Mojon and Peersman (2003), our use of non-recursive identification restrictions marks a difference with the latter two authors who instead employ a Cholesky identification approach.[18]

Table 6 reports the accumulated responses from oil shocks derived from this alternative approach (panel A) alongside counterfactual experiments (panel B). With regard to the former, we observe that impulse response results are broadly in line with those resulting from the Cholesky ordering as shown above in Table 4. In particular, the short-term interest rate responses to an exogenous oil price hike again suggest that monetary policy has responded by tightening since 1986.[19] The impulse response for the nominal interest rate points to an only very gradual increase that is perceived only between the first two years and the third. The degree of smoothness implied by our results are even stronger than the already very high one detected by López's (2002) Taylor rule estimation over 1984-1998. In contrast to the period since 1986, it appears that monetary policy has been accommodative in the full sample.

Based on our short-run restriction identification, we perform a monetary policy counterfactual exercise. The latter assumes that the real short-term interest rate does not react to the shock. The counterfactual results, which are also shown in panel B of Table 6, are reasonable. They indicate that, in the period since 1986, where the prediction is that of tightening in monetary policy, the counterfactual projection indicates higher values of both real output growth and inflation compared to the baseline scenario. In quantitative terms, our counterfactual results suggest that the fraction of macroeconomic variability induced by the oil shock indirectly via monetary policy changes appears to be rather modest, in line with Hamilton and Herrera's (2004) results for the US. In contrast to our results for the period since 1986, in the full sample case the counterfactual exercise points to an accommodative policy, as the implied projection consists of lower levels of both real output growth and inflation.

4. CONCLUDING REMARKS

This paper studies the role of oil price shocks in shaping interest rates in Spain. The main empirical findings for the period since Spain's EU accession in 1986 are the following. The preferred specification is the linear model, which is found to beat leading non-linear approaches. Real short-term interest rates tend to rise following an unexpected oil price hike, while nominal interest rates increase very gradually. The share of real interest rate variability explained by oil prices is around 10%. Historical decompositions show that oil prices impacted both real and nominal interest rates at around the 1990 oil price spike. With regard to the latest episode of high oil prices, nominal interest rates are found to be pushed upwards at two times, namely, in 1999 and 2005-2006. In light of higher inflationary pressures, the increase of nominal interest rates in 1999 appears not to have prevented a fall in real rates, which are found to rise in response to the shock only in 2000-2001. Turning to counterfactual analysis, the period since 1986 can be characterised as one of tightening of interest rates in response to oil shocks, with interest rate hikes contributing to reducing inflation and making the economic slowdown more marked. It is worth saying, however, that the fraction of macroeconomic variability induced by the oil shock indirectly via monetary policy changes appears to be rather modest.

The main results from this paper are not robust to estimating the model over a longer sample going back to 1970. Over this sample, it is found that oil prices have non-linear impacts, real interest rates are little affected by oil shocks and monetary policy appears to be accommodative. In line with the latter, the evidence conclusively shows that interest rates were cut at the time of the sizeable oil price increases of 1974-1975. Future research may attempt to corroborate the specific features of Spain's monetary targeting regime captured here; one possibility would be to set up a regime-specific structural model to be taken to data from that period (see e.g. Sánchez, 2011, for the case of the – admittedly much smaller – Romanian economy).

Our sample period contains a number of diverse energy crisis episodes. Our estimation results highlight that the monetary policy response differed depending on the strategy adopted by the authorities in charge. The most important energy shock – i.e. the one of the mid-1970s – was met in Spain by an accommodative monetary policy stance: by attempting to moderate the plunge in real economic activity triggered by this shock, the monetary authorities allowed the inflationary outburst to be quite protracted. In contrast, the monetary authority resorted to restrictive interest rates whenever Spain was confronted with oil shocks after 1986 – concretely, during the 1990 spike in the oil price and the more moderate but persistent increases recorded in these prices from 1999 and into the early 2000s.

Our study of the Spanish economy has thus focused on two main aspects: first, on the response of interest rates to oil prices, and second on structural change linked to a shift in monetary policy regime at the time of EU accession. Our results support the notion that the then novel use of interest rates as the monetary policy instrument modified in a substantial manner the way in which the Spanish economy had been operating. Future research will study the separate impact of yet another structural change, namely, that brought about by the economic instability brought about by the financial crisis of 2007. We have been careful to exclude not only the period since this crisis broke out, but also a full year of data before any slowdown was noticeable in 2007. We trust that the lessons learned from Spain's monetary policy transition can not only be contrasted with the experience of other countries that have adopted some sort of inflation targeting strategy, but also shed light on the challenges faced by those countries that will go through comparable transition processes.

FUNDING

Rebeca Jiménez-Rodríguez acknowledges support from Ministerio de Ciencia e Innovación under Research Grant PID2022-143170OB-I00.

ACKNOWLEDGMENT

A previous version of the present article circulated under the title "Oil Prices and Spanish Interest Rates". The views expressed in this paper are those of the authors and do not necessarily reflect the position of the European Central Bank. The usual disclaimer applies.

REFERENCES

Alonso, F., Ayuso, J., & Martínez-Pagés, J. (2000). The informational content of inflation for Spanish interest rates. *Investigacion Economica*, *24*, 455–471.

Álvarez, L., Hurtado, S., Sánchez, I., & Thomas, C. (2011). The impact of oil price changes on Spanish and euro area consumer price inflation. *Economic Modelling*, *28*(1-2), 422–431. doi:10.1016/j.econmod.2010.08.006

Ayuso, J., & Escrivá, J. (1998). Trends in the monetary policy strategy in Spain. In Monetary policy and inflation in Spain. St. Martin's Press.

Barrell, R., & Pomerantz, O. (2004). *Oil prices and the world economy*. NIESR Discussion Paper No. 242.

Bernanke, B., Gertler, M., Watson, M., Sims, C. A., & Friedman, B. M. (1997). Systematic monetary policy and the effects of oil price shocks. *Brookings Papers on Economic Activity*, *1*(1), 91–158. doi:10.2307/2534702

Camarero, M., Ordóñez, J., & Tamarit, J. (2002). Monetary transmission in Spain: A structural cointegrated VAR approach. *Applied Economics*, *34*(17), 2201–2212. doi:10.1080/00036840210138419

Camarero, M., & Tamarit, J. (2002a). Oil prices and Spanish competitiveness: A cointegrated panel analysis. *Journal of Policy Modeling*, *24*(6), 591–605. doi:10.1016/S0161-8938(02)00128-X

Camarero, M., & Tamarit, J. (2002b). A panel cointegration approach to the estimation of the peseta real exchange rate. *Journal of Macroeconomics*, *24*(3), 371–393. doi:10.1016/S0164-0704(02)00043-5

Cuñado, J., & Pérez de Gracia, F. (2003). Do oil price shocks matter? Evidence from some European countries. *Energy Economics*, *25*(2), 137–154. doi:10.1016/S0140-9883(02)00099-3

Cushman, D., & Zha, T. (1997). Identifying monetary policy in a small open economy under flexible exchange rates. *Journal of Monetary Economics*, *39*(3), 433–448. doi:10.1016/S0304-3932(97)00029-9

De Miguel, C., Manzano, B., & Martín-Moreno, J. (2003). Oil price shocks and aggregate fluctuations. *The Energy Journal (Cambridge, Mass.)*, *24*(2), 47–61. doi:10.5547/ISSN0195-6574-EJ-Vol24-No2-2

De Miguel, C., Manzano, B., & Martín-Moreno, J. (2006). Oil shocks and the business cycle in Europe. In C. De Miguel, X. Labandeira, & B. Manzano (Eds.), *Economic modelling of climate change and energy policies*. Edward Elgar Publishing. doi:10.4337/9781781958957.00021

Elliott, G. (1999). Efficient tests for a unit root when the initial observation is drawn from its unconditional distribution. *International Economic Review*, *40*(3), 767–783. doi:10.1111/1468-2354.00039

Elliott, G., Rothenberg, T., & Stock, J. (1996). Efficient tests for an autoregressive unit root. *Econometrica*, *64*(4), 813–836. doi:10.2307/2171846

Gómez-Loscos, A., Montañés, A., & Gadea, M. D. (2011). The impact of oil shocks on the Spanish economy. *Energy Economics*, *33*(6), 1070–1081. doi:10.1016/j.eneco.2011.05.016

Hamilton, J. (1983). Oil and macroeconomy since World War II. *Journal of Political Economy*, *91*(2), 228–248. doi:10.1086/261140

Hamilton, J. (1996). This is what happened to the oil price-macroeconomy relationship. *Journal of Monetary Economics*, *38*(2), 215–220. doi:10.1016/S0304-3932(96)01282-2

Hamilton, J., & Herrera, A. (2004). Oil shocks and aggregate macroeconomic behavior: The role of monetary policy. *Journal of Money, Credit and Banking*, *36*(2), 265–286. doi:10.1353/mcb.2004.0012

Herrera, A. M., Karaki, M. B., & Rangaraju, S. K. (2019). Oil price shocks and U.S. economic activity. *Energy Policy*, *129*, 89–99. doi:10.1016/j.enpol.2019.02.011

Hooker, M. (1996). What happened to the oil price-macroeconomy relationship? *Journal of Monetary Economics*, *38*(2), 195–213. doi:10.1016/S0304-3932(96)01281-0

Jiménez-Rodríguez, R., & Sánchez, M. (2005). Oil price shocks and real GDP growth: Empirical evidence for some OECD countries. *Applied Economics*, *37*(2), 201–228. doi:10.1080/0003684042000281561

Kilian, L. (2008). A comparison of the effects of exogenous oil supply shocks on output and inflation in the G7 countries. *Journal of the European Economic Association*, *6*(1), 78–121. doi:10.1162/JEEA.2008.6.1.78

Kim, S., & Roubini, N. (2000). Exchange rate anomalies in the industrial countries: A solution with a structural VAR approach. *Journal of Monetary Economics*, *45*(3), 561–586. doi:10.1016/S0304-3932(00)00010-6

Lee, K., Ni, S., & Ratti, R. (1995). Oil shocks and the macroeconomy: The role of price variability. *The Energy Journal (Cambridge, Mass.)*, *16*(4), 39–56. doi:10.5547/ISSN0195-6574-EJ-Vol16-No4-2

López, V. (2002). Has Banco de España followed a Taylor rule using real-time information? *Investigaciones económicas*, *26*, 475-496.

Mæhle, N., & King, D. (2022). Transitioning Operational Targets: From Reserve Money to Interest Rates. In Technical Assistance Handbook. Monetary and Capital Markets Department, International Monetary Fund.

Mojon, B., & Peersman, G. (2003). A VAR description of the effects of monetary policy in the individual countries of the euro area. In I. Angeloni, A. Kashyap, & B. Mojon (Eds.), *Monetary transmission in the euro area* (pp. 56–74). Cambridge University Press. doi:10.1017/CBO9780511492372.005

Mork, K. (1989). Oil and macroeconomy when prices go up and down: An extension of Hamilton's results. *Journal of Political Economy*, *97*(3), 740–744. doi:10.1086/261625

Mork, K., Olsen, O., & Mysen, H. (1994). Macroeconomic responses to oil price increases and decreases in seven OECD countries. *Energy Journal*, *15*, 19–35.

Qu, Z., & Perron, P. (2007). Estimating and testing structural changes in multivariate regressions. *Econometrica*, *75*(2), 459–502. doi:10.1111/j.1468-0262.2006.00754.x

Sánchez, M. (2011). Modelling anti-inflationary monetary targeting in Romania. *International Economic Journal*, *25*(1), 125–145. doi:10.1080/10168737.2010.487541

Smets, F. (1997). Measuring monetary policy shocks in France, Germany and Italy: The role of exchange rate. *SSRN*, *133*, 597–616. doi:10.2139srn.860664

Smets, F., & Wouters, R. (1999). The exchange rate and the monetary transmission mechanism in Germany. *De Economist*, *147*(4), 489–521. doi:10.1023/A:1003803228309

ENDNOTES

1. It is worth citing the seminal paper by Hamilton (1983) for the US economy; for a recent overview of the literature on that country, see Herrera et al. (2019). For evidence on countries outside the US, see Mork et al. (1994), Cuñado and Pérez de Gracia (2003), Jiménez-Rodríguez and Sánchez (2005), and Kilian (2008), among others.
2. For other references relating to the structural break towards the mid-1980s in the US case, see Hooker (1996) and Hamilton (1996).
3. Back in time, the initial favourable effect of EU accession on Spanish economic activity may have been overemphasised in the literature, given that the second half of the 1980s also was a period of relatively low oil prices (see e.g. Camarero and Tamarit, 2002a).
4. As for efficiency in oil use – another source of potential structural change – it is worth mentioning that Spain's oil consumption fluctuated and even declined for ten years after the energy crisis of the mid-1970s, but it resumed steady growth since the mid-1980s until the onset of the financial crisis in 2007 (rising from somewhat above 40 to 80 million tonnes of oil equivalent). See e.g. *BP Statistical Review of World Energy* (various editions).

5 Identified VARs of the type undertaken in the present paper are known to offer the advantage of uncovering selected structural features of the economy, while at the same time not imposing too strong assumptions about the environment in which economic agents operate.

6 It is worth noting that CPI inflation is defined as the first log-difference of the CPI.

7 Oil prices are used directly in the linear approach to VAR estimation, and are transformed - in ways discussed below - for their use in non-linear models. The choice of a readily available Producer Price Index for the denominator of our oil price measure helps reduce the possibility that the identified oil shock mistakenly captures an inflation uncertainty component. The GDP deflator has the advantage of being more comprehensive, but it is also reported with a long lag.

8 The unit root tests in Table 1 correspond to the entire period since 1970. Qualitatively similar results were obtained for the shorter sample starting in 1986, which is the focus of our analysis. These results are available from the authors upon request.

9 In connection with this, Alonso et al. (2000) find that real short-term interest rates have information for inflation. This does not mean that we lose track of nominal interest rates, given that they can be traced from developments in real rates and inflation.

10 Other periods in which relevant changes to monetary policy took place include the enactment of central bank autonomy in 1994 and the introduction of inflation targets in January 1995.

11 We similarly construct scaled and net oil price decrease variables, that is, $SOPD_t$ and $NOPD_t$, respectively. As we show in the next section, neither of the two is however found to have statistically significant macroeconomic effects in most of the cases.

12 The optimal lag length was found to be six in all models for Spain, except those estimated over the period 1970-1998 in which case the optimal lag is four.

13 To our knowledge, the only previous study testing for asymmetric effects of oil prices in Spain is Cuñado and Pérez de Gracia (2003). They find that such effects are significant using a model for industrial production, inflation and oil prices, which they estimate using quarterly data for 1960-1999.

14 The result concerning model selection for the full sample and the period 1970-1998 suggests that it is important to consider not just whether oil prices increase or decline (and by how much), but also the environment in which the movements take place. An oil shock in a stable price environment is likely to have larger economic consequences than one in a volatile price environment. In this regard, the scaled model more specifically highlights the importance of controlling for the time-varying conditional variability of oil price shocks.

15 Granger-causality results in Cuñado and Pérez de Gracia (2003) point to the lack of significance in the lagged macroeconomic effects of oil prices in Spain.

16 Historical decompositions reported in the top panel of Figures 1 and 2 start in 1989:1, while those in the corresponding lower panels start in 1972:3. We also computed decompositions using different conditional forecasts, which tended to broadly corroborate our substantive results.

17 We thus assume that policymakers have serious difficulties assessing ongoing real-side developments within the quarter. This is a reasonable assumption given the lack of reliable indicators for both GDP components and sectoral output beyond the relatively small industrial sector.

18 We also differ from Mojon and Peersman (2003) in that they need to include German interest rate shocks to eliminate the price puzzle, which arises when monetary policy tightening – say – induces higher inflation. Instead, this puzzle is absent from our results regardless of whether such German shocks are included or not. This is in line with previous studies including commodity prices (such

as oil prices here) to get rid of this puzzle. Another puzzle usually featuring in structural VARs is the exchange rate puzzle (interest rate hikes - say - lead to an exchange rate depreciation). While this puzzle is present in our full sample results, the evidence for post-1986 sample is mixed, with the puzzle showing only for some time horizons. All of these results are available from the authors upon request.

19 This result can be interpreted as a more price-stability-oriented monetary policy approach in Spain following EU membership. One factor playing a role at an early stage in the post-1986 period is the monetary tightening 1989-1992 phase over which the anti-inflationary bias inflation was reinforced via REER appreciation of the peseta (see Camarero and Tamarit, 2002b).

Chapter 6
EU's Energy Policy and Assessing Europe's Spiraling Energy Security Crises

Mukesh Shankar Bharti
https://orcid.org/0000-0002-3693-7247
Amity University, India

ABSTRACT

This chapter analyzes the energy crisis in Europe, which has been an emerging problem in recent years. Though it has been making efforts to reduce its dependence on fossil fuels, especially on Russia, it has not been able to achieve much success. A primary reason for this is that energy demand has increased while investments in renewable resources and other forms of alternative energy have not kept pace. This chapter implies a qualitative approach to explaining empirical data of the EU's policy on energy security. The study also focuses on to what extent the EU maintains energy issues during this crisis. What is the relationship between the EU and Russia during the war on energy issues? This research also answers the following question: What are the EU measures on the energy crisis in Europe?

INTRODUCTION

The European Union (EU) has shown its commitment to work on energy security in recent years on future sustainability in the energy sector. EU policy is to work on energy saving, clean energy production and diversification of energy supplies. The EU has focused on the area of renewable energy in the power generation, industry, buildings and transport sectors. By 2020, the EU aims to achieve a form of climate neutrality, however, the European Commission (EC) also want to work together with the European countries to stop future energy crisis. The EU's aim is to cut down its reliance on Russian gas by two-thirds from the last financial year of 2022-23. By 2030, the EU has swift plans to make it independent of Russian fossil fuels. Thus, the EU and its sister institutions are working on an alternative plan to fill the gap of the energy crisis through the promotion of green alternatives. The EU believes that it is necessary to find out an alternative source of energy with the implementation of the laws of the

DOI: 10.4018/979-8-3693-0440-2.ch006

Union by boosting efficiency and transitioning to renewable energy. Russia is recorded as the leading supplier of both petroleum oil and natural gas to the EU in 2020-21. In the financial year 2020-2021, the EU imported 24.8% of crude oil from Russia (Dutta, 2022a). The majority of crude oil from Russia is shipped to Europe by sea, and the rest of the crude oil is transported through the Druzhba pipeline in central Europe. The Druzhba pipeline supplies refineries in Poland, Germany, Hungary, Slovakia and the Czech Republic.

The EU has been importing natural gas from Russia through the Yamal and Nord Stream pipelines. The Yamal pipeline enters in European Union from Belarus to Poland and the Nord Stream gas pipeline enters the EU through Germany. Ukraine provides another route for the Russian gas pipeline to the EU, namely the Brotherhood and Soyuz gas pipelines. The EU imported natural gas from Russia at around 39.2 percent in 2021. Furthermore, the EU imported 62 percent of its energy resources from Russia in 2021, i.e., coal, crude oil and natural gas. Which accounted for around 99 billion Euros of trade between the EU and Russia

The Russian invasion of Ukraine caused energy crises in EU member states due to a disrupted supply chain. On the other hand, the reduction of Russian supply to the EU caused the price rate of gas to increase. The question of energy security has been the prime concern of the EU since the war happened in Ukraine. Prices have climbed over the past two years and continue to accelerate in the European market. It has been affecting the common people to stop consuming, known as "demand destruction." European energy markets have tightened to the point where small changes in supply have large effects on prices. This is why wholesale energy prices have been so volatile and have skyrocketed (Zettelmeyer et al., 2022).

The EU has refocused its public diplomacy to transform energy security policy to accelerate deeper partnerships in countries across Asia, Africa and other Pacific regions to reduce dependence on Russia (Bharti & Goswami, 2023). The Russian invasion of Ukraine has made the burning issue of energy security one of the EU's top priorities in recent years. That is why the EU's diplomacy has been changed towards the other parts of the world to cooperate in the area of renewable energy and other resources. Since last year, Russia has reduced gas flows to the EU and other European countries as well (Zachmann et al., 2023). Until 2021, according to Eurostat data, Russia was the largest supplier of coal, oil and natural gas to EU member states (Eurostat, 2022). This war brought havoc in prices and has been creating major turbulence for the EU energy system. At present, the EU and other non-EU European countries are suffering from soaring energy prices (European Commission, 2022a).

REVIEW OF LITERATURE AND CONCEPTUAL BACKGROUND

Giuli and Oberthür (2023) talk about the EU assessment on sustainable energy security should focus on the long-term with suitable structural response measures. Coal-fired power plants could drive short-term emergency measures that will meet temporary needs (Giuli & Oberthür, 2023). The energy security crisis has been guiding the major economies to adopt the roots of renewable and nuclear energy to make them less dependent on fossil fuels (Jewell et al., 2014). There are various pieces of literature from academic and policy consensus reveal that it is impossible to nurture long-term future scenarios on how to assess energy security and evaluate it. In spite of the various circumstances, the EU seems to extend its support to the future course of the agenda on energy security. Most of the research and think tank reports talk about energy security and the future scarcity of oil and gas. There is a need to work on the management of alternative resources for energy security instead of oil, coal and gas by the international communities (Bollen et al., 2010; Costantini et al., 2007; Rozenberg et al., 2010; Turton & Barreto, 2006).

This research provides useful insights, it doesn't matter and accounts for the fact that if the global energy systems undergo radical transformations, it seems that oil and other conventional energy sources will no longer be the dominant fuel in the transport sector in the upcoming decades. The trade-in biofuels will take place as a new energy security concern worldwide. "Other studies provide a more generic approach to evaluating future energy security based on overall net import dependency." Thus, the EU's bilateral cooperation at the regional level has been focusing on new sources of energy talks with like-minded countries and regional organisations (McCollum et al., 2011). This study indicates that import dependency is going to drastically decrease through the development of alternative sources of energy and different approaches combining the interests of the countries into a single indicator as well (McCollum et al., 2013). This study highlights through the assessing of literature that long-term energy security requires a concrete, preferably quantitative, representation of the future. It needs to incorporate of proper range of potential futures. Over the past several years the global community has tried to the development of Integrated Assessment Models (Bosetti et al., 2011; Leimbach et al., 2010; Rao & Riahi, 2006; van Vuuren et al., 2011).

Numerous of the European Union's energy initiatives have had limited success or have failed to maintain momentum, while concerns regarding energy security persist. "The European Union (EU) member states have not only put sanctions on Russian energy resources, but are also exploring alternative sources to secure the supply of essential energy resources and, implementing various policies and initiatives in place to cushion the blow of high energy prices" (Dutta, 2022b). The Russian aggression against Ukraine has highlighted the critical concern of energy security and Europe's overreliance on Russia. The European Commission (EC) President Ursula van der Leyen said in March 2022, "We must become independent from Russian oil, coal and gas. We simply cannot rely on a supplier who explicitly threatens us. We need to act now to mitigate the impact of rising energy prices, diversify our gas supply for next winter and accelerate the clean energy transition. The quicker we switch to renewables and hydrogen, combined with more energy efficiency, the quicker we will be truly independent and master our energy system. I will be discussing the Commission's ideas with European leaders at Versailles later this week, and then working to swiftly implement them with my team" (European Commission, 2022b).

This study uses qualitative analysis to elaborate on energy security and the concurrent energy crisis in the European Union. An empirical approach is utilised to discuss the core agenda of the EU on energy security and its related problems across Europe. Further, this study discusses the implementation of the inductive and deductive nature of methods to highlight concrete recommendations and key findings. This study relies on various data from different sources to investigate energy-related issues in the EU and answer the research questions. The primary and secondary resources were collected from the online libraries of universities, think tanks, government institutions bodies, newspaper editorials, and public and private research institutions to use in this study to discuss the scarcity of energy after the Russian invasion of Ukraine in February 2022. Apart from this, the study also includes data from online published journals' articles, archival reports, European Commission's regular reports, Eurostat data and books. This study also utilises online available news, television debates and documentaries. This study incorporates empirical data sourced from reputable academic databases such as Taylor & Francis, Wiley Online Library, Sage, Springer Nature, ScienceDirect, as well as the online libraries of Oxford and Cambridge publications.

The review and assessment of EU Energy Security and current energy crisis issues are based on the Web of Science and Scopus databases to collect publications on EU energy efficiency policies that are deeply related to the energy security of buildings, including a qualitative approach to the assessment of energy security, economic, climatic and environmental efficiency. Thus, the pragmatic nature of the EU's explanation of futuristic energy and environmental security.

The present study offers a theoretically grounded examination and discourse on the energy security of the European Union (EU). It aims to explore the role of supranational policies within the EU framework, specifically focusing on the Commission. Moreover, this analysis contributes to the ongoing discourse on European Union integration and the dynamics of authority and policy responsibilities between member states and their respective policies. Notably, the study highlights the significant achievements attained through extensive cooperation and international connections. The EU's soft power policy explores the area of diplomatic connections in Asia, Africa and Latin America. In spite of these initiatives, the EU is focusing on cooperation with Central Asian countries and Pacific and Caribbean countries. The EU's foreign policy uses the soft power element and exercises different legacies in third-world countries to the establishment of deeper engagement (Nye, 2004). The provision of the EU's Copenhagen criteria focuses on a liberal world with a vibrant democracy, rule of law, human rights respect for minorities and preservation of women's rights etc. The EU's supranational approach uses the norms of high politics to unite the member states under one common legislation which is benefitted for all the common people of the continent (Hoffmann, 1966). On the issue of the "Paris Agreement" on climate, all the member states are on the same page to implement the accord and support the EU to adopt a clear-cut policy on energy security. The EU and its supranational policy could be understood under the provision and commitment to energy policy (Kingdon & Stano, 1984). In recent years, the EU has initiated all suitable policies to work on energy crises and the future availability of alternative resources.

EU'S ENERGY POLICY

The development of energy security policy is at the heart of the European project, with the ECSC Treaty (European Coal and Steel Community) in 1951 and the Euratom Treaty (European Atomic Energy Community) in 1957 (Economidou et al., 2020). During 1970-80, the EU's initial focus was to enhance and emphasise energy policy as a core approach and energy security was a key concern of the EU through the 'Oil Embargo' in the 1980s. Thus, at the initial level, EU policies have been searching for alternative security of energy in Europe (Alpanda & Peralta-Alva, 2010; Bluszcz, 2017; Vivoda, 2009). The oil crisis of the 1970s in the Organisation for Economic Co-operation and Development (OECD) countries started energy efficiency to achieve the goal of policy response to enhance oil and energy security in Europe (Blumstein et al., 1980; Brown & Huntington, 2017; Papadopoulos, 2016). On the other hand, energy is a demanding sector in the era of geopolitical and geoeconomics at the global level. Energy security is deeply rooted in the "security of oil supply" in the international system but in this new liberal economic world which has been associated with economic development need to manage an alternative source of energy security (Månsson et al., 2014; Papadopoulos, 2016).

The international community agreed on the first Intergovernmental Panel on Climate Change (IPCC) Assessment report and the establishment of the United Nations Framework Convention on Climate Change (UNFCCC) at the Rio Summit in 1992, this summit impacted the EU energy policy under the provision of the mitigation of climate change. The EU also started various programs on the security of energy management and its supply as well (Sovacool & Saunders, 2014; Wiel et al., 1998). The 1993 'SAVE Directive' (93/76/EEC) represents it's kind of the first prominent EU pragmatic and broader concept of energy efficiency policy and member states also supported the EU's policy on energy security (Elagöz, 1992; Kestner, 1991; van Wees et al., 2002). The EU Member States have a common consensus to consider a common framework of energy security policy of the Union. There are supportive stances of the Member States that are paving the way for enhancing several policies for proper implementation by the EU (Elagöz, 1994; Swisher, 1996).

The EU adopted the 'Kyoto Protocol' in 1997, and since then EU has implemented the agreement of the protocol and is committed to a binding eight percent Greenhouse Gas (GHG) emission reduction target during 2008-2012 compared to 1990. This is also called the EU's prompt response to the norms of the protocol (Bertoldi, 2022). The "Kyoto Protocol" agreement on reducing CO2 emissions renewed the need for a more active commitment and promotion of energy efficiency COM (2000)247 final) (Geller et al., 2006; Zgajewski, 2014). In 2006, the European Commission started a real investigation of the results of the action plan. Finally, Commission published its 2nd Energy Efficiency Action Plan (EEAP) in the year of 2006 (Backlund et al., 2012; De Paepe et al., 2013; Fawcett et al., 2019). Its scope was to control and reduce energy demand and take targeted measures on consumption and supply with the intention of saving 20 percent of annual primary energy consumption by 2020 compared to baseline energy consumption forecasts for 2020. In addition, the EU policy is also paving the way for other European institutions to act like this to improve the policy and work towards energy saving for the future course of work. This goal corresponded to achieving approximately 1.5 percent annual savings through 2020.

THE EUROPEAN UNION ENERGY EFFICIENCY ACTION PLAN 2011

In 2011, the roadmap was presented by the new Commission for enhancing the future agenda for a competitive low-carbon economy in 2050. However, the European Community also suggested that it is necessary to do needful work for energy security. The Commission has implemented a series of comprehensive initiatives aimed at advancing energy fairness, enhancing energy security, and fostering sustainable practices in order to mitigate the effects of global warming. The current pressing concern within the European community pertains to the imperative of upholding environmental sustainability in order to enhance the quality of human existence. The objective is to achieve a reduction in greenhouse gas emissions of 40 percent by the year 2030, followed by a further reduction of 60 percent by 2040, and ultimately reaching a range of 80 to 95 percent reduction by 2050, all in comparison to the emission levels recorded in 1990 (da Graça Carvalho, 2012; Economidou et al., 2020). At the same time, the European Commission has agreed to adopt a new action plan for energy efficiency (Backlund et al., 2012).

In 2014, the EU agreed to future energy security and climate targets for 2030 as part of the Intended Nationally Determined Contributions (INDCs) to the UNFCCC process leading to the Paris Agreement. EU has been also encouraging other non-EU European countries to follow the ethics of the Paris Agreement and its directives for a sustainable environment and energy security. These were defined as a 40 percent reduction in greenhouse gas emissions compared to 1990 levels, a minimum share of 27 percent of renewable energy consumption and at least 27 percent energy savings. By and large, the EU has a clear approach to the implementation of the Paris Agreement and countries from other parts of the world also agreed with the EU's position and they have also adopted the policy on energy security and saving the environment (Veum & Bauknecht, 2019). In 2018, the EU amended to meet the renewable energy and energy efficiency target at 32.5 percent.

The Energy Union (2015) decided to work following five key areas as the EU's energy policy.

- The EU policy is to ensure solidarity and cooperation between member states for energy security and diversify Europe's different sources of renewable energy;
- EU to ensure the functioning of a fully equipped internal integrated policy on the energy market, allowing the free flow of energy through a well-equipped and adequate infrastructure which would be established without technical or regulatory errors.
- The EU is enabling energy efficiency and reducing dependency on energy imports, reducing emissions and boosting jobs and growth;
- Decarbonise the economy and move towards a low-carbon economy in accordance with the Paris Agreement;
- The EU wants to work more deeply on promoting and accelerating research into low-carbon and clean energy technologies and prioritise research and innovation to drive the energy transition and improve competitiveness (European Parliament, 2023).

From 2004-07, the EU has been developing a new concept as a common policy on "European Energy Policy." Energy is a key legislative focus of the EU which has seen energy as a "matter of sovereignty". Since Russia has been aggressing towards the Ukrainian territory it is resulting in a tense situation between the EU and Russia. The normal supply chain has also been disrupted to stop the normal flow of energy to the EU member states. EU Energy Policy has main three pillars for strengthening energy security i.e., the establishment of the internal market, the mitigation of climate-related transformation, and the security of supply. The EU has been working positively on energy security and climate for many years, and its policy by strengthening the common roots of real problems among member states, the EU also became one of the pioneers of action aimed at mitigating emissions. The EU-developed climate and energy package is a set of binding legislation, the aim of which is to secure targets for 2020. It is known as the "20-20-20" targets, they set out three key targets for 2020, including a reduction of 20 percent in EU emissions from 1990 levels; an increase in the proportion of EU energy consumption produced from renewable resources to 20 percent; and a 20 percent improvement in energy efficiency in the EU (ECf18). Increased attention to alternative energy also reflects broad European support for green modernization, as well as grassroots concerns (Kopnina, 2016).

The Green Deal launched by the new Commission in 2019 aims to fundamentally reshape the energy diplomacy of the European Union (EU). However, even if the EU will have to adapt to the new political direction determined by the Green Deal, it cannot be reduced to it. EU energy diplomacy will have to deal with the profound and diverse geoeconomics and geopolitical changes triggered by the energy transition, which include, but go even beyond, the objectives of the Green Deal. The current EU Energy Diplomacy Action Plan is awaiting revision. In recent years, the EU's public diplomacy has been working to partnerships with South and Southeast Asian countries under the Asia-Europe connectivity to achieve mutual goals and opportunities together. That's why the EU's prominent members have cooperated with regional partners to boost energy security and economic prosperity (Bharti & Bharti, 2022). When defining new priorities, the Union will have to find a balance between global aspirations and limited financial means. The German-led EU Presidency is called upon to step up its efforts to improve EU energy diplomacy along three lines. First, revise the set of existing priorities in light of new challenges.

Table 1. Share of renewable energies (RE) in gross final energy consumption and in gross final electrical energy consumption

Countries	RE shares of gross final energy consumption (%)						RE share of gross final energy consumption (%)				
	2005	2010	2017	2018	2019	2020	2005	2010	2017	2018	2019
Austria	24.4	31.2	33.1	33.8	33.6	13	62.9	66.4	71.6	74.2	75.1
Belgium	2.3	6.0	9.1	9.5	9.9	16	2.4	7.2	17.3	18.9	20.8
Bulgaria	9.2	13.9	18.7	20.6	21.6	30	8.7	12.4	19.0	22.4	23.5
Croatia	23.7	25.1	27.3	28.0	28.5	18	35.2	37.5	46.4	48.1	49.8
Cyprus	3.1	6.2	10.5	13.9	13.8	25	0.0	1.4	8.9	9.4	9.8
Czech Republic	7.1	10.5	14.8	15.1	16.2	38	3.8	7.5	13.7	13.7	14.0
Denmark	16.0	21.9	34.7	35.4	37.2	23	24.6	32.7	59.9	62.4	65.4
Estonia	17.4	24.6	29.2	30.0	31.9	18	1.1	10.3	17.0	19.7	22.0
Finland	28.8	32.3	40.9	41.2	43.1	16	26.9	27.7	35.2	36.8	38.1
France	9.6	12.7	15.9	16.4	17.2	17	13.7	14.8	19.9	21.1	22.4
Germany	7.2	11.7	15.5	16.7	17.4	20	10.6	18.2	34.6	37.8	40.8
Greece	7.3	10.1	17.3	18.1	19.7	40	8.2	12.3	24.5	26.0	31.3
Hungary	6.9	12.7	13.5	12.5	12.6	23	4.4	7.1	7.5	8.3	10.0
Ireland	2.8	5.8	10.5	10.9	12.0	11	7.2	15.6	30.1	33.3	36.5
Italy	7.5	13.0	18.3	17.8	18.2	10	6.3	20.1	34.1	33.9	35.0
Latvia	32.3	30.4	39.0	40.0	41.0	14	43.0	42.1	54.4	53.5	53.4
Lithuania	16.8	19.6	26.0	24.7	25.5	34	3.8	7.4	18.3	18.4	18.8
Luxembourg	1.4	2.9	6.2	9.0	7.0	15	3.2	3.8	8.1	9.1	10.9
Malta	0.1	1.0	7.2	8.0	8.5	31	0.0	0.0	6.8	7.7	8.0
Netherlands	2.5	3.9	6.5	7.3	8.8	24	6.3	9.6	13.8	15.2	18.2
Poland	6.9	9.3	11.1	11.5	12.2	49	2.7	6.6	13.1	13.0	14.4
Portugal	19.5	24.2	30.6	30.2	30.6	14	27.7	40.6	54.2	52.2	53.8
Romania	17.6	22.8	24.5	23.9	24.3	25	28.8	30.4	42.0	41.8	41.7
Slovakia	6.4	9.1	11.5	11.9	16.9	20	15.7	17.8	21.3	21.5	21.9
Slovenia	19.8	21.1	21.7	21.4	22.0	13	28.7	32.2	32.4	32.3	32.6
Spain	8.4	13.8	17.6	17.5	18.4	13	19.1	29.8	36.3	35.1	36.9
Sweden	40.3	46.6	54.2	54.7	56.4	13	50.9	55.8	65.9	66.2	71.2
EU-27	10.2	14.4	18.5	18.9	19.7	20	16.4	21.3	31.1	32.2	34.1

Source: https://www.bmwk.de/Redaktion/EN/Publikationen/Energie/renewable-energy-sources-in-figures-2020.pdf?__blob=publicationFile&v=1

Table 2. Share of renewables in gross final energy consumption for heating and cooling and in final energy consumption for transport

EU Countries	Renewable energy shares of gross final energy consumption in the heating/cooling sector (%)					RE shares of gross FEC for transport in percent					
	2005	2010	2017	2018	2019	2005	2010	2017	2018	2019	Target
Austria	17.9	27.2	26.6	25.4	25.7	5.1	10.7	9.7	9.9	9.8	All countries 10%
Belgium	3.4	6.7	8.1	8.3	8.3	0.7	4.8	6.6	6.7	6.8	
Bulgaria	14.3	24.3	29.9	33.3	35.5	0.9	1.5	7.3	8.1	7.9	
Croatia	30.0	32.9	36.6	36.7	36.8	1.0	1.1	1.2	2.6	5.9	
Cyprus	29.3	32.5	46.5	46.0	47.4	0.0	2.0	2.6	2.7	3.3	
Czech Republic	22.8	30.4	44.6	45.5	48.0	1.1	5.2	6.6	6.6	7.8	
Denmark	7.7	12.1	13.4	14.1	14.6	0.4	1.1	6.9	6.9	7.2	
Estonia	39.1	44.0	54.6	54.6	57.5	0.2	0.4	0.4	3.3	5.1	
Finland	9.9	18.1	19.9	18.2	18.1	0.9	4.4	18.8	17.7	21.3	
France	8.2	15.6	20.1	19.3	19.7	2.1	6.6	8.8	9.0	9.2	
Germany	32.2	43.2	51.7	53.7	52.3	4.0	6.4	7.0	7.9	7.7	
Greece	13.4	18.7	28.2	30.3	30.2	0.1	1.9	4.0	4.1	4.0	
Hungary	22.8	31.0	33.7	34.2	33.8	1.0	6.2	7.7	7.7	8.0	
Ireland	12.4	16.2	20.7	21.4	22.5	0.1	2.5	7.4	7.2	8.9	
Italy	42.7	40.7	54.6	55.4	57.8	1.0	4.9	6.5	7.7	9.0	
Latvia	3.6	4.7	7.5	8.5	8.7	2.4	4.0	2.3	4.7	5.1	
Lithuania	1.0	7.3	19.3	23.3	25.7	0.7	3.8	4.3	4.3	4.0	
Luxembourg	2.4	3.1	5.7	6.1	7.1	0.2	2.1	6.5	6.6	7.7	
Malta	10.2	11.8	14.9	15.1	16.0	0.0	0.0	6.8	8.0	8.7	
Netherlands	32.1	33.8	41.0	40.9	41.6	0.5	3.4	6.0	9.6	12.5	
Poland	49.8	58.5	65.8	65.3	66.1	1.7	6.6	4.2	5.7	6.1	
Portugal	5.0	7.9	9.8	10.6	19.7	0.5	5.5	7.9	9.0	9.1	
Romania	26.4	29.5	34.6	32.3	32.2	1.9	1.4	6.6	6.3	7.8	
Slovakia	10.8	14.1	19.7	20.6	22.6	1.7	5.3	6.9	7.0	8.3	
Slovenia	9.4	12.6	17.7	17.6	18.9	0.8	3.1	2.6	5.5	8.0	
Spain	3.4	4.3	6.6	6.3	6.3	1.3	5.0	5.8	6.9	7.6	
Sweden	10.0	18.8	26.5	37.2	35.1	6.6	9.6	26.8	29.7	30.3	
EU-27	12.4	17.0	20.9	21.2	22.1	2.0	5.5	7.5	8.3	8.9	

Source: https://www.bmwk.de/Redaktion/EN/Publikationen/Energie/renewable-energy-sources-in-figures-2020.pdf?__blob=publicationFile&v=1

Table 3. Production of electricity from renewable energy sources in the EU-27 (Primary energy (TWh))

RE Sectors	2005	2010	2011	2012	2013	2014	2015	2016	2017	2018	2019	2020
Biomass	70.1	111.6	119.0	132.9	139.2	144.3	149.4	151.2	153.7	155.5 9	159.9	158.3
Hydropower	348.4	401.3	332.8	359.6	396.7	398.6	363.2	372.7	322.5	370.3	345.3	373.3
Wind energy	71.0	139.8	165.3	187.5	209.5	222.4	263.2	266.8	312.3	320.5	367.1	397.1
Geoth. energy	5.4	5.6	5.9	5.8	6.0	6.3	6.6	6.7	6.7	6.7	6.7	6.7
Photovoltaics	1.5	22.5	45.3	66.4	79.3	88.7	95.3	95.5	102.0	110.5	120.0	140.2
Solar thermal	0.0	0.8	2.0	3.8	4.8	5.5	5.6	5.6	5.9	4.9	5.7	5.0
Ocean energy	0.5	0.5	0.5	0.5	0.4	0.5	0.5	0.5	0.5	0.5	0.5	0.5
RE total	496.9	682.0	670.9	756.4	835.8	866.2	883.8	899.0	903.6	968.9	1005.3	1081.1
RE share of gross electricity consumption	14.9 %	22.8 %	22.8 %	25.7 %	28.6 %	30.3 %	30.5 %	30.7 %	30.6 %	32.8 %	34.5 %	38.5 %
New Energy (TWh)												
EU-gross final electricity consumption	3,316.0	2,985.4	2,941.8	2,939.1	2,921.1	2,861.5	2,906.8	2,928.3	2,961.0	2,945.3	2,908.9	2,791.3
Import	335.1	291.5	321.1	349.5	332.1	363.7	387.6	362.5	366.6	372.3	369.4	381.1
Export	319.4	286.6	320.1	342.7	333.9	368.7	394.3	361.9	371.1	363.5	366.5	367.9

Source: German Environment Agency (UBA) [32] based on the sources quoted therein

Second, to expand the geographical radius of its actions beyond its direct neighbourhood by focusing on twelve anchor partners across the Afro-Eurasian ellipse. Third, update its toolkit of instruments around five new areas of action, moving away from an exclusively prescriptive and ideological approach towards a more realistic and country-specific approach (Pastukhova et al., 2020).

Table 4. Electricity production from renewable energy sources in the EU-27, 2020

Countries	Hydro Power	Wind Energy	Solid Bio-mass	Biogas	Liquid biogenic fuels	Photo-voltaics	Solar Thermal	Geoth. Energy	Ocean Energy	Total
(TWh)										
Austria	45.3	6.8	4.0	0.6	0.0001	2.0	-	0.0001	-	58.8
Belgium	1.3	12.9	4.3	1.0	0.02	5.0	-	-	-	24.4
Bulgaria	3.3	1.5	1.5	0.2	-	1.5	-	-	-	8.0
Croatia	5.8	1.7	0.6	0.4	-	0.1	-	0.1	-	8.7
Cyprus	-	0.2	-	0.1	-	0.3	-	-	-	0.6
Czech Republic	3.4	0.7	2.6	2.6	-	2.2	-	-	-	11.6
Denmark	0.02	16.4	5.2	0.7	-	1.2	-	-	-	23.5
Estonia	0.03	0.8	1.5	0.03	-	0.1	-	-	-	2.5
Finland	15.9	7.9	11.1	0.3	0.001	0.3	-	-	-	35.5
France	66.7	40.7	5.8	2.8	0.0001	13.6	-	0.1	0.5	130.2
Germany	24.9	131.0	17.1	33.0	0.4	50.6	-	0.2	-	257.2
Greece	3.4	9.3	0.02	0.3	-	4.4	-	-	-	17.5
Hungary	0.2	0.7	1.8	0.3	-	2.5	-	0.02	-	5.5
Ireland	1.2	11.5	0.7	0.2	-	0.06	-	-	-	13.7
Italy	48.6	18.7	6.8	8.2	4.7	24.9	-	6.0	-	117.9
Latvia	2.6	18.7	0.5	0.3	-	0.005	-	-	-	3.6
Lithuania	1.1	0.2	0.4	0.1	-	0.1	-	-	-	3.4
Luxembourg	1.1	1.6	0.3	0.1	-	0.2	-	-	-	2.0
Malta	-	0.3	-	0.01	-	0.2	-	-	-	0.2
Netherlands	0.05	0.0001	7.9	0.9	-	8.0	-	-	-	32.2
Poland	2.9	15.8	7.0	1.2	0.002	2.0	-	-	--	28.9
Portugal	14.0	12.3	3.5	0.3	-	1.7	-	0.2	-	31.9
Romania	15.7	6.9	0.4	-	-	1.7	-	-	-	24.8
Slovakia	4.7	0.004	1.0	0.5	-	0.7	-	-	-	6.9
Slovenia	5.2	0.01	0.2	0.1	0.01	0.4	-	-	-	5.9
Spain	33.9	56.3	4.8	0.8	0.01	15.6	5.0	-	0.03	116.4
Sweden	71.8	27.5	8.8	0.01	0.01	1.0	-	-	-	109.1
EU 27	**373.3**	**397.1**	**98.1**	**55.1**	**5.1**	**140.2**	**5.0**	**6.7**	**0.5**	**1081.1**

Source: Eurostat (Production of electricity and derived heat by type of fuel)

The Commission deeply understands the importance of scale to energy security, that is a 'supranational scale' which is appropriate in response to the context of energy security and a sustainable environment. This is promoted with passion as 'purposefully constructed' to achieve appropriate scale on energy security and could create a crisis management approach to future scarcity of oil and natural gases. It may be possible with a courage so different that it requires political consensus and legislative development to execute through the executive bodies, which may lead to "creeping powers", "a steady, if surreptitious, growth in the powers of the Commission" (Majone, 2002; Maltby, 2013; Mayer, 2008). The supranational scale of institutions is in a position to implement the legislative provisions with the landmark decision for energy security. The energy-based government can justify the supranational approach of energy governance for a proper solution to upcoming scarcity and restrictions (Niemann, 2021; Schmitter, 2002).

The United Kingdom's withdrawal from the European Union on January 1, 2021, is concurrently linked to alterations in statistical data pertaining to the utilisation of renewable energy sources inside the European Union. Table 1 shows this edition of "Renewable Energy Sources in Numbers", so the presentation is for the EU-27 without the UK. In order to determine the shares of renewable energies in the gross electricity consumption, the production of electricity from wind and hydraulic origin was calculated using the standardization rule defined in the European directive.

The Table two shows that the EU's member states have been using renewable energy share in the area of cooling and heating sectors. Austria, Sweden, Finland and the Netherlands are the main countries in the EU where consumption rates are higher than those of other Member States.

Table 3 shows that hydropower, wind energy, biomass and photovoltaics are the highest resources of renewable energy in the EU. Thus, this figure is showing that the EU has been accelerating at the appropriate level to its dependency.

Table four shows that with 257.2 terawatt hours (calculated according to EU directive), Germany alone contributed almost 24% of the total electricity production from renewable energies in the EU-27 in 2020 It was followed by France with 130.2 terawatt hours and, just behind, Italy (117.9), Spain (116.4) and Sweden (109.1 terawatt hours).

RUSSIAN AND UKRAINIAN WAR AND ENERGY ISSUES FOR THE EU

The Russian invasion of Ukraine brought a high rate of energy prices in the EU. That's why the EU has been managing an alternate source of energy supply in Europe since the Ukrainian crisis occurred. The cost of energy at least increased to 63 percent and affected households brutally. This contributes to an increase in overall household spending of between 2.7 percent and 4.8 percent (IEA, 2022). It is more than doubled the actual price of oils, gas and coal. France is in favour of the EU to cooperate with like-minded countries across the world for less dependency on Russia. France's presidency of the EU has started deeper cooperation in Asia, Africa and countries from the Pacific region. France wants deeper cooperation in the region of the Gulf, South Asia and Central Asia. That is EU's position would strong in the comparison of China and Russia's geopolitical stability in this region which is naturally rich in the context of oils, gas and other sources of energy. France and Germany both countries have common concerns with perfection in the Indo-Pacific region to cooperate with regional partners. Thus, the EU and its stronger member states want the EU should be major stakeholders through the expansion of trade and economic cooperation with India, Japan, South Korea, the Association of Southeast Asian Nations (ASEAN), and Australia (Bharti & Singh, 2023).

DISCUSSION

The EU's key objectives are to achieve security of supply, competitiveness and sustainability. The EU countries have a long-lasting agenda to reach and achieve the ultimate goals. On 25th February 2015, the European Union formed the "Resilient Energy Union" which is part of the energy policy of the union. This policy is also forwarding some sort of legacy on the climate policy as well. In the current world order, there is a growing need for natural resources in EU countries from Central Asian countries to fill the energy gap after the Russian invasion of Ukraine. The EU Energy Union can succeed following the EU's fruitful and deepening relations with important like-minded partner countries around the world. There are many Western European EU countries that during its EU presidency favour working with Central Asian countries in the area of energy security. In the Eurasia region, China and Russia are stronger sides through their communist legacy and geopolitically dominated over the Western powers in this region. However, the EU has started better work at the bilateral level with these five Central Asian countries. China's Belt and Road Initiative (BRI) framework of economic and trade cooperation has attracted the Central Asian countries and all five countries are members of the BRI Forum. Therefore, this research indicates that China's geopolitics and strategy are deeply rooted in these former Soviet Union countries. At the geopolitical level of diplomacy, Russia and China support each other's interests in the Eurasia region. On February 24, 2022, Russian military aggression against several regions of Ukraine's eastern county (the Donbas region) caused diplomatic tensions between the EU and its member states with Moscow and the supply chain has been disrupted since then. This Russian invasion of Ukraine has created several problems at the global level, not for only the EU. These crises have been exacerbated since then when Russia started an unprovoked war against Ukraine. The Western and EU countries rushed to impose sanctions against the Russian Federation. (Bharti, 2023a, 2023b; Mišík, 2022).

The EU and the United States have agreed to work on energy security together as settled joint "US and EU Task Force on Energy Security" which was launched by US President Joe Biden and President of the European Commission Ursula von der Leyen. This Task Force's main objective is to reduce the EU's member countries' dependency on Russian energy. The EU and the US policy is to diversify its natural gas supplies in alignment with the objectives of climate and work on reducing its overall demand for natural oil and gas. The US has been exporting liquefied natural gas to the EU member countries more than doubled. Since the implementation of the "Task Force on Energy Security" the US delivered an additional fifteen billion cubic meters of LNG to the EU. The EU has considered importing LNG from the United States as the highest amount of import. The EU is the largest destination for US exports in the energy sector after the Russian invasion of Ukraine. At the end of the financial year 2022-23, the US LNG exports to the EU recorded 52 percent of total supplies. On the other hand, the EU had imported Russian gas which accounts for around 16 percent of only. In March 2022, the Russian gas export to the EU down to 37 percent. (The White House, 2023).

The US and EU have a common understanding of the issues of energy security to cooperation at the transatlantic level. The joint EU and the US Task Force on Energy Security build on long-standing cooperation at the continental level under the guidance and framework of the 'US-EU Energy Council.' This has been supporting the EU's energy needs and the joint commitment of both sides to the reduce

EU's reliance on Russian energy. This joint energy programme of the US and the EU is working with other countries towards the global transition to the achievement of clean energy in the wake of the unprovoked and unjustified Russian invasion of Ukraine. The European Union and its member states are committed to the implementation of the "Paris Agreement" to achieve the key principles of net zero emission by 2050. In the fold of the EU, the individual countries are working on energy security issues through bilateral, trilateral and multilateral levels of partnership with like-minded countries at the global level. Germany is one of the key EU countries which have achieved the highest level of stored renewable energy sources. Other EU countries also follow Germany and EU countries also get support for installation of the renewable energy support centers (Heshmati & Abolhosseini, 2017).

A disruption in the energy market has been occurring everywhere worldwide. This kind of energy disruption is becoming a regular phenomenon in the upcoming decades. The war between Russia and Ukraine has been going on since February 2023. This has caused significant energy disruptions in Europe and EU member states have now entered into deeper partnerships with Central Asian countries to fulfilment of oil and gas. The EU's bilateral, trilateral and multilateral cooperation with countries in Asia and Africa reinforces its diverse aspirations to minimises the energy gap in Europe (Popkostova, 2022).

CONCLUSION

This study reveals that Russia's invasion of Ukraine strained diplomatic relations between the EU and Russia. Since February 2022, EU countries have been facing a huge number of Ukrainian refugees and Central and Eastern European countries have adopted a large number of Ukrainians into their country. Basically, Poland is the largest EU recipient country and has received more than eight thousand refugees in their country and Romania, Hungary, Slovakia, Baltic and Nordic countries have provided shelter to these war-affected people. Since the start of the Russian aggression on Ukrainian territory, the EU has criticised at the highest level and favoured the Ukrainian side in the United Nations. This study also traced that the EU is very serious about the issue of the energy crisis in Europe and about the price caps, exceptional taxes and subsidies which have contributed to reducing costs for consumers in Europe. Based on the European Commission's Energy Price Toolkit published in October 2022, all Member States have taken national fiscal policy measures to soften the blow of energy price increases on consumers and businesses. The EU has increased renewable energy production to fill the Russian supply gap which was not normal as usual before the Ukrainian crisis. EU member states have therefore accelerated emergency regulation to deal with high energy prices. Thus, the EU wants to ensure energy security through the adoption of new policies and the transport of natural resources from other sources. The new rules were quickly adopted by European energy ministers in the Council. The aforementioned regulation will be in effect starting from December 1, 2022, and will remain in force until March 31, 2023.

This book chapter brought a major recommendation on the Russian invasion of Ukraine, EU countries suffered from the almost double rate of domestic energy. Russia has brought political instability to Europe and innocent people have lost their lives in different parts of Eastern Europe. This study also reveals that Russia's unprovocative war has created an energy security crisis and that the EU is considering how to fill the void and reduce dependence on Russia. This study has also incorporated Germany into the primary sphere, and Berlin is currently progressing in the establishment of its own infrastructure for importing liquefied Natural Gas (LNG). The initial direct injection of LNG into the country's gas network is anticipated to occur by the conclusion of 2022. Additionally, Germany aims to enhance trade and establish fresh agreements with alternative suppliers as a means to substitute the Russian gas pipeline. The French and German governments have been referred to as the driving forces behind the European Union. However, despite their influential positions, these two nations have thus far been unable to establish substantive accords and engage in meaningful conversation to bring an end to the ongoing conflict. In general, this study asserts that Russia continues to exhibit aggression against Ukraine's Donbass region, while the international community has been ineffective in halting the ongoing conflict. The European Union continues to face an energy crisis due to the cessation of oil and gas delivery from Russia to European nations.

REFERENCES

Alpanda, S., & Peralta-Alva, A. (2010). Oil crisis, energy-saving technological change and the stock market crash of 1973–74. *Review of Economic Dynamics*, *13*(4), 824–842. doi:10.1016/j.red.2010.04.003

Backlund, S., Thollander, P., Palm, J., & Ottosson, M. (2012). Extending the energy efficiency gap. *Energy Policy*, *51*, 392–396. doi:10.1016/j.enpol.2012.08.042

Bertoldi, P. (2022). Policies for energy conservation and sufficiency: Review of existing policies and recommendations for new and effective policies in OECD countries. *Energy and Building*, *264*, 112075. doi:10.1016/j.enbuild.2022.112075

Bharti, M. S. (2023a). The European Union's Economic Development Strategy and Cooperation with the Countries of Central Asia. *Nowa Polityka Wschodnia*, *36*(1), 220–244. doi:10.15804/npw20233611

Bharti, M. S. (2023b). The Sustainable Development and Economic Impact of China's Belt and Road Initiative in Ethiopia. *East Asia (Piscataway, N.J.)*, *40*(2), 175–194. doi:10.100712140-023-09402-y PMID:37065271

Bharti, M. S., & Bharti, S. S. (2022). The EU Public Diplomacy in the Time of Virtual Reality: Political, Social and Economic Implications. In B. Olbrych (Ed.), *Life in Virtual Reality, Chances and dangers* (Vol. 2, pp. 13–25). Akademia Handlowa Nauk Stosowanych w Radomiu.

Bharti, M. S., & Goswami, A. (2023). Geopolitical Perspective of the EU's Post-Pandemic Public Diplomacy: Prospects and Challenges. In S. Kavoğlu & E. Köksoy (Eds.), *Global Perspectives on the Emerging Trends in Public Diplomacy* (pp. 24–49). IGI Global. doi:10.4018/978-1-6684-9161-4.ch002

Bharti, M. S., & Singh, A. (2023). India and France bilateral partnership for advancing strategic autonomy in the Indo-Pacific region: Special reference to the Indo-French strategic partnership. *Cogent Social Sciences*, *9*(1), 2215561. doi:10.1080/23311886.2023.2215561

Blumstein, C., Krieg, B., Schipper, L., & York, C. (1980). Overcoming social and institutional barriers to energy conservation. *Energy*, *5*(4), 355–371. doi:10.1016/0360-5442(80)90036-5

Bluszcz, A. (2017). European economies in terms of energy dependence. *Quality & Quantity*, *51*(4), 1531–1548. doi:10.100711135-016-0350-1 PMID:28725090

Bollen, J., Hers, S., & van der Zwaan, B. (2010). An integrated assessment of climate change, air pollution, and energy security policy. *Energy Policy*, *38*(8), 4021–4030. doi:10.1016/j.enpol.2010.03.026

Bosetti, V., Carraro, C., Duval, R., & Tavoni, M. (2011). What should we expect from innovation? A model-based assessment of the environmental and mitigation cost implications of climate-related R&D. *Energy Economics*, *33*(6), 1313–1320. doi:10.1016/j.eneco.2011.02.010

Brown, S. P. A., & Huntington, H. G. (2017). OPEC and world oil security. *Energy Policy*, *108*, 512–523. doi:10.1016/j.enpol.2017.06.034

Costantini, V., Gracceva, F., Markandya, A., & Vicini, G. (2007). Security of energy supply: Comparing scenarios from a European perspective. *Energy Policy*, *35*(1), 210–226. doi:10.1016/j.enpol.2005.11.002

Da Graça Carvalho, M. (2012). EU energy and climate change strategy. *Energy*, *40*(1), 19–22. doi:10.1016/j.energy.2012.01.012

De Paepe, M., T'Joen, C., Huisseune, H., Van Belleghem, M., & Kessen, V. (2013). Comparison of different testing methods for gas fired domestic boiler efficiency determination. *Applied Thermal Engineering, 50*(1), 275–281. https://doi.org/https://doi.org/10.1016/j.applthermaleng.2012.06.027

Dutta, A. (2022a, June 13). *Europe's Energy Security in the Aftermath of Ukrainian Crisis.* Indian Council of World Affairs. Retrieved from https://www.icwa.in/show_content.php?lang=1&level=3&ls_id=7471&lid=5009#:~:text=The%20plans%20put%20forward%20by,and%20transitioning%20to%20green%20alternatives

Dutta, A. (2022b, September 28). *Assessing Europe's spiralling energy crisis*. Observer Research Foundation. Retrieved from https://www.orfonline.org/expert-speak/assessing-europes-spiralling-energy-crisis/

Economidou, M., Todeschi, V., Bertoldi, P., D'Agostino, D., Zangheri, P., & Castellazzi, L. (2020). Review of 50 years of EU energy efficiency policies for buildings. *Energy and Building*, *225*, 110322. doi:10.1016/j.enbuild.2020.110322

Elagöz, A. (1992). Energy savings training in the member states of the EC. *Proceedings*, *2*, 2140–2145.

Elagöz, A. (1994). Legal and administrative measures for energy savings in non-industrial buildings in the member states of the EC. *Renewable Energy*, *4*(1), 109–112. doi:10.1016/0960-1481(94)90071-X

European Commission. (2022a). *RePowereu Plan, COM(2022)230*. Retrieved from https://eur-lex.europa.eu/legal-content/EN/TXT/?uri=COM%3A2022%3A230%3AFIN&qid=1653033742483

European Commission. (2022b, March 8). *REPowerEU: Joint European action for more affordable, secure and sustainable energy*. Retrieved from https://ec.europa.eu/commission/presscorner/detail/en/ip_22_1511

European Parliament. (2023, February 9). *Energy policy: general principles*. Retrieved from https://www.europarl.europa.eu/ftu/pdf/en/FTU_2.4.7.pdf

Eurostat. (2022). *Imports of Natural Gas by Partner Country*. Retrieved from https://appsso.eurostat.ec.europa.eu/nui/submitViewTableAction.do

Fawcett, T., Rosenow, J., & Bertoldi, P. (2019). Energy efficiency obligation schemes: Their future in the EU. *Energy Efficiency*, *12*(1), 57–71. doi:10.100712053-018-9657-1

Geller, H., Harrington, P., Rosenfeld, A. H., Tanishima, S., & Unander, F. (2006). Polices for increasing energy efficiency: Thirty years of experience in OECD countries. *Energy Policy*, *34*(5), 556–573. doi:10.1016/j.enpol.2005.11.010

Giuli, M., & Oberthür, S. (2023). Third time lucky? Reconciling EU climate and external energy policy during energy security crises. *Journal of European Integration*, *45*(3), 395–412. doi:10.1080/07036337.2023.2190588

Heshmati, A., & Abolhosseini, S. (2017). European Energy Security: Challenges and Green Opportunities. In The Political Economy of Clean Energy Transitions (pp. 292–310). doi:10.1093/oso/9780198802242.003.0015

Hoffmann, S. (1966). Obstinate or obsolete? The fate of the nation-state and the case of Western Europe. *Daedalus*, *95*(3), 862–916.

IEA. (2022, December 12). *How the European Union can avoid natural gas shortages in 2023*. Retrieved from https://www.iea.org/news/how-the-european-union-can-avoid-natural-gas-shortages-in-2023

Jewell, J., Cherp, A., & Riahi, K. (2014). Energy security under de-carbonization scenarios: An assessment framework and evaluation under different technology and policy choices. *Energy Policy*, *65*, 743–760. doi:10.1016/j.enpol.2013.10.051

Kestner, M. (1991). First energy efficiency directives under SAVE programme. *Energy in Europe*, *1*(7), 25.

Kingdon, J. W., & Stano, E. (1984). *Agendas, alternatives, and public policies* (Vol. 45). Little, Brown.

Kopnina, H. (2016). Energy Policy in the European Union: Renewable Energy and the Risks of Subversion. In J. de Zwaan, M. Lak, A. Makinwa, & P. Willems (Eds.), Governance and Security Issues of the European Union: Challenges Ahead (pp. 167–184). T.M.C. Asser Press. doi:10.1007/978-94-6265-144-9_10

Leimbach, M., Bauer, N., Baumstark, L., & Edenhofer, O. (2010). Mitigation Costs in a Globalized World: Climate Policy Analysis with REMIND-R. *Environmental Modeling and Assessment*, *15*(3), 155–173. doi:10.100710666-009-9204-8

Majone, G. (2002). The European Commission: The Limits of Centralization and the Perils of Parliamentarization. *Governance: An International Journal of Policy, Administration and Institutions*, *15*(3), 375–392. doi:10.1111/0952-1895.00193

Maltby, T. (2013). European Union energy policy integration: A case of European Commission policy entrepreneurship and increasing supranationalism. *Energy Policy*, *55*, 435–444. doi:10.1016/j.enpol.2012.12.031 PMID:24926115

Månsson, A., Johansson, B., & Nilsson, L. J. (2014). Assessing energy security: An overview of commonly used methodologies. *Energy*, *73*, 1–14. doi:10.1016/j.energy.2014.06.073

Mayer, S. (2008). Path dependence and Commission activism in the evolution of the European Union's external energy policy. *Journal of International Relations and Development*, *11*(3), 251–278. doi:10.1057/jird.2008.12

McCollum, D. L., Krey, V., & Riahi, K. (2011). An integrated approach to energy sustainability. *Nature Climate Change*, *1*(9), 428–429. doi:10.1038/nclimate1297

McCollum, D. L., Krey, V., Riahi, K., Kolp, P., Grubler, A., Makowski, M., & Nakicenovic, N. (2013). Climate policies can help resolve energy security and air pollution challenges. *Climatic Change*, *119*(2), 479–494. doi:10.100710584-013-0710-y

Mišík, M. (2022). The EU needs to improve its external energy security. *Energy Policy*, *165*, 112930. doi:10.1016/j.enpol.2022.112930

Niemann, A. (2021). Neofunctionalism. In M. Riddervold, J. Trondal, & A. Newsome (Eds.), *The Palgrave Handbook of EU Crises* (pp. 115–133). Springer International Publishing. doi:10.1007/978-3-030-51791-5_6

Nye, J. (2004). *Soft Power: The means to success in world politics*. Public Affairs.

Papadopoulos, A. M. (2016). Forty years of regulations on the thermal performance of the building envelope in Europe: Achievements, perspectives and challenges. *Energy and Building*, *127*, 942–952. doi:10.1016/j.enbuild.2016.06.051

Pastukhova, M., Pepe, J., & Westphal, K. (2020, June 31). *Beyond the Green Deal: Upgrading the EU's Energy Diplomacy for a New Era*. SWP Comment. Retrieved from https://www.energiewende-global.com/fileadmin/user_upload/giz-website/Media_Library/Erneuerbare_Energien/Beyond_the_Green_Deal_Upgrading_the_EUs_Energy_Diplomacy_for_a_New_Era.pdf

Popkostova, Y. (2022, January). *Europe's Energy Crisis Conundrum*. The EUISS Is an Agency of the European Union. Retrieved from https://www.iss.europa.eu/sites/default/files/EUISSFiles/Brief_2_Energy%20Crisis.pdf

Rao, S., & Riahi, K. (2006). The role of non-CO2 greenhouse gases in climate change mitigation: Long-term scenarios for the 21st century. *The Energy Journal (Cambridge, Mass.)*, *27*(3), 177–200. doi:10.5547/ISSN0195-6574-EJ-VolSI2006-NoSI3-9

Rozenberg, J., Hallegatte, S., Vogt-Schilb, A., Sassi, O., Guivarch, C., Waisman, H., & Hourcade, J.-C. (2010). Climate policies as a hedge against the uncertainty on future oil supply. *Climatic Change*, *101*(3), 663–668. doi:10.100710584-010-9868-8

Schmitter, P. C. (2002, July). *Neo-Functionalism*. European University Institute. Retrieved from https://www.eui.eu/Documents/DepartmentsCentres/SPS/Profiles/Schmitter/NeoNeoFunctionalismRev.pdf

Sovacool, B. K., & Saunders, H. (2014). Competing policy packages and the complexity of energy security. *Energy*, *67*, 641–651. doi:10.1016/j.energy.2014.01.039

Swisher, J. N. (1996). Regulatory and Mixed Policy Options for Reducing Energy Use and Carbon Emissions. *Mitigation and Adaptation Strategies for Global Change*, *1*(1), 23–49. doi:10.1007/BF00625614

The White House. (2023, April 3). *Joint Statement on U.S.-EU Task Force on Energy Security*. Retrieved from https://www.whitehouse.gov/briefing-room/statements-releases/2023/04/03/joint-statement-on-u-s-eu-task-force-on-energy-security/

Turton, H., & Barreto, L. (2006). Long-term security of energy supply and climate change. *Energy Policy*, *34*(15), 2232–2250. doi:10.1016/j.enpol.2005.03.016

van Vuuren, D. P., Stehfest, E., den Elzen, M. G. J., Kram, T., van Vliet, J., Deetman, S., Isaac, M., Klein Goldewijk, K., Hof, A., Mendoza Beltran, A., Oostenrijk, R., & van Ruijven, B. (2011). RCP2.6: Exploring the possibility to keep global mean temperature increase below 2°C. *Climatic Change*, *109*(1), 95–116. doi:10.100710584-011-0152-3

van Wees, M. T., Uyterlinde, M. A., & Maly, M. (2002). Energy efficiency and renewable energy policy in the Czech Republic within the framework of accession to the European Union. *Energy*, *27*(11), 1057–1067. doi:10.1016/S0360-5442(02)00068-3

Veum, K., & Bauknecht, D. (2019). How to reach the EU renewables target by 2030? An analysis of the governance framework. *Energy Policy*, *127*, 299–307. doi:10.1016/j.enpol.2018.12.013

Vivoda, V. (2009). Diversification of oil import sources and energy security: A key strategy or an elusive objective? *Energy Policy*, *37*(11), 4615–4623. doi:10.1016/j.enpol.2009.06.007

Wiel, S., Martin, N., Levine, M., Price, L., & Sathaye, J. (1998). The role of building energy efficiency in managing atmospheric carbon dioxide. *Environmental Science & Policy, 1*(1), 27–38. https://doi.org/https://doi.org/10.1016/S1462-9011(98)00004-5

Zachmann, G., Sgaravatti, G., & McWilliams, B. (2023, July 27). *European natural gas imports*. Bruegel. Retrieved from https://www.bruegel.org/dataset/european-natural-gas-imports

Zettelmeyer, J., Tagliapietra, S., Zachmann, G., & Heussaff, C. (2022, December). *Beating the European Energy Crisis*. International Monetary Fund. Retrieved from https://www.imf.org/en/Publications/fandd/issues/2022/12/beating-the-european-energy-crisis-Zettelmeyer

Zgajewski, T. (2014, June). *Energy Efficiency: The Ever-Neglected Priority of The European Energy Strategy*. Egmont Paper 66: The Royal Institute for International Relations. Retrieved from https://www.egmontinstitute.be/app/uploads/2014/05/ep66.pdf?type=pdf+2014

Chapter 7
The Impact of Russia-Ukraine War on the Global Energy Crisis

Ejazul Haq Ateed
https://orcid.org/0000-0003-4802-2586
Kirikkale University, Turkey

ABSTRACT

The Russia-Ukraine war has profoundly affected the global energy crisis, leading to significant disruptions and uncertainties in energy flows both domestically and internationally. The escalation of tensions in 2022 made crucial energy infrastructure vulnerable, causing a reduction in natural gas and energy supplies to European countries heavily reliant on Russian exports. This disruption has resulted in fluctuating energy prices and increased volatility in global markets, pushing importing nations to explore alternative sources and focus on renewable energy and domestic production. Geopolitical tensions have risen as countries compete for energy resources and prioritize their energy security, prompting efforts to enhance resilience and develop contingency plans. This chapter analyzes the multi-faceted impacts of the Russia-Ukraine war on the global energy crisis, stressing the importance of proactive measures to address vulnerabilities, enhance energy security, and foster international cooperation for a more resilient and sustainable future.

INTRODUCTION

The war between Russia and Ukraine has not only greatly affected the immediate neighbor of Ukraine, Europe, but also shocked the world. Energy security has been one of the major issues affected by this war more than anything else. The conflict which escalated Russia-Ukraine tensions caused disruptions to natural gas supplies, through the pipelines that traverse Ukrainian territory. Given that Russia is a leading natural gas exporting county to Europe, the hostilities caused concerns about energy security and supply reliability across the continent. Several European countries that were about 40% reliant on Russian gas saw their energy prices surge, and fears of potential shortages emerged. This war made European countries reconsider their energy policies. In particular, the EU, which has directly coordinated with the US in Russia's energy sanctions, adopted a two-sided policy. This policy includes changing the

DOI: 10.4018/979-8-3693-0440-2.ch007

energy source geographically and investing in the renewable domestic energy sector. The goal is to protect these countries in the best possible way in the future against the damage caused by geopolitical changes.

Moreover, the war intensified debates about the broader energy transition. Indeed, one of the important consequences of this war is the excessive attention of countries on the stability and instability of fossil fuels. As countries reevaluated their reliance on Russian oil and gas, some governments accelerated their efforts to shift towards cleaner and more sustainable energy sources, such as renewables and nuclear power. This shift, coupled with increased energy conservation measures, further influenced the global energy market by altering demand dynamics and pushing for greater innovation in the energy sector. Ultimately, the war between Russia and Ukraine acted as a catalyst for changes in energy policies and strategies worldwide, highlighting the need for greater resilience and cooperation to address the complexities of energy security in an interconnected world.

In this chapter, the main effects of the war between Russia and Ukraine on the global energy crisis are examined. The conflict triggered a series of events that reverberated throughout the energy markets worldwide, affecting both supply and demand dynamics. By delving into the complexities of this crisis, the chapter aims to shed light on how geopolitical tensions between Russia and Ukraine disrupted the flow of natural gas and oil, causing significant ripple effects on the global energy landscape. Through an in-depth examination of the war's consequences, this chapter comprehensively analyzes the challenges of different countries in energy supply, the policies employed to mitigate risks, and the opportunities it presented for accelerating the transition towards sustainable and alternative energy sources. By analyzing the case of the Russia-Ukraine War, the chapter aims to draw valuable lessons for policymakers, energy analysts, and stakeholders, emphasizing the need for a resilient and diversified energy sector that can withstand geopolitical shocks and contribute to a more sustainable and secure global energy future.

ENERGY BACKGROUND ON THE WAR

The Russia-Ukraine War possesses profound historical and geopolitical underpinnings, which can be meticulously delineated to emanate from the disintegration of the Union of Soviet Socialist Republics in 1991. The disintegration of the USSR led to the emergence of Ukraine as an independent nation, a development that complicated the relations between Russia and Ukraine. Historical tensions over issues such as territorial claims, cultural identity, and the status of the Russian-speaking population in Ukraine have been persistent sources of friction between the two countries (Kuzio, 2002). Additionally, the contested status of Crimea, an autonomous region with historical ties to both Russia and Ukraine, further exacerbated the situation. Russia's action to annex Crimea to its soil in 2014 caused further escalation and set the stage for the 2022 conflict. This key juncture served as a watershed moment in the dynamics of Russia-Ukraine relations, precipitating a notable divergence. The condemnation of Russia's actions by Western powers, coupled with the consequential imposition of economic sanctions, engendered resurgence reminiscent of a new Cold War, characterized by the rekindling of geopolitical tensions between the Eastern and Western blocs.

The Russia-Ukraine conflict drew substantial attention from political and academic circles due to its energy crisis implications. However, it is essential to recognize that prior to the military confrontation both nations were already engaged in an energy-centered rivalry, a point emphasized by Ukrainian Deputy Energy Minister Maxim Nemchinov in November 2021. A pivotal aspect of this struggle was Ukraine's strategic aim to enhance energy supply diversification, notably through liquefied natural gas

(LNG) imports from Qatar. This drive for diversification significantly contributed to the conflict. Hence, geopolitical interests and disputes over energy resources, particularly natural gas, played a key role in fueling the conflict. In order to reduce energy dependence on Russian natural gas, Ukraine sought to diversify the source of energy supply and considered importing LNG from Qatar. This in turn exacerbated the tensions between the two countries (Tass, 2021). This strategic maneuver to lessen dependency on Russian energy imports heightened the existing strain in bilateral relations, ultimately culminating in the Russia-Ukraine military confrontation. In response, Russia sought to assert its influence in the region and maintain control over critical energy transit routes through Ukraine. The disagreement over the terms of the gas transit contract between Gazprom, the Russian state-owned gas company, and Naftogaz, the Ukrainian state energy company, further escalated the crisis (Reuters, 2018).

The resolution of the Gazprom-Naftogaz dispute in December 2019 marked a significant development in the energy dynamics between Russia and Ukraine. The settlement, however, leaned more favorably towards Ukraine, which contributed to Russia's dissatisfaction. The dispute's resolution entailed concessions from Gazprom, potentially involving pricing, transit terms, and other commercial aspects. This outcome hindered Russia's ability to exert its traditional energy leverage over Ukraine, thereby challenging Moscow's influence in the region. Thus, the unfavorable settlement was perceived as a setback for Russia's energy interests and geopolitical influence, prompting a strategic reassessment of its approach towards Ukraine (Arbitration Journal, 2021). This discontent arising from the Gazprom-Naftogaz settlement could be seen as one of the nuanced factors that prompted Russia to attack Ukraine in February 2022. Geopolitical calculations are seldom driven by a single cause; rather, they result from a confluence of various motives and circumstances. The energy element, intertwined with broader geopolitical considerations, could have influenced Russia's strategic calculus. A perceived weakening of Russia's energy leverage, compounded by other geopolitical tensions and perceived threats, might have pushed Moscow towards more aggressive actions to safeguard its interests and reassert control in the region. Thus, the Gazprom-Naftogaz settlement's aftermath may have played a role in the complex tapestry of events that led to the Russia-Ukraine conflict in 2022.

The Russian move to attack Ukraine elicited strong international reactions and had significant implications on the global stage. As the conflict escalated, different countries supported Ukraine by condemning Russia's invasion, and besides sending military equipment and financial aid to Ukraine, in particular western countries imposed economic sanctions that targeted most of Russia's energy sector (Atlantic Council). These sanctions aimed to exert pressure on Russia and demonstrate solidarity with Ukraine, but they also had repercussions on global trade and energy markets. The sanctions caused disruptions in energy flows, affecting not only Russia's oil and gas exports but also creating uncertainties in the global energy supply chain, leading to price fluctuations and concerns about energy security (IEA, 2022).

In sum, the energy implications of the war were profound. European countries, highly reliant on Russian gas supplies, sought to reduce their vulnerability to geopolitical disruptions. This led to accelerated efforts to diversify energy sources and enhance energy security by investing in renewable energy, expanding LNG terminals, and promoting domestic production (IEA, 2023). Additionally, the crisis highlighted the importance of addressing climate change and transitioning away from fossil fuels to reduce dependency on volatile energy suppliers. Consequently, the Russia-Ukraine War of 2022 served as a catalyst for reshaping global energy policies and accelerating the transition towards a more sustainable and resilient energy future.

RUSSIA'S ROLE IN GLOBAL ENERGY MARKETS

Russia holds a prominent position as a major energy exporter in the global market. The country possesses vast reserves of fossil fuels particularly oil and natural gas. To be very specific, Russia has the largest reserves of natural gas in the world and is second only to the US in terms of production. In 2021, the country was recognized as the largest natural gas exporter in the world. As far as oil production is concerned, this country obtained the third place in 2022 after the US and Saudi Arabia (IEA, 2022). With oil reserves of 80 billion barrels, this country ranks sixth and is the largest oil exporter in the world (Slav, 2023). Russia's role as a major energy exporter has also led to complex geopolitical dynamics, as it leverages its energy resources to gain influence on the global stage. The existence of a huge network of energy pipelines in this country, particularly those supplying Europe, grants it significant geopolitical leverage. Russia's energy exports are often used as a tool for advancing its foreign policy objectives, which can lead to tensions and concerns among importing countries about energy security. Moreover, its dominant position in the European gas market has raised debates about the potential risks of over-reliance on Russian gas, driving European countries to seek alternative sources and enhance energy diversification strategies (ECFR, 2023).

In recent years, Russia has also expanded its energy exports to growing markets in Asia, particularly China. For example, as one of the export destination diversification policies, the Power of Siberia gas pipeline was included in Russia's agenda. With the launch of this gas transmission project in late 2019, China became one of Russia's major export destinations. This gas pipeline with a length of 3000 km pumps 22 billion cubic meters of gas to China in 2023, and this capacity is supposed to reach 38 billion cubic meters by 2027. In this connection, the visit of Chinese President Xi Jinping to Russia in March 2023 is noteworthy that encompassed various economic issues, including the construction of a new pipeline called Power of Siberia 2. This proposed project with a length of 2600 km is supposed to transport 50 billion cubic meters of gas annually from Yamal Peninsula in Russia to North China (Reuters, 2023). The pipeline has gained significance due to Russia's stranded gas reserves resulting from the war in Ukraine and disrupted trade with Europe. While negotiations and contract terms are secretive, the existing Russian-Chinese gas contract, particularly the original Power of Siberia pipeline, offers insights into the future pricing formula. The project aims to address Russia's changing energy export strategy and the geopolitical context shaping energy trade in the region (Vakulenko, 2023). This shift in focus towards Asian markets has diversified Russia's customer base and reduced its dependence on traditional European markets, providing the country with additional geopolitical leverage.

Broadly speaking, considering the fossil resources, Russia is among the energy giants in the oil, natural gas and coal global markets. Russia's unique position in terms of oil resources has made this country to have a crucial impact on global oil markets and energy security. According to the IEA, this country is in the third place in terms of oil production, which constitutes 14% of the global oil production. The significance of Russia's oil resources lies not only in meeting domestic energy needs but also in its role as a major exporter, supplying oil to various countries, including those in Europe and Asia, and influencing global oil prices and supply dynamics. In 2021, the country exported about 4.7 million barrels per day worldwide (IEA, 2022).

Another vital energy resource in Russia is natural gas. In 2020, the country's proven natural gas reserves were estimated to be 37.4 trillion cubic meters, giving it a crucial role in meeting both national and international demands. On the other hand, the existence of a large network of gas transmission to the east and west has placed this country in an important geopolitical position. International Energy Agency

Figure 1. Energy exports of Russia (2021)
Source: US Energy Information Administration.

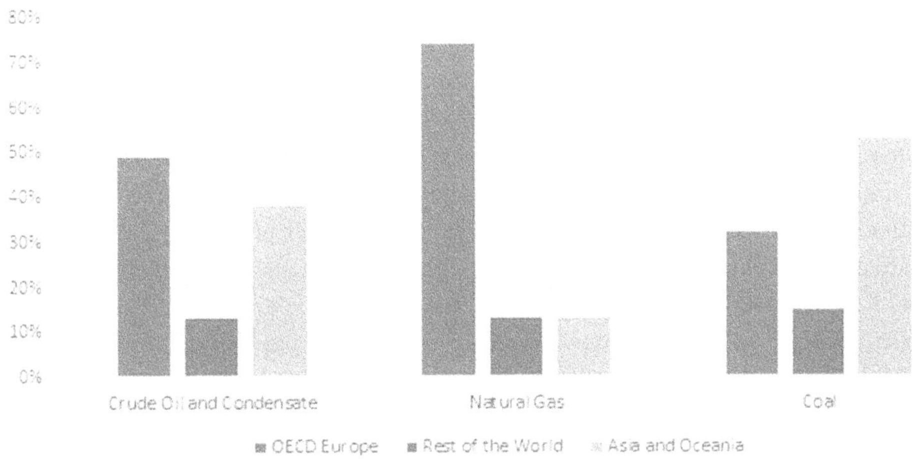

reports that Russia consistently ranks among the top three producers of oil globally, with its production accounting for a significant share of the world's total output (IEA, 2022). In 2021, it was the largest gas-exporting country whose 74% was exported to Europe. Given its substantial energy exports, any disruptions to Russia's energy supply chain can have profound implications for global energy markets and security. All this shows how natural gas reserves in Russia affect the global markets and play an important role as an energy supplier to Europe and Asia.

Apart from oil and gas, Russia also holds considerable reserves of coal, which is another essential energy resource. While the global focus has been shifting towards cleaner energy sources, coal still holds a vital position in Russia's energy mix and economy. Russia possesses the second-largest proven coal reserves globally, trailing only the US. Notably Russian vast deposits of coal located in Siberia and the Far East make its production substantial. This activity contributes to Russia's sixth-ranked position worldwide in both coal production and consumption (Statista, 2022). Despite the push towards reducing carbon emissions and transitioning to renewable energy, coal remains an essential resource for Russia's energy security and economic stability, especially in regions heavily reliant on coal-fired power generation.

Russia's energy partnerships and customer countries play a crucial role in its position as a major energy exporter. Over the years, Russia has established significant energy relations with various countries, particularly in Europe and Asia. The EU is one of the key regions heavily dependent on Russian energy supplies. Russia's natural gas exports to Europe are primarily facilitated through pipelines, with Gazprom, the Russian state-owned gas company, being a major player in these transactions. Prior to the war, Germany, in particular, was one of Russia's largest customers, receiving a substantial portion of its gas imports from Russia (IEA, 2022).

The presented data offers insights into Russia's energy export distribution across various regions, including OECD Europe, Asia and Oceania, and the other parts of the world. Remarkably, energy exports of Russia to OECD Europe are dominated by gas, constituting a substantial 74% of the total exports, followed by crude oil and condensate at 49%, and coal at 32%. In the context of Asia and Oceania, gas continues to play a significant role, accounting for 13% of the exports, accompanied by crude oil and condensate at 38%, and coal at a notably higher percentage of 53%. Conversely, in other parts of the world, the distribution of energy exports appears more balanced, with oil and condensate sharing 13% each, followed by gas at 13%, and coal at 15% (EIA, 2021).

This data analysis highlights several key trends in Russia's energy export strategy. Firstly, natural gas is one of the most important exports of Russia to OECD Europe and Asia/Oceania, which makes this country the most important source of gas supply, indicating its substantial infrastructural and contractual ties in these regions. Secondly, the varied energy composition across regions reflects Russia's adaptability to cater to the energy demands and preferences of different markets. The dominance of coal in the Asia/Oceania region may reflect the energy mix preferences or the industrial requirements of these countries. Lastly, the relatively balanced distribution of energy exports to other parts of the world suggests that Russia aims to diversify its export destinations, reducing reliance on any single market.

Furthermore, Russia's energy partnerships extend beyond Europe and Asia. The country has also engaged in collaborations with other energy-importing countries in the regions other than Europe i.e. Africa and the Middle East. For example, Russia has signed agreements with Algeria to enhance cooperation in the oil and gas sectors (Tass, 2023). These partnerships provide Russia with access to diverse markets and enhance its geopolitical influence in regions critical to global energy supply and demand.

UKRAINE'S IMPORTANCE IN ENERGY TRANSIT

While Russia acts as a major source of fossil energy in the region, Ukraine plays the role of a transit passage for this energy to Europe. The country's strategic geographic location makes it a critical conduit for Russian gas pipelines that supply European markets. The Bratstvo or the Brotherhood pipeline, later replaced by the Soyuz and the Urengoy–Pomary–Uzhhorod pipeline systems, have been instrumental in transporting Russian natural gas to Europe through Ukrainian territory. Ukraine's gas transit dynamics exhibited significant fluctuations during this critical period. On February 28 2023 there was an increase, in the amount of gas flowing from Russia to Europe through the Sudzha route reaching a volume of 43.1 million meters However, a substantial decline of around 28% was observed on May 21, 2022, compared to the preceding day. Hence, the escalation of conflict in 2022 significantly impacted gas transit, as illustrated by the transit of nearly 110 million cubic meters to European nations on February 25, 2022, amid the onset of hostilities. In this situation as of May 2022 two focal points emerged; the Novopskov Border Compressor Station and Sokhranivka gas transit point located in the occupied Luhansk Region. In response to these developments Ukraines Gas Transmission System Operator was forced to declare a force majeure and relinquish control over these facilities. As a result, gas transportation through this route stopped on May 11 2022. The reason behind these changes lies in Gazproms agreement with Ukraine, which stated that 65 billion cubic meters of gas would be transported in 2020 and then a yearly amount of 40 billion meters, until 2024. In 2021, Ukraine played a role in allowing the transportation of 37 billion meters of Russian gas directly to the EU. This route has now become the important channel for Russian gas supply to the EU right after Nord Stream (Statista, 2023). According to the IEA (2021), Ukraine accounted for approximately 40% of all Russian gas exports to Europe in recent years. This dependency on Ukrainian transit has made Europe vulnerable to potential disruptions in gas flows during periods of geopolitical tensions between Russia and Ukraine, as is evident during the current Russia-Ukraine War.

Moreover, Ukraine's transit role has not been limited to Russia-Europe gas exports. The country has also been a key link for Russian gas supplies to several Eastern and Central European nations. The Trans-Balkan pipeline, which runs through Ukraine, has facilitated gas deliveries to countries such as

Figure 2. Ukraine's major natural gas transit pipelines from Russia
Source: EIA.

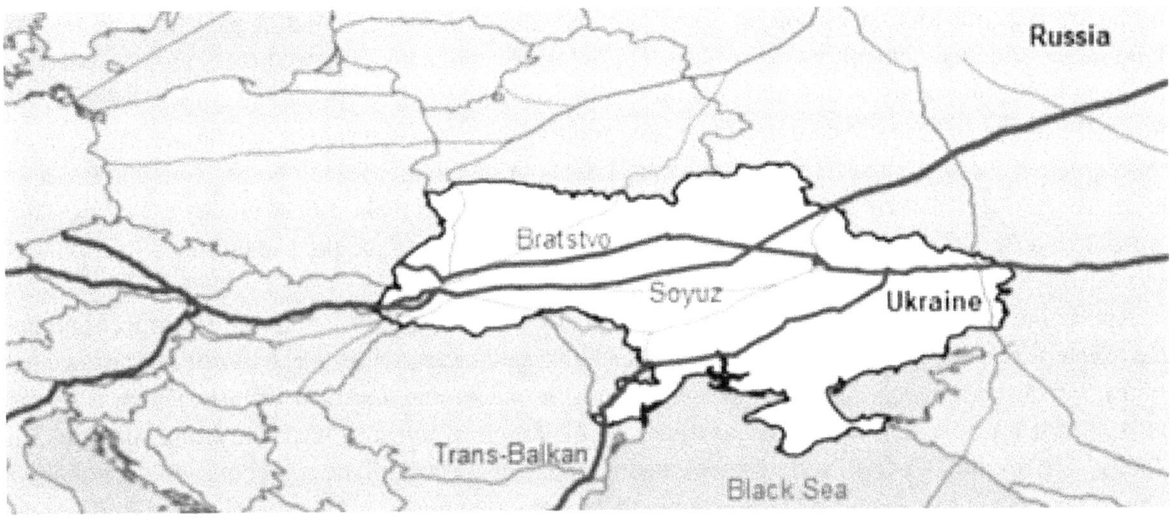

Bulgaria, Greece, and Türkiye. As a result, Ukraine's status as a vital transit country has positioned it at the center of energy security discussions, with European countries seeking to diversify transit routes and decrease their reliance on Ukrainian territory for gas transportation. These concerns have caused the European countries to look for an alternative way to transfer Russian gas, one of which is Nord Stream 2. By bypassing Ukraine, both Russia and the EU aimed to keep their energy economy away from geopolitical disputes (European Parliament, 2021).

The importance of Ukrainian pipelines was brought to the forefront during the 2006 and 2009 Russia-Ukraine gas disputes. This was the time when Russian gas supplies to Europe were seriously disrupted. These incidents raised concerns among European countries about their vulnerability to energy supply disruptions and underscored the need for diversified energy supply routes (Kerr, 2017). The crisis spurred European efforts to explore alternative energy sources, enhance interconnectivity between countries, and invest in LNG infrastructure to reduce dependency on the Ukrainian transit route. Additionally, these incidents led to discussions about modernizing and expanding existing pipeline infrastructure and exploring the potential for bypassing Ukraine altogether, further highlighting the pivotal role of Ukrainian pipelines in shaping European energy policies (Knodt & Kemmerzell, 2022). In more recent times, the 2014 annexation of Crimea by Russia further heightened concerns over energy transit through Ukraine. The annexation led to uncertainties about the future use of the critical gas transit route in the Black Sea region, known as the Trans-Balkan pipeline, which had previously been the prime conduit for Russian gas exports to Europe (Prontera, 2017). This development exacerbated existing geopolitical tensions and raised questions about the long-term reliability of gas supplies to European countries, contributing to discussions on the diversification of energy supplies and routes.

The importance of Ukraine as a transit country that delivers Russian gas to Europe has also intertwined energy dynamics with geopolitical considerations. The ongoing Russia-Ukraine tensions have, at times, translated into disputes over gas transit terms and tariffs. Moreover, conflicts over pricing and transit conditions between Gazprom and Naftogaz, the respective Russian and Ukrainian state energy companies, have led to disruptions in gas exports to Europe, prompting concerns about the reliability of the Ukrainian territory as a transit route. Consequently, the bridging role of Ukraine for Russian gas has not only affected energy security in Europe but also shaped geopolitical dynamics in the region due to the extended reliance on Russian natural gas across various economic sectors, including industrial consumers, regional governments, and other stakeholders. This interconnection underscores how energy has become a critical factor intricately woven into economic interests and broader geopolitical considerations. Additionally, the dependence of core manufacturing industries on Russian energy heightened the urgency for alternative energy sources. The war's impact is not confined to the EU and North America; Russia's ability to seek new markets in China and India demonstrates the global reach of energy concerns. This conflict underscores the multifaceted nature of geopolitical conflicts and their intertwined relationship with energy dynamics on a global scale (Dizikes, 2022).

Amidst the ongoing conflict, Ukraine has strategically engaged in negotiations with European nations and Western powers, leveraging its advantageous geographic location as a key transit hub for energy routes. For instance, according to the Energy Minister of Ukraine, German Galushchenko, it seems unlikely that Ukraine will accept the gas transit deal through its territory with Gazprom. As stated by Oleksiy Chernyshov, CEO of Naftogaz the existing transit deal between the two countries, according to which Gazprom is able export 40 billion cubic meters of gas annually to Europe through Ukraine, and Kiev gets $7 billion, is set to terminate by the end of 2024. In fact, Ukraine wants to become a primary energy source of Europe by exporting its own domestic gas to Europe in the long term (Gavin, 2023).

Moreover, the integrity and stability of Ukrainian pipelines have implications for broader regional security and stability. The ongoing Russia-Ukraine conflict has heightened concerns about the security of critical energy infrastructure in the region. The vulnerability of pipelines to sabotage, cyber-attacks, or direct military actions during times of conflict poses risks to energy flows and can escalate tensions between Russia and Europe (European Parliament, 2021). Ensuring the safety and reliability of Ukrainian pipelines is, therefore, crucial not only for energy security but also for fostering stability in the broader European neighborhood.

IMPACT OF THE WAR ON ENERGY SUPPLIES

The Russia-Ukraine War resulted in significant disruptions in energy production and export from Russia. Particularly the oil and gas sectors are being affected by different measures taken by energy-producing and energy-consuming countries worldwide. Amidst the crisis, Russia experienced shutdown of critical energy infrastructure that affected major oil and gas fields in the country. For instance, the Urengoy-Pomary-Uzhhorod pipeline, a crucial transit route that delivers gas from northwest Siberia Basin to Europe through Ukraine, experienced disruptions due to the hostilities (Reuters, 2022). These disruptions were caused by a combination of sanctions imposed on Russia, deliberate energy supply cut-offs of by belligerents, and ongoing conflicts in Ukraine. One significant event that shook the energy sector was the Nord Stream 2 pipeline explosion in September 2022. In fact, the war in Ukraine acted as a trigger, after which not only European countries, but the whole world, including Russia, paid more attention to energy supplies and the resulting economy.

Likewise, the Togliatti-Odessa pipeline, which used to transport up to 2.5 million tons of ammonia annually from Togliatti in western Russia to Ukraine's Pivdennyi port on the Black Sea for global export, has been inactive since the beginning of the war in February of the previous year. This extended period of inactivity has had repercussions for both Russia's ammonia exports and Ukraine's access to

Figure 3. Fall and rise of Russian crude oil exports (2022-2023)
Source: Bruegel

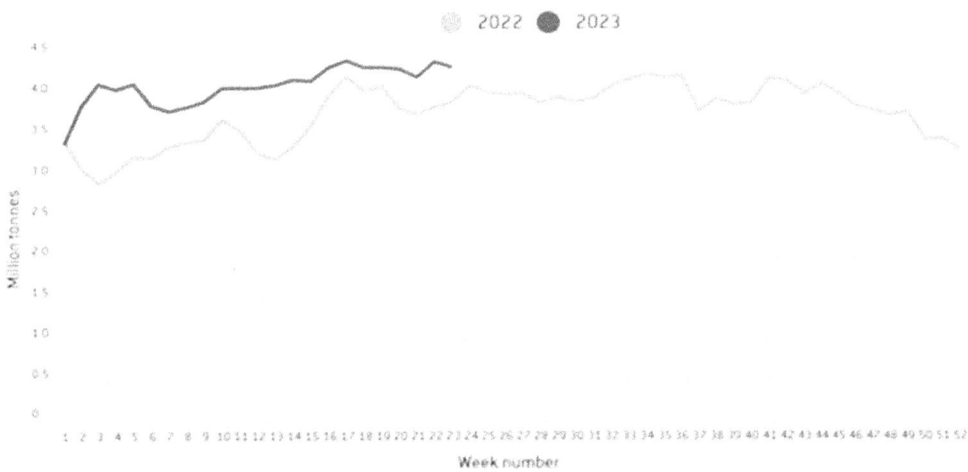

this critical energy resource. In addition to that, the crisis also impacted gas supplies to neighboring countries beyond Europe. As tensions mounted in the Black Sea region, concerns arose about potential disruptions to gas flows to Türkiye, which receives a significant portion of its gas from Russia via the Turk Stream pipeline (Ibid, 2022). As a result, one can argue that the geopolitical tensions in the region brought serious concerns, after which countries turned to review their energy policies in order to reduce political and economic vulnerabilities.

The conflict also had implications on global oil markets. As a global prominent oil producer, Russia experienced disruptions in its oil exports because of the war. The uncertainty surrounding energy supplies from Russia led to fluctuations in oil prices and increased volatility in the global oil market. This further exacerbated concerns about energy security and supply stability, with some countries seeking alternative sources of oil to mitigate potential risks associated with disruptions in Russian oil exports.

As a result of these ups and downs in Russian exports, crude oil prices experienced sharp fluctuations as traders closely monitored developments in the region (Bloomberg, 2022). Geopolitical tensions and uncertainties over the duration and intensity of the conflict led to increased speculative trading, further contributing to market volatility. However, due to the US release of strategic reserves and increased production of oil by OPEC countries, the rise in the price of oil has been temporary. The sharp hike in the global crude oil exceeded $120 per barrel last year, but now it reached pre-war price range about $80 per barrel.

Compared to last year, in the first half of 2023, natural gas production in Russia shows a 13% decrease. The main reason for that was Moscow's decision to stop the country's gas exports to most European countries. During this period, Russia produced 319.3 billion cubic meters of gas. This production decline began last year when Russia significantly reduced gas output following the cessation of most pipeline exports to Europe amid the conflict over Ukraine. In June, Russia's gas production was down 8.6% year-on-year, with this decrease narrowing in magnitude due to export constraints already being in place in 2022. The Energy Ministry's historical calculation method excludes burned-off or flared volumes. The major contributor to the production drop is Gazprom PJSC, accounting for over 20% of the reduction. Novatek PJSC, the second-largest gas producer, decreased output by 1.9%. Rosneft PJSC, a non-exporter of gas, increased its production by 44%, primarily due to specific projects. This overall drop in production and exports caused a 46% decline in Russia's budget revenue from main gas taxes in comparison to the previous year (Bloomberg, 2023).

By learning from the disruptions of energy production and export in Russia, the energy policy of many countries in the world experienced a big change. In order to reduce the effects of geopolitical crisis, the consuming countries either sought to change the geographical source of fossil energy supply, or they put investment in renewable energies on the agenda with a long-term strategy. It also sparked renewed interest in accelerating the transition towards renewable and sustainable energy sources to reduce dependence on volatile fossil fuel exporters. However, the transition to renewables has not been a generally accepted option for European countries. As one effect of the conflict has been an increase in fossil fuel usage, some consumer countries has sought alternative energy sources to compensate for the shortfall in gas supplies. The uncertainty surrounding gas availability and the escalating prices prompted some countries to turn to coal and oil as readily available substitutes for meeting their energy demands (EIA, 2022). For example, during the winter months when demand for heating is high, European countries increased coal consumption, leading to a surge in carbon emissions (Bloomberg, 2022). The use of fossil fuels to bridge the gap left by reduced gas supplies highlights the challenges in ensuring energy security during geopolitical conflicts in an interconnected global energy market.

The disruptions in gas supplies also affected the operations of gas-dependent industries, such as power generation and manufacturing. As a result of this trend, the demand of businesses and industries for other alternative energy sources increased, among which oil and coal are at the top of the list. For example, European industries and power plants that previously used natural gas faced fuel shortages, compelling them to switch to coal-fired power generation to maintain electricity supply stability (Tan, 2022). This increased reliance on coal not only raised environmental concerns but also intensified competition in the coal market, leading to higher prices and further impacting global energy markets.

The global LNG market also experienced repercussions. With Europe seeking alternative sources of natural gas and competing for LNG imports, LNG prices surged to record highs. However, the increased reliance on LNG, being a globally traded commodity, has rendered European energy prices more susceptible to disruptions in supply, encompassing disturbances originating from distant regions (Financial Times, 2023). This surge in prices had implications for energy markets worldwide, impacting countries that relied on LNG imports for their energy needs.

GEOPOLITICAL RAMIFICATIONS OF THE CRISIS

International responses to Russia's attack on Ukraine in 2022 were swift and assertive. In response to the war, other countries adopted four different positions, which include condemning Russia; political, military and economic support for Ukraine; neutrality policy; and support for Russia against Ukraine. Given that the West is a primary belligerent of the war, one of the most significant measures taken by westerners is the imposition of sanctions on Russia, targeting key sectors of its economy, including the energy sector. In this regard, the EU and the US came to the fore in applying economic pressure on Russia (BBC, 2022). These sanctions aimed to limit Russia's access to global financial markets, block trade with certain companies and individuals, and freeze assets belonging to Russian officials and oligarchs. Importantly, the energy sector was a major target of these sanctions.

Specifically, the western bloc targeted Russia's oil and gas industry, which is vital to its economy and a key source of revenue. The sanctions limited the ability of Russian energy companies, such as Gazprom and Lukoil, to access international markets and conduct business with Western companies. Furthermore, restrictions were placed on the delivery of energy-related technologies and equipment that were intended for Russia, thereby hampering the country's oil and gas production capabilities (European Council, 2023). To counter Russian oil revenue, Western allies also established an oil price cap, preventing Russia from receiving more than $60 per barrel of crude oil. However, this cap might not be the primary reason for the current oil price decline; the EU oil embargo on Russian imports plays a more significant role.

On the other hand, the EU targeted the Russian gas sector with a plan to cut gas from Russia by two-thirds within a year. The financial system of Russian banks was also affected by global financial sanctions on this country, and as a result, its banks were excluded from the international SWIFT system. However, on the contrary, China, India and Türkiye enhanced their energy deals with Russia, increasing purchases of Russian oil, accounting for 70% of Russian crude flows by sea. These countries have taken advantage of lower-priced Russian oil and have sometimes conducted transactions in their local currencies.

As mentioned before, in 2021, Russia exported half of its crude oil to European countries. However, the amount dropped remarkably after the war when the most hawk countries of Europe such as UK decreased their Russian energy imports in 2022. Despite efforts to diversify energy sources, some European countries like the Slovak Republic and Hungary remain heavily reliant on Russian energy. Before the war in 2021, the EU was importing 40% of its natural gas from Russia, but just 6 months after the war in August 2022, this amount dropped to around 17%. The UK's reliance on Russian gas dropped from 4% in 2021 to none. European countries are turning to LNG imports from producers like the US and Qatar, although the limited number of LNG terminals in Europe remains a challenge for ensuring consistent supply (BBC, 2023).

The impact of these sanctions was significant. Russia, heavily reliant on oil and gas exports, saw its energy revenues decline sharply. The restrictions on energy-related technologies also affected the maintenance and expansion of Russia's energy infrastructure, leading to concerns about the country's ability to meet its energy export commitments. However, the sanctions also had broader global implications. The reduction in Russian oil and gas exports affected global energy markets and contributed to higher oil and gas prices. In response to the sanctions, Russia attempted to find alternative markets for its energy exports, particularly in Asia. Albeit, the shift was not without challenges, as Russia faced competition from other major energy exporters like the United States and OPEC (Reuters, 2022).

With Russia being a key energy exporter and the conflict disrupting energy flows, OPEC countries recognized the opportunity to increase their market share and influence. OPEC's response to the crisis was a calculated effort to capitalize on the situation and potentially gain a stronger foothold in the global energy market. As Russia faced international sanctions and its energy exports were affected, OPEC members sought to increase their oil production to meet the growing demand and fill the void left by Russia's reduced exports. For countries like Saudi Arabia, this presented an opportunity to assert their role as a reliable and stable supplier of oil during times of geopolitical uncertainty (Wilson, 2022).

However, OPEC's act of increasing crude oil production was a temporary measure after the war. The cartel's highest post-war crude oil production was seen in August 2022, when it produced 29.65 million barrels of oil per day. Compared to August 2021, in which 26.705 million barrels were produced per day, this amount shows an increase of 2.945 million barrels. If this amount is compared with a month before the war, it is an increase of 1.705 million barrels. OPEC's decision to reduce oil production by

Figure 4. OPEC's total crude oil production (August 2021 – January 2024)

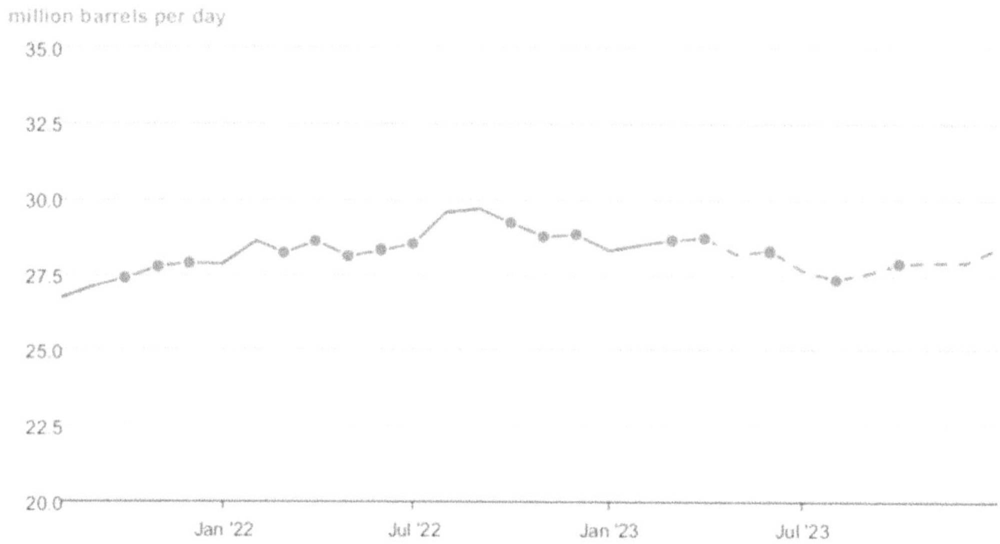

2 million barrels per day in October 2022 in order to support oil prices caused disputes between Saudi Arabia and the United States, and despite Washington's efforts, Riyadh did not give up on its decision to reduce oil production. OPEC+ countries' decision again in June 2023 to extend the reduction until 2024 has made the oil producing giants more aligned with Russia (Hernandez, 2023; EIA, 2023).

Source: EIA (2023).

One of the important consequences of the war in Ukraine in terms of the energy market relates the US Strategic Petroleum Reserves. In order for the US to be able to alleviate the shock of the global energy market and especially European markets, it entered the scene and accelerated the release of its strategic reserves, which had started at the end of 2021. As a result, the US stood in a position to export more energy to international markets, reducing the dependence of some countries on Russian supplies. The Biden administration took steps to boost domestic oil production and increase LNG exports to Europe, thereby offering an alternative to Russian gas imports and supporting European energy security (EIA, 2022). Additionally, Washington actively engaged in diplomatic efforts to facilitate the movement of energy supplies and ensure that vital energy transit routes, such as the Druzhba pipeline, remained operational during the crisis (Reuters, 2022).

Hence, European countries have taken steps to reduce reliance on Russian energy products such particularly oil, gas and coal, driving the deployment of low-carbon technologies such as renewables and heat pumps. However, some countries temporarily turned to carbon-intensive coal due to gas price hikes. The crisis disproved fears of widespread shortages, partly due to the fortunate mild weather that reduced heating demand. While Europe's energy transition had positive effects, the crisis inflicted severe economic pain. Industries like fertilizer production, reliant on natural gas, faced a 70% decline. Energy price hikes triggered by the crisis rippled through global economies, raising input costs and impacting food prices, particularly in poorer nations. The shift away from Russian crude and the G7-imposed "price cap" in Europe redirected Russian oil exports toward China and India. The change in Europe's gas supply mix has permanently altered global gas trade and energy markets, disadvantaging Russia. The International Energy Agency (IEA) revised downward its projections for Russian gas and oil exports due to market shifts (German, 2023).

Although the initial oil price surge retreated, Europe's pivot away from Russia has bolstered the geopolitical significance of US LNG exports, crucial for filling the void left by Russian supplies. The IEA's recent oil market analysis identifies Russia as one of the two "wildcards" dominating the global oil market in 2023, alongside China.

Overall, the war triggered responses from major energy players like OPEC and the US, influencing their energy policies and market strategies. OPEC members saw an opportunity to enhance their market position, while the USA sought to strengthen energy security for itself and its allies, especially in Europe, amid geopolitical tensions and supply disruptions caused by the conflict.

DOUBLE POLICY: DIVERSIFICATION OF SOURCES AND ROUTES

The European countries, which were badly shaken by the war in Ukraine, increased their efforts to reduce the dependence on Russian energy and enhance energy security. The conflict highlighted the vulnerabilities of relying heavily on a single energy supplier and underscored the importance of diversifying energy sources and supply routes. To achieve decreasing Europe's reliance on Russian energy, several strategies and initiatives were adopted by these countries. The most important strategies are summarized as follow:

Investment in Renewable Energy: European nations accelerated their investments in renewable energy sources that include wind, solar, and hydroelectric power. These efforts aimed to increase the share of renewables in the energy mix and decrease reliance on traditional sources of energy exemplified by fossil fuels mainly natural gas from Russia (European Commission, 2022). Countries like Germany and Denmark, for instance, are among the leading nations who are expanding their renewable energy capacity, enabling them to reduce their dependency on gas imports.

Expansion of LNG Infrastructure: European countries invested in expanding their LNG infrastructure to diversify gas supply sources. The development of new LNG terminals and regasification facilities allowed Europe to import LNG from a more diverse range of global suppliers, including the US and Qatar. Nevertheless, by 2030, the extensive capacity of LNG terminals might experience substantial underuse. Predictions indicate the potential for an unused capacity reaching 250 bcm, surpassing more than half of the EU's total gas consumption in 2021. This potential underutilization arises despite differing demand projections for LNG in 2030, ranging between 150 bcm and 190 bcm (IEEFA, 2023). In spite of that, these facilities offer flexibility in sourcing gas from various parts of the world, reducing Europe's reliance on pipeline gas from Russia.

Promotion of Domestic Gas Production: Some European countries focused on increasing their domestic gas production to bolster energy security. For instance, countries like the Netherlands and the United Kingdom explored opportunities to boost their own gas production from domestic reserves (Lockwood & Devenish, 2022). By relying more on domestic sources, these countries aimed to reduce their dependence on imported Russian gas.

These strategies collectively aimed to enhance Europe's energy security and resilience, minimizing the potential impacts of geopolitical crises on energy supply and prices. The recognition that energy security is closely tied to political stability and economic prosperity has led European countries to accelerate the implementation of policies intended at diversification of energy sources and reduction of dependency on Russian energy.

More specifically, LNG has emerged as a crucial component of the energy security strategy for many countries due to its ability to be transported over long distances and stored for future use. The increased use of LNG terminals and facilities allowed European nations to access gas from a variety of global suppliers, reducing their reliance on pipeline gas from Russia. For instance, countries like Poland and Lithuania invested in LNG infrastructure, enabling them to import gas from diverse sources and bolstering their energy security (European Commission, 2022).

Moreover, the post-war period saw an uptick in LNG trade and investment globally. Countries like the US, Australia, and Qatar expanded their LNG production capacities to meet the growing demand for LNG in Europe and other regions. The increased supply of LNG provided more options for countries to secure reliable energy sources and mitigate the potential risks associated with geopolitical disruptions in gas supplies. According to CEDIGAZ data, in 2022, global LNG trade increased 5% compared to 2021 with an average of 51.7 Bcf/d, thus hitting a record high. This surge was driven by expanded liquefaction capacity in the US and increased LNG demand in Europe. As for Moscow, the implication was unavoidable as it was able to substitute exports of Russian pipelined natural gas (EIA, 2023).

On the other hand, several alternative pipelines and energy corridors were proposed to bypass Ukraine and enhance energy security in the region. Albeit some of these projects had been launched before the war, interruption of Ukrainian routes made these projects at the forefront of policymakers:

Nord Stream 2: The EU and Russia, fed up with the Ukraine's unstable geopolitical situation, have been looking for a more peaceful route for their energy trade. Therefore, Nord Stream 2 gas pipeline project was designed to connect Russian energy directly to Germany. This pipeline is actually alternative to Nord Stream 1 to transfer energy through the Baltic Sea to Europe, bypassing the Ukraine soil. However, this project faced controversies and opposition from some European countries and the US due to concerns over increased dependency on Russian gas and potential energy security risks. However, the blowing up of the Nord Streams 1 and 2 pipelines in last September has sparked a controversy between Russia and the West. This act, which resulted in significant damage to an underwater pipeline transporting Russian gas to Germany, has raised suspicions and debates about its origin and potential political implications. The incident has led to speculations, investigations, and accusations, contributing to the ongoing tensions between Russia and Western countries (Camut, 2023).

Turk Stream: Turk Stream is another gas pipeline project that began operating in 2020, delivering Russian gas to Türkiye and further into Southeastern Europe. The pipeline has the capacity to supply gas to countries in the region and offers an alternative route that avoids Ukraine (TurkStream, 2023). In fact, the vital role of this gas pipeline in enhancing diversification and ensuring energy security in the Balkans and Southern Europe cannot be underestimated.

Southern Gas Corridor (SGC): It is a major infrastructure project designed to transport gas from Azerbaijan to Europe through a series of pipelines, including the Trans-Adriatic Pipeline (TAP) and the Trans-Anatolian Natural Gas Pipeline (TANAP). The SGC diversifies Europe's gas supply by providing an alternative route from the Caspian region, bypassing Russia and Ukraine (Yorucu & Mehmet, 2018).

These alternative pipelines and energy corridors are part of a broader strategy to enhance energy security and reduce geopolitical risks in the aftermath of the Russia-Ukraine War. By diversifying sources and routes, countries aim to ensure a stable and resilient energy supply, mitigating the impact of future geopolitical conflicts on their energy markets.

As part of their efforts to supply energy from alternative sources, some European countries have considered investment on offshore wind energy. European countries with access to coastlines have been exploring the potential of offshore wind farms to harness the strong and consistent wind resources in the region. The expansion of offshore wind energy can offer a reliable and indigenous source of electricity, reducing dependence on energy imports from volatile regions (Soukissian et al., 2023). For instance, countries like the United Kingdom, Denmark, and Germany have already made significant strides in offshore wind projects, and the crisis further incentivized investment in this sector.

Another area of opportunity is solar energy. Despite being less prevalent in some European countries due to the region's climate, solar energy can still have a vital effect on diversifying the energy mix and enhancing energy security. Advancements in solar technology, coupled with falling solar panel costs, have made solar energy more attractive and economically viable. Moreover, the crisis has ignited greater attention towards energy storage technologies as a means to guarantee a consistent and dependable provision of renewable energy. Energy storage systems, including batteries and pumped hydro storage, play a significant role in reducing the intermittent characteristics of renewable sources such as wind and solar power. These technologies enable the storage of surplus energy during times of excess generation and discharge it when demand exceeds supply, ensuring a consistent power supply. Countries have been exploring energy storage initiatives to integrate more renewable energy into their grids and enhance grid stability.

CONCLUSION AND RECOMMENDATIONS

The Russia-Ukraine War of 2022 had profound and lasting implications for global energy security. It exposed the vulnerability of energy supply chains to geopolitical disruptions, particularly in regions heavily reliant on Russian oil and gas. This war made different countries to pay special attention to the diversification of the geographical supply source and the type of the energy source. In order to ensure energy security in the long term, both states and industries have taken different measures and revised their existing energy policies.

While diversification of suppliers and transit routes are the main agenda for consumer countries, the accelerated shift towards renewable energy sources and the decoupling from fossil fuels are more rational option. The conflict served as a wake-up call for many countries, especially in Europe, to prioritize long-term solutions. A change in the supplier or transit route can fulfill the immediate needs of consumer countries, but as geopolitical considerations are always ripe to trigger a conflict, this option sounds imperfect. The development and adoption of clean energy technologies to decrease dependence on fossil fuel imports from politically unstable regions offers a rational option. Governments and businesses have been investing more in renewable energy projects including solar, wind and hydropower, to bolster energy security and minimize the potential impact of future geopolitical disruptions.

The war also prompted increased investments in energy infrastructure to facilitate the diversification of energy supply routes. Several European countries have been expanding their LNG import terminals to accommodate more diversified sources of natural gas from global markets. This effort aims to reduce the dependence on pipeline gas from Russia and enhance flexibility in energy sourcing.

Furthermore, the Russia-Ukraine War led to a reevaluation of regional energy partnerships and cooperation. Countries in Europe and beyond have been seeking to strengthen energy alliances and cooperation agreements with more stable and reliable suppliers. For instance, the EU has been engaging in energy dialogues and partnerships with energy-rich countries like Norway, Algeria, and Qatar to enhance energy security and mitigate risks associated with geopolitical uncertainties.

In sum, the Russia-Ukraine War of 2022 had far-reaching consequences for global energy security. The conflict underscored the importance of diversifying energy sources, transitioning away from fossil fuels, and investing in resilient energy infrastructure. It also prompted greater regional cooperation and partnerships to ensure stable and secure energy supplies. These long-term implications will continue to shape energy policies and strategies worldwide, as nations work towards building a more sustainable and secure global energy future.

In light of the discussion of this chapter, some recommendations can be presented so that governments and industries can insure themselves against damages caused by geopolitical crises:

Energy Diversification and Investment in Renewable Sources: The energy crisis following the Russia-Ukraine War highlighted the vulnerability of countries heavily reliant on Russian gas supplies. As a response, energy consuming countries should accelerate their efforts to expand their energy resources and diminish reliance on fossil fuels. Commitment to investing in renewable energy technologies like solar, wind, and hydropower should gain momentum as nations aim to bolster their energy stability and decrease carbon emissions. Transitioning to renewable energy not only improves resilience against geopolitical disruptions but also aligns with global climate goals, contributing to the de-carbonization of the energy sector.

Expansion of LNG Infrastructure: To bolster energy security, energy consuming countries should increase investment in expanding LNG terminals and infrastructure. By increasing their capacity to import LNG, nations can access a broader range of global gas suppliers, reducing the dominance of a single supplier like Russia and enhancing competition in the energy market. This move can provide more flexibility in sourcing energy, mitigate supply disruptions, and potentially lead to lower energy prices for consumers.

Regional Energy Cooperation and Solidarity: One of the consequences of the Russia-Ukraine War is its role in underscoring the importance of regional energy cooperation. Particularly, European countries explored ways to strengthen energy solidarity within the EU, creating mechanisms to back member states in times of crisis. However, some EU members such as Hungary and Germany have been reluctant to cut Russian energy import. In order to have an uninterrupted and smooth flow of energy, there should be a common mechanism through which shared gains are secured. Though, initiatives such as the Energy Union, aimed at ensuring a secure, sustainable, and interconnected energy market within the EU, gained renewed attention, by pooling resources and collaborating on energy projects, countries can increase their collective energy security and reduce vulnerability to external pressures.

Geopolitical Realignment and Energy Partnerships: The energy crisis following the Russia-Ukraine War prompted some countries to reevaluate their geopolitical alliances and energy partnerships. Efforts to diversify energy suppliers and strengthen ties with non-traditional gas-exporting nations gained prominence. For example, some European countries explored closer energy cooperation with countries in the Eastern Mediterranean and the Caspian region, potentially tapping into new gas resources. This geopolitical realignment may have broader implications on the global energy market and reshape regional dynamics.

REFERENCES

Arbitration Journal. (2021, February 11). *The Naftogaz - Gazprom Saga, Debunking Myths about the Arbitration Awards*. Retrieved from https://journal.arbitration.ru/analytics/the-naftogaz-gazprom-saga-debunking-myths-about-the-arbitration-awards/

Atlantic Council. (n.d.). *Russia Sanctions Database*. Retrieved from https://www.atlanticcouncil.org/blogs/econographics/russia-sanctions-database/

BBC. (2022, March 1). *Ukraine Conflict: EU and US Impose Sanctions over Invasion*. Retrieved from https://www.bbc.com/news/world-europe-60506681

BBC. (2023, January 26). *Russia Sanctions: What Impact Have They Had on its Oil and Gas Exports?* Retrieved from https://www.bbc.com/news/58888451

Bloomberg. (2022, March 1). *Brent Oil Gains, US Crude Falls amid Market Volatility*. Retrieved from https://www.bloomberg.com/news/articles/2022-03-03/oil-extends-gain-as-investors-weigh-strain-of-ukraine-conflict

Bloomberg. (2022, March 3). *Europe's Gas Prices Head for Highest since 2018 with Russia Sidelined*. Retrieved from https://www.bloomberg.com/news/articles/2022-03-04/europe-s-gas-prices-head-for-highest-since-2018-with-russia-sidelined

Bloomberg. (2022, March 4). *Russia Gas Output Down 13% in First Half after EU Exports Cut*. Retrieved from https://www.bloomberg.com/news/articles/2023-07-26/russia-gas-output-down-13-in-first-half-after-eu-exports-cut#xj4y7vzkg

Camu, N. (2023, June 13). *CIA Warned Ukraine Not to Blow Up Nord Stream, Reports Say*. Retrieved from https://www.politico.eu/article/cia-warned-ukraine-not-to-blow-up-nord-stream-reports-pipeline/

EIA (US Energy Information Administration). (2022). *Short-Term Energy Outlook*. Retrieved from https://www.eia.gov/outlooks/steo/

EIA (US Energy Information Administration). (2023, July 5). *Global Liquefied Natural Gas Trade Volumes Set A New Record in 2022*. Retrieved from https://www.eia.gov/todayinenergy/detail.php?id=57000

European Commission. (2021). *European Energy Security Strategy*. Retrieved from https://www.europarl.europa.eu/factsheets/en/sheet/142/european-energy-security-strategy

European Commission. (2022). *European Green Deal*. Retrieved from https://ec.europa.eu/info/strategy/priorities-2019-2024/european-green-deal_en

European Commission. (2022, May 5). *Inauguration of Gas Interconnection between Poland and Lithuania*. Retrieved from https://commission.europa.eu/news/inauguration-gas-interconnection-between-poland-and-lithuania-2022-05-05_en

European Council. (2023, June 26). *EU Sanctions against Russia Explained*. Retrieved from https://www.consilium.europa.eu/en/policies/sanctions/restrictive-measures-against-russia-over-ukraine/sanctions-against-russia-explained/

European Parliament. (2021). *Security of Gas Supply in the EU*. Retrieved from https://www.europarl.europa.eu/factsheets/en/sheet/66/security-of-gas-supply-in-the-eu

Financial Times. (2023, August 10). *Gas Price Spike Underscores Europe's Vulnerability to Global Energy Shocks*. https://www.ft.com/content/452f2664-fd70-4f91-b8a2-1a208f72c4e4

Gavin, G. (2023, July 12). *Ukraine Warns Key Russian Gas Supply to Europe Will Be Cut*. Politico. Retrieved from https://www.politico.eu/article/ukraine-warns-it-wont-negotiate-new-russian-gas-transit-deal/

German, B. (2023, January 23). *Ukraine War Upended Energy Markets Forever*. Axios. https://www.axios.com/2023/01/23/ukraine-war-russia-energy-markets

Hernandez, J. (2023, June 4). *Saudi Arabia Cuts Oil Production again to Shore Up Prices — This Time on its Own*. NPR. https://www.npr.org/2023/06/04/1180056198/saudi-arabia-oil-opec

IEEFA. (2023, March 21). *Over Half of Europe's LNG Infrastructure Assets Could Be Left Unused By 2030*. Retrieved from https://ieefa.org/articles/over-half-europes-lng-infrastructure-assets-could-be-left-unused-2030#:~:text=Europe's%20LNG%20terminal%20capacity%20could,at%20the%20end%20of%202022

International Energy Agency (IEA). (2022 November 16). *Frequently Asked Questions on Energy Security*. Retrieved from https://www.iea.org/articles/frequently-asked-questions-on-energy-security

International Energy Agency (IEA). (2022). *Oil Market and Russian Supply*. Retrieved from https://www.iea.org/reports/russian-supplies-to-global-energy-markets/oil-market-and-russian-supply-2

Irina, S. (2023, April 24). *Top 10 Countries With Largest Oil Reserves*. Retrieved from https://oilprice.com/Energy/Crude-Oil/Top-10-Countries-With-Largest-Oil-Reserves.html

Kardaś, S. (2023, May 4). *Keeping the Lights On: The EU's Energy Relationships since Russia's Invasion of Ukraine*. European Council on Foreign Relations. Retrieved from https://ecfr.eu/publication/keeping-the-lights-on-the-eus-energy-relationships-since-russias-invasion-of-ukraine/

Kerr, J. (2017). *Introduction to Energy and Climate: Developing a Sustainable Environment*. CRC Press. doi:10.1201/9781315151885

Knodt, M., & Kemmerzell, J. (2022). *Handbook of Energy Governance in Europe*. Springer Nature. doi:10.1007/978-3-030-43250-8

Kuzio, T. (2002). Ukraine: State and Nation Building. Routledge.

Lockwood, M., & Devenish, A. (2022, April 28). *Dutch and British Responses to the Gas Crisis*. Retrieved from https://ukerc.ac.uk/news/dutch-and-british-responses-to-the-gas-crisis/

Peter Dizikes. (2022, December 13). *Energy, War, and the Crisis in Ukraine*. Retrieved from https://news.mit.edu/2022/energy-war-and-crisis-ukraine-1213

Prontera, A. (2017). *The New Politics of Energy Security in the European Union and Beyond: States, Markets, Institutions*. Taylor & Francis. doi:10.4324/9781315555126

Reuters. (2023, March 22). *Explainer: Does China need more Russian gas via the Power-of-Siberia 2 pipeline?* Retrieved from https://www.reuters.com/business/energy/does-china-need-more-russian-gas-via-power-of-siberia-2-pipeline-2023-03-22/

Reuters. (2018, February 28). *Ukraine's Naftogaz Claims $2.56 Billion Victory in Gazprom Legal Battle.* Retrieved from https://www.reuters.com/article/us-ukraine-crisis-russia-gazprom-idUSKCN1GC2Z8

Reuters. (2022a, March 1). *Russia Says No Need for Western Banks, but Will Adjust.* Retrieved from https://www.reuters.com/markets/europe/russias-lukoil-says-oil-and-gas-sector-targeted-by-sanctions-2022-03-10/

Reuters. (2022b, March 10). *European Gas, Coal and Power Prices Hit Record Highs.* Retrieved from https://www.reuters.com/business/european-gas-coal-power-prices-hit-record-highs-2022-03-10/

Russian Crude Oil Tracker. (2023, July 27). *Bruegel | The Brussels-based Economic Think Tank.* Retrieved from https://www.bruegel.org/dataset/russian-crude-oil-tracker#:~:text=In%202021%2C%20Russia%20produced%20540,comprising%2013%25%20of%20global%20exports

SoukissianT.O'HaganA. M.AzzellinoA.BoeroF.Brito e MeloA.ComiskeyP.GaoZ.HowellD.Le BoulluecM. MaisondieuC.ScottB.TedeschiE.MaheriA.PennockS. (2023). European Offshore Renewable Energy: Towards a Sustainable Future. Zenodo. https://doi.org/ doi:10.5281/ZENODO.7561906

Statista. (2023, March 2). *Gas Inflow for Transit from Russia to Europe in Ukraine from February 1, 2022 to February 28, 2023, By Entry Point.* Retrieved from https://www.statista.com/statistics/1308480/ukraine-russian-gas-transit-volume-by-route/

Statista. (2022, November 21). *Coal Mining in Russia – Statistics and Facts.* Retrieved from https://www.statista.com/topics/7049/coal-mining-in-russia/#topicOverview

Stern, J. (2007). The 2006 Russian–Ukrainian Gas Crisis: Implications for Europe. *Oxford Review of Economic Policy*, *23*(2), 226–240.

Stern, J., & Zafirakis, D. (2010). The 2009 Russia–Ukraine Gas Dispute: Implications for EU-Russia Gas Relations. *International Affairs*, *86*(4), 887–909.

Tan, H. (2022, June 21). *Europe is Drawing Up Emergency Plans to Switch Back to Coal after Russia Cuts Natural-Gas Supplies.* Business Insider. Retrieved from https://www.businessinsider.com/europe-energy-emergency-plans-coal-power-russia-cuts-gas-supply-2022-6

Tass. (2023, July 27). *Russia, Algeria Agree on Extension of Russian Companies' Participation in Gas Projects.* Retrieved from https://tass.com/economy/1653073

Tass. (2021, November 21). *Ukrainian Government Claims it is at 'Energy War' with Russia.* Retrieved from https://tass.com/world/1360437

US Energy Information Administration (EIA). (2021, February 12). *Top World Oil Producers, Exporters, and Consumers.* Retrieved from https://www.eia.gov/todayinenergy/detail.php?id=47776

US Energy Information Administration (EIA). (2023, June 16). *Russia.* Retrieved from https://www.eia.gov/international/analysis/country/RUS

US Energy Information Administration (EIA). (2023, July 2). *Europe is A Key Destination for Russia's Energy Exports.* Retrieved from https://www.eia.gov/todayinenergy/detail.php?id=51618

Vakulenko, S. (2023, April 18). *What Russia's First Gas Pipeline to China Reveals About a Planned Second One.* Carnegie Endowment for International Peace. Retrieved from https://carnegieendowment.org/politika/89552

Wilson, T. (2022, October 25). Saudi Arabia Willing to Pump More Oil if Global Energy Crisis Worsens. *Financial Times.* Retrieved from https://www.ft.com/content/8598d326-2989-4468-9bcd-a9a905ca4f67

Yorucu, V., & Mehmet, O. (2018). *The Southern Energy Corridor: Turkey's Role in European Energy Security* (Vol. 60). Springer International Publishing. doi:10.1007/978-3-319-63636-8

Chapter 8
China's Energy Conundrum: Navigating Through Crises, Policy Responses, and Global Impact

Mohamad Zreik
https://orcid.org/0000-0002-6812-6529
Sun Yat-sen University, China

ABSTRACT

China's energy dilemma is examined in this chapter, along with its historical and geopolitical settings. China's energy initiatives have a major impact on international energy stability because of the country's position as the world's largest energy consumer. The energy challenges caused by fast industrial growth and dependency on fossil fuels are discussed after a brief history of China's energy sector is presented. China's reaction to these challenges is dissected, including the measures it has taken to diversify its energy supply, increase the use of renewable energy, boost energy efficiency, and get involved in global energy governance. The chapter analyzes the effects of these policies on China's economy, social stability, environment, and foreign relations, both at home and abroad. The chapter wraps up with a glimpse into the future of China's energy plans. A sustainable and secure global energy system is the goal of the analysis, and it can help guide stakeholders in the right direction.

1. INTRODUCTION

The energy sector in China is a complex web of tradition, innovation, and explosive development. China's influence on the international energy market is significant because it is the largest energy consumer and the world's second largest economy (Zreik, 2023a). An ever-increasing need for energy is being driven by the country's large population and fast rising economy, necessitating the development of a diverse and sustainable energy mix (Akhtar et al., 2022). According to the International Energy Agency (IEA) data for 2019, China consumed approximately 3.9 billion tons of oil equivalent in primary energy, with coal accounting for 57.7% of this consumption (Clark & Zhang, 2022).

DOI: 10.4018/979-8-3693-0440-2.ch008

China used to get most of its energy from coal mined within the country. However, the country's industrialization and urbanization required a switch to cleaner energy sources due to the environmental problems linked with coal usage. As a result, the nation shifted its focus to investigating and perhaps investing in alternative energy sources like oil, natural gas, nuclear power, and various renewables (Wang, Sun, & Iqbal, 2022).

Coal, oil, natural gas, hydroelectric electricity, nuclear power, and renewable sources like wind and solar all factor into China's current energy mix (Wang et al., 2023). Coal is still an important element of China's energy mix, but the government has taken major steps in recent years to lessen reliance on it, in part because of concerns about the country's impact on the environment (Wang, Sun, & Iqbal, 2022).

China is now the largest coal producer, consumer, and importer, as well as a major oil and natural gas user and importer. It's leading the way toward a cleaner energy future by investing heavily in renewable energy and manufacturing renewable energy technologies.

However, China's energy sector faces its fair share of obstacles. China's energy industry is facing serious challenges, including the need to meet the rising energy demands of the country's expanding middle class, maintain energy security, cut greenhouse gas emissions, and move toward a low-carbon economy. The way China handles these issues and implements its energy policies will have far-reaching effects on the energy landscape worldwide.

Due to the country's outsized position in both energy use and production, China's energy policies carry considerable weight on a worldwide scale. Energy costs, investment trends, and the rate at which countries embrace renewable energy are all affected by China's policies to meet its domestic energy demands, battle climate change, and secure its energy supplies (Stern & Xie, 2023).

China consumes a lot of energy, therefore its domestic energy decisions, including whether to keep using coal or switch to renewables, have an outsized effect on global energy output, demand, and carbon emission levels. Its energy policies, likewise, have the potential to influence global developments. For instance, China's heavy spending on renewable energy has helped bring down the price of such technology around the world, speeding up their widespread acceptance (Gielen et al., 2019).

China is a major oil importer, and its oil consumption and procurement policies have the potential to affect prices worldwide (Liadze et al., 2023). The country's ties to oil-producing countries might also affect international affairs. It is possible that global energy trade patterns and alliances will change as a result of China's efforts to ensure its own energy security through the diversification of supply sources and foreign relationships.

This chapter will look deeper into the nuanced nature of China's energy environment, the nature of its energy crises, and the measures the country has put in place to deal with them. It will examine the development of China's energy sector across time, address the difficulties caused by the country's rapid industrialization and its disproportionate reliance on fossil fuels, and evaluate China's policy responses.

Implications for international relations and the global energy landscape, as well as China's economic development, social stability, and environmental sustainability, will be explored in this chapter. By looking ahead at where China's energy policies are headed, it is hoped to provide light on how the country's energy initiatives may affect international energy security and geopolitics in the years to come.

2. HISTORICAL CONTEXT OF CHINA'S ENERGY SECTOR

2.1. Discovery of Oil and Rise of Industrialization

The development of China's energy industry is inextricably linked to the country's modern industrialization. Coal is the obvious starting point for any discussion of China's energy history. The discovery of oil, however, radically altered the energy environment and sparked a major surge in industry (Zou et al., 2016).

For centuries, coal was China's main source of energy for both residential and commercial use. Although China drilled its first oil well in the late 19th century, oil didn't become a major player in the country's energy landscape until the 1950s (Hou, 2020). China's march toward oil as a vital energy source may be traced back to 1959, when the large Daqing oilfield was discovered. China's industrialization was propelled by the country's increasing exploitation of its oil reserves (Hou, 2020).

China's fast economic growth and urbanization in the second half of the 20th century propelled the country into the ranks of the world's leading industrial powers. China has become one of the world's greatest energy consumers as its industrialization has led to a sharp increase in demand for power. Demand for fossil fuels increased because of the prevalence of energy-intensive industries like manufacturing, steel, and construction (Zreik, 2021).

This industrial expansion was driven, in great part, by homegrown means. China's massive coal reserves and substantial oil production have been key to the country's rapid economic growth (Zou et al., 2016). The rapid rate of industrialization, however, has also resulted in an increased reliance on fossil fuels, particularly coal and oil, which has created severe environmental issues and an energy security conundrum. China's energy sector has seen significant changes over the past few decades, resulting in a number of crises and prompting the implementation of new regulations designed to help the country weather the storm.

2.2. Transformations in the Energy Landscape

China has shown tremendous flexibility and strategic acumen in its energy sector restructuring. To ensure that its expanding energy needs could be supplied in a sustainable and secure manner, China was forced to regularly examine its energy policies as the 20th century progressed (Bown, 2021).

The first major shift occurred when it became clear that continuing to rely on coal posed serious risks to the environment and the reliability of our energy supply. To offset its reliance on coal, China began looking into and investing in alternative fossil fuels including oil and natural gas. This shift was facilitated by the discovery of large domestic oil and natural gas reserves, which decreased the economy's reliance on coal while adding new energy options.

The worldwide energy shortages of the 1970s also caused a significant paradigm shift. China began investigating nuclear and hydroelectric power possibilities after realizing the danger of relying too much on fossil fuels (Kanwal et al., 2022). The environmental problems caused by burning fossil fuels and the energy security concerns caused by a strong reliance on imported energy both have potential solutions that might be implemented with the help of these alternative energy sources.

However, China's shift toward renewable energy sources has likely been the most consequential change. China, in the early 21st century, began a program of strong investment in renewable technologies like wind and solar power in response to the dual concerns of climate change and energy security.

China is now at the forefront of renewable energy production and technology because to the country's decision to focus on this area (Yu, 2023).

Changes like this show how China is adapting to its changing energy demands and obstacles. What we see now is largely the result of their efforts; the country's energy landscape is more diverse than ever, with a gradual but steady trend toward low-carbon sources.

2.3. Introduction to the Emergence of Energy Crises

China's rapid economic growth in the late 20th and early 21st centuries, powered predominantly by fossil fuels, has been both a marvel and a source of concern (Sachs, 2015). As the country transformed into a global manufacturing hub, its demand for energy surged dramatically. By 2010, China surpassed the United States as the world's largest energy consumer (Cui, Peng, & Zhu, 2015).

In the years 2000-2010, China's energy consumption doubled, leading to frequent power blackouts in major cities like Beijing, Shanghai, and Guangzhou (Qinhua & Chung, 2016). Imported energy dependency grew, with oil imports, for example, rising from 1.5 million barrels per day in 1995 to over 9 million barrels per day by 2018 (Zreik, 2023b). China's reliance on global fossil fuel markets exposed its economy to price fluctuations. For instance, in 2008, global crude oil prices peaked at $147 a barrel, burdening the Chinese economy and its energy-intensive industries (Heinberg & Fridley, 2016). China's coal-dominated energy production led to significant logistical challenges. Coal transport by rail became congested, leading to coal shortages in key power plants.

Environmental issues, though crucial, were symptoms of this broader energy crisis. The urgency to address this multifaceted energy crisis led to a series of reforms in China's energy policy, a shift towards renewable energy, and a reconsideration of energy consumption patterns. Significant changes in China's energy sector have not prevented the country from facing a slew of energy crises. Rapid industrialization, urbanization, population growth, and economic development all contributed to an extraordinary surge in the demand for energy, which in turn precipitated the aforementioned crises (Sun, 2020).

China's massive population and economy mean that it uses a lot of energy, and this has put a strain on the country's energy infrastructure. A variety of economic, environmental, and geopolitical challenges have culminated in what might be considered energy crises due to the overreliance on coal and, later, oil and natural gas.

The rising ecological consequences of coal use were the first warning sign of an imminent energy crisis. Significant air and water pollution arose from the intensive use of coal as a primary energy source, causing substantial environmental and public health concerns (Yang & Liu, 2019). Because of the severity of the pollution problem, the government had to reconsider its energy regulations and look into more eco-friendly options.

Second, because local energy supply couldn't keep up with the soaring demand brought on by growing industrialization and urbanization, more and more energy had to be imported. When it comes to oil, China went from being a net exporter to an importer of energy (Taylor, 2021). Concerns about energy security and economic fragility were sparked by the change, especially in light of the recent ups and downs in oil prices and geopolitical tensions throughout the world.

Finally, China's energy issue was given a new dimension by the growing awareness of climate change and the role of greenhouse gas emissions in exacerbating it. Since China is the world's greatest contributor to greenhouse gas emissions due to its heavy reliance on coal, it has been under increasing pressure to curb these emissions (Lin & Guan, 2023). The combination of these variables has led to a complicated energy crisis in China.

3. EXAMINATION OF CHINA'S ENERGY CRISES

3.1. Industrial Growth and Middle-Class Expansion

China's energy difficulties have been exacerbated by the country's tremendous industrial boom and increase of the middle class over the past few decades. Rapid industrialization boosted the economy and improved people's standard of life, but at the expense of a massive increase in energy consumption (Zreik, 2022).

Manufacturing, building, and steel production—all of which use a lot of energy—grew rapidly as China's economy developed. These sectors drove China's economic expansion and expansion in energy use (Xu et al., 2021). Since domestic energy production couldn't keep up with demand, more and more energy, especially fossil fuels like coal and oil, had to be imported.

China's energy demand was also significantly affected by the growth of the country's middle class, which is now one of the largest in the world. The middle class has become more consumerist as a result of rising incomes and shifting priorities. Energy consumption has increased due to the rising demand for consumer items, vehicles, and better housing (Zhao et al., 2020).

The growth of cities to house the expanding middle class has led to an increase in energy use. Large amounts of energy were used during the construction of new buildings, transportation infrastructure, and utilities. More people living in metropolitan areas means a higher demand for electricity to power their homes' heating, cooling, and other electrical appliances (Huo et al., 2022).

Furthermore, the need for healthier environments and cleaner air increases in tandem with the expansion of the middle class. As a result, the government is under more pressure than ever to cut emissions and wean itself off of coal, further complicating the energy crisis. The rise of China's industrial sector and the size of its middle class has contributed to the country's economic success, but it has also exacerbated the country's environmental and energy security problems.

3.2. Rising Energy Demand

The growing energy needs of the country play a major role in China's current energy crisis. China's energy infrastructure and resources are under immense strain due to the country's growing industrialization, urbanization, and economic growth.

China's rising energy demand can mostly be attributed to the country's rapid industrialization. Energy-intensive industries like steel, cement, and chemical production grew rapidly as China became a global manufacturing powerhouse (Jenkins, 2022). These sectors' heavy reliance on fossil fuels, especially coal, contributed to a dramatic increase in energy demand.

At the same time, urbanization in China is a major reason for the increase in energy consumption. The need for energy to fuel urban centers has skyrocketed as millions have relocated from the countryside to the city in quest of better prospects. New building and transportation infrastructure, combined with increased appliance use in urban households, has significantly increased the need for power.

Furthermore, there have been major shifts in energy consumption patterns as a result of China's rapidly expanding economy and rising population standards. The rising purchasing power of the middle class has fueled increased demand for products and services that are heavy consumers of energy.

As a result of these developments, China's overall energy demand has skyrocketed, far exceeding the country's ability to meet this demand with its own resources. As a result, China has shifted from being a net exporter to an importer of energy, creating new sources of worry about the country's energy security and economic precarity (Liu et al., 2021).

Given the reliance on fossil fuels and the associated greenhouse gas emissions, meeting the increasing energy demand also presents substantial environmental challenges. The complexity of China's energy crisis is exacerbated by these factors, highlighting the importance of thorough and effective governmental responses.

3.3. Over-Reliance on Fossil Fuels

The overuse of fossil fuels, especially coal, has played a major role in China's energy challenges. China faces significant economic, environmental, and geopolitical concerns as a result of its reliance on coal as the world's largest consumer of coal and oil as the world's second-largest consumer of oil (Boyd & Ufimtseva, 2021).

China's massive population has relied heavily on coal as a cheap and abundant energy source since the country's industrialization began. This coal reliance, however, has had serious ecological effects. Air pollution in China is mostly caused by burning coal, which is a major cause of illness and death every year (Fan, He, & Zhou, 2020). Moreover, China is under pressure to minimize its carbon footprint in the face of climate change as it is the greatest worldwide emitter of greenhouse gases, mostly from coal combustion.

While not as significant as coal, the country's reliance on oil has also brought significant issues. Due to the country's rapid industrialization and rising demand from its burgeoning middle class, local oil supply has been unable to keep up with consumption. This has led to China being one of the world's largest buyers of oil (Hu et al., 2022). China's growing reliance on imported oil raises energy security worries because of the country's vulnerability to supply disruptions, price volatility, and geopolitical conflicts.

China's energy difficulties are complex due to the interplay between environmental concerns, energy security concerns, and international pressures linked with an over reliance on fossil fuels. In response to these threats, the Chinese government has enacted a number of policies to broaden the country's energy base, boost efficiency, and advance renewable sources of power.

3.4. Environmental and Greenhouse Gas Challenges

China's energy problems are exacerbated by the country's reliance on coal, which has led to severe environmental and greenhouse gas concerns. China's energy consumption patterns have far-reaching effects on the environment, including on air quality, water resources, and their contribution to global climate change.

China's energy use is a major contributor to one of the most obvious environmental problems: air pollution. Pollutants such sulfur dioxide, nitrogen oxides, and particulate matter are produced when coal is burned in power plants and factories. Smog and acid rain, both of which are made worse by these pollutants, are also bad for people's health (Saraswat, Sharma, & Saraswat, 2022). Air pollution is a major problem in China, especially in the country's cities, where it has been linked to thousands of premature deaths and a huge economic cost.

China's energy policies also have an effect on the country's water supply. Water scarcity is a problem in some areas due to the high demand for it from industries like coal mining and power generation. Coal waste disposal also poses a threat to aquatic ecosystems and human health due to water contamination (Wang et al., 2020).

China's impact on global warming as a result of its energy need is one of the gravest problems for the planet. China's contribution in climate change mitigation is crucial because it is the world's greatest producer of carbon dioxide. The burning of fossil fuels, especially coal, is responsible for the great bulk of China's greenhouse gas emissions (Zhao et al., 2022). China is under pressure to make the switch to a more sustainable and low-carbon energy system due to rising worldwide emphasis on climate change and domestic environmental and public health issues.

3.5. Importance of Energy Security in China

China's energy dilemma has shifted the focus of the country's energy policies and goals to the concept of energy security. As China's economy and population have expanded, so has the importance placed on maintaining a steady, reliable, and cost-effective energy supply.

The problem of China's energy security is intricate and multifaceted. It includes not just the accessibility of energy supplies physically, but also the cost-effectiveness of energy, the dependability of energy supply, and the sustainability of energy sources.

Concerns over China's energy security have been heightened by the country's rapid rise in energy consumption and its heavy reliance on fossil fuels. China faces the difficulty of servicing its increasing energy consumption as the world's top energy consumer. The country increasingly relies on foreign supplies of energy to complement domestic output, particularly oil and natural gas (Caineng, Songqi, & Qun, 2020). Concerns have been raised concerning the stability and reliability of China's energy supply due to its reliance on imported energy, which leaves it vulnerable to supply disruptions and price volatility on international energy markets.

Moreover, China's environmental and public health problems, as well as international criticism over its carbon emissions, have resulted from the country's reliance on coal, a highly polluting and carbon-intensive energy source. Because of these challenges, China must now seek other, greener, and more long-term energy sources to ensure its energy security. China has invested heavily in domestic energy production and infrastructure, engaged in international energy diplomacy, and shifted toward renewable energy sources in large part because of the country's commitment to energy security (Liu et al., 2021).

4. ANALYSIS OF CHINA'S ENERGY POLICIES

4.1. Diversification of Energy Sources

In recent years, China has strategically diversified its fossil fuel supply sources beyond its traditional reliance on the Middle East to bolster energy security. This shift has been motivated by factors such as geopolitical tensions, supply uncertainties, and the desire for stable energy prices. As a result, China has intensified its energy ties with Central Asia, Russia, Africa, and South America, establishing pipelines and making investments in oil infrastructure and exploration projects. Furthermore, China has ramped up its domestic oil and gas exploration efforts, exemplified by developments in the Sichuan Basin's shale gas resources. This diversification strategy not only ensures a steady energy supply for China's burgeoning economy but also mitigates potential geopolitical risks and price volatilities. China's diversification of its energy sources is one of the primary tactics it has adopted in response to the energy crises and the accompanying environmental, economic, and geopolitical challenges. This plan's objectives include not only ensuring a steady and consistent energy supply, but also lessening the strategy's energy footprint.

Reducing China's dependency on coal has been a primary goal of the country's diversification plan, which has prioritized the use of natural gas and renewable energy (Zhang et al., 2023). Natural gas is viewed as a 'bridge fuel' that can aid China in making the switch from coal to more environmentally friendly energy sources. It can be utilized for power generating, household heating, and transportation, and produces fewer greenhouse gases and air pollution than coal does. China has made substantial investments in natural gas infrastructure and tried to ensure reliable imports via pipelines and liquefied natural gas (LNG) contracts in order to expand the amount of natural gas in its energy mix (Wang, Kong, & Li, 2022).

China's strategic partnerships with Russia have become increasingly prominent in its energy diversification efforts. A testament to this is the Power of Siberia pipeline, which began operations in 2019. This multi-billion-dollar gas pipeline stretches over 3,000 kilometers, connecting Siberian gas fields to northeast China, ensuring a direct and stable energy supply for the next 30 years. Such collaboration reinforces the two nations' mutual interests in energy security and economic development. Furthermore, China has been reaching out to the Pacific islands, tapping into their vast potential of underexplored offshore oil and gas reserves. For instance, China's engagement with Papua New Guinea in liquefied natural gas projects showcases its approach to securing energy ties in the Pacific region. These partnerships not only provide China with alternate energy sources but also hold geopolitical significance, strengthening its influence and ties in these regions.

Recognizing the vulnerabilities of over-reliance on Middle Eastern oil, China has made significant strides in diversifying its fossil fuel supply sources. A prime example is its deepening energy ties with Russia. By the end of 2019, the Power of Siberia gas pipeline became operational, facilitating a 30-year deal for Russian gas supplies to China, further cementing energy relations between the two neighbors. Additionally, China has invested heavily in oil fields in Russia's Far East and Siberia (Mehmet & Yorucu, 2020; Pepe, 2020). As per data from the Chinese Ministry of Commerce, China's investment in the oil fields of Russia's Far East and Siberia reached nearly $10 billion by the end of 2020 (Chen & Galkin, 2023). Beyond this northern neighbor, China has expanded its energy diplomacy to the Pacific islands. Countries like Papua New Guinea have seen significant Chinese investments in natural gas exploration and infrastructure development (Doaemo et al., 2021). These strategic shifts underscore China's proactive approach to safeguarding its energy security by broadening its supply chain and reducing dependency on any single region.

However, renewable energy promotion has been central to China's efforts to diversify its energy supply. China has surpassed the United States as the leading investor in clean energy sources like wind, solar, and hydro (Li & Han, 2023). Feed-in tariffs, subsidies, and mandated market shares are just a few of the policies the government has put in place to encourage the use of renewable energy. As a result, renewable sources now account for a much larger percentage of China's power generation than they did a decade ago, even if they still make up a very small fraction of the country's overall energy mix (Mastoi et al., 2022).

Also, China has been putting a lot of money into nuclear power as a long-term answer to its energy and environmental security concerns. The low-carbon base-load power provided by nuclear energy can supplement the unreliable output of renewable sources like wind and solar (Zhang, Andrews-Speed, & Perera, 2015).

4.2. Promotion of Renewable Energy

The promotion of renewable energy sources is a major manifestation of China's commitment to diversifying its energy sources. China's renewable energy sector has experienced unprecedented growth thanks to the country's proactive policies and increased investment, making it the top investor in renewable energy globally. China's National Energy Administration reported that in 2020, the country added 120 GW of wind and solar power capacity, making it a global leader in renewable energy installation (Pan et al., 2023).

China has made great strides in the development of renewable energy sources, particularly wind and solar power. The Chinese government has set lofty goals for the use of renewable energy sources like wind and solar, and it has backed these goals up with strong legislative support. This consists of subsidies to manufacturers and developers of renewable energy systems as well as feed-in tariffs that ensure set, premium pricing for renewable power. As a result of these regulations, the number of wind and solar farms has exploded (Liu, 2019).

In addition, China has poured a lot of money on hydroelectric electricity. China considers hydro power to be an important component of its energy mix, and the country is home to the world's largest hydroelectric power station, the Three Gorges Dam (Cheng, Shi, & Yu, 2021). Hydroelectric development, while providing a source of renewable, low-carbon power, has been mired in social and environmental controversy due to its impact on local ecosystems and the relocation of residents (Lo, 2021).

Bioenergy and geothermal power are two other renewable energy sources that China is investigating (Gyamfi, Bein, & Bekun, 2020). However, these are in the preliminary research and development stages at the present time.

Despite the progress, renewable energy in China still confronts a number of obstacles. Wind and solar power generation can be unpredictable, so there is a pressing need for energy storage solutions and grid integration concerns. Even while wind and solar technologies have become increasingly cost-competitive in recent years, their long-term viability has been called into question as the government moves to eliminate subsidies.

China's efforts to boost renewable energy have far-reaching consequences for the world beyond the country's borders, where they help provide energy security and promote environmental sustainability. China's policies and practices in the renewable energy sector have an outsized impact on worldwide renewable energy trends, international climate change efforts, and the dynamics of the global energy market because of the country's position as a pioneer in these areas.

4.3. Enhancement of Energy Efficiency

Improving energy efficiency is also an important part of China's approach to the energy crisis. China has begun a number of steps targeted at enhancing efficiency across diverse sectors in an effort to meet its energy consumption, reduce greenhouse gas emissions, and boost economic competitiveness.

Most of China's energy goes toward the manufacturing sector, thus the government has mandated energy-saving targets for big businesses and encouraged the use of energy-saving equipment. One such program is the "Top-10,000 Program," which mandates that the largest energy consumers in the country meet certain energy efficiency standards (Xiang et al., 2021). China's 13th Five-Year Plan (2016-2020) set a target to reduce its energy intensity by 15% compared to 2015 levels. By the end of 2019, China had achieved a reduction of approximately 13.5% (Liu et al., 2022).

Energy efficiency regulations for residential buildings have been passed to cut back on the amount of power used for heating, cooling, and household appliances. The "Green Lights Program" and similar initiatives educate the public on the benefits of energy-efficient lighting products and work toward eliminating the usage of inefficient incandescent bulbs (Wang et al., 2021).

The energy efficiency of China's transportation systems has also improved greatly. It has encouraged the widespread use of electric vehicles and plug-in hybrids, as well as established fuel economy regulations for cars and trucks.

The administration has also prioritized increasing electricity sector efficiency. Updating power facilities, encouraging cogeneration, and launching demand-side management initiatives are all part of the effort to lower peak demand for electricity.

As a result of these initiatives, China has reduced its energy intensity (energy consumption as a percentage of GDP), but there are still many obstacles to overcome (Shen & Lin, 2021). A few examples are the need for more consistent investment in energy-efficient technologies and the requirement for stricter enforcement of efficiency requirements.

Improving energy efficiency aids China in solving its energy problems and aids international initiatives to reduce greenhouse gas emissions. For countries facing similar energy and environmental difficulties, China's experiences and lessons learnt through its energy efficiency measures can be invaluable.

4.4. Participation in International Energy Governance

China is becoming more active in international energy governance as the country realizes its importance in the worldwide energy market. Its policies and practices in the energy sector have international implications.

China has participated in international energy organizations like the International Energy Agency (IEA) and the Organization of the Petroleum Exporting Countries (OPEC) since it is the world's largest energy consumer and a major importer of oil and natural gas. China has extended its involvement with the IEA, even though it is not a full member, by taking part in a number of its programs and activities (Downie, 2020). China's engagements with OPEC have increased as the country works to ensure the reliability of its oil imports and increase its influence in the international oil market (Yu et al., 2023).

China has participated in the International Renewable Energy Agency (IRENA) and the United Nations Framework Convention on Climate Change (UNFCCC) in addition to more conventional energy forums. A growing readiness to participate in international climate governance and a desire to move toward a low-carbon economy are reflected in China's pledges under the Paris Agreement (Papadis & Tsatsaronis, 2020).

Additionally, China has both led and participated in regional energy cooperation platforms. China, Russia, and Central Asian countries may work together on energy issues thanks to the Shanghai Cooperation Organization (SCO).

China's involvement in global energy regulation, however, is not without obstacles. It has been a difficult process for the country to strike a balance between protecting its oil interests, easing environmental worries, and easing geopolitical tensions. As China becomes more involved in international energy administration, it will have far-reaching effects on both energy security and geopolitics. China's influence on global energy trends and standards is projected to increase as the country continues to manage its energy challenges and shape its energy policies.

4.5. Evaluation of Policy Effectiveness and Impact

China's energy policies have had a tremendous influence and impact, from increasing the country's use of renewable energy to its involvement in global energy governance. There have been beneficial outcomes from utilizing many energy sources. China is the world's biggest investor in renewable energy due to its huge growth of wind, solar, and hydroelectric electricity. Natural gas is being actively pursued as a 'bridge fuel' to help the country transition away from coal, but at a slower rate than renewables (Aleluia et al., 2022). However, problems still exist, such as the high cost and unreliability of natural gas and the difficulty of integrating renewable energy sources into the grid.

Overall, China's efforts to improve energy efficiency have paid off, resulting in a significant drop in energy intensity. Industries, homes, and the transportation sectors have all been encouraged by the sector-specific efficiency targets to use more energy-efficient practices and technologies. However, there are still issues to be concerned about, including the implementation of these standards, regional differences, and the ongoing investment in energy-efficient technologies.

Chinese involvement in international energy governance has increased the country's clout in the development of energy policies and procedures around the world. Energy security and climate change mitigation are two areas where it has actively participated through its involvement with conventional energy groups and climate change forums. However, it faces persistent difficulties in striking a balance between its domestic energy interests and its foreign commitments.

Energy policy in China have an international impact. Energy markets, emission trends, and international attempts to combat climate change are all significantly impacted by China's energy policies because of the country's position as the world's largest consumer and emitter of greenhouse gases (Jia, 2023). Its energy use, for example, has an effect on both international energy prices and the policies of energy-exporting countries due to the country's investment in renewable technologies.

5. IMPLICATIONS OF CHINA'S ENERGY CRISES AND POLICIES

5.1. Influence on Economic Growth

The impact on China's economic development of the country's energy crises and the government's reactions to such crises is substantial. Energy, the driving force behind all economic activity, is intrinsically linked to China's development path.

China's rise to the ranks of the world's largest economies may be attributed in large part to the country's huge industrial boom during the previous few decades, which in turn was fueled by coal (Al Shaher & Zreik, 2022a). Over-reliance on fossil fuels, however, has led to unpredictability in the energy supply, environmental degradation, and climate change hazards, all of which endanger long-term economic expansion. China has made a conscious decision to move toward a more diverse and sustainable energy mix in light of these dangers (Wang, Sun, & Iqbal, 2022).

Renewable energy and energy efficiency improvements in particular have been singled out as potential new growth drivers for the economy. Jobs and capital have been created and invested heavily in the renewable energy sector. By fostering renewable energy sources like wind and solar power, as well as alternative fuels like electric vehicles, the 'green economy' has grown in recent years, helping to ensure the long-term health of both economies and ecosystems.

Moreover, there have been significant economic benefits from increased energy efficiency in a number of different industries. The cost of energy services has decreased, industrial competitiveness has increased, and technological innovation has been sparked in part due to energy efficiency techniques that have increased productivity in energy consumption (Gitelman, Kozhevnikov, & Visotskaya, 2023).

There are consequences for China's economic development from the country's growing role in global energy regulation. It helps China's energy-intensive economy by securing reliable energy imports and influencing global energy prices. However, this strategy leaves China vulnerable to geopolitical threats and the unpredictable nature of global energy markets, both of which threaten the country's economic stability. Moreover, there are financial hurdles to overcome as we shift to a more diversified, low-carbon energy system. Energy transition costs, the elimination of fossil fuel businesses, and the requirement for infrastructure modifications all fall under this category.

5.2. Impact on Social Stability

There are serious consequences for societal stability from China's energy challenges and the policies implemented to address them. Energy, a fundamental component of modern life, affects many dimensions of social welfare, including the quality of people's lives, their ability to earn a living, and their health.

While the rapidly rising middle class has contributed to improved living standards, it has also put enormous strain on the energy supply, which could lead to shortages and price fluctuations. If energy becomes more difficult to get or more expensive for low-income households, this can worsen socioeconomic inequalities.

The over use of fossil fuels in China has also led to significant environmental and public health problems. Coal combustion is a major source of air and water pollution, which has led to an increase in public health issues and contributed to growing social unrest (Sonone et al., 2020). Therefore, the Chinese government's drive toward cleaner energy sources is not only good for the environment, but also essential for protecting the health of the population and maintaining social harmony.

The shift to a "green economy" in China will have far-reaching effects on the country's social fabric. One positive effect of research into alternative energies and energy-saving technology has been the creation of new employment opportunities, which in turn has boosted wage and salary levels (Khan et al., 2022). However, steps to manage this transition and help affected people are necessary because a transition away from fossil fuels may cause job losses in traditional energy businesses like coal mining.

China's involvement in global energy regulation has a knock-on effect on the country's social stability. China's involvement in global energy politics can make the country vulnerable to external shocks and instabilities, but it also helps keep domestic energy costs and living standards stable.

5.3. Contribution to Environmental Sustainability

There are far-reaching and nuanced policy responses to China's energy challenges that have ramifications for environmental sustainability. China has a significant impact on international climate change mitigation efforts as the world's greatest emitter of greenhouse gases, largely as a result of its vast use of coal.

China's over use of fossil fuels has caused severe environmental damage, including pollution of air and water supplies, erosion of soil, and related health problems (Azam, Khan, & Ali, 2023). In light of these environmental consequences, the Chinese government has launched ambitious efforts to switch to a low-carbon energy system.

Renewable energy promotion is a major pillar of these efforts. Not only has China begun to lessen its reliance on coal, but it has also laid the groundwork for a future in which renewable, nonpolluting energy sources take center stage. The transition to renewable energy sources is essential to lowering greenhouse gas emissions and halting global warming.

Also important in fostering environmental sustainability are China's measures aimed at improving energy efficiency. These regulations help reduce carbon emissions and lessen the effects of climate change by encouraging more efficient energy use and curbing unnecessary energy consumption (Wang & Zhang, 2022). All industries, homes, and vehicles can benefit from this efficiency shift because of the energy and pollution savings they can achieve.

However, there are several obstacles on the path to a sustainable energy future. Transitioning away from fossil fuel industries requires careful management of issues including the intermittent nature of renewable energy sources, the need for substantial changes to energy infrastructure, and the like. Despite these obstacles, China's energy policies aimed at achieving environmental sustainability are an essential part of the worldwide fight against climate change.

5.4. Changes in International Relations

The energy issues and the government's response in China have significantly altered the country's diplomatic standing. China is the greatest consumer of energy in the world, and its energy policies have far-reaching effects on the country's contacts with and connections to other nations and international organizations (Coenen et al., 2021).

China has strengthened its ties with energy-producing countries and areas due to its growing reliance on imported energy, especially oil and natural gas. Numerous energy trade agreements and infrastructure initiatives, including as the Belt and Road Initiative, have contributed to the strengthening of ties between China and nations in the Middle East, Russia, and Central Asia (Al Shaher & Zreik, 2022b).

As a result of its policy of energy diversification and increased investment in renewable energy technologies, China has emerged as a world leader in the clean energy sector. Because of its prominence in the industry, it is able to affect global energy markets, prices, and regulations, especially those pertaining to the shift to renewable sources.

China's prominence on the global scene can also be attributed to its work in international energy governance. China plays a pivotal role in shaping global energy security and climate change policies through its interactions with global energy organizations like the International Energy Agency and the Organization of the Petroleum Exporting Countries and its commitments under climate change agreements like the Paris Agreement (Yao, 2022).

However, China's expanding role in the international energy market is not without controversy. China's international relations are complicated by, among other things, competition for energy supplies, tensions over energy infrastructure projects, and divergent positions on climate change obligations.

6. FUTURE TRAJECTORY OF CHINA'S ENERGY POLICIES

6.1. Predicted Path of Energy Policies

It is difficult to foresee the future course of China's energy policies due to the interplay of numerous economic, social, environmental, and geopolitical elements. Nonetheless, China is committed to a future in which its energy system is both sustainable and secure.

China will likely increase diversification of its energy sources to deal with its energy shortages. China's energy mix will remain heavily reliant on fossil fuels, notably coal, but the percentage of renewable energy sources is predicted to increase dramatically. Accelerating progress in wind, solar, hydro, and nuclear energy generation will be the result of both technology advances and encouraging governmental policies.

China's energy policies will continue to place a premium on conserving resources. The energy intensity of China's industrial, residential, and transport sectors is expected to continue decreasing thanks to sector-specific efficiency objectives and the rising use of cutting-edge technologies.

It's also expected that China's participation in global energy governance will increase. China will keep forging strategic energy relationships and influencing global energy policies and practices as it works to safeguard its energy imports and lessen the effects of volatility in the global energy market.

China's future energy plans will be influenced by the country's pledge to meet its national and international obligations to reduce emissions of greenhouse gases. According to the Global Carbon Atlas, in 2019, China's carbon dioxide emissions reached 10.06 gigatons, accounting for roughly 28% of global CO2 emissions (Alaloul et al., 2022). More ambitious climate goals, the elimination of high-carbon energy sources, and massive investment in low-carbon technology and green sectors are all things to anticipate. However, there will be obstacles to overcome on the path to a more sustainable and secure energy system, such as dealing with the social implications of the transition, improving the energy infrastructure, and striking a balance between economic growth and environmental sustainability.

6.2. Potential Global Impact

The trajectory of China's energy policies has important implications for global energy security and geopolitics because China is the world's largest energy consumer and a prominent player in the global energy market.

Energy security in the world would benefit greatly from a Chinese energy system that is both sustainable and secure. Reducing worldwide demand for fossil fuels as a result of China's continued diversification of energy sources and promotion of renewable energy and efficiency may lessen price pressures and volatility in international energy markets.

Furthermore, China's dedication to a green transition can encourage global adoption of renewables because of the country's position as a global leader in renewable energy technologies. China's efforts in renewables have already had a global impact, bringing down the price of technology like solar panels and wind turbines and making them more accessible to people all over the world.

China's energy policies may also have a global impact on efforts to reduce the effects of climate change. China's attempts to reduce emissions through deployment of renewable energy and energy efficiency are crucial for global efforts to control temperature rises because China is the greatest greenhouse gas emitter.

China's energy policy and the country's rising influence in international energy governance have the potential to alter the global balance of power. China plays a pivotal role in shaping the future of global energy governance as a result of its strategic energy relationships, investments in energy infrastructure overseas, and involvement in global energy debates.

Resource competitiveness, disagreements over energy trade and infrastructure projects, and contrasting views on energy and climate policy are just a few examples of the potential tensions and conflicts that could arise as a result. These difficulties highlight the intricate relationship between China's energy policy and international politics, and they highlight the need for ongoing conversation, collaboration, and creativity in the quest for global energy security and sustainability.

7. CONCLUSION

This chapter has presented a critical analysis of China's energy policy, as well as its historical development of the energy sector and its investigation of its energy challenges. China's centrality in changing the local and worldwide energy landscapes has been highlighted by this exploration.

Rapid industrialization, urbanization, and economic expansion have been the primary forces shaping China's energy sector today. China has become the world's greatest consumer of energy due to the country's growing middle class and massive industrial sector. Overreliance on fossil fuels, especially coal, in the face of rising demand has led to a string of energy crises marked by fluctuating supplies, increased pollution, and rising greenhouse gas emissions. As a result of these issues, China has made ensuring reliable access to energy a top priority.

The Chinese government has taken several measures in response to the energy crisis, including increasing energy efficiency, supporting renewable energy, and diversifying energy sources. These initiatives have helped significantly with China's energy problems, but their effects can be seen much beyond the country's borders. China is a prominent player in the global energy market, and its activities have a profound effect on energy security and geopolitics around the world.

China's efforts to diversify its energy sources and promote renewable energy have the potential to reduce global demand for fossil fuels, stabilizing energy prices and ensuring a steady supply. Additionally, other countries may be encouraged and equipped to make a similar green transformation by China's dedication to renewables and energy efficiency. National interests and global energy stability need to be carefully navigated in light of China's rising influence and active participation in international energy governance, which may lead to problems.

Going forward, we advise all parties involved in the global energy system, including governments, energy corporations, and international organizations, to keep a close eye on China's energy policy and open lines of communication and cooperation with the country. Cooperation among nations is essential in order to address global problems like climate change and energy independence. Both the accomplishments and failures of China's energy crisis management and transition to a more sustainable energy system should be studied by stakeholders.

As China's energy influence grows, it is imperative that the country's actions and policies be factored into global energy strategies and climate pledges. In the future, China will be a large consumer and a major player in global energy policy, thus stakeholders must be ready for this.

REFERENCES

Akhtar, M. Z., Khan, H. U. R., Sriyanto, S., Jabor, M. K., Rashid, A., & Zaman, K. (2022). How do industrial ecology, energy efficiency, and waste recycling technology (circular economy) fit into China's plan to protect the environment? Up to speed. *Recycling*, *7*(6), 83. doi:10.3390/recycling7060083

Al Shaher, S., & Zreik, M. (2022a). The Belt and Road Initiative in Lebanon: A Promising Initiative in a Complex Society. *The Journal of Asian Finance Economics and Business*, *9*(2), 151–158.

Al Shaher, S., & Zreik, M. (2022b). Sino-Iranian Relations: More Cooperation Despite Sanctions. *Res-militaris, 12*(2), 637-649.

Alaloul, W. S., Musarat, M. A., Rabbani, M. B. A., Altaf, M., Alzubi, K. M., & Al Salaheen, M. (2022). Assessment of Economic Sustainability in the Construction Sector: Evidence from Three Developed Countries (the USA, China, and the UK). *Sustainability (Basel)*, *14*(10), 6326. doi:10.3390u14106326

Aleluia, J., Tharakan, P., Chikkatur, A. P., Shrimali, G., & Chen, X. (2022). Accelerating a clean energy transition in Southeast Asia: Role of governments and public policy. *Renewable & Sustainable Energy Reviews*, *159*, 112226. doi:10.1016/j.rser.2022.112226

Azam, W., Khan, I., & Ali, S. A. (2023). Alternative energy and natural resources in determining environmental sustainability: A look at the role of government final consumption expenditures in France. *Environmental Science and Pollution Research International*, *30*(1), 1949–1965. doi:10.100711356-022-22334-z PMID:35925458

Bown, C. P. (2021). The US–China trade war and Phase One agreement. *Journal of Policy Modeling*, *43*(4), 805–843. doi:10.1016/j.jpolmod.2021.02.009

Boyd, R., & Ufimtseva, A. (2021). Facilitating peaceful rise: The increasing role of geopolitics and domestic legitimacy in China's energy policy. *Energy Policy*, *158*, 112532. doi:10.1016/j.enpol.2021.112532

Caineng, Z. O. U., Songqi, P. A. N., & Qun, H. A. O. (2020). On the connotation, challenge and significance of China's "energy independence" strategy. *Petroleum Exploration and Development*, *47*(2), 449–462. doi:10.1016/S1876-3804(20)60062-3

Chen, D., & Galkin, P. (2023). China's energy investment through the lens of the Belt and Road Initiative. In *A Research Agenda for Energy Politics* (pp. 93–126). Edward Elgar Publishing. doi:10.4337/9781789901764.00015

Cheng, D., Shi, X., & Yu, J. (2021). The impact of green energy infrastructure on firm productivity: Evidence from the Three Gorges Project in China. *International Review of Economics & Finance*, *71*, 385–406. doi:10.1016/j.iref.2020.09.022

Clark, A., & Zhang, W. (2022). Estimating the employment and fiscal consequences of thermal coal phase-out in china. *Energies*, *15*(3), 800. doi:10.3390/en15030800

Coenen, J., Bager, S., Meyfroidt, P., Newig, J., & Challies, E. (2021). Environmental governance of China's belt and road initiative. *Environmental Policy and Governance*, *31*(1), 3–17. doi:10.1002/eet.1901

Cui, L. B., Peng, P., & Zhu, L. (2015). Embodied energy, export policy adjustment and China's sustainable development: A multi-regional input-output analysis. *Energy*, *82*, 457–467. doi:10.1016/j.energy.2015.01.056

Doaemo, W., Dhiman, S., Borovskis, A., Zhang, W., Bhat, S., Jaipuria, S., & Betasolo, M. (2021). Assessment of municipal solid waste management system in Lae City, Papua New Guinea in the context of sustainable development. *Environment, Development and Sustainability*, *23*(12), 18509–18539. doi:10.100710668-021-01465-2 PMID:33942012

Downie, C. (2020). Strategies for Survival: The International Energy Agency's response to a new world. *Energy Policy*, *141*, 111452. doi:10.1016/j.enpol.2020.111452

Fan, M., He, G., & Zhou, M. (2020). The winter choke: Coal-Fired heating, air pollution, and mortality in China. *Journal of Health Economics*, *71*, 102316. doi:10.1016/j.jhealeco.2020.102316 PMID:32179329

Gielen, D., Boshell, F., Saygin, D., Bazilian, M. D., Wagner, N., & Gorini, R. (2019). The role of renewable energy in the global energy transformation. *Energy Strategy Reviews, 24*, 38-50.

Gitelman, L., Kozhevnikov, M., & Visotskaya, Y. (2023). Diversification as a Method of Ensuring the Sustainability of Energy Supply within the Energy Transition. *Resources*, *12*(2), 19. doi:10.3390/resources12020019

Gyamfi, B. A., Bein, M. A., & Bekun, F. V. (2020). Investigating the nexus between hydroelectricity energy, renewable energy, nonrenewable energy consumption on output: Evidence from E7 countries. *Environmental Science and Pollution Research International*, *27*(20), 25327–25339. doi:10.100711356-020-08909-8 PMID:32347487

Heinberg, R., & Fridley, D. (2016). *Our renewable future: Laying the path for one hundred percent clean energy*. Island Press. doi:10.5822/978-1-61091-780-3

Hou, L. (2020). *Building for oil: Daqing and the formation of the Chinese socialist state*. BRILL.

Hu, J., Wang, K. H., Su, C. W., & Umar, M. (2022). Oil price, green innovation and institutional pressure: A China's perspective. *Resources Policy*, *78*, 102788. doi:10.1016/j.resourpol.2022.102788

Huo, T., Ma, Y., Xu, L., Feng, W., & Cai, W. (2022). Carbon emissions in China's urban residential building sector through 2060: A dynamic scenario simulation. *Energy*, *254*, 124395. doi:10.1016/j.energy.2022.124395

Jenkins, R. (2022). *How China is reshaping the global economy: Development impacts in Africa and Latin America*. Oxford University Press. doi:10.1093/oso/9780192866356.001.0001

Jia, Q. (2023). The impact of green finance on the level of decarbonization of the economies: An analysis of the United States', China's, and Russia's current agenda. *Business Strategy and the Environment*, *32*(1), 110–119. doi:10.1002/bse.3120

Kanwal, S., Mehran, M. T., Hassan, M., Anwar, M., Naqvi, S. R., & Khoja, A. H. (2022). An integrated future approach for the energy security of Pakistan: Replacement of fossil fuels with syngas for better environment and socio-economic development. *Renewable & Sustainable Energy Reviews*, *156*, 111978. doi:10.1016/j.rser.2021.111978

Khan, S. A. R., Godil, D. I., Yu, Z., Abbas, F., & Shamim, M. A. (2022). Adoption of renewable energy sources, low-carbon initiatives, and advanced logistical infrastructure—An step toward integrated global progress. *Sustainable Development (Bradford)*, *30*(1), 275–288. doi:10.1002d.2243

Li, W., & Han, M. (2023). Mapping renewable energy transition worldwide: Gravity trajectory, contribution decomposition and income levels. *Renewable Energy*, *206*, 1265–1274. doi:10.1016/j.renene.2023.02.119

Liadze, I., Macchiarelli, C., Mortimer-Lee, P., & Sanchez Juanino, P. (2023). Economic costs of the Russia-Ukraine war. *World Economy*, *46*(4), 874–886. doi:10.1111/twec.13336

Lin, B., & Guan, C. (2023). Evaluation and determinants of total unified efficiency of China's manufacturing sector under the carbon neutrality target. *Energy Economics*, *119*, 106539. doi:10.1016/j.eneco.2023.106539

Liu, J. (2019). China's renewable energy law and policy: A critical review. *Renewable & Sustainable Energy Reviews*, *99*, 212–219. doi:10.1016/j.rser.2018.10.007

Liu, S. Q., Huang, X., Li, X., Masoud, M., Chung, S. H., & Yin, Y. (2021). How is China's energy security affected by exogenous shocks? Evidence of China–US trade dispute and COVID-19 pandemic. *Discover Energy*, *1*(1), 1–23. doi:10.100743937-021-00002-6

Liu, Z., Deng, Z., He, G., Wang, H., Zhang, X., Lin, J., Qi, Y., & Liang, X. (2022). Challenges and opportunities for carbon neutrality in China. *Nature Reviews. Earth & Environment*, *3*(2), 141–155. doi:10.103843017-021-00244-x

Lo, K. (2021). Authoritarian environmentalism, just transition, and the tension between environmental protection and social justice in China's forestry reform. *Forest Policy and Economics*, *131*, 102574. doi:10.1016/j.forpol.2021.102574

Mastoi, M. S., Munir, H. M., Zhuang, S., Hassan, M., Usman, M., Alahmadi, A., & Alamri, B. (2022). A comprehensive analysis of the power demand–supply situation, electricity usage patterns, and the recent development of renewable energy in China. *Sustainability (Basel)*, *14*(6), 3391. doi:10.3390u14063391

Mehmet, O., & Yorucu, V. (2020). *Modern geopolitics of Eastern Mediterranean hydrocarbons in an age of energy transformation* (Vol. 78). Springer Nature. doi:10.1007/978-3-030-43585-1

Pan, J., Li, Y., Zhang, Y., & Ji, Z. (2023). China's Revolutionary Transition towards Carbon Neutrality and Prevention of Relevant Risks. *Chinese Journal of Urban and Environmental Studies*, 2350003.

Papadis, E., & Tsatsaronis, G. (2020). Challenges in the decarbonization of the energy sector. *Energy*, *205*, 118025. doi:10.1016/j.energy.2020.118025

Pepe, J. M. (2020). The "Eastern Polygon" of the Trans-Siberian rail line: A critical factor for assessing Russia's strategy toward Eurasia and the Asia-Pacific. *Asia Europe Journal*, *18*(3), 305–324. doi:10.100710308-019-00543-5

Qinhua, X. U., & Chung, W. (2016). *China's Energy Policy from National and International Perspectives: The Energy Revolution and One Belt One Road Initiative*. City University of HK Press.

Sachs, J. D. (2015). *The age of sustainable development*. Columbia University Press. doi:10.7312ach17314

Saraswat, R., Sharma, S., & Saraswat, D. (2022). Effect of air pollution on climate. *International Journal of Research in Engineering and Scienc*, *10*(5), 22–25.

Shen, X., & Lin, B. (2021). Does industrial structure distortion impact the energy intensity in China? *Sustainable Production and Consumption*, *25*, 551–562. doi:10.1016/j.spc.2020.12.012

Sonone, S. S., Jadhav, S., Sankhla, M. S., & Kumar, R. (2020). Water contamination by heavy metals and their toxic effect on aquaculture and human health through food Chain. *Lett. Appl. NanoBioScience*, *10*(2), 2148–2166.

Stern, N., & Xie, C. (2023). China's new growth story: Linking the 14th Five-Year Plan with the 2060 carbon neutrality pledge. *Journal of Chinese Economic and Business Studies*, *21*(1), 5–25. doi:10.1080/14765284.2022.2073172

Sun, Y. (2020). The achievement, significance and future prospect of China's renewable energy initiative. *International Journal of Energy Research*, *44*(15), 12209–12244. doi:10.1002/er.5243

Taylor, M. (2021). China's evolving energy security strategy. *Asian Affairs*, *52*(4), 890–913. doi:10.1080/03068374.2021.2004031

Wang, C., Raza, S. A., Adebayo, T. S., Yi, S., & Shah, M. I. (2023). The roles of hydro, nuclear and biomass energy towards carbon neutrality target in China: A policy-based analysis. *Energy*, *262*, 125303. doi:10.1016/j.energy.2022.125303

Wang, H., & Zhang, R. (2022). Effects of environmental regulation on CO2 emissions: An empirical analysis of 282 cities in China. *Sustainable Production and Consumption*, *29*, 259–272. doi:10.1016/j.spc.2021.10.016

Wang, K., Zhang, Y., Lei, L., & Qiu, S. (2021). Evaluation on the efficiency of LED energy enterprises in China by employing the DEA model. *Mathematics*, *9*(19), 2356. doi:10.3390/math9192356

Wang, S., Sun, L., & Iqbal, S. (2022). Green financing role on renewable energy dependence and energy transition in E7 economies. *Renewable Energy*, *200*, 1561–1572. doi:10.1016/j.renene.2022.10.067

Wang, X. C., Klemeš, J. J., Wang, Y., Dong, X., Wei, H., Xu, Z., & Varbanov, P. S. (2020). Water-Energy-Carbon Emissions nexus analysis of China: An environmental input-output model-based approach. *Applied Energy*, *261*, 114431. doi:10.1016/j.apenergy.2019.114431

Wang, Z., Kong, Y., & Li, W. (2022). Review on the development of China's natural gas industry in the background of "carbon neutrality. *Natural Gas Industry B*, *9*(2), 132–140. doi:10.1016/j.ngib.2021.08.021

Xiang, N., Wang, L., Zhong, S., Zheng, C., Wang, B., & Qu, Q. (2021). How does the world view China's carbon policy? A sentiment analysis on Twitter data. *Energies, 14*(22), 7782. doi:10.3390/en14227782

Xu, B., Luo, Y., Xu, R., & Chen, J. (2021). Exploring the driving forces of distributed energy resources in China: Using a semiparametric regression model. *Energy, 236*, 121452. doi:10.1016/j.energy.2021.121452

Yang, T., & Liu, W. (2019). Health effects of energy intensive sectors and the potential health co-benefits of a low carbon industrial transition in China. *International Journal of Environmental Research and Public Health, 16*(17), 3022. doi:10.3390/ijerph16173022 PMID:31438537

Yao, L. (2022). Domestic dynamics and china's engagement in global renewable energy governance. *The Chinese Journal of International Politics, 15*(1), 69–86. doi:10.1093/cjip/poac004

Yu, K. (2023). *China's Energy Security in the Twenty-First Century: The Role of Global Governance and Climate Change* (Vol. 2). Hong Kong University Press. doi:10.2307/jj.4303780

Yu, Z., Ridwan, I. L., Tanveer, M., & Khan, S. A. R. (2023). Investigating the nexuses between transportation Infrastructure, renewable energy Sources, and economic Growth: Striving towards sustainable development. *Ain Shams Engineering Journal, 14*(2), 101843. doi:10.1016/j.asej.2022.101843

Zhang, H., Xiong, P., Yang, S., & Yu, J. (2023). Renewable energy utilization, green finance and agricultural land expansion in China. *Resources Policy, 80*, 103163. doi:10.1016/j.resourpol.2022.103163

Zhang, S., Andrews-Speed, P., & Perera, P. (2015). The evolving policy regime for pumped storage hydroelectricity in China: A key support for low-carbon energy. *Applied Energy, 150*, 15–24. doi:10.1016/j.apenergy.2015.03.103

Zhao, C., Ju, S., Xue, Y., Ren, T., Ji, Y., & Chen, X. (2022). China's energy transitions for carbon neutrality: Challenges and opportunities. *Carbon Neutrality, 1*(1), 7. doi:10.100743979-022-00010-y

Zhao, P., Lu, Z., Fang, J., Paramati, S. R., & Jiang, K. (2020). Determinants of renewable and non-renewable energy demand in China. *Structural Change and Economic Dynamics, 54*, 202–209. doi:10.1016/j.strueco.2020.05.002

Zou, C., Zhao, Q., Zhang, G., & Xiong, B. (2016). Energy revolution: From a fossil energy era to a new energy era. *Natural Gas Industry B, 3*(1), 1–11. doi:10.1016/j.ngib.2016.02.001

Zreik, M. (2021). China and Europe in Africa: Competition or Cooperation? *Malaysian Journal of International Relations, 9*(1), 51-67.

Zreik, M. (2022). US-China Relations in The Era of Multi-Polarism: Trade War Between the Two Economic Giants. *Eurasian Research Journal, 4*(2), 43–65. doi:10.53277/2519-2442-2022.2-03

Zreik, M. (2023). Analytical study on Foreign Direct Investment Divestment Inflows and Outflows in Developing Economies: Evidence of China. *Chinese Economy, 56*(6), 1–16. doi:10.1080/10971475.2023.2193118

Zreik, M. (2023b). The Integration of China's Belt and Road Initiative into Global Supply Chains: New Pathways for Social and Environmental Responsibility. In A. Taghipour (Ed.), *Government Impact on Sustainable and Responsible Supply Chain Management* (pp. 74–94). IGI Global. doi:10.4018/978-1-6684-9062-4.ch005

KEY TERMS AND DEFINITIONS

Carbon Neutrality: A state in which the net amount of carbon dioxide or other greenhouse gases emitted into the atmosphere is zero, often achieved by offsetting emissions with carbon removal or simply reducing emissions to zero.

Energy Diversification: The strategy of increasing the variety of energy sources used to meet a country's energy needs, thereby reducing dependency on a single or limited sources of energy.

Energy Efficiency: Using less energy to perform the same task, thereby reducing energy waste. It often involves technological, behavioral, and economic changes.

Energy Intensity: The amount of energy consumed for each unit of economic activity or GDP. A decrease in energy intensity indicates a more energy-efficient economy.

Energy Security: The uninterrupted availability of energy sources at an affordable price. It also concerns the risks associated with energy supply disruptions.

Energy Transition: The long-term structural change in energy systems, often referring to the shift from fossil-based systems of energy production and consumption to renewable energy sources.

Fossil Fuels: Natural fuels such as coal, oil, or natural gas, formed in the geological past from the remains of living organisms.

Global Energy Governance: The collective processes and mechanisms by which countries and other stakeholders make decisions about the production, distribution, and consumption of energy resources on a global scale.

Greenhouse Gas Emissions: Gases that trap heat in the atmosphere, including carbon dioxide, methane, and nitrous oxide, which contribute to the greenhouse effect and global warming.

Renewable Energy: Energy derived from natural processes that are replenished at a faster rate than they are consumed, such as sunlight, wind, rain, tides, and geothermal heat.

Chapter 9
Environmental and Ecological Challenges in Central Asia: A Comparative Analysis of the Renewable Energy Policies of Central Asian Nations

Ayushi Saini
Jawaharlal Nehru University, India

Rajoli Siddharth Jayaprakash
Jawaharlal Nehru University, India

ABSTRACT

Oil was discovered in Uzbekistan in 1885, in Kazakhstan and Turkmenistan in the 1900s, and since then the geopolitical interests of these hydrocarbon-rich states have always remained predominant. During the Soviet era, they were energy peripheries of the Union. Post dissolution, these nations reaped the rents generated from hydrocarbons which translated to economic development in the region. However, Kyrgyzstan and Tajikistan are hydrocarbon energy poor and do not dominate the geopolitics of Central Asia. However, it is critical to note that the ecology of Central Asia was massively impacted by Soviet projects in the regions, for instance the nuclear waste in Kazakhstan or the drying up of the Aral Sea and the Belt and Road Initiative projects since 2013. Nations have announced their net-zero targets and doled out renewable energy projects. This chapter will compare the renewable energy policies of Central Asian countries.

INTRODUCTION

The environment and economy of Central Asian nations stand at a critical juncture. This group comprises five landlocked nations, with Kyrgyzstan and Tajikistan situated as upper riparian states and the remaining three as lower riparian states. Among these nations, some possess abundant natural resources, including hydrocarbons, as seen in the cases of Uzbekistan, Kazakhstan, and Turkmenistan; while others rely on hydropower, exemplified by Kyrgyzstan and Tajikistan. Despite the region's economic development

DOI: 10.4018/979-8-3693-0440-2.ch009

variance, nations must make a difficult trade-off to invest in clean technologies to lower emissions at a high cost or compromise the ecology of the region through utilization of cheap energy.

Since the discovery of oil and natural gas, Central Asian nations were pivotal to the preponderance of the Soviet Union. Countries rich in hydrocarbons were supplying oil and natural gas. At the same time, Kyrgyzstan and Tajikistan generated hydroelectric power for the Soviet Union. The tasks were assigned to nations presuming a possible dissolution, that a balancer would be required to de-escalate the tensions manifested in Central Asia's politics. The Soviet projects and operations in Central Asia have lasting effects on the ecology of Central Asian region. Upon the dissolution of the Soviet Union, the five nations got total control over their natural resources and the resources of their ontological prior -Soviet Union- present in their countries. Despite that challenges remain, such as the damming of the Amu Darya and Syr Darya rivers is affecting the upstream nations due to the shortage of supply. These nations have been growing as their economies took off after a tumultuous 1990s. By the early 2010s, their growth rates averaged 6%. Increased growth rate was accompanied by increased demand for energy. As the domestic demand for energy grows, and multi-modal connectivity projects such as BRI emerge, the ecology of the region tends to be damaged. Kazakhstan is responsible for more than 50% of Central Asia's emissions, and the energy intensity of Uzbekistan is four times higher than the EU's average and twice the world average, as per International Energy Agency.

In 2019, Uzbekistan launched the concept of Environmental protection. In 2021, President Kassam-Jomart Tokayev unveiled the Environmental Code, which introduced the best available techniques (BAT). Such policy intervention acts as a precursor for designing renewable energy policies, such as Kazakhstan's carbon-neutral strategy 2060, which this chapter will focus on. It is essential to compare the renewable energy policies of Central Asian nations, as it can help a researcher ascertain the political processes involved in understanding the demand for clean energy strategies by understanding the lobbying of environmental NGOs, the strength of the civil society, state capacity, and the influence of domestic energy actors and trans-national actors in renewable energy policymaking and implementation. In the aftermath of the comparison, an emphasis will be laid on the political process of Kazakhstan, as it is a significant emitter of CO2 in the region.

Kazakhstan stands out as the most important country in Central Asia when it comes to renewable energy policies and its evolving environmental landscape. This distinction is grounded in several key factors. Firstly, Kazakhstan boasts vast and diverse renewable energy potential, particularly in wind and solar resources, which surpasses that of its Central Asian neighbours such as Uzbekistan, Turkmenistan, Tajikistan, and Kyrgyzstan (IRENA, 2018). These reserves provide a unique opportunity for Kazakhstan to lead the region in transitioning towards sustainable energy sources, aligning with global efforts to combat climate change. Moreover, Kazakhstan has demonstrated a commitment to fostering a conducive regulatory environment for renewable energy investments, attracting both domestic and international stakeholders. However, despite these promising developments, the nation faces the challenge of balancing its renewable energy ambitions with concerns over environmental deterioration, as the extraction of mineral resources and land degradation persist (Strikeleva, 2018; Hu et. al, 2020). Thus, Kazakhstan's role as a pivotal player in Central Asia's renewable energy landscape underscores the need for comprehensive environmental policies to mitigate potential ecological repercussions while harnessing its green energy potential effectively.

Furthermore, it is critical to understand why more and more actors are showing interest in the renewable energy of the region. One must also realise the lasting ecological impacts of the Soviet developmental projects across Central Asia and the effects of BRI.

ENVIRONMENTAL CRISES IN CENTRAL ASIA: FROM SOVIET LEGACY TO POST-SOVIET REALITIES

The states of Central Asia are facing severe environmental challenges, which are being further exacerbated by climate change. These issues are complex, intertwined, and often rooted in the countries' shared Soviet legacy (Tursumbayeva et al., 2022). The world today faces many challenges, with environmental issues being one of the most pressing and critical problems. Climate change, deforestation, pollution, and loss of biodiversity are all significant concerns affecting not just the planet but also the livelihoods and well-being of millions worldwide. Analysts and experts are paying increasing attention to this ecological problem.

Nuclear waste- Over three decades have passed since the dissolution of the Soviet Union, a monumental event in history. As the Soviet Union disintegrated into 15 separate states, a pressing concern revolved around the fate of the nuclear weapons and materials dispersed throughout the constituent states. Kazakhstan and Ukraine took center stage as the states hosting Soviet nuclear weapons. Pavel Podvig in a report for Nuclear Threat Initiative (2018) notes that with independence, "Kazakhstan inherited 1,410 nuclear warheads and the Semipalatinsk nuclear weapon test site which was used as a primary above-and below-ground testing site for the Soviets between 1949 and 1989" (NTI, 2018).

Semipalatinsk served as the site for over 450 nuclear tests by the Soviet Union, with their inaugural test taking place there. The Soviet Union's nuclear presence in Central Asia extended beyond testing and missile operations, encompassing a significant uranium industry that spanned the region. A 2010 report by the International Atomic Energy Agency on the Soviet Union's uranium heritage in Central Asia revealed that during the 1970s and 1980s, over a third of the Soviet Union's uranium production transpired in this region. Upon gaining their independence, the region's nations possessed uranium mining, processing, and waste facilities. According to the report, the closure of these mines and processing plants occurred between 1961 and 1995, with only those waste sites in proximity to densely populated areas receiving any remediation efforts. In contrast, some sites were left completely abandoned, as per the findings in the IAEA report (IAEA 2010). Many of these sites are clustered alongside the tributaries of the Syr Darya River, which meanders through the densely populated Fergana Valley. This region is the agricultural heartland, shared among the Kyrgyz, Tajik, and Uzbek Republics. At present, these abandoned mining and processing sites pose significant environmental and public health risks while also hindering economic progress. The very real threat exists that radioactive pollutants and heavy metals might infiltrate the transnational river system, potentially leading to an ecological catastrophe.

Aral Sea- During the Soviet era, Central Asia served as an essential reservoir of resources for the Soviet Union. The extraction of resources and the usage of the land of Kazakhstan particularly, resulted in the resource scarcity and piling up of nuclear waste in Kazakhstan. The Aral Sea, once one of the world's largest inland bodies of water, bore the brunt of Soviet irrigation schemes designed to transform arid landscapes into fertile agricultural zones. The result was catastrophic. By diverting water from the two major rivers that fed the Aral Sea, the Amu Darya and the Syr Darya, to support cotton and rice cultivation, the Soviet government unwittingly set in motion one of the most significant environmental disasters of the 20th century (White, 2013). The Aral Sea began to shrink dramatically, leaving behind a desolate landscape of salt flats and a drastically altered climate (Hanks, 2021; Mambra 2022). Regions like Semipalatinsk in Kazakhstan became infamous for nuclear testing, resulting in long-lasting contamination and health hazards for local populations (Aidarkhanova, 2022). The sprawling cotton monoculture, particularly in Uzbekistan, also led to soil degradation and chemical pollution, impacting both human health and the environment (Hanks, 2021).

The collapse of the Soviet Union in 1991 brought some other challenges also to the region. Water disputes emerged as a critical post-Soviet challenge. The division of the Aral Sea basin among five countries—Kazakhstan, Uzbekistan, Turkmenistan, Kyrgyzstan, and Tajikistan—created a complex web of competing interests (World Meteorological Organization 2014). Water became a precious and contentious resource, with disputes often triggering political tensions and regional rivalries. For example, the construction of dams and reservoirs on the Amu Darya and Syr Darya rivers by upstream countries threatened the water supply of downstream nations, further straining relationships in an already fragile region (Pena-Ramos, 2021).

Kazakhstan and Uzbekistan, the two largest economies in the region, continue to heavily rely on fossil fuel-based power generation, a practice that releases carbon dioxide, contributing to the heat-trapping effect in the atmosphere (Wishart and Abidi, 2021). According to the US Department of Commerce data, Kazakhstan predominantly relies on coal-burning power plants for nearly 80% of its electricity. Renewable sources, including water, solar, and wind installations, contribute to less than 13% of Kazakhstan's power generation (US Dept of Commerce, 2019). In Kyrgyzstan, as observed by Ulan Ismailov, antiquated and pollution-intensive factories have given rise to substantial environmental issues. The air quality in the vicinity of these facilities significantly surpasses permissible pollution limits by several orders of magnitude. Such a heavy reliance on these industrial operations poses a significant environmental and public health hazard in the context of global warming and the associated greenhouse effect (Ismailov, 2019). Uzbekistan's electricity supply is almost entirely derived from hydrocarbons. In 2016, approximately 79.7% of its power was sourced from oil, coal, or natural gas, with hydroelectric power constituting the remainder (IEA, 2021).

Kazakhstan's water sources have faced widespread pollution due to industrial and agricultural runoff, and some regions grapple with radioactivity. Desertification has led to the loss of significant agricultural expanses. Industrial areas often lack adequate controls on emissions that affect both air and water quality. The Semey region in the northeast, home to Semipalatinsk, bears the enduring consequences of radiation contamination resulting from Soviet-era weapons testing (Lukashenko et al., 2020). Kazakhstan, historically a nomadic society relying on agriculture, contends with the pressing issue of desertification. This challenge is further compounded by problems such as erosion and overgrazing. The impact of desertification has resulted in the loss of extensive agricultural land. Wind erosion has notably affected the northern and central regions due to the widespread adoption of dryland wheat farming (Hu, 2020).

In 2016, all five Central Asian nations signed and ratified the Paris agreement within the UNFCC. However, with the current level of hydrocarbon consumption and increment in per capita emissions, it is difficult to limit the impacts of global warming. At the current state, the over-utilization of hydrocarbons can be potentially fatal for the ecology of the region. The only panacea is green transition, which is highly linked to the social transformation of the Central Asian nations. These countries are on the path of green transition, say to renewables since the per capita incomes of these nations have been increasing (Wishart & Abidi, 2021).

In Economics, the inverted Kuznets curve is used to delineate the correlation between inequality and GDP growth rate in a country. Prior to the industrialization of a country, inequality will be high in society, and it will decline as GDP growth rates increase (Kuznets, 1950). A similar Environmental inverted Kuznets curve can be seen in the case of Central Asia (refer to Figure 1). The hypothesis is that the environmental degradation in a given country will worsen as the country undergoes industri-

Figure 1. The environmental Kuznets curve
Source: A literature survey of environmental Kuznets curve, June 2019, Economic analysis

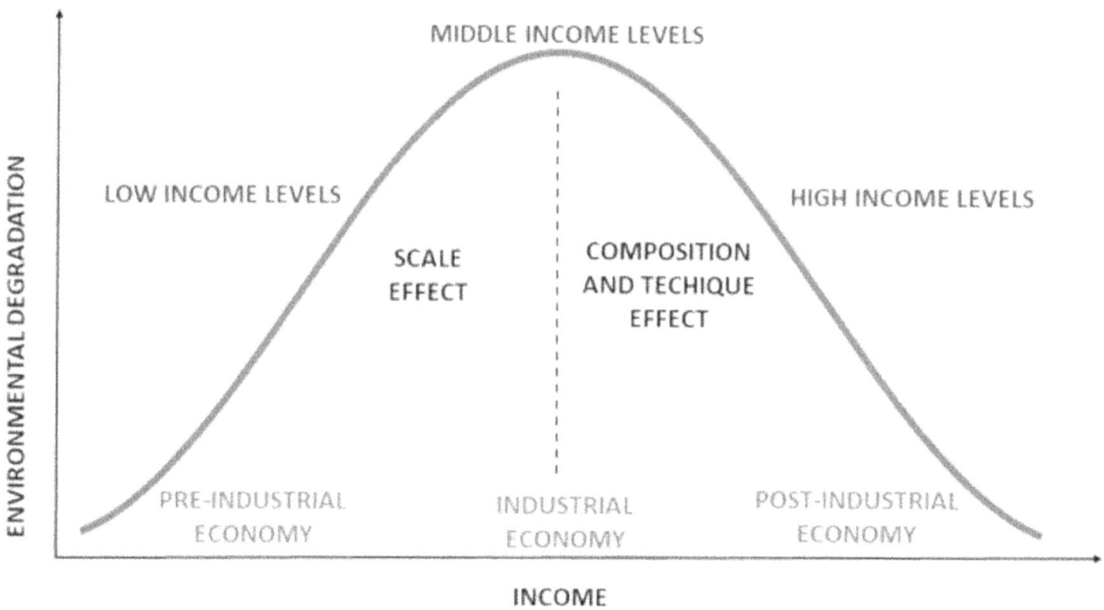

alization. However, as the per capita incomes of the people improve alongside industrial growth, the environmental degradation of a country will reduce, as the marginal propensity to purchase cleaner technology increases. This approach has its shortcomings, where nations have attained income equality but still have high per capita emissions. In Central Asia, the GDP per capita of Kazakhstan is $11,290, which is in the category of upper middle-income country, while Uzbekistan's GDP per capita is $2,255, which is only continuing to grow majorly due to the good governance and economic reforms initiated in the mid-2010s. A wave of liberalization persists in Uzbekistan this year. Tashkent plans to liberalize energy tariffs, which is indicative of further economic growth. Turkmenistan's GDP per capita is $7,400. However, the energy-poor countries of Central Asia, Tajikistan and Kyrgyzstan have per capita incomes of $900 and $1300, respectively (CEIC data, 2022 https://www.ceicdata.com/en). These two are reliant on the remittances from migrant labourers and agriculture. We observe a high standard of living among the middle-income countries of Central Asia. However, the hydrocarbon dependence in these countries is very high. That being said, the governments in Kazakhstan and Uzbekistan have not wholly dismissed renewable energy adoption.

The poor air quality is another reason as to why renewable energy is being prioritised by actors. Dushanbe, Tashkent, Ashgabat, Bishkek, Almaty, and Asthana have very poor air quality. Tajikistan and Kyrgyzstan rank 4th and 7th worldwide on the poor air quality index based on PM 2.5 exposure (IQAir, 2022a). Other Central Asian nations are not far behind on this index either. Energy tariffs in Central Asia are very cheap due to swathes of hydrocarbon reserves and transportation infrastructure through pipelines. Therefore, we observe a higher energy intensity in Uzbekistan and Kazakhstan. In the short run, it is unlikely that consumers will be able to pay higher tariffs across Central Asia. So, a trade-off presents. Here the capability approach, developed by Amartya Sen, which emphasizes individuals'

Table 1. The environmental performance index (Central Asian countries)

Country	Rank	EPI Score	10-Year Change
Kazakhstan	93	40.90	11.80
Uzbekistan	107	38.20	1.90
Turkmenistan	118	37.00	8.90
Tajikistan	117	37.10	-1.60
Kyrgyzstan	126	35.70	1.20

Source: *Environmental performance index,* https://epi.yale.edu/epi-results/2022/component/epi

subjective well-being, makes sense (Sen, 2008). In the case of Central Asia, where massive ecological destruction is taking place, the question does emerge of the bargaining capacity of the individual with the state in form of lobbying and activism, which can be correlated to the level of Human development of the people in across Central Asia.

The Human Development Index collates the mean years of schooling with life expectancy at birth and the GNI per capita to ascertain a nation's level of development. The Human Development Index helps understand the quality of life in Central Asian countries because a healthy, educated populace has more bargaining power with the state through lobbying and activism. All Central Asian countries are ranked between medium (0.550-0.699) to very high category (>0.800). Kazakhstan ranks the highest at 46 and Tajikistan at the lowest at 122. It is to be noted that higher HDI does not correlate to better environmental performance (Samimi et al., 2018). Rather, it correlates to better bargaining power for an individual in the process of green transition of a country. For example, a nation with a good economy and education will see a change in consumer behaviour, where several individuals may purchase an EV automobile. As more consumers purchase it, the demand for charging stations increases, where the state will be forced to create an infrastructure for EVs, and other car-making companies may be incentivised to manufacture more vehicles that run on electricity.

Another helpful index related to this research is the Environment Performance Index, which measures the environmental health and sustainability of countries. The EPI has forty performance indicators looking at a country's environmental profile in totality.

According to Table 1, one can observe that Kazakhstan is ranked higher in the EPI in comparison to the other Central Asian countries; it is also crucial to note that Turkmenistan and Kazakhstan have improved since the previous decade. Kazakhstan ranked higher in ecosystem vitality, Environmental Health, Climate Change policy objectives, and Climate change mitigation. One can extrapolate from the EPI data that there is a growing demand for cleaner energy in the near future.

The bargaining power of people can be seen in terms of environmental activism as well. Environmental activism is increasing in Central Asia, unlike in the Soviet period, where environmental activists were part of the state system. Post-dissolution of the USSR, a new trend emerged where the environmental activists coupled the national law with international conventions, such as the Aarhus convention. This convention protects the right of an individual to live in a healthy environment, and it involved the transnational actors, which created an interdependent system in fighting environmental issues in Central Asia (Weinthal & Watters, 2010). For instance, the residents of Berezovka in Kazakhstan, where Karachaganak Petroleum Operating (KPO) exploited an oilfield 5km close to people's homes, were impacted. It resulted in the health crisis of the individuals (BHRRC, 2021). The residents fought with the support of transnational E-NGOs and won against a big hydrocarbon firm. The demand for renewables is not directly from the people; it can better be stated that the per capita incomes are reaching a point where the people in Central Asia are demanding for a better quality of life, and these demands complement net neutrality advocated by the UNFCCC.

China's Belt and Road Initiative and its Ecological Impact- Giulia Sciorati claims that, "in Central Asia, China's role as the main external economic actor through its Belt and Road Initiative (BRI) risks aggravating existing environmental challenges. China's projects in Central Asia imply expanding transport infrastructures by land, while its regional energy projects continue to be mainly based on coal, oil, and gas." Hence, she argues that China could not keep up with its aim to build greener societies along with the BRI (Sciorati, 2021). Among various reasons that are aggravating this threat to the global environment, China's Belt and Road Initiative (BRI) has caught the special attention of security analysts. Due to the rapid expansion of BRI, issues such as deforestation, loss of biodiversity, displacement of people, migration, increased carbon emissions, degradation of natural habitats and ecosystems, air pollution, and water scarcity are becoming increasingly prevalent. The BRI is having a significant impact on the ecology of Central Asian states (Laruelle, 2018; Simonov, 2020). Central Asia, which was once a critical hub for trade along the Great Silk Road during the Middle Ages, has been on the periphery of world geo-economics for the last couple of centuries (Sadovskaya & Utyasheva, 2018; Kurbanov, 2018).

The multiple-connectivity of Kazakhstan to China has given rise to various geopolitical, societal, and ecological issues in the region, such as problems related to trans-border rivers, concerns about water pollution, soil erosion, cultural displacement, loss of traditional livelihoods, and loss of employment due to BRI-related development and Beijing's lack of attention to climate change (Sadovskaya & Utyasheva, 2018; Kurbanov, 2018; Dave, 2018). The ecological problems created by various BRI projects in Kazakhstan threaten human security in these countries. These ecological problems could lead to social, economic, and political instability in Kazakhstan, exacerbating the human security challenges faced by local communities. Some human security problems that the BRI may exacerbate in Kazakhstan include displacement and loss of livelihoods, loss and inaccessibility of natural resources, water scarcity, land degradation, various types of pollution, loss of employment, etc. (Laruelle, 2018; Simonov, 2019; Chellaney, 2013).

Though BRI provides an opportunity for Kazakhstan to improve its domestic infrastructure (CSIS, 2017; World Bank, 2022), at the same time, it poses risks such as potential job loss for local people, leading to unemployment, foreign competition, debt trap, and negative environmental impact (Yellinek, 2020). Many of the industries that Chinese investors and citizens are also involved in can have a negative impact. Besides gas, many Chinese people in Kazakhstan are engaged in crypto mining. Questions remain about how increased oil production and crypto mining might affect the environmental health of Kazakhstan (Goldstein, 2022). Similarly, the apprehension about the BRI and its impact on climate change has been raised (McBride et al., 2023).

Environmental activism- According to the International Partnership for Human Rights (IPHR), the situation for civic freedoms in Uzbekistan and Turkmenistan can be marked as "closed," Kazakhstan and Tajikistan as "repressed", and Kyrgyzstan as "obstructed" (IPHR, 2023). Freedom House also ranks all the Central Asian countries as "unfree," except for Kyrgyzstan, which is "partly free." In other words, civil society activists in Central Asia are under constant pressure, and NGOs and activists are rarely able to effectively work on sensitive cases related to the environment. This means that civil society -including the civil society groups working on environmental problems and climate change- often face severe difficulties in their working conditions. According to Professor Sebastien Peyrouse of George

Washington University, the lack of safe civil society space in which to raise and address environmental problems, significantly hinders the effectiveness of measures to mitigate climate change and protect the environment (Payrouse, 2022).

RENEWABLE ENERGY POTENTIAL, POLICIES, AND TARGETS OF CENTRAL ASIAN COUNTRIES

Elena Shadrina argues that, "the Central Asian region holds significant untapped potential for various forms of non-hydropower renewable energy, including solar, wind, and biogas, among others. Despite the considerable promise of these resources, their full utilization has yet to be realized" (Shadrina, 2020). In addition to the region's abundant fossil fuel reserves, Central Asia boasts substantial potential for renewable energy sources supporting sustainable energy generation. In particular, the intricate network of rivers in Tajikistan and Kyrgyzstan positions these countries favourably for hydroelectric power (Abylkasymova et al., 2019). Beyond hydro resources, these nations also exhibit a high potential for solar energy, thanks to their elevated geographical features. The potential for solar energy is not confined to Tajikistan and Kyrgyzstan; it extends across a broad spectrum in Kazakhstan, Uzbekistan, and Turkmenistan. Furthermore, Kazakhstan and Turkmenistan exhibit significant wind energy potential, with solar energy resources following closely behind (Nabiyeva, 2015; Nurdavletova, 2018; Eschanov, 2013)

Figure 2 manifests the level of economic development co-related to the demand for clean energy. It is to be noted that Tajikistan and Kyrgyzstan are nations that are powered by hydroelectric river projects. Their CO2 emissions bunched together does not cross 12 mt, whereas Kazakhstan alone accounts for 225.78 mt of CO2, which is solely due to the hydrocarbon-backed energy intensity in Kazakhstan. At a glance, all Central Asian nations apart from Turkmenistan have renewable energy targets. Where Kazakhstan is the only country with net metering, Kyrgyzstan and Tajikistan are the only nations with tradable renewable energy certificates. Kazakhstan and Kyrgyzstan have feed-in tariffs. None of the Central Asian nations have capital subsidies for renewable energy. However, Kazakhstan, Tajikistan and Kyrgyzstan have significant public investment in loans and grants, reduction of taxes, energy production payment, and tax credits.

Uzbekistan's Renewable Energy Policy

Paris Agreement was ratified by Tashkent in 2018. Uzbekistan adopted a national commitment to reduce Green House Gas emission per capita by 10% of 2010 levels maximum by 2030. It has drafted a strategy in transitioning to green economy between 2019-2030, where the target entails that Uzbekistan will attempt to attain 25% of its electricity generated through Renewable Energy Sources (RES). Uzbekistan is looking to reduce its carbon intensity. The RES potential for Uzbekistan is 117984 Mtoe. Solar energy has the highest potential due to the topographical features of Uzbekistan. In 2018, renewable energy potential of Uzbekistan was 1844 MW which covered 3% of the total energy consumption. However, 10-12% of country's energy generated is through RES (IEA, 2020).

The challenges in implementing renewable energy systems in Uzbekistan is majorly due to the high costs associated with installation and the lack of scale of economies. Considering the current non-renewable energy (hydrocarbons) tariffs being low, the transition into high-cost short-run renewable energy is hard and presents itself as a major challenge in the energy transition. There are less sources for financing

Figure 2. Renewable energy consumption vs. income in Central Asia
Elena Shadrina: Renewable energy in Central Asian Economies; role in reducing regional energy insecurity, ADBI working paper series

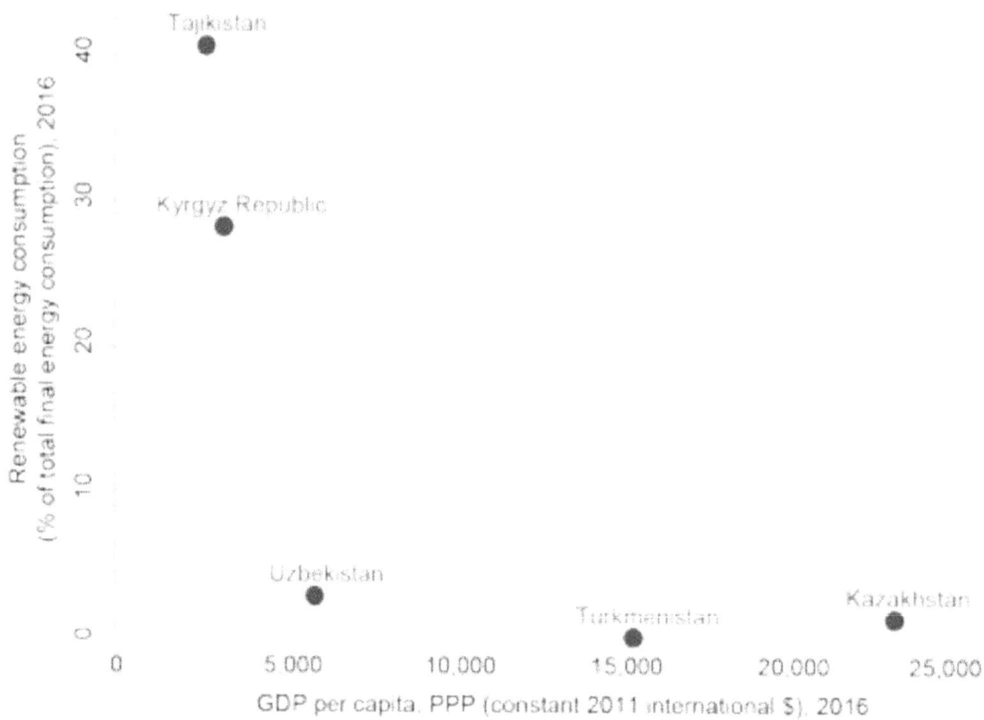

such large-scale projects due to the economy of Uzbekistan. Unlike Kazakhstan, the per capita income of Uzbekistan is still in the lower middle-income category, and the short-run costs outweigh the future benefits. Lastly, nuclear power dominates the discourse over renewable energy sources as the cost of operations is lower (IEA, 2020; Biennial Report of the Republic of Uzbekistan, 2021).

However, there are success stories in the green transition in Uzbekistan. In 2019, the government of Uzbekistan launched a programme for converting vehicles to natural gas fuel systems. The discourse of clean energy and the utilization of renewable energy is trickling into the nation of Uzbekistan. The global reliance on hydrocarbons and the increasing needs of Uzbekistan's economy may prove to be a hurdle to attaining its vision by 2030 (Biennial Report of Republic of Uzbekistan, 2021).

Renewable Energy Policy of Kyrgyzstan

In 2008, Kyrgyzstan introduced a legal framework titled the "Renewable Energy Sources" law, which was subsequently amended in 2019. This law was designed to establish the groundwork for renewable energy feed-in tariffs, aiming to cover investment costs for a period of up to eight years (Ministry of Justice of Kyrgyz Republic, 2008). Nonetheless, full implementation of this law remains pending, with certain aspects, such as tariff calculation and determination, still in the process of development through the creation of bylaws, which are presently under review by the government. Kyrgyzstan has primarily focused on large hydropower projects. However, from 2010 to 2025, plans were initiated for the establishment and enhancement of 132 small-scale hydropower plants, collectively delivering 275 MW of capacity (UNIDO and ICSHP, 2016). In 2008, a proposal was presented for the reconstruction of 24 plants with a combined capacity of 200 MW (Baum, 2008). Additionally, Isaev and Tolomushev have identified potential for constructing 92 new small-scale hydropower plants, with a combined capacity of 178 MW and an estimated annual energy production of up to 1 billion kWh. Furthermore, there is the possibility of constructing seven hydroelectric power stations on irrigation reservoirs, with an installed capacity of 75 MW and an average annual electricity generation of about 220 million kWh (Isaev and Tolomushev, 2016).

Tajikistan and Turkmenistan

Tajikistan has formulated several significant documents, including the "National Development Strategy to 2030," the "Program for Development in Mid-term Perspective 2016–2020," the "Power Sector Development Master Plan," and the "Sustainable Development Transition Concept to 2022". While acknowledging the need for energy source diversification, these documents primarily emphasize hydropower, with brief mentions of solar, wind, biomass, and biogas. Notably, a notable disparity exists among these documents (Shadrina, 2020). Despite the overarching focus on large-scale hydropower development, Tajikistan has shown interest in exploring alternative renewable energy sources, particularly small-scale hydropower.

In contrast, Turkmenistan's stance on renewable energy remains somewhat opaque, owing to a lack of available information and comprehensive policy frameworks for renewables (Eshchanov et al., 2019). However, they have formulated the "National Socioeconomic Development Program for 2011–2030," supplemented by a shorter-term plan from 2019 to 2021, considering the need for energy diversification. Regrettably, these documents fall short of providing concrete measures or assigning responsibility for their implementation, as highlighted by Shadrina in 2020. Nonetheless, there have been proposals for nine small-scale hydropower plants possessing a potential capacity of 57 MW, though clear execution dates are yet to be determined (UNIDO and ICSHP, 2016). The flagship of Turkmenistan's electric power industry is the Mary high-tech combined cycle power plant with a capacity of 1,574 MW, and it has only one hydropower plant with very less installed capacity (https://www.newscentralasia.net/ 2023).

Kazakhstan's Renewable Energy Policy and Role of Other Actors

The institutionalization of renewable energy policy and governance in Kazakhstan dates back to 2006, but progress has been sluggish. Despite over a decade of policy implementation marked by an evolving and incomplete governance structure, the utilization of renewable energy sources remains marginal, with limited advancements. In 2018, the energy composition in Kazakhstan was primarily fossil fuels at 81.3%, followed by hydro at 9.7%, gas turbine at 8.5%, and solar, wind, and bioenergy contributing a mere 0.5% (KEGOC, 2019). Kazakhstan is often characterized as an authoritarian state, renowned for its robust administrative capacity to execute government directives. However, in the context of renewable energy, development has been slow. It would be an oversimplification to attribute the lack of progress in renewable energy generation solely to the dominance of the oil sector. While the dominance of the oil sector is evident in Kazakhstan, the government has proactively shaped its renewable energy policy, passed relevant legislation, and established institutional frameworks, reflecting a clear endeavor to align the nation with industrialized world economies. Nazarbayev's policy commitment is underscored by the Kazakhstan-2050 strategy (Nazarbayev, 2012). Despite the institutionalization of renewable energy policy and governance since 2006, the root causes of their ineffectiveness must be discerned.

The rapid growth of the renewable energy sector in Kazakhstan over the past decade can be attributed to the proactive implementation of support and regulatory measures, both domestically and in the global context. The sustained influx of investments, marked by substantial growth and stable capitalization, underscores the pivotal role that the private sector can assume in this transformative process. Presently, development banks and foreign investors serve as the primary backers of renewable energy projects in Kazakhstan, primarily in terms of capacity. The nation's abundant natural resources provide a strong foundation for the sector's ongoing expansion. Notably, Kazakhstan holds a strategic position within the Silk Road economic belt, occupying a unique place as a key neighbor and vital access route to Europe for China. Furthermore, it fulfils a crucial logistical and transit role along this path and plays a significant role in meeting China's energy requirements. These comparative advantages, in conjunction with the country's geo-economic positioning and its proactive and well-balanced foreign policy, have paved the way for its distinctive involvement in the Silk Road initiative.

However, there is a caveat. The 2060 carbon neutrality plan of Kazakhstan entails the use of Hydrogen in industry, transport, and power. In January 2022, KazMunayGas and a German firm Linde signed an MOU to develop clean energy projects in Kazakhstan through the production of blue hydrogen and green hydrogen using electrolysis. KMG and Eni SPA are developing a renewable gas power plant. In 2022, Karachaganak Green energy Cooperation was established to devise a new project for the valorization of excess gas produced in Karachaganak (ENI, 2023; Teodoro, 2023). With a mission to assist the decarbonization efforts of Kazakhstan, this development is radical and is observed where Gas companies are designing plans to develop low-carbon intensive hydrogen. Gazprom, having a significant stake in the Kazakhstan energy market, is not keen to buy the renewables, citing that the demand for natural gas was higher. Despite the quality of life and income being better in Kazakhstan, the geopolitical location of Kazakhstan and the increasing demand for natural gas and oil will not see the energy intensity of Kazakhstan go down majorly due to the dependence on these sectors in the generation of rents.

Kazakhstan has large oil reserves, primarily located in the Caspian Sea region and the western part of the country. Russia is a crucial partner for Kazakhstan in exporting its oil. The Caspian Pipeline Consortium (CPC) pipeline, which runs from Kazakhstan's Tengiz field to the Russian port of Novorossiysk on the Black Sea, is a vital route for Kazakhstan's oil exports. Russia's influence on energy prices, particularly in the oil and gas markets, tends to affect Kazakhstan's energy revenues and budget (Charrel, 2022). Changes in global oil prices, which are influenced by Russia as one of the world's largest oil producers, can have significant economic implications for Kazakhstan. The energy-rich Central Asian nation remains economically dependent on Russia, especially regarding oil exports. However, amid recent Russian 'Special Military Operation' in Ukraine, Kazakhstan has grown apprehensive of its relations with Russia, where there are fears regarding its energy exports getting affected.

COMPARATIVE ANALYSIS OF ECOLOGICAL CHALLENGES AND RENEWABLE ENERGY TRANSITION IN CENTRAL ASIAN COUNTRIES

1. *Negative impact on environment*: Central Asian countries face distinct environmental challenges, reflecting their varied landscapes and economic activities. Kazakhstan wrestles with extensive industrial pollution, including toxic waste and soil contamination, primarily due to its large resource

extraction and heavy industry sectors. Uzbekistan grapples with inadequate solid waste management, leading to land and water pollution, aggravated by its dense population (UNDP, 2023). In Uzbekistan, anthropogenic activities have resulted in the accumulation of substantial amounts of industrial waste, alongside the improper disposal of solid domestic waste in substandard landfills, dumps, and sludge storage facilities. The most detrimental industrial byproducts originate from sectors such as mining, oil and gas production, coal mining, and the chemical industry (IEA, 2020). Turkmenistan confronts hazardous waste concerns stemming from its petrochemical industry. Kyrgyzstan faces ecological degradation from mining activities and associated pollution, impacting its mountainous terrain. In contrast, Tajikistan struggles with water-related issues, including pollution and resource mismanagement, partly caused by inefficient sewage systems and agriculture practices (UNDP, 2023).

2. *Renewable energy*: Renewable energy holds the potential to address the escalating energy needs of Central Asian nations while mitigating the adverse environmental effects associated with fossil fuel consumption. The advancement of renewable energy in the region faces several obstacles encompassing regulatory framework, infrastructure, financial constraints, technical proficiency, awareness, support, as well as data and information.
    a) Kazakhstan leads in the deployment of renewable energy, as others lag in their efforts (Laldjebaev, 2021). The cost of producing electricity from RESs is still high in developing countries, and Uzbekistan leads the group of countries supplying their populations with inexpensive electricity.
    b) Innovative renewable energy technologies are being developed in Central Asia. Where Kazakhstan is the leading country in terms of innovative technology adaptation, it is too rapid for Uzbekistan to keep up. Because there is no local renewable energy technology manufacturing in Uzbekistan, purchase, installation, and maintenance costs remain high.
    c) There are various types of barriers that these five countries face with varying intensities, such as those related to- regulatory framework, infrastructure, finances, expertise & and awareness. Where Kazakhstan has a proper regulatory framework and long-term development strategy, Uzbekistan lacks that. Uzbekistan and Tajikistan face uncertainty due to the monopoly of state-owned electricity companies. Where Kyrgyzstan suffers from a clear framework, regulations, and enforcement, Turkmenistan's energy sector is characterized by the absence of any renewable energy regulatory framework at all (Dikambaev, 2019; Energy Charter Secretariat, 2013a & b; Karatayev et al., 2016; Kashkinbekov, 2017; QazaqSolar, 2020; Shadrina, 2020). Almost every country faces challenges related to infrastructure. Due to the lack of technical requirements for the integration of RE facilities into the grid, Kazakhstan faces the challenge of transporting RE-generated electricity through the transmission system and to the consumption centres of the country. Uzbekistan has abundance of outdated energy infrastructure. At present, hydroelectric power plants (HPPs) are the primary source of renewable energy, contributing just over 10% to the nation's overall electricity generation. Although Uzbekistan possesses substantial potential for renewable energy sources (RESs), such as solar and wind power, it has yet to harness these resources to their full extent. The government has set ambitious objectives: the construction of solar and wind power facilities, totaling 8 GW in capacity by 2030, and the attraction of investments. Furthermore, there is a plan to augment the capacity of hydroelectric power plants to 1935 GW (Statistics Agency under the President of Uzbekistan, 2020; IEA, 2021). The obsolete infrastructure results in

Figure 3. The trend of installed renewable energy capacity in Central Asian countries (IRENA, 2020)

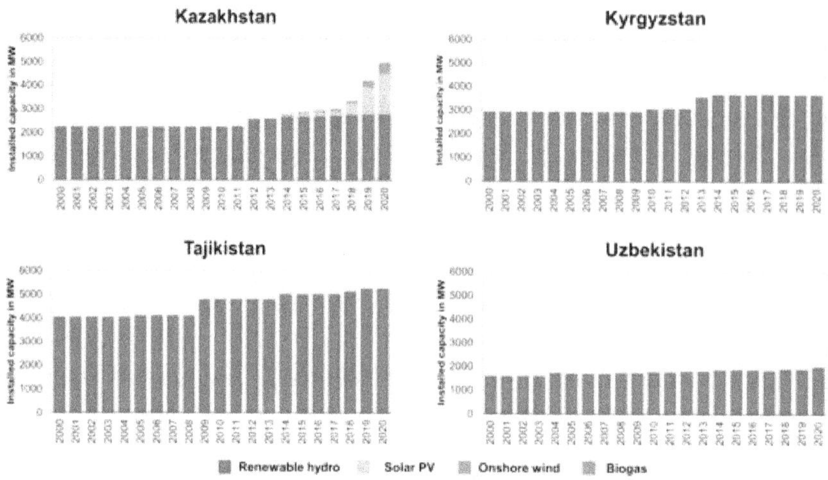

high electricity losses, estimated at 20 percent of net generation, and frequent power outages undermining economic activities and the well-being of citizens across the country. Kyrgyzstan and Tajikistan have outdated, overloaded and dilapidated infrastructure. Because of difficult mountain terrain, there is lack of roads to built road to transport RE equipment (Laldjebaev et al., 2021; Shadrina, 2020). Turkmenistan has potential for wind and solar power. The country has 300 sunny days per year and wind potential equal to the country's fossil fuel potential, but 100% of its electricity generation is fossil fuel-fire based. It has virtually no renewable energy power plants. Turkmenistan's only hydropower plant, the Hindu Kush located on the Murghab River is one of the oldest operating hydropower plants in the world, but its installed capacity is only 1.2 MW (https://www.newscentralasia.net/ 2023).

Figure 3 portrays the trend of the installed renewable energy capacity in Central Asia over the last 20 years. Turkmenistan does not have significant RE sources. It can be determined from Figure 3 that apart from hydro-energy, the employment of other RE resources is mainly untapped. However, Kazakhstan has noticeable progress in RE development.

Kazakhstan grapples with a shortage of funding for scientific research in renewable energy, and it faces substantial initial capital outlays for new renewable energy equipment. In Uzbekistan, the challenge is exacerbated by low electricity prices and a dearth of financial resources and investments to facilitate the transition to renewables. In Turkmenistan, unused utility quotas have failed to stimulate private sector investments in renewable energy sources, leading to a lack of interest and promotion in this sector. Similarly, the combination of insufficient funds and low current electricity tariffs in Kyrgyzstan and Tajikistan hampers the implementation of renewable energy policies (Dikambaev, 2019).

Regarding Tajikistan, Kyrgyzstan, and Uzbekistan, a shortage of local expertise and qualified specialists for project development and equipment maintenance poses a significant challenge. In Kazakhstan, the absence of qualified local professionals capable of overseeing renewable energy project development, design, financing, construction, operation, and maintenance is a notable issue. Although there is a growing acknowledgement of the role of renewable energy at the policy level in Kazakhstan, this awareness has yet to penetrate the general population. Uzbekistan faces a lack of clear support mechanisms for renewable energy development. The remaining three countries, Tajikistan, Kyrgyzstan, and Uzbekistan, are also characterized by a lack of awareness regarding the potential significance of renewable energy technology in reducing energy insecurity (Laldjebaev, 2021; Shadina, 2020; Dikambaev, 2019).

d) Tajikistan and Kyrgyzstan, situated in the upper reaches of the Syr Darya and Amu Darya rivers, are endowed with abundant water resources, primarily utilized for winter hydropower generation. In contrast, Kazakhstan, Turkmenistan, and Uzbekistan rely predominantly on water for summer crop irrigation. This disparity in water usage patterns is a key factor contributing to potential tensions regarding water distribution in the region (Imagambetova, 2022). Due to the economic disparity, it becomes harder for Tajikistan, Kyrgyzstan, and Turkmenistan to implement renewable energy policies as compared to economically better Kazakhstan and Uzbekistan.

3. *Plausible impact on health, societies, and economies*: The region might face several challenges, while transitioning to cleaner energy is critical for reducing greenhouse gas emissions and mitigating climate change. The construction and operation of renewable energy infrastructure, such as hydropower dams and wind farms, can still have localized environmental and health effects, including habitat disruption and water quality concerns. Large-scale renewable energy projects can lead to social displacement, as communities may need to be relocated to make way for infrastructure development. This can disrupt traditional livelihoods and social structures. The economic consequences of renewable energy adoption are mixed. On one hand, investments in renewable energy can stimulate job creation and economic growth. On the other hand, the initial capital costs of renewable energy projects can be high, potentially straining national budgets in these countries (Li et al., 2023; Shadrina, 2020).

CONCLUSION

In conclusion, this chapter has delved into the intricate web of environmental and ecological challenges facing Central Asia, a region marked by a complex history of Soviet influence, hydrocarbon wealth, and a burgeoning energy demand. The legacies of Soviet-era projects, such as nuclear waste sites, the desiccation of the Aral Sea, and the geopolitical ramifications of energy production, continue to cast long shadows over the region's ecology. Central Asian nations, rich and poor in hydrocarbons, are at a crossroads. They must grapple with the difficult choice between investing in clean technologies to reduce emissions, albeit at a high cost or continuing to rely on cheap but ecologically damaging energy sources. As these nations experience economic growth and increased domestic energy demand, the ecological toll of their energy production becomes increasingly evident. The chapter highlights the emergence of renewable energy policies across Central Asia, driven by global commitments like the Paris Agreement and a growing awareness of environmental issues. Uzbekistan's transition towards a green economy and Kazakhstan's carbon-neutral strategy are significant steps in this direction. These policies underscore the importance of comparing and analyzing the approaches of Central Asian nations to understand the role of environmental NGOs, civil society, state capacity, and domestic and transnational actors in shaping renewable energy policies.

Moreover, the chapter sheds light on the region's changing dynamics of environmental activism. Post-Soviet environmental activists have adopted a more transnational approach, leveraging international conventions and support to address local environmental issues. The demand for renewable energy is not merely a result of ecological concerns but also reflects the rising aspirations of Central Asian populations for a higher quality of life. China's Belt and Road Initiative (BRI) looms large in the discussion, as it contributes to and exacerbates environmental challenges in Central Asia. The BRI's expansion of transport infrastructures and energy projects, mainly reliant on fossil fuels, poses a significant threat to the region's ecology. The ecological consequences of various BRI projects, including deforestation, loss of biodiversity, and pollution, further complicate the region's environmental landscape.

Finally, the chapter examines the renewable energy policies and targets of Central Asian countries. The data illustrates a correlation between economic development and the demand for clean energy, with Kazakhstan's high per capita emissions standing in stark contrast to the hydroelectric-dependent nations of Tajikistan and Kyrgyzstan. While all Central Asian countries have renewable energy targets, challenges such as high installation costs, low energy tariffs, and the dominance of fossil fuels in energy production hinder their transition towards greener energy sources. Central Asia faces a formidable environmental and ecological challenge as it grapples with the past's legacies and the present's imperatives. Despite domestic Kazakh firms working on renewable solutions such as the development of green hydrogen, the region's journey towards renewable energy and ecological sustainability is marked by complex geopolitical, economic, and environmental factors. The bottom line is that the energy-intensive Central Asian nations are at a crossroads: to pay a high price for development or a substantially cheaper one for environmental degradation.

REFERENCES

Abylkasymova, A. (2019). *Hydropower Potential of the Central Asian Countries*. Central Asia Data-Gathering and Analysis Team. https://www.researchgate.net/publication/331716216_Hydropower_Potential_of_the_Central_Asian_Countries

Aidarkhanova, A., Larionova, N., Tleukanova, Z., Mamyrbaeva, A., Ermakova, R., Svetacheva, Y., Aktayev, M., & Panitskiy, A. (2022). The character of radionuclide contamination of natural lakes at the territory of the Semipalatinsk test site. *Journal of Environmental Radioactivity*, *255*, 107041. Advance online publication. doi:10.1016/j.jenvrad.2022.107041 PMID:36265400

Dave, B. (2018). Silk Road Economic Belt: Effects of China's Soft Power Diplomacy in Kazakhstan. In M. Laruelle (Ed.), *China's Belt and Road Initiative and its Impact in Central Asia* (pp. 97–108). The George Washington University. https://www.fpri.org/wp-content/uploads/2022/01/louthan-1.pdf

Decree of the President of the Republic of Kazakhstan. (2013). *On the Concept of transition of the Republic of Kazakhstan to 'green economy'. No 577*. https://gbpp.org/wp-content/uploads/2014/04/Green_Concept_En.pdf

Eshchanov, B. (2019). *Renewable energy policies of the Central Asian countries*. Norwegian Institute of International Affairs (NUPI).

Eshchanov, B.R. (2013). Prospects of renewable energy penetration in Uzbekistan—Perception of the Khorezmian people. *Renewable and Sustainable Energy Reviews*, *21*, 789–797. doi:10.1016/j.rser.2013.01.023

Goldstein, E. (2022). What does China want in Kazakhstan? *Harvard International Review*. https://hir.harvard.edu/chinas-kazakhstan-gambit/

Hanks, R. R. (2021). "Louder than Words": A Profile of the Destruction of the Aral Sea and Its Consequences. *Association of Asian Studies*, *26*(1). https://www.asianstudies.org/publications/eaa/archives/louder-than-words-a-profile-of-the-destruction-of-the-aral-sea-and-its-consequences/

Hu, Y., Han, Y., & Zhang, Y. (2020). Land desertification and its influencing factors in Kazakhstan. *Journal of Arid Environments*, *180*, 104203. Advance online publication. doi:10.1016/j.jaridenv.2020.104203

IEA. (2020). *Uzbekistan energy profile*. IEA. https://www.iea.org/reports/uzbekistan-energy-profile

Imagambetova, A. (2022). Problems of sharing transboundary water resources in Central Asia. *Journal of Academic Approaches*, *13*(2). https://dergipark.org.tr/tr/pub/ayd

Isaev, R. E., & Tolomushev, A. E. (2016). The potential and resources of renewable energy sources in the Kyrgyz Republic and the problems of their development. *Proceedings of the Kyrgyz State Technical University named after I. Razzakov*, 112–119.

Karachaganak Petroleum Operating. (2021). *Business and Human Rights Resource Centre*. https://www.business-humanrights.org/documents/36055/Karachaganak_Petroleum_Operating.pdf

Karatayev, M., Hall, S., Kalyuzhnova, Y., & Clarke, M. L. (2016). Renewable energy technology uptake in Kazakhstan: Policy drivers and barriers in a transitional economy. *Renewable & Sustainable Energy Reviews*, *66*, 120–136. doi:10.1016/j.rser.2016.07.057

Kazakhstan, P. W. C. (2021). *Renewable Energy Market in Kazakhstan: Potential, Challenges, and Prospects*. PWC Eurasia Deals.

Laldjebaev, M. (2021). *Renewable energy in Central Asia: An overview of potentials, deployment, outlook, and barriers. Energy Reports*. doi:10.1016/j.egyr.2021.05.014

Laruelle, M. (2018). *China's Belt and Road Initiative and its Impact in Central Asia*. The George Washington University.

Li, Q. (2023). The impact of energy transition on economy and health and its fairness. *Journal of Cleaner Production*, *425*. doi:10.1016/j.jclepro.2023.138953

Lukashenko, S., Kabdyrakova, A., Lind, O. C., Gorlachev, I., Kunduzbayeva, A., Kvochkina, T., Janssens, K., De Nolf, W., Yakovenko, Y., & Salbu, B. (2020). Radioactive particles released from different sources in the Semipalatinsk Test Site. *Journal of Environmental Radioactivity*, *216*, 106160. Advance online publication. doi:10.1016/j.jenvrad.2020.106160 PMID:32217195

Mambra, S. (2022). Aral Sea Disaster: Why One of the Biggest Inland Seas Dried Up? *Marine Insight*. https://www.marineinsight.com/environment/aral-sea-disaster-why-one-of-the-biggest-inland-seas-dried-up/

Ministry of Energy of the Republic of Kazakhstan. (2022). *Razvitiye vozobnovlyayemykh istochnikov energii* [Development of renewable energy sources]. https://www.gov.kz/memleket/entities/energo/activities/4910?lang=ru

Murshed, M. (2021). Can regional trade integration facilitate renewable energy transition to ensure energy sustainability in South Asia? *Energy Reports*, *7*, 808–821. doi:10.1016/j.egyr.2021.01.038

Musiał, W., Zioło, M., Luty, L., & Musiał, K. (2021). Energy policy of European Union member states in the context of renewable energy sources development. *Energies*, *14*(10), 28–64. doi:10.3390/en14102864

Nabiyeva, K. (2015). *Renewable Energy and Energy Efficiency in Central Asia: Prospects for German Engagement*. Michael Succow Foundation.

Narayan, D. (2018). *Kyrgyz Republic-Energy sector review*. Academic Press.

Normatov, I. (2010). Geothermal water resources of the Republic of Tajikistan and a perspective on their use. *Proceedings World Geothermal Congress*, 25-29.

Nurdavletova, S., & Akatayeva, A. (2018). The renewable energy in the regional development of Central Asia. *Society and Security Insights*, 162–185. https://cyberleninka.ru/article/n/the-renewable-energy-in-the-regional-development-of-centralasia/viewer

Painuly, J. P. (2001). Barriers to renewable energy penetration; a framework for analysis. *Renewable Energy*, *24*(1), 73–89. doi:10.1016/S0960-1481(00)00186-5

Peña-Ramos, J.A. (2021). Water Conflicts in Central Asia: Some Recommendations on the Non-Conflictual Use of Water. *Sustainability*, *13*(6), 3479. doi:10.3390/su13063479

Radovanovic, M., Filipović, S., & Andrejević Panić, A. (2021). Sustainable energy transition in Central Asia: Status and challenges. *Energy, Sustainability and Society*, *11*(1), 49. doi:10.118613705-021-00324-2

Sadovskaya, Y., & Utyasheva, L. (2017). Human Silk Road. In M. Laruelle (Ed.), *The People-to-People Aspect of the Belt and Road Initiative in China's Belt and Road Initiative and its Impact in Central Asia* (pp. 109–125). The George Washington University Press.

Saltybayev, Y. (2018). BRI and Kazakhstan. *Journal for International Relations and Sustainable Development*, *10*, 76–85.

Samimi, A. J. (2011). Environmental Performance and HDI: Evidence from Countries Around the World. *Middle East Journal of Scientific Research*, *10*(3), 249–301. https://idosi.org/mejsr/mejsr10(3)11/3.pdf

Sciorati, G. (2021). *Time to Talk Climate Change in the Post-Soviet Region*. Italian Institute for International Political Studies. https://www.ispionline.it/en/publication/time-talk-climate-change-post-soviet-region-30008

Secretariat, E. C. (2013). *Investment climate and market structure review in the energy sector of Kazakhstan*. Brussels: Energy Charter Secretariat. www. energy charter. org/fileadmin/DocumentsMedia/ICMS/ICMS-Kazakhstan_2013_en.

Shadrina, E. (2019). *Renewable energy in Central Asian economies: role in reducing regional energy insecurity* (No. 993). ADBI Working Paper Series.

Shadrina, E. (2020). Non-hydropower renewable energy in central Asia: Assessment of deployment status and analysis of underlying factors. *Energies*, *13*(11), 2963. doi:10.3390/en13112963

Simonov, E. (2020). Environmental Aspects of Belt and Road Projects in Central Asia. *Crude Accountability Environmental Justice*. https://crudeaccountability.org/environmental-aspects-of-belt-and-road-projects-incentral-asia/

Sorbello, P. (2015). *The Role of Energy in Russian Foreign Policy towards Kazakhstan*. Energy Brains.

Strikeleva, E. (2018). Influence of Land and Water Rights on Land Degradation in Central Asia. *Hydrological Impacts of Climate Change and Land Use/Land Cover Change*, *10*(9), 1242. doi:10.3390/w10091242

Teodoro, R. (2023). Eni Inks Deal to Build Hybrid Renewables-Gas Plant in Kazakhstan. *Rigzone*. https://www.rigzone.com/news/eni_inks_deal_to_build_hybrid_renewablesgas_plant_in_kazakhstan-09-jun-2023-173013-article/

The Kazakhstan energy politics: is oil diversification a geopolitical conundrum? (2022). *Special Eurasia*.

Tursumbayeva, M., Muratuly, A., Baimatova, N., Karaca, F., & Kerimray, A. (2022). Cities of Central Asia: New Hotspots of Air Pollution in the World. SSRN *Electronic Journal*. doi:10.2139/ssrn.4208086

Vakulchuk, R., Øverland, I., Aminjonov, F., Abylkasymova, A., Eshchanov, B., & Moldokanov, D. (2019). *BRI in central Asia: Overview of Chinese projects. Central Asia Data-Gathering and Analysis Team*. CADGAT.

Weinthal, E., & Watters, K. (2010). Transnational environmental activism in Central Asia: The coupling of domestic law and international conventions. *Environmental Politics*, *19*(5), 782–807. doi:10.1080/09644016.2010.508311

Wolff, P. (2016). *China's 'Belt and Road' Initiative- Challenges and Opportunities*. German Development Institute.

Zabanova, Y. (2023). Towards a Geoeconomics of Energy Transition in Central Asia's Hydrocarbon-Producing Countries. In R. Sabyrbekov, I. Overland, & R. Vakulchuk (Eds.), *Climate Change in Central Asia. SpringerBriefs in Climate Studies*. Springer. doi:10.1007/978-3-031-29831-8_8

Chapter 10
Climate Crisis and The Future of Renewable Energy in the Turkic Republics

Baybarshan Ali Kazancı
https://orcid.org/0000-0002-3407-3692
Kırıkkale University, Turkey

Osman Furkan Furkan Arslan
https://orcid.org/0000-0001-7639-5377
Kırıkkale University, Turkey

Selin Dinçer
https://orcid.org/0000-0003-3233-493X
Kırıkkale University, Turkey

ABSTRACT

The continuation of the worsening climate crisis and the severe environmental degradation caused by fossil fuels is not sustainable for the world. It is important for major energy suppliers and importing countries to turn to renewable energy to meet the intense demand for energy and for future generations. In addition, governments are turning to renewable energy sources and increasing their investments in order to reduce foreign dependency in an economic and political context. Therefore, renewable energy strategies offer new opportunities for competitive strategies and cooperation in the world. This study evaluates the current renewable energy studies and investments of the Turkish Republics. In addition, policy recommendations will be made within the framework of the possible economic/political effects of these resources, which will create potential in the long run for the countries.

DOI: 10.4018/979-8-3693-0440-2.ch010

INTRODUCTION

Energy sector has always occupied the world's economic agenda and has become an indispensable part of global system. The concept of energy is the dynamo of sustainable development, affecting every field from international politics to economy. Countries with rich fossil resources earn high incomes through energy exports and can use energy factor in their favor in international policies. Thus, these countries can allocate a budget for financing sustainable development and quality living standards. For developed countries are dependent on foreign energy, importing natural gas and oil used in areas such as industry, heating, transport, and electricity generation may cause current account deficits. In addition, if energy supply security is negatively affected by foreign policy, inflation problem may threaten the economy of the country.

Energy market, of which fossil fuels account for 82% (BP, 2022), is now at the center of multi-vector policies. Increasing world population, regional and global wars, and economic crises disrupt the energy supply-demand balance and create major problems. In addition, while the reserves of fossil fuels are decreasing, on the other hand, the emission of greenhouse gases after the processing of these fuels increases global warming. The Intergovernmental Panel on Climate Change (IPCC) (2014) states that if greenhouse gas emissions continue to increase at the current rate, the world will be adversely affected by rising sea levels, shifts in seasons, loss of biodiversity, and increased frequency and intensity (Godfrey and Tunhuma, 2020: 3).

Regionally and globally, changing climate and environmental conditions directly or indirectly affects the lives of individuals residing in the relevant areas. Factors such as the world's population increase, wars, regional conflicts, energy struggles, and industrialization serve as driving forces for environmental pollution, consequently leading to global warming and climate change. In this context, environmental pollution, directly or indirectly linked to human activities in the global atmosphere, has undergone extensive analysis in numerous scientific studies. It is observable that climate and environmental disasters caused by human activities have escalated since the Industrial Revolution. However, examination of the relevant literature reveals conflicting perspectives: proponents attributing these disasters to human activities and skeptics contending otherwise. Moreover, the current concern regarding anthropogenic changes in greenhouse gases in the Earth's atmosphere is highly debated, particularly the impact of human activities augmenting the natural formation of the greenhouse effect and its correlation to global warming.

Numerous scientists concur that global warming represents the primary environmental challenge confronting life on Earth. While the existence of a natural greenhouse effect is well acknowledged, the perturbation in the composition and abundance of atmospheric greenhouse gases due to human activity raises significant concerns. The terms 'global warming' and 'increasing greenhouse effect' imply human-induced climate change. Given that the primary human contribution to climate change stems from greenhouse gas emissions through fossil fuel combustion, mitigating this impact will necessitate substantial alterations in energy production and consumption. Various methods aimed at pollution reduction can yield short-term improvements. For instance, enhancing energy efficiency across economic sectors and transitioning from high-carbon to low-carbon fuels offer alternatives. However, achieving a long-term solution requires incentivizing technological progress appropriately to ensure climate-friendly advancements. Conversely, accurately predicting the ultimate physical impacts of climate change remains challenging. There exists substantial global uncertainty regarding the repercussions of climate change, amplifying the climate crisis. This uncertainty complicates decision-making, as it is challenging to determine the most prudent course of action. Decision-makers tend to postpone action until more precise scientific evidence of potential damage becomes available. The uncertainty surrounding changing agricultural practices, weather conditions, the unconscious utilization of energy resources, and other ripple effects further complicates estimations of potential damages.

It is not sustainable for the world that the climate crisis continues to increase in severity and that the sociological damage caused by fossil fuels on environment is severe. It is important for the main energy suppliers and importer countries to turn towards renewable energy in order to meet the intense demand for energy for future generations. In addition, governments are turning towards renewable energy sources and increasing their investments to reduce their external dependence in the economic and political context. With the decrease in costs in the coming years, long-term global renewable energy policies will be able to create new dynamics. Therefore, renewable energy strategies offer new opportunities for competition strategies and cooperation in the world. With increasing investments, technological progress is accelerating, product diversity is expanding through R&D, new employment areas are being created, and idle land and sea areas are participating in electricity generation. The demand for electrical energy used in almost every field is increasing every year. As a matter of fact, by 2022, global electricity consumption was 24,398 TWh (IEA, 2023) and it increased by 6.07% compared to 2018.

The Turkic Republics constitute the subject of this study, it has different characteristics in both fossil and renewable energy resources. Members (Azerbaijan, Kazakhstan, Kyrgyzstan, Uzbekistan, Türkiye) and observer countries (Hungary, Turkmenistan) gathered under the umbrella of the Organization of Turkic States (OST) contribute to energy supply security. Azerbaijan, Kazakhstan, Uzbekistan, and Turkmenistan earns income from energy exports in Central Asia. Kyrgyzstan, Hungary and Türkiye are countries that are dependent on foreign energy. This group of countries is looking for alternative solutions in the face of increasing energy demands. In recent years, meetings have been held to increase natural gas exploration and production, strengthen the infrastructure to diversify supply sources and develop the use of renewable energy.

In this study, the current renewable energy studies and investments of the Turkic Republics will be evaluated. In addition, policy recommendations will be made within the scope of the possible economic/political effects of these resources that will create potential in long term. In this context, in the first part, strategic importance of renewable energy resources in the world will be mentioned. In the second part, current renewable energy production and consumption of the Turkish states will be determined with quantitative data and energy investments will be explained. In the last part, determinations will be made about the future of renewable energy resources in relevant countries with the data obtained.

1. STRATEGIC IMPORTANCE OF RENEWABLE ENERGY IN THE WORLD

Global climate change has an increasing effect on the world. Droughts, and depletion of fossil fuels, have started to be questioned in energy markets. On the other hand, the self-interested behavior of energy-exporting countries regarding price policies poses serious risks for energy-demanding countries. Thus, renewable energy is becoming attractive in terms of having very low environmental damage compared to fossil fuels and reducing foreign dependence on energy. In addition, countries demanding renewable energy resources can also ensure energy supply security by turning to domestic opportunities (Bayraç, 2011: 248). In addition, as Önal (2020: 79) states, energy supply transformation has become popular worldwide due to the environmental damage caused by fossil fuels. Recently, the surprise production cut by the Organisation of Petroleum Exporting Countries (OPEC) (Bloomberg HT, 2023), and with

Figure 1. Share of cumulative power capacity by technology in the world, 2010-2027
Source: IEA, 2023

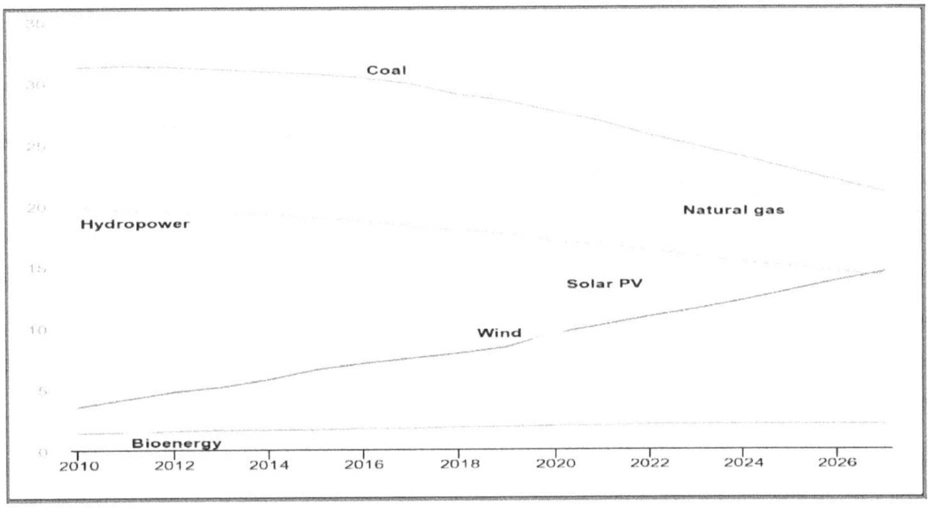

the Russia-Ukraine war, Russia, the world's largest gas supplier, reducing its gas supply to countries that oppose it and using this situation as a political pressure tool have led to global energy supply crises. With this war, European countries imposed economic sanctions on Moscow. In response, the Moscow administration used the natural gas as a political weapon and started restricting gas flow to Europe. With this decision taken in the winter months, serious escalations were experienced in energy prices. (BBC Türkçe, 2023). In the global arena where the need for energy is increasing day by day, these approaches bring security of energy supply to the top and increases in energy prices accompanied by interruptions seriously affect countries dependent on foreign energy. As a result, world economic balances have deteriorated and the risk of recession has increased along with inflation. In this context, developed countries with high energy demand have initiated studies on renewable energy. To ensure that production processes are not interrupted, and not affected by cyclical fluctuations and to ensure the continuity of energy supply security, countries should turn to renewable energy sources.

Energy that does not decrease in nature as it is consumed and has the potential to renew itself sustainably is called renewable energy. Renewable energy sources can be counted as solar energy, biomass energy, wave energy, wind energy, hydroelectric energy, and geothermal energy (Bekar, 2020: 43). The easy availability of substitutes for renewable energy sources will increase the diversity of energy supply. Investments in this field will open new employment areas in long term and support the current account deficit by reducing the foreign trade deficit.

When Figure 1 is analyzed, the world is seen that renewable energy resources obtained from solar and wind are increasing in a foreseeable way. Coal, natural gas, and hydroelectric power are in a downward trend. By 2026, solar energy is expected to surpass coal and natural gas.

Renewable resources, including solar, wind, hydropower, biofuels, etc., are at the center of transition to less carbon-intensive and more sustainable energy systems. Generation capacity has increased rapidly in recent years with policy support and sharp cost reductions, especially for solar and wind energy. Deployment of renewable energy in heat and transport sectors is one of the main drivers for keeping the increase in average global temperatures below 1.5 degrees Celsius. In the "Net Zero Emissions by 2050" scenario, renewables enable electricity generation to be almost completely decarbonized. Meanwhile, renewable transport fuels and renewable heat contribute to significant emission reductions in transportation, buildings, and industry.

The International Renewable Energy Agency (IRENA) states that the investment of 131 billion dollars in renewable energy will meet 86% of global energy by 2050 (IRENA, 2023The European Union (EU) has been at the forefront of global policy, increasing the rate of transition to renewable energy from less than 2% in 2005 to more than 10% in 2020 (IRENA, 2023). Again, the EU has formulated new policies to accelerate renewable energy activities. In this context, energy policy is based on the establishment of a competitive energy market, sustainable development, and security of energy supply. The 1973 and 1979 crises in the global markets seriously affected the EU members like other states and brought the single market understanding and environmentally friendly clean energy agenda to the forefront. Some incentives are provided for renewable energy within the EU. Premium system and fixed price and tariff guarantee are provided. In addition to these, investment incentives and subsidies should be supported by fiscal policies and regulatory studies should be carried out. (Bayraç & Çildir, 2017: 204).). In 2021, global energy strategies and incentives have gained momentum with energy consumption reaching an all-time high.

In energy markets where fossil fuels account for 82%, the remaining 6.8% is renewable energy from hydroelectricity, solar energy, etc., 6.7%, and the share of nuclear energy is 4.2%. The share of renewable energy increased by 15 percent, reaching a record level. Wind and solar energy accounted for 10.2 percent of world electricity generation (BP, 2022). In the renewable energy industry, the wind and solar energy industry has a great advantage in terms of employment. In Türkiye, it provides employment for 1.2 million people, including 670 thousand direct, 253 thousand induced, and 270 thousand indirect employments (İzmir Kalkınma Ajansı, 2023). According to the IRENA report, the legal infrastructure has been prepared in Germany to switch to 100% renewable energy by 2030. In this context, renewable energy is expected to employ 38 million people by 2030 (İklim Haber, 2023). As can be understood from the information obtained, the oil and natural gas industry lags far behind renewable energy sources in terms of employment opportunities (Ağpak & Özçiçek, 2018: 116).

The production and consumption of electricity is one of the main targets that brings the international strategy of renewable energy to the forefront. States need electrical energy, which they focus on to ensure the sustainability of the industrial, residential, transport, and service sectors. In 2019, total final electricity consumption in the world increased by 1.7% compared to 2018 and reached 22,848 THW. In the same year, electricity consumption by sectors was 9.56 TWH for industry, 6.07 TWH for residential, 4.8 TWH for commercial and public services, and 0.4 TWH for transport. By 2022, global electricity consumption continued to increase to 24,398 TWH (IEA, 2023).

The geographical potential of renewable energy focuses on generating electrical energy. Renewable energy also increases its geostrategic importance. Countries invest according to electricity generation capacity in accordance with the flow power of water, the number of sunny days, and wind speed. Renewable energy resources (such as solar, wind, water, etc.) has great opportunities, especially for countries that lack fossil resources. The efficient and planned use of these resources will both reduce the share of energy in imports and enable the formation of an economic cycle in the region where they are invested in.

Solar panel is a technology that can be produced in large facilities, creating economies of scale, and can also be deployed over large areas. It has a wide range of applications, from small residential rooftop systems to power generation installations. Despite increasing investment costs due to rising commodity prices, solar energy is the least-cost option for electricity generation (IEA, 2023). To generate electricity from the sun, it is necessary to select lands suitable for the number of sunny days. Countries continue their investments to ensure ecological balance and economic transformation of idle desert lands without harming nature. China has become the world's largest producer with giant solar farms placed on desert lands. Considering that this capacity can meet the electricity needs of the whole UK many times over, it is seen that the world solar energy capacity is very high considering the amount of desert lands. According to the drought index, desert areas constitute 33% of the total global land area. The largest desert lands in every continent of the world are the Sahara Desert in North Africa and the Kalahari and Namibia areas in South Africa (Cherlet, at all, 2018). Therefore, desert areas that seem idle in the coming years may turn into large investment areas to generate electricity in all seasons.

Wind energy is a proven technology with a comprehensive supply chain. Electricity generation from offshore winds is expected to increase rapidly, with wind turbines being developed to maximize the electricity generated in the last five years. In 2022, China claimed half of the world's wind power capacity and secured the top position in offshore installations. In the same year, electricity generation from wind increased by 14 percent to more than 265TWh, the second largest growth among all renewable energy technologies after solar energy (IEA, 2023). According to the map prepared by the Global Wind Atlas, offshore coasts, deserts, and arid areas seem to be the most suitable regions for electricity generation to obtain high efficiency from wind turbines (Global Wind Atlas, 2023). To achieve this level of capacity increase, governments should support the private sector by preparing an environment conducive to investment through international/national policies.

Hydropower provides many purposes beyond electricity generation, including infrastructure to provide clean water for housing, industry, and agriculture. It is also used to store water to reduce the impact of extreme weather events such as floods and droughts. Hydropower plants are among the cleanest sources of electricity compared to other forms of energy. Using hydropower instead of fossil fuels for electricity generation has helped to avoid more than 100 billion tonnes of carbon dioxide over the last 50 years. Globally, 60% of all renewable electricity is generated by hydropower. In total, it accounts for about 16% of global electricity generation (International Hydropower Association, 2023). China ranks first in world electricity generation with 159 GW. Hydropower currently generates more electricity than all other renewable technologies combined and is expected to remain the world's largest renewable electricity generation source until the 2030s. Hydropower is expected to eventually be overtaken by wind and solar (IEA, 2023). Irregular rainfall, global warming, and inefficient use of water cause drought in the world. In addition, the share of hydroelectric power plants in renewable energy will decrease in the coming years due to the long duration of dam construction, which constitutes a huge investment.

Countries that earn large revenues from oil and natural gas can become serious actors if they allocate financing to renewable energy. Especially the desert areas in the African continent and the Middle East stand out as the most suitable geography for the lowest-cost solar panels among renewable energies. Therefore, as states turn to new energy systems due to oil embargoes and natural gas shortages, international power balances will change and new geopolitical models will be developed. Large oil companies will be replaced by global companies that dominate the fields that will convert renewable energy into electricity.

Considering the geography and strategic importance of the energy resources it possesses, the Turkic States within the Organization of Turkic States draw attention in terms of having a say in the future of renewable energy. They have the investment potential to make the current transformation in terms of renewable energy in terms of both the underground resources they have and the geographical conditions they are in, and the financial infrastructure to meet these investments. It is thought that the CIS states, which currently play a pivotal role in the current energy market in the world, will also play a key role in the energy markets of the next century if they integrate and adapt to new developments by considering this energy transformation.

2. RENEWABLE ENERGY RESOURCES AND POTENTIAL IN TURKIC STATES

In today's world, most of the energy used in industry, housing, and transportation consists of oil and natural gas. The limitations of these two resources and the need of countries for energy resources make energy policies important. When necessary, the use of energy resources by energy supplier countries as a means of political pressure threatens energy trade and the security of supply. From the perspective of blocked global/regional energy policies, renewable energy investments are increasing day by day. In addition, considering the increasing climate crisis and the environmental damage caused by fossil fuels, renewable resources representing green energy are important.

Considering the developed countries in the world, it is seen that they have pioneering studies and breakthroughs in this field. The solar energy sector is the most easily obtained among renewable energy sources. China ranks first as the country with the production base and the highest energy demand. China is followed by America, Japan, and Germany, the other three industry and production giants (Kayışoğlu & Diken, 2019: 63). China ranks first in wind and hydroelectricity production, followed by the US and EU. In today's world, investments in renewable energy tend to increase every year. In 2008, the amount of investment made in the field of renewable energy was 155.4 billion dollars, while the investment made in 2018 was 600 billion dollars (REN21, 2019).

Growth in global electricity consumption increases in line with economic growth. Transition to energy-intensive sectors, increase in industrial production, lighting, and household appliances used in households affect electricity consumption. Electricity consumption in the world is 25.343 billion kHw in a year. The share of the Turkish countries listed in Table 1 in total electricity consumption is approximately 2.11%. The countries with the highest electricity consumption among these countries are Türkiye (284 billion kHw), Kazakhstan (92 billion kHw), Uzbekistan (58 billion kHw), Hungary (44 billion kHw), Azerbaijan (25 billion kHw), Turkmenistan (15 kHw), Kyrgyzstan (12 billion kHw). In terms of economic size, industrialization, and population, Türkiye consumes more electricity than other countries. Kazakhstan has the largest economy and industry among the Turkic countries in Central Asia,

Table 1. Electricity consumption of Turkic countries in 2021 (billion kHw)

Countries	Billion kHw
Azerbaijan	25
Kazakhstan	92
Kyrgyzstan	12
Hungary	44
Uzbekistan	58
Türkiye	284
Turkmenistan	15

Source: EIA, 2023

its also ranks second in electricity consumption. Uzbekistan ranks third in this consumption and has the largest population in the region.

Azerbaijan, which has gained geo-economic power with its investments in oil and natural gas sectors, plans to diversify exports and establish environmentally friendly economic models by developing renewable energy resources. Azerbaijan has a wind energy potential of 37 GWh from wind and sun and 157 GWh from the Caspian Sea, including the lands liberated from occupation (Anadolu Ajansı, 2023). The country's technical potential is around 23,000 MW with 2400-3200 sunshine hours per year. The wind blowing along the Caspian Sea coast is capable of generating 3,000 MW of energy. At the economic level, it can save fuel by generating 2.4 TWh of electricity. The technical potential for hydroelectricity, today's largest renewable energy source, is determined to be 3.2 TWh (IEA, 2023).

Kazakhstan has a very high renewable energy potential in terms of its geographical location and landforms. Kazakh government wants to utilize its potential and this field is making breakthroughs (Syzdykova, 2020: 80). The country has 97 renewable energy projects with a total capacity of 1260 MW and the government has approved 19 more projects (Satubaldina, 2020). Kazakhstan's renewable energy capacity was estimated at 3.1 GW in 2019. Renewable energy accounts for 8% of the country's electricity supply. The most efficient renewable energy source used in Kazakhstan is hydropower. It is thought to correspond to 13% of potential energy production in the country. The existing hydroelectric potential is determined as 2.248 GW. The Kordai wind power plant in the country has a capacity of 1500 KW (Syzdykova, 2020: 83).

Solar energy has significant potential as a renewable energy source due to its large sparsely populated areas and climatic conditions, especially in southern Kazakhstan receives 2200 to 3000 hours of sunshine per year. The northern parts of the country receive about 2,000 hours of sunshine. The southern cities called Kyzylorda and Shymkent receive 2,936 and 2,892 hours of sunshine per year. This potential is enough to meet the electricity needs of southern Kazakhstan. Current research suggests that Kazakhstan may have 1 trillion Kw of potential wind energy (Euronews, 2023). Kazakhstan met 3% of its annual energy production from renewable energy in 2020. This country aims to increase this share to 15% in 2030 and 50% in 2050 (ANKASAM, 2023). Speaking in the UAE, Kazakhstan President Tokayev said that they plan to provide 6.5 GW of renewable energy resources in their country in 2035 (Temiz Enerji Haber Portalı, 2023). However, despite having such a high potential within the scope of renewable energy, Kazakhstan provides a large part of its energy production from fossil fuels. Although the renewable energy potential is high, the share of these resources in total energy production is very limited (Syzdykova, 2020: 79).

Kyrgyzstan does not have fossil resources as much as other Turkic states in the region. (Bostan & Yılmaz & Ravanoğlu, 2015). According to the data of the Ministry of Industry of Kyrgyzstan, it has the capacity to produce 1.3 billion kWh of energy per year from biomass energy, 490 million kWh per year from solar power plants, and 46.6 million kWh per year from wind energy. Kyrgyzstan hydroelectricity has an important place, has the richest water deposits in Turkestan region. The current hydroelectric energy potential is 5.8 billion kWh (State Committee for Industry, Energy and Subsoil Utilization of the Kyrgyz Republic, 2018). Despite this potential, Kyrgyzstan meets 70% of its electricity generation needs from imported natural gas, oil, and coal (Cabbarov, 2018). Kyrgyzstan is advantageous in the field of renewable energy due to its geographical location. Renewable energy potential is thought to be 840.2 million TOE per year (Report of the Ministry of Energy and Industry of the Kyrgyz Republic, 2013). This current figure corresponds to 142.5 billion kWh. When compared to the countries in the region, it is right after Russia and Tajikistan in the Commonwealth of Independent States (Dikambayev, 2019).

Despite these data, Kyrgyzstan's utilization rate of non-fossil fuel energy remains below 1% (Akhmet Yassavi University, 2023).

In Hungary, as an observer state of the organization, nuclear energy accounts for almost half of electricity generation. Hungary also set a solar energy target of 6500 MW for 2030 and reached 3000 MW of this target in 2020 (Republic of Türkiye Ministry of Trade, 2022). In 2021, 3,793 GWH of energy was produced from solar energy. Hungary meets 10.6% of its total energy from renewable energy. The stakeholders of this renewable energy were solar, biomass, and wind energy, respectively (Mordor Intelligence, 2023). It is still a country with the lowest renewable energy production in the EU. Currently, solar power plant projects are ongoing. The capacity of wind power plants is approximately 330 Megawatts. However, wind farms cannot be established at the desired level due to restrictive legislation.

In 2021, 55.5 billion kWh of electricity was generated from hydroelectricity in Türkiye. As of the end of May 2022, hydroelectric electricity generation reached approximately 35.2 billion kWh. By the end of June 2022, the installed capacity of electricity based on wind energy was 10,976 MW and its share in total installed capacity was 10.81%. Türkiye's average annual total sunshine duration is calculated as 2,741 hours. As of the same period, the installed capacity of electricity based on solar energy has reached 8,479 MW, and its share in the total installed capacity is 8.35% (Republic of Türkiye Ministry of Energy and Natural Resources, 2023).

Uzbekistan updated its energy policies with the Ministry of Energy established in 2019. However, the natural gas sector accounts for 85% of total energy production. The remaining energy production consists of hydroelectricity (10.2%) and coal (3.7%). Almost all renewable energy is met by hydroelectricity. Wind and solar energy are neglected. However, the potential of solar energy is 88 times higher than hydroelectricity. Uzbekistan receives a large amount of sunlight compared to many European countries. and has taken action to implement large-scale solar energy projects in 2021. Tender processes are being carried out with investments to be made in the south of the country totaling 2050 MW (IEA, 2023). Uzbekistan aims to increase electricity generation from renewable energy by 25 percent by 2030 (Republic of Türkiye Ministry of Trade, 2022). Uzbek President Mirzoyev has taken new steps to utilize the renewable energy potential and announced an investment of 2,000 MW capacity from solar energy panels. In addition, the installation of solar panels in industrial zones and large enterprises is planned to generate 400 million kWh and 75 KHw energy for social facilities and public buildings (UZ Daily, 2023).

Turkmenistan, another country in the region rich in underground resources, has one of the largest natural gas reserves in the world. After Russia (47.57 trillion cubic meters), Iran (29.6 trillion cubic meters), and Qatar (25.47 trillion cubic meters), Turkmenistan comes next with 24.3 trillion cubic meters. Turkmenistan has 11.7% of the world's natural gas resources (Williams, 2013). Turkmenistan, has a very low demand for renewable energy. Due to its geographical characteristics, it has a very low potential for hydroelectric and geothermal energy. However, Turkmenistan has a magnificent solar and wind energy potential due to its 300 days of sunshine per year. Even though this potential energy is considered to produce energy equivalent to fossil fuels, renewable energy has not gained as much importance as fossil fuels (Asia Wind Energy Association, 2022). While 99% of the electricity generated in the country is obtained from natural gas power plants, 1% is met from hydroelectricity (European Bank for Reconstruction and Development, 2012). Realizing its deficiency in this field, Turkmenistan has started to accelerate its efforts in the field of renewable energy and to offer a future perspective. Through the agreement inked between the United Arab Emirates and Turkmenistan, a deal was established to invest in a hundred megawatts of solar panels. (Atavatan Turkmenistan, 2023). Turkmenistan plans to reach a serious point

Tables 2. Renewable energy generation of Turkic Republics (2020, GW)

Countries	Solar	Hydro	Wind
Türkiye	10953	78094	24.828
Azerbaijan	47	1070	96
Kazakhstan	1789	9660	1077
Uzbekistan	-	5000	16
Kygyzstan	-	13979	-
Turkmenistan	-	3	-
Hungary	2.459	244	655

Resource: IRENA, 2022
Prepared by compiling from the relevant source.

in wind energy by 2030 and to meet 100% of its energy from renewable energy by obtaining solar energy from its vast desert plains in 2050 (Satymov & Bogdanov & Breyer, 2020: 13590).

When the situation of electricity generation from water (hydro), solar, and wind in the Turkic Republics is examined in general, hydroelectric energy comes to the fore. According to the data in Table 2, Hungary and Azerbaijan's production from hydroelectric energy is weak. Turkmenistan, most of whose lands is covered with desert, has almost no production. The highest hydroelectric production is realized by Türkiye (78.094 GW) and Kyrgyzstan (13979). Türkiye, Hungary, and Kazakhstan are in the top three in terms of solar power generation. Kyrgyzstan, Uzbekistan, and Turkmenistan have no production from solar energy in 2020 according to the current table. Electricity generation from wind energy is quite high in Türkiye compared to other countries. It is observed that Kyrgyzstan and Uzbekistan cannot get efficiency from this type of energy.

Although the Turkic Republics in Central Asia seem to produce hydroelectric energy, their electricity production from solar and wind energy is at very low levels. Geographically, Turkmenistan is not in a good position in renewable energy electricity production due to its barren lands and rich natural gas deposits. Türkiye has reached quite good levels in these three sectors compared to all other countries. Hungary, a European country, has relatively focused on solar energy. Therefore, considering that renewable energy will occupy the agenda in international politics in the medium term, it is crucial to shift future planning to this field.

3. POSSIBLE PARAMETERS OF RENEWABLE ENERGY POLICIES OF TURKISH COUNTRIES

Most of the available energy in the world is met from fossil fuels. Fossil fuels have been used in energy supply for about 150 years, provided 80% of the world's energy production in 2021 (Environmental and Energy Study Institute, 2021). Developed countries account for most of the energy demand. These demands for fossil fuels manifest themselves in the climate change phase. While 45% of the current carbon emissions belong to two countries, China and the US, greenhouse gas emissions correspond to 11% of the total share (Yılmaz & Can, 2018: 525). Global powers such as the US and the EU, which are among the leading countries in the world, have set 2030 targets to reduce greenhouse gas emissions in the medium term. Gas emissions from fossil fuels pose a threat to the world and especially developed countries are looking for solutions to this problem. Thus, renewable energy sources have been placed on the global agenda and investments have been concentrated in this field in the context of global targets.

In addition to the damages caused by fossil fuels to the ecosystem, the fact that they are limited resources pushes countries to increase the diversity of energy supply. In this context, because it is a sustainable energy source, renewable energy gains great importance to leave a more livable world to future generations. Some countries are trying to increase the proportion of renewable energy in their current energy shares by reducing their fossil fuel consumption compared to previous years (Gürbüz, 2014).

The damages caused by the energy obtained from fossil fuels to the environment and nature should be taken into consideration by all countries and a solution should be reached together. In this context, countries need to turn to sustainable energy sources with low environmental damage values with the common agreements reached (Uzun, 2023). In line with these consensus studies, the Paris Climate Agreement was signed within the scope of global climate regulations for a more livable future. With this agreement, the countries party to the convention have declared that they will reduce their emissions rapidly (Republic of Türkiye Ministry of Foreign Affairs, 2022). In addition to the negative effects of existing fossil fuels on the climate crisis, the fact that these resources are extracted in a limited number of countries causes the countries with these resources to raise prices from time to time with a monopolistic approach and to use their power as a political sanction tool when necessary. In this axis, such developments lead to serious problems on the energy supply security issue (Gürbüz, 2014). In addition, since fossil fuels are limited resources, it is obvious that new problems in the energy supply will come to agenda with the depletion of existing stocks in the coming years. Even from the most positive point of view, it is thought that oil reserves will run out in 50 years, while a similar prediction is made for natural gas and coal. This reduction will naturally be reflected in prices and fossil fuel-based energy costs will increase (WWF, 2011).

With their fossil fuel reserves and geographical features, CIS members and observers have important positions in terms of renewable energy. Even though some of the current members of the CIS are rich in fossil fuels, they need to realize the future in terms of energy and take precautions by taking into account the threat of global warming, which is increasing its impact on the world. Therefore, as investments in renewable energy increase with each passing year, the importance of fossil fuels will gradually decrease in the long run. In this case, Turkish countries need to integrate into global climate and renewable energy policies without delay. Especially with the energy transformation to be experienced, it is imperative to make these policies sustainable.

In the renewable energy sector requires large investments, existing countries do not have sufficient financing. Spending the income obtained from fossil energy for economic development creates the need for investment. Regionally, the continuation of relations with Russia and China in Central Asia based on fossil fuels, the establishment of multilateral relations with companies making global investments in renewable energy, and the return of foreign investments to the CIS countries will accelerate developments.

Taking necessary steps in the field of renewable energy within the CIS has been included in the 2040 Vision document. In the field of renewable energy such as solar, wind, and hydroelectricity, it is mentioned to ensure information exchange between member countries, to ensure the necessary technological transfers, to achieve cooperation in issues such as diversification of supply in energy (Türk Devletleri Teşkilatı, 2021).

The world population is increasing day by day, increasing the need for energy in the world. This situation increases the current importance of the CIS in future projections and strengthens the idea that it will play a key role in the field of energy.

Azerbaijan is a geo-economic and geostrategic regional power in the natural gas sector and is a country that provides energy to neighboring countries through energy exports. The military conflicts with Armenia since the independence process have caused Azerbaijan to allocate a budget for defense expenditures. In this axis, the income items obtained from energy resources turn into defense expenditures. In particular, large investments are required for the reconstruction of the territories gained as a result of the victory in the Second Karabakh War. In this process, the suitability of new areas, especially high areas for wind farms and sunny areas for panels should be investigated, and renewable energy investments should not be ignored in the short term. It should be taken into consideration that the income obtained from fossil resources will decrease in the medium term, efficient sectors should be supported, and electrical energy to be produced should reach out to exportable levels. The wind capacity in the Caspian Sea should be supported by R&D studies within the maritime jurisdictions and necessary steps should be taken.

Kazakhstan, one of the largest countries of the Asian continent in terms of area, is a regional power due to its energy exports. Semi-desert and desert areas covering approximately 1/3 of Kazakhstan combined with steppe erode agricultural lands and dust storms occur (ADB, 2010). If the extreme temperatures experienced are combined with this situation, the current electricity generation from solar and wind energy remains well below the electricity generation potential. Solar panels and windmills to be installed will also contribute to the reduction of natural disasters. When Kazakhstan reaches the desired capacity in renewable energy, it will be able to diversify its trade items by providing energy to the countries in the region that need electricity.

Kyrgyzstan, blessed with abundant water resources, effectively harnesses hydroelectric energy in comparison to its regional counterparts. However, this country, lacking significant fossil fuel resources, grapples with water-sharing disputes and border conflicts with neighboring nations at times. The Kyrgyz economy, unable to make substantial investments in renewable energy, currently relies on fossil fuels for about three-quarters of its energy production. Given its smaller land size compared to other Turkic countries, Kyrgyzstan could consider establishing wind farms in its mountainous regions and installing solar panels in its sun-drenched wastelands. Nevertheless, the major obstacle lies in the limited financial resources available for such investments in Kyrgyzstan.

In Hungary, the only European observer state of the Organization of Turkic States, investments in renewable energy are increasing. However, production from solar panels and wind turbines is not at a sufficient level. In line with the political analyses made by the International Energy Agency, Hungary's orientation towards renewable energy will reduce its energy dependence on Russia. In addition, this inclination becomes important in terms of taking a different step in the joint actions of the EU members and preventing some political disputes among the member states. In line with these developments and analyses, the Hungarian government has taken some steps and set a very ambitious target of 90% clean energy in line with the 2030 National Energy Strategy (International Energy Agency, 2022). Being reliant on external sources for energy, Hungary stands to gain from investment and incentive initiatives facilitated by its membership in the EU. Therefore, it seems illogical to keep Hungary separate from EU policies. Hungary can act as a bridge in terms of joint projects to be carried out between the CIS and the EU in renewable energy policies.

Uzbekistan meets its current energy needs from fossil fuels and does not have as many fossil fuel reserves as other countries in the region. This situation leads Uzbekistan to supply diversity in energy. Investments in sustainable energy have not been achieved at the desired level. Three large desert lands in Uzbekistan provide potential in terms of wind energy and hydroelectricity. If the border problems with neighboring countries are completely resolved, joint consortiums will be able to add momentum to sustainable energy.

Türkiye is the energy-dependent country that stands out among Turkic countries with its population, economic structure and geographical location. However, it ranks at the top among Turkic countries in terms of electricity generation from solar, wind, and water resources. Türkiye attaches great importance to the development of renewable energy resources. According to the 2017 National Energy Policy, increasing the use of domestic and renewable energy resources is among the main priorities. Türkiye ranked 5th in Europe and 12th in the world in terms of installed capacity in renewable energy. By the end of 2022, 54% of Türkiye's installed capacity is composed of renewable resources (Republic of Türkiye Ministry of Foreign Affairs, 2023). Türkiye's rise to the world league in clean energy is an opportunity for CSA observers and members. Thanks to the consortiums to be formed under the leadership of Türkiye, technology transfer and energy investments can be the dynamo of regional development.

Turkmenistan, less fortunate than some other states in terms of renewable energy potential, currently relies heavily on natural gas for its economy. This reliance has led to significant carbon emissions, contributing to the global warming crisis. However, Turkmenistan possesses the highest solar energy potential in the region, estimated at 655 GW (ANKASAM, 2023). The vast Karakum desert, covering 70% of the country, presents an ideal opportunity for the installation of solar energy panels and windmills. With substantial income generated from its natural gas resources, Turkmenistan is well-positioned to finance such investments. Given the right technological investments, the nation has the potential to emerge as a major player in the energy sector.

In general, it seems important for Turkic countries to initiate renewable energy transformation projects under a common roof to create independent policies in the future. It is highly probable that energy, which is an indispensable sector for every country, will occupy the world agenda in the coming years because it requires high technological investments and provides great income.

CONCLUSION AND RECOMMENDATIONS

Energy resources are an indispensable sector for developed and developing countries. This sector of directly affects the dynamics of global/regional economic policies, will play an active role in the coming centuries. The use of today's hydrocarbon resources as a political trump card by supplier states against energy-importing countries and the difficulty of substituting fossil fuels create serious energy crises. On the other hand, greenhouse gases generated in energy production cause the global climate crisis. These consequences may disrupt foreign trade, liberalization, technological developments, and foreign policies. If the economic, political, and environmental crises are not resolved in the short term, the spread of sociological depression will become a possibility. As a result, it is a compulsory option to supply the energy needed from renewable resources in the shortest period with the slogan "Clean World, Clean Environment". Since electricity consumption in the world is increasing every year, countries investing in solar, wind, and water resources will both contribute to the reduction of the global warming problem and will be instrumental in reducing global energy conflicts.

Looking at the general outlook, it is foreseen that the hydroelectricity sector in renewable energy will enter a downward trend and that there will be a period in which the relatively lowest-cost solar panels will peak. Wind roses, on the other hand, are considered by countries as a second option. Countries and global companies that are actors in these two sectors will shape the world energy markets and become global powers.

Turkic Republics are late in renewable energy investments and are affected by energy policies in terms of both fossil resources and geographical location. In terms of renewable energy, these countries should prioritize solar panels considering the number of sunny days and desert areas. However, with the exception of Hungary and Türkiye, electricity generation from renewable resources is not sufficient. Azerbaijan, Kazakhstan, Uzbekistan, and Turkmenistan should direct their revenues from fossil resources to renewable energy resources considering the depletion of underground reserves. Countries rich in fossil resources depend on this field for their energy production and have difficulty switching their policies to renewable energy. Türkiye is making a breakthrough in renewable energy. Therefore, this country should establish a joint consortium with the integration of the Organization of Turkic States and activate R&D incubation centers to be supported by the renewable energy fund in which all countries participate. Otherwise, making investments that require high costs seems weak in the current conjuncture. Hungary, a member of the EU dependent on foreign energy, can act as a bridge to the Asian continent for the transformation of European capital into renewable energy investments.

REFERENCES

Ağpak, F., & Özçiçek, Ö. (2018). Bir istihdam politikası aracı olarak yenilenebilir enerji. *Ömer Halisdemir Üniversitesi İktisadi ve İdari Bilimler Fakültesi Dergisi, 11*(2), 112-128.

Akhmet Yassavi University. (2023). *Kırgızistan'ın Yenilenebilir Enerji Sektöründeki Gelişmeler.* Eurasian Research Institute: www.eurasian-research.org/publication/kirgizistanin-yenilenebilir-enerji-sektorundeki-gelismeler/?lang=tr#wpcf7-f20009

Anadolu Ajansı. (2023, June 28). *İlham Aliyev: Azerbaycan'ın şimdiki hedefi yenilenebilir enerji.* AA: https://www.aa.com.tr/tr/dunya/ilham-aliyev-azerbaycanin-simdiki-hedefi-yenilenebilir-enerji/2788986

ANKASAM. (2023a). *Orta Asya'nın Artan Enerji İhtiyacı ve Alternatif Yöntemler.* https://www.ankasam.org/orta-asyanin-artan-enerji-ihtiyaci-ve-alternatif-yontemler/

ANKASAM. (2023b). *Rusya-Kazakistan Arasında İvme Kazanan Enerji İlişkileri.* https://www.ankasam.org/rusya-kazakistan-arasinda-ivme-kazanan-enerji-iliskileri/

Asia Wind Energy Association. (2022). *Turkmenistan.* https://www.asiawind.org/research-data/market-overview/turkmenistan/

Atavatan Türkmenistan. (2023). *Türkmenistan ile BAE arasında yenilenebilir enerji alanındaki ortaklık yeni bir aşamaya giriyor.* https://www.atavatan-turkmenistan.com/tr/turkmenistan-ile-bae-arasinda-yenilenebilir-enerji-alanindaki-ortaklik-yeni-bir-asamaya-giriyor/

Bayraç, H. N., & Çildir, M. (2017). AB Yenilenebilir Enerji Politikalarının Ekonomik Büyüme Üzerindeki Etkisi. *Uluslararası Yönetim İktisat ve İşletme Dergisi, 13*(13), 201–212.

Bekar, N. (2020). Yenilenebilir Enerji Kaynakları Açısından Türkiye'nin Enerji Jeopolitiği. *Türkiye Siyaset Bilimi Dergisi, 3*(1), 37–54.

Bloomberg, H. T. (2023, April 4). *Petrol fiyatları OPEC+ kararı sonrası rallide.* https://www.bloomberght.com/petrol-fiyatlari-opec-karari-sonrasi-rallide-2329305

Bostan, A., Yilmaz, A., & Ravanoğlu, G. A. (2015). Kırgızistan Enerji Tüketiminin Ayrıştırma Yöntemiyle Analizi (2002-2011). *Ege Academic Review, 15*(1), 39. doi:10.21121/eab.2015117998

British Petroleum. (2022). *BP Statistical Review of World Energy.* 71 st. Edition. Author.

Cabbarov, F. R. (2018). *Ekonomik Büyüme ve Enerji Tüketimi İlişkisi. G. Üniversitesi içinde, 1.* Uluslararası Ekonomi ve İşletme Sempozyumu.

Cherlet, M., Hutchinson, C., Reynolds, J., Hill, J., Sommer, S., & von Maltitz, G. (2018). *World Atlas of Desertification.* Publication Office of the European Union.

DailyU. Z. (2023, June 20). *внедрение ВЭИ в Ташкенте планируется направить $1 млрд.* https://www.uzdaily.uz/ru/post/75414

Dikambayev, Ş. (2019). *Kırgız Cumhuriyeti Ulusal Sürdürülebilir Enerji Eylem.* https://unece.org/fileadmin/DAM/project-monitoring/unda/16_17X/E2_A2.3/NSEAP_Kyrgyzstan_RUS.pdf

Environmental and Energy Study Institute. (2021). *Fossil Fuels.* Environmental and Energy Study Institute: https://www.eesi.org/topics/fossil-fuels/description#:~:text=Fossil%20fuels%E2%80%94including%20coal%2C%20oil,percent%20of%20the%20world's%20energy

Euronews. (2023, June 10). *Kazakistan yeşil enerjiye geçişte rüzgar ve güneş enerjisi potansiyeline güveniyor.* https://tr.euronews.com/next/2022/12/02/kazakistan-yesil-enerjiye-geciste-ruzgar-ve-gunes-enerjisi-potansiyeline-guveniyor

European Bank for Reconstruction and Development. (2012). *Turkmenistan Country Profile.* Author.

Global Wind Atlas. (2023, July 10). *Welcome to the Global Wind Atlas.* Global Wind Atlas: https://globalwindatlas.info/en

Godfrey, S., & Tunhuma, F. A. (2020). İklim krizi: Sahra Altı Afrika'daki çocukların iklim değişikliği etkileri, eğilimleri ve savunmasızlıkları. Nairobi: Birleşmiş Milletler Çocuklara Yardım Fonu Doğu ve Güney Afrika Bölge Ofisi.

Gürbüz, Ö. (2014). *ABD ve Çin'in iklim hamlesi Türkiye'yi masaya çağırıyor.* BBC Türkçe: https://www.bbc.com/turkce/ekonomi/2014/11/141113_iklim_turkiye

İklim Haber. (2023, April 28). *Almanya 2035'e Kadar %100 Yenilenebilir Enerjiye Geçmesini Sağlayacak Yasayı Hazırladı.* İklim Haber: https://www.iklimhaber.org/almanya-2035e-kadar-0-yenilenebilir-enerjiye-gecmesini-saglayacak-yasayi-hazirladi/

International Energy Agency. (2023, July 13). *Electricity consumption.* https://www.iea.org/reports/electricity-information-overview/electricity-consumption2023

International Energy Agency. (2023, July 15). *Azerbaijan Energy Profile.* IEA: https://www.iea.org/reports/azerbaijan-energy-profile

International Energy Agency. (2023, July 15). *Context of renewable energy in Uzbekistan* IEA: https://www.iea.org/reports/solar-energy-policy-in-uzbekistan-a-roadmap/context-of-renewable-energy-in-uzbekistan

International Energy Agency. (2023a, July 15). *Solar PV.* IEA: https://www.iea.org/energy-system/renewables/solar-pv

International Energy Agency. (2023b, July 15). *Wind.* IEA: https://www.iea.org/energy-system/renewables/wind

International Hydropower Association. (2023, August 1). *Hydropower and the pathway to net zero.* IHA: https://www.hydropower.org/net-zero

IRENA. (2023a, April 28). *Finance & investment.* International Renewable Energy Agency: https://www.irena.org/Energy-Transition/Finance-and-investment

IRENA. (2023b, April 28). *Use of renewable energy for transport in Europe.* International Renewable Energy Agency: https://www.eea.europa.eu/ims/use-of-renewable-energy-for

İzmir Kalkınma Ajansı. (2023, April 28). *Yenilenebilir Enerjinin Yarattığı İstihdam Potansiyeli.* İzmir Kalkınma Ajansı: https://kalkinmaguncesi.izka.org.tr/index.php/2021/08/05/yenilenebilir-enerjinin-yarattigi-istihdam-potansiyeli/

Kayişoğlu, B., & Diken, B. (2019). Türkiye'de yenilenebilir enerji kullanımının mevcut durumu ve sorunları. *Tarım Makinaları Bilimi Dergisi, 15*(2), 61–65.

Ministry of Foreign Affairs of the Republic of Türkiye. (2023). *Türkiye'nin uluslararası Stratejisi.* https://www.mfa.gov.tr/turkiye_nin-enerji-stratejisi.tr.mfa#:~:text=%C3%96te%20yandan%2C%20T%C3%BCrkiye%20enerji%20talebini,alanda%20uluslararas%C4%B1%20ili%C5%9Fkilerin%20%C3%B6nemini%20art%C4%B1rmaktad%C4%B1r

Mordor İntelligence. (2023). *Hungary Geothermal Energy Market Sıze & Share Analysıs - Growth Trends & Forecasts (2023 - 2028).* https://www.mordorintelligence.com/industry-reports/hungary-geothermal-energy-market#:~:text=According%20to%20preliminary%20statistics%20by,a%20Y-o-Y%20increase%20of%2054.3%25

Öziç, E. A. (2018). *Türkiye'nin Yenilenebilir Enerji Potansiyeli ve Gelecek Hedefleri.* Ordu Üniversitesi Sosyal Bilimler Araştırmaları Dergisi.

Renewables Now 21. (2023, August 2). *Renewables 2019 Global Status Report.* REN21: https://www.ren21.net/gsr-2019

Report of the Ministry of Energy and Industry of the Kyrgyz Republic. (2013). *Development of Renewable Resources.* https://www.unescap.org/sites/default/files/C_Kyrgyz_Orozaliev_R.pdf

Republic of Türkiye Ministry of Energy and Natural Resources. (2023, August 1). *Hidrolik.* https://enerji.gov.tr/bilgi-merkezi-enerji-hidrolik

Republic of Türkiye Ministry of Trade. (2022a). *Macaristan'da Güneş Enerjisi Kapasitesi 3.000 MW'ın Üzerine Çıktı.* https://dtybs.ticaret.gov.tr/blog/post/12260/

Republic of Türkiye Ministry of Trade. (2022b). *Özbekistan 8 GW Kapasiteli Yenilenebilir Enerji Üretmeyi Planlıyor*. https://dtybs.ticaret.gov.tr/blog/post/13477/#

Satymov, R., Bogdanov, D., & Breyer, C. (2021). The value of fast transitioning to a fully sustainable energy system: The case of Turkmenistan. *IEEE Access : Practical Innovations, Open Solutions, 9*, 13590–13611. doi:10.1109/ACCESS.2021.3050817

State Committee for Industry, Energy and Subsoil Utilisation of the Kyrgyz Republic. (2018). http://ptfcar.org/wp-content/uploads/2018/06/5-Kyrgyzstan-State-Committee-on-Energy-Industry-and-Subsoil-Use-Marat-Chalponkulov-EN.pdf

Syzdykova, A. (2020). Kazakistan'ın Yenilenebilir Enerji Potansiyeli. *Ekonomi İşletme ve Maliye Araştırmaları Dergisi, 2*(1), 79–88. doi:10.38009/ekimad.699911

Türk Devletleri Teşkilatı. (2021). *Türk Dünyası 2040 Vizyonu*. https://turkicstates.org/assets/pdf/haberler/turk-dunyasi-2040-vizyonu-2396-98.pdf

Türkçe, B. B. C. (2023, April 28). *Avrupa'da enerji krizi: Rusya Kuzey Akımı'nı kesti, AB ne yapacak?* BBC News Türkçe: https://www.bbc.com/turkce/haberler-dunya-62971871

U.S Energy Information Administration. (2023, July 19). *Electricity*. EIA: https://www.eia.gov/international/data/world/electricity/electricity-consumption?pd=2&p=0000002&u=0&f=A&v=mapbubble&a=-&i=none&vo=value&t=C&g=00000000000000000000000000000000000000000001&l=249-ruvvvvvfvtvnvv1vrvvvvfvvvvvvfvvvou20evvvvvvvvvvnvvvs0008&s=315532800000&e=1609459200000&

Uzun, Y. (2023). Yenilenebilir Enerji-Sürdürülebilir Kalkınma: Rusya Örneği. *Ekonomik Büyüme ve Verimlilik Politikaları*, 46-67.

Williams, S. (2013). Turkmenistan Natural Gas Reserves Estimates. *The Wall Street Journal, 12*.

WWF. (2011). *2050 Yılında %100 Yenilenebilir Enerji*. https://www.wwf.org.tr/?1410/2050deyuzde100yenilenebilirenerji

Yilmaz, E. A., & Hatice, C. A. N. (2018). Türkiye'nin yenilenebilir enerji potansiyeli ve gelecek hedefleri. *Ordu Üniversitesi Sosyal Bilimler Enstitüsü Sosyal Bilimler Araştırmaları Dergisi, 8*(3), 525–535.

Chapter 11
The Locomotives of the Algerian Hydrocarbon Industry:
Anti-Colonialism, Nationalism, and Rentierism

Mustafa Yasir Kurt
https://orcid.org/0000-0001-8811-9193
Social Sciences University of Ankara, Turkey

Mürsel Bayram
Social Sciences University of Ankara, Turkey

ABSTRACT

The aim of this chapter is to shed light on the industry-politics nexus in resource-rich Algeria with emphasis on the connection between hydrocarbon processing industry and the economic-political goals of the Algerian state. The chapter involves a historical and political inquiry by focusing on the change in economic and technological capacity of the industry over the years, drawing attention to the relevant developments in domestic and foreign policy, as well as their reflections in Algeria's energy policy. The development of the Algerian hydrocarbon industry within a period of 70 years is investigated in terms of anti-colonialism, nationalism, and rentier relations between the state and interest groups (i.e., elites, foreign states, and international companies).

INTRODUCTION

Algeria ranks second in Africa and eleventh in the world with 4.5 trillion cubic meters of proven gas reserves. The North African country ranks third in Africa and sixteenth in the world with 12.2 billion barrels of proven oil reserves as well (CIA World Factbook, 2023). The income derived from this "gift of nature" accounts for 95% of the country's total exports and 30% of the GDP. The nationalist zeal to monopolize the rent derived from natural resources has culminated in growing state control over the

DOI: 10.4018/979-8-3693-0440-2.ch011

hydrocarbon industry. Eventually, the hydrocarbon industry has been a guarantee for Algeria's economic independence and a crucial part of its national interests.

Algeria's construction of hydrocarbon industry on a nationalist and protectionist discourse is related not only to the strategic importance of oil, but also to a political reflex rooted in the colonial period. The oil reserves discovered in the Sahara in the 1950s laid the foundations of Algerian hydrocarbon industry, while aggravating the conditions of colonial rule and reinforcing the struggle for independence. France extended the colonization of Algerian territory despite local resistance and international pressure. Nationalist policies on hydrocarbon resources emerged as a consequence of the post-independence goal of building an industry free from foreign interference and completely under state control. What necessitated this nationalist zeal was France's continued dominance and power over the "independent Algerian" economy and oil resources. Besides economic investments and development, a political struggle was inevitable to build an independent hydrocarbon industry. Therefore, the first section of the chapter will elaborate the reasons behind and the political and economic repercussions of the decision by President Houari Boumédiène on 24 February 1971 to scale Algeria's share in the oil business up to 51% and to nationalize all the natural gas fields and pipelines within the national borders.

The political dynamics that shaped the development of Algerian hydrocarbon industry are not limited to the struggle against foreign presence and its nationalist implications. The strong orientation of economic and political representatives/elites involved in hydrocarbon activities towards predatory behaviors, regardless of the fact that revenues are derived from a non-renewable natural resource, is another factor that makes the industry the focus of political relations. This orientation ultimately led to the questions of how and by whom hydrocarbon revenues are allocated. Alvarez (2010), Martinez (2010), and Shabafrouz (2010) argue that the rent-elite relationship between the state and the national oil company Sonatrach contributed to the construction of a repressive political order, the consolidation of a military regime, and the emergence of a predatory mindset. In this framework, the last section of the chapter is about the rent politics that have shaped Algeria's political and economic life.

THE BIRTH OF THE ALGERIAN HYDROCARBON INDUSTRY AND THE TRANSFORMATION OF HYDROCARBON RESOURCES INTO A COMMODITY OF EXPLOITATION

Although the existence of hydrocarbon resources in Algeria was known centuries ago (Aissaoui, 2001: 40), the transformation of these resources into an industrial product was materialized within the framework of France's colonial goals and policies. In the nineteenth century, when oil production became an indicator of power for modern nation-states, France lacked an integrated oil industry with production and distribution activities and managed to join the international oil market following a delayed and painful process compared to the US, Britain and Russia. It was only after the World War I that France was able to come up with a rival company to compete with Standard Oil and Royal Dutch-Shell, which had established regional monopolies through shares in international oil production (Sassi, 2003). The position of France among the victorious states at the end of the war provided it with advantages in the field of energy as well as many other political issues. Two important developments in the post-war period marked a new beginning for the French oil industry: the granting of shares to the Turkish Petroleum Company (TPC) in Iraq in 1920 and the establishment of *Compagnie française des pétroles* (CFP) in 1924. Due

Table 1. Oil production in Hassi Messaoud oil field (tons)

	CFP (A)	SN REPAL	TOTAL
1957-1958	216.096	220.205	436.301
1959	601.578	689.005	1.290.583
1960	2.373.343	4.271.422	6.644.765
1961 (first 8 months)	2.085.819	3.163.453	5.249.272

Source: Salut (2006)

to the involvement of American companies in the sharing of Iraqi oil and the outbreak of a new world war soon after, France's hopes for the continuity of energy supply were replaced by security problems.

Following the World War II, France's share and influence over the Middle Eastern oil declined and its partnerships in the TPC shifted in favor of the US. As its position in the Middle East consortium was jeopardized due to the problems in energy supply, France turned to its colonial territories in the Sahara. The main reason behind this change in strategy was the expectation that every discovery in these occupied territories would reduce its external dependence (Cantoni & Veneer, 2014: 46-51). The oil discoveries and the first industrial activities in Algeria were in line with this strategy and orientation.

France had expected significant oil resources in the Sahara, which was the source of geological studies carried out in the region from the 1920s onwards. However, discoveries ushering in production only started to materialize in the second half of the twentieth century (Musso, 2017: 67). The first significant discovery was made by *Compagnie de recherches et d'exploration de pétrole au Sahara* (C.R.E.P.S.) in June 1956. In Edjeleh, a region close to the Libyan border, a reserve of 500 million tons was found at a depth of approximately 450 meters. Within three months following this discovery, two more important reserves were found. The first was the discovery of 600 million tons of oil in Hassi-Messaoud by CFP(A) and SN Repal, and the second was the discovery of natural gas in Hassi R'mel, which even today hosts Algeria's largest reserves (Salut, 2006: 365; Gaillard and Lebois, 2015: 19).

France's dependence on foreign oil fell from 90% in 1960 to 60% within a few years (Malti, 2010: 19), which encouraged the French rulers to increase investments in the Sahara. French Minister Jacques Soustelle (1959) confirmed that "In the years to come, not only France, but most of Europe will depend on the Sahara for cheap energy it needs for industrial growth". France's hydrocarbon investment in Algeria increased from 8.5% in 1954 to 27% in 1961 (Bendib, 1998: 83).

Following oil discoveries, the Sahara represented a strategic and psychological value for France. The oil fields controlled in the region were seen as a guarantee of supply security and as a victory over the Anglo-American cartel. However, despite the establishment of an energy supply scheme protected against external threats, the threats in Algeria had become increasingly visible. The more production activities were conducted in the region, the more reaction and resistance came from the real owners of natural resources, the Algerian people. The war of independence by the resistance groups united under the umbrella of *Front de libération nationale* (FLN) continued in a wider and more violent way after the discoveries in the Sahara. The FLN, which organized and carried out actions in densely populated areas, strategically turned towards oil production facilities in the south (Adjel-Debbich, 2018: 133-134).

As the resistance against the colonial rule grew stronger and spread to a wider area, protests against the French presence rose in intensity. Although the oil industry was unaffected in the early years of the war and was expected - by the French - to continue to be so, several sabotages with the support of local population soon demonstrated the FLN's determination for independence (Stein, 2014: 120). As attacks on labor camps, pipelines and railways increased, production facilities were either abandoned or guarded by military forces (Musso, 2017: 76). The FLN not only fought militarily to protect its rights over the Sahara, but also made various diplomatic initiatives by bringing the oil issue to the forefront. During these initiatives, FLN representatives stated that any agreements made with the French authorities by the oil companies operating in this region after independence would be deemed invalid and reminded that they could only maintain their rights in the Sahara if they supported them in the war of independence. An article published in the FLN publication AlMoudjahid is noteworthy:

For the development of such a vast territory, the technical and financial means provided by France would be insufficient, let alone for a nation that has been subjected to foreign domination for more than 125 years. But the Algerians themselves intend to set the conditions and modalities of this indispensable foreign assistance. Only a free Algerian government would have the right to ratify such contracts and make concessions on national territory. Foreign companies investing their capital in the Sahara, and those applying to the French government for permission to explore, are building their investments on sand. (ElMoudjahid, 1958)

The most serious response to the FLN's call came from the Italian oil company *Ente Nazionale Idrocarburi* (ENI). With its operational capacity and productivity declining in the face of growing French pressure and restrictions, ENI contacted with the FLN in the expectation of a payoff in the near future. The meeting in 1958 between Enrico Mattei, one of the founders of ENI, and Taieb Bonlahronf, the FLN Representative in Rome, was the beginning of a long-lasting relationship (Cantoni and Veneer, 2014: 173-174). The FLN welcomed Italy's offer of cooperation in order to turn France's weakening control and sovereignty in the region in its favor (Musso, 2017: 80).

Against the backdrop of shifting balance, France started to evaluate the possibility of losing the war and oil resources, and made some political moves to guarantee its presence in the Sahara region. One of those moves was the establishment of *Organization commune des régions sahariennes* (OCRS) in 1957 to reorganize the administrative borders and structures of colonial territories, i.e., Algeria, Chad, Niger, Mali and Mauritania. By drawing new borders within the framework of this organization, France aimed to separate the Sahara region, including the oil fields, from Algeria and to maintain its dominance over the Saharan oil regardless of the outcome of the war (Sèbe, 2010: 314). This idea of division was soon reflected in the rhetoric of French officials, who began to refer to the non-Saharan part of the country as northern Algeria (Malti, 2010: 23).

Another political move by France came when it became clear that the OCSR plan had failed and independence was inevitable. De Gaulle's failed policy of dividing Algeria into two parts was replaced by attempts to establish an oil industry that could control Algeria even after independence. It is possible to see the reflections of this political move in the 1962 Evian Agreement that formalized Algeria's independence. The agreement provided France with significant concessions regarding the hydrocarbon industry.

Since 1830, the Algerian people had been living under colonial rule, and it was only in 1962 that they were able to successfully conclude their long struggle for independence. However, it soon became clear that colonialism, which had permeated every part of society for more than a century, would continue in various forms after independence (Naylor, 1985: 179). The continuation of France's authority over oil exploration, production and distribution in the first years of independence is the most striking example of this situation. France's uncompromising stance at the negotiating table regarding important refineries

Table 2. Oil and natural gas production in Algeria between 1962 and 1965

	1962	1963	1964	1965
Oil	20,452	23,568	26,670	26,365
Natural Gas	-	-	809	1,839

Note: Oil production is calculated in thousand cubic meters, and natural gas production is calculated in million cubic meters. **Source:** Naylor, 2000: 66.

built during the colonial period, such as Hassi Messaoud and Hassi R'Mel, as well as Algeria's lack of the technological and economic means to operate them, delayed the process of building an independent industry and economy (Bendib, 2018: 121). To better understand this process, it is important to examine the terms of independence, namely the articles of the Evian Agreement.

During the peace talks held in Evian, Switzerland in May 1961, the Sahara was among the issues that caused disagreement between the FLN and France. According to the plan prepared by the French side, the Sahara would remain under French sovereignty; Algeria would be a country neighboring the Sahara and a transfer point hosting pipelines to Europe (Sönmez, 2007: 82-83). Algeria rejected this offer but conceded during the preparation of the Evian Agreement (Malti, 2020: 57). The concessions are presented in the following articles of the agreement:

- For the export of hydrocarbons in the Sahara, transactions will be carried out in French francs
- Algeria will refrain from any initiative that harms French companies and their subsidiaries in exploration, exploitation or transportation of hydrocarbons in liquid or gaseous form
- Algeria will give priority to French companies in the event of equal bids for allocated or repossessed areas for a period of six years
- Oil industry disputes will be transferred to an international arbitration tribunal instead of the Algerian Supreme Court
- Algeria will ratify the *Code pétrolier saharien* (CPS) which set out the rules of government over the territory demarcated by the OCSR (Agreements Relating to Algerian Independence, 1962).

While the agreement ostensibly offered a partnership between Algeria and France over hydrocarbon resources in the Sahara, in reality it was a guarantee of France's presence in the region. With the implementation of the Agreement, the French companies Elf-Erap and CFP came to control 90% of the oil production in the region and a significant part of the exploration and marketing activities. In return, Algeria was given a small share in the Arzew gas refinery and a 40.5% stake in SN Repal (Iratni, 1986: 182- 183).

With the Agreement, the OCRS ceased to exist. All the privileges of the OCRS were transferred to a body called *Organisme saharien* (Cornat, 1965: 4). The new body was tasked with protecting the rights defined in the Saharan Petroleum Law, developing infrastructure systems, drafting mining-related legislation and advising on regulations ((Grimaud, 1972: 1282; Aissaoui, 2001: 59).

The foreign control of a strategic sector called into question the political and economic independence of the state and damaged the political image of the ruling elite. The resultant discomfort and reactionary attitude caused the Algerian hydrocarbon industry to be built on nationalist and statist foundations. This attitude is closely related to the adoption of socialism as a state ideology. The founding government adopted a socialist development model, put forward oil as an important target for state ownership and control, with a state ideology of controlling and directing the economy. Nationalism and socialism, which gained a sacred status among the political elite (Entelis, 1981: 194), were the main concepts that shaped Algeria's hydrocarbon policies. The "expropriation of mineral and energy wealth" in the Tripoli Programme of June 1962 and the statements in the Algerian Charter of April 1964 that "the Evian Agreement was an obstacle to the development of the Algerian state" and that "imperialism still reigns in the country" were the first signs of the new orientation (Tripoli Programme, 1962; Les éditions de l'asymétrie, 1964). The theme in meetings and communiqués was soon reflected on the ground. A new era of nationalization began in the industry with the establishment of Sonatrach company in 1963.

In the years following independence, Algerian leaders repeatedly expressed their desire to revise the articles of the Evian Agreement regulating the oil industry (Salut, 2006: 373). Their desire, at least at the initial stage, was not shaped by the idea of expelling France from the country once and for all. The lack of economic means and experience to run the industry necessitated a gradual termination of the French presence. Therefore, in the first phase, the aim was to participate in the French-run industry with national assets and values. An institutional organization to integrate Algeria into oil activities on its territory, in other words a national oil company, was the most visible manifestation of this objective. The goal of ending the French presence was a long-term process (Iratni, 1986: 212).

The order established by the Evian Agreement was put to the test for the first time when the Algerian government wanted to take part in the oil pipeline project connecting the Haoud El Hamra oil facilities near Hassi Messaoud to the port of Arzew. Crude oil transportation, albeit the weakest link in the hydrocarbon production chain, was considered an important starting point for Algeria to gradually expand into the entire sector and end the French presence on its territory. It was a political move and was protested by sixteen foreign companies operating in the region and the French government itself (Aïssaoui, 2001: 66-67). Despite economic and political pressure from foreign investors and France, the Algerian government had already created a company, ostensibly to take part in pipeline projects, but in reality to compete directly with private companies and eventually to form the basis of the national industry with *Société nationale pour la recherche, la production, le transport, la transformation, et la commercialisation des hydrocarbures* (Sonatrach) (McDougall, 2017: 257). The 800 km pipeline project between Haoud El Hamra and Arzew was the company's first project. Thus, Sonatrach took its place in Algerian history as an economic and political instrument (Belhoul, 1984: 292).

Sonatrach became one of the largest hydrocarbon companies in Africa shortly after its establishment in 1963. Although Sonatrach was established to operate in all areas of the hydrocarbon sector, it was able to complete the projects it was involved in with the help of foreign companies, mainly French ones, due to administrative and technological inadequacies in its early years (Bendib, 1988: 165). In those years, Sonatrach's share in production was limited to 12%, while French companies such as CFP, SN Repal, CREPS and SNPA accounted for 71% and other foreign companies such as Shell for around 17% (Aissaoui, 2001: 67).

Table 1 shows the declining investment of the French company CFP following the establishment of Sonatrach, which is indicative of the changing balance in Algeria. The reactions against the conditions imposed by the Evian Agreement forced France to renegotiate. Thus, in 1965, the hydrocarbon issue was put back on the table with amendments in favor of Algeria, and Sonatrach was accepted as the new actor of hydrocarbon production in the region.

Ahmed Ben Bella, the first president of Algeria, repeatedly warned the French and other foreign investors operating in the region not to engage in activities with colonialist objectives, reminding them of both the changing conditions and the fact that they were operating in an independent country. Alge-

Table 3. CFP's investment regions and annual investment amount (million Francs)

	1963	1964	1965
Europe	453	487	587
Algeria	177	91	106

Source: Salut, 2006, s. 375.

ria announced three goals to send the message that Algeria would be more active in the field: Active participation in hydrocarbon sector, increasing financial gains from the sector, and the preparation of a special regulation for the development of natural gas production (Aissaoui, 2001: 68). In line with these statements and objectives, the Algerian government requested negotiations at the state level to reorganize and redefine the hydrocarbon industry which was demarcated by the Evian Agreement. Realizing that it was amidst an unavoidable change, the French government was forced to come to the table to protect the interests of its companies. As a result of the negotiations, an agreement with new regulations was signed in June 1965 (Naylor, 2000: 69).

After nearly two years of negotiations, the Franco-Algerian Oil Accord was signed by the heads of state on July 29, 1965. With this agreement, Sonatrach became the operator of all newly discovered oil fields, while Algeria became the state responsible for the purchase, transportation and sale of oil. The agreement introduced new tax provisions for foreign companies, approved concession rights, and established the Association Coopérative (ASCOOP), which established a new exploration and production regime for resources not included in existing concession contracts (Tordo, et al., 2011: 109). Under the new arrangements, the tax rates on the profits of French companies were adjusted to 53% in 1965-67, 54% in 1968 and 55% in 1969 (Bendib, 1988: 168). The main task of ASCOOP, which represented the partnership between Sonatrach and the French company SOPEFAL, was to organize oil exploration and production activities over an area of 180,000 km (Malti, 2010: 64). ASCOOP played an important role in the discovery of 364 million tons of reserves and 4 million tons of production between 1966 and 1970 (Salut, 2006: 378).

Sonatrach grew rapidly and expanded its operations following the ratification of the 1965 Agreement. The latter gave Sonatrach the opportunity to gain direct experience and invest in research and development. The goals of national development and resource nationalism outlined in the Tripoli Program and the Algerian Charter finally began to pay off. As a complement to this process, the concessions of other foreign companies excluded by the 1965 Agreement were terminated and their assets were taken over. American and British companies were particularly targeted during the takeovers. In interpreting this decision, the government's ideological stance and foreign policy objectives, as well as the statist policies implemented since independence, should be taken into account. The fact that these states supported Israel during the Six-Day War (1967) contradicts Algeria's uncompromising stance on Palestine. Algeria imposed an oil embargo on the two states and decided to confiscate their assets in the country. Within a few years after the decision, all Anglo-American enterprises, except El Paso and Getty, were nationalized (Grimaud, 1972: 1286). Eventually Sonatrach's assets quadrupled, while the British and American governments refrained from intervening, fearing an escalation of conflict (Musso, 2017: 87).

Conflicts arising from Sonatrach's determination to expand its control over the oil industry and the reluctance of French oil companies to give up their advantages continued despite the 1965 Agreement and ASCOOP. Algeria's main complaint about ASCOOP was the high profits that France, as an investor,

Table 4. Companies nationalized between 1967-1970

Date	Company
1967	BP
1967	ESSO Algeria ESSO Africa ESSO Sahara Mobil
1968	Domestic Distribution Networks
1968	Shell
1969	Sinclair
1970	SOFRAPEL, AMIF, Phillips,
1970	Newmont Overseas Petroleum

Source: Bendib, 1988, s. 349.

received for the small amount of money invested. From 1965 to 1968, French oil companies earned 380 billion francs from oil production while investing only 20 billion francs (Iratni, 1986: 214). Considering the competition and conflict of interest in many other areas, it is possible to say that the parties anticipated the end of the compromise long before. Naylor (2000) interprets the 1965 Agreement as a political maneuver by the Algerian government, aware of the dubious nature of the "partnership" with France, before nationalizing the entire industry. The agreement and partnership initiative, which kept French postcolonial activities under wraps for a while, was short-lived due to international developments and growing discontent on the Algerian side.

By the end of the 1960s, despite France's unchanged colonial ambitions and continued energy dependence, Algeria experienced significant changes and developments compared to the early years of its independence. The North African country gained the ability and opportunity to act more independently in domestic politics and started to become more visible and active in the international arena. Membership to OPEC is one of the turning points of the new period.

Algeria participated as an observer in OPEC high consultative meetings since the early years of its independence, but did not warm to the idea of joining the organization. The first reason was its reservation that the trust between OPEC members had not been built due to the different regimes and political objectives. Another reason was that a state whose main concern since the early years of its independence was to increase state participation and control in the oil industry did not want the presence of another superior authority besides France (Malti, 2020: 58). Even if these reasons were eliminated or softened, Algeria did not have the power to violate or abrogate the Evian and 1965 Agreements (Aissaoui, 2001: 72). Therefore, Algeria waited until 1969 for domestic conditions to mature and for OPEC to become a more stable organization in line with its policies (Skeet, 1988:29).

In February 1969, Algeria wanted to raise the price CFP and ERAP paid per barrel from 2.08 USD to 2.65 USD and then to 2.85 USD, the limit set by OPEC. However, the French government rejected these prices announced by Algeria. When the parties did not back down on the price issue, tensions in bilateral relations escalated further. While the price crisis continued, Algeria adjusted its tax rates. These steps were interpreted as Algeria's efforts to harmonize its hydrocarbon sector with OPEC's fiscal guidelines (Naylor, 2000: 91).

Algeria's reservation of supreme authority came to an end when OPEC's 1968 Statement on Petroleum Policy in Member Countries gave the green light to member countries' demands for control over prices. The text committed OPEC to be more flexible and less interventionist (in favor of member countries) in areas such as development, participation, tax rates and protection of hydrocarbon resources (Guidelines for Petroleum Policy in OPEC Member Countries, 1968). Thus, in 1969, domestic conditions became favorable for membership, and OPEC's policies found common ground with Algeria's objectives. By July 1969, Algeria's application for full membership was accepted and the country was included in the organization as the 11th member.

As the "Mecca of revolutionaries" (Byrne, 2016) due to its experience in the struggle against France and its support for organizations fighting against occupation and exploitation in different parts of the world, especially in Palestine, Algeria kept its revolutionary and combative attitude against imperialism within OPEC. In this context, after independence, it attempted to spread its "oil wars" against foreign companies with Sonatrach within the organization. The cooperation agreement with the US company Getty Oil set a precedent for other OPEC members in this sense. According to the agreement, the company operating in the Rhourde El Baguel oil field agreed to sell 51% of its concession to Sonatrach, increase the announced price by 20% and revise the tax rate (Grimaud, 1972: 1286; Malti, 2020: 59). In a few years, Algeria turned this strategy to an official policy and applied it to all other foreign companies operating in the country.

NATIONALIZATION AND GROWING STATE INTERVENTION IN INDUSTRY

Given that one of the objectives of Algeria's joining OPEC was to strengthen its bargaining position against foreign companies, the previous concessions and agreements were not expected to last much longer (Bendid, 1988, 171). On February 3, 1971, Algerian President Houari Boumedienne defined the framework for new cooperation with foreign companies as follows: "We are ready to make agreements with anyone who wants to cooperate with us on the basis of mutual interests, but everyone should know that threats and pressure will have no effect on us" (Naylor, 2000: 96). Sid Ahmed Ghozali, general manager of Sonatrach, described Algeria's goals for the new period as follows: "We have a development plan that will be implemented by maximizing the potential of our country, including crude oil. This plan must be realized in the field of production, industrial transformation and finance. The rents must go to Algeria, the owner of this natural wealth" (Garavani, 2015: 85).

The statements of Boumédiène and Ghozali did not find any response from the French and the negotiations for the revision of the 1965 Agreement did not yield any results. Boumédiène announced on 24 February 1971 the increase of Algeria's share in the oil business to 51% and the complete nationalization of natural gas fields and pipelines within the national borders. According to this decision, foreign oil companies wishing to operate in Algeria could only do so under the supervision of Sonatrach, with a maximum stake of 49% (Gaillard and Lebois, 2015: 21). As a result of this decision, Sonatrach's share in crude oil production increased from 30% to 77% (Iratni, 1986: 221). By 1980, all hydrocarbon facilities, with the exception of the Hassi Messaoud refinery, were nationalized and placed under Sonatrach's control (Belhoul, 1984: 293).

Boumédiène's nationalization of the hydrocarbon industry, like many other sectors, caused contraction in Algerian economy. Even though the nationalization policy did not completely ban the activities of international oil companies, the restrictive conditions resulted in a noticeable decrease in capital transfers from investors. Since then, Sonatrach's area of responsibility expanded to include investment as well as production, refining, distribution and marketing (Entelis, 2012: 561).

Sonatrach was empowered by nationalization owing to the broad powers it assumed. It also empowered the elites who had been amassing power through hydrocarbon rents. The elites (patrimonial and military elites) controlled almost all the revenues from the oil and gas sector, which has been Sonatrach's responsibility since its establishment (Shabafrouz, 2010: 16). The control allowed the elites to become almost untouchable, especially in the 1970s, when oil prices rose and Sonatrach was given more power through nationalization policies. In the following years, the military regime became increasingly reliant and dependent on the rents and power obtained through Sonatrach (Lowi, 2009: 91).

The 1970s saw not only a change in the structure of hydrocarbon industry and the competencies of actors, but also a change in the nature of production commodities. In fact, oil-centered production started to give way to natural gas by this period. Years after the establishment of hydrocarbon industry, Algeria turned to natural gas liquefaction and transportation of Liquefied Natural Gas (LNG) and quickly became one of the major trading partners of the European market thanks to the pipelines built in the Mediterranean (Laframboise et al., 1998: 71). Algeria, which hosted the world's first commercial LNG plant, exported gas to France, the UK and the US for years (Sutton, 1979: 115). In the following years, Algeria has become increasingly involved in the international energy market with the natural gas pipeline projects it has invested in. 37 pipeline projects with a total length of 19,623 km have been realized (Oirere, 2020). These include international pipelines in which Algeria is a project partner and operates. The Transmed Pipeline between Algeria and Italy with a length of 1650 km and a transportation capacity of 38 bcm/y, the Maghreb-Europe Pipeline between Algeria and Spain with a length of 523 km and a transportation capacity of 11 bcm/y, and the Medgaz Pipeline to Spain with a length of 201 km and a transportation capacity of 8 bcm/y are the international projects currently in operation (Oirere, 2020). The Galsi Natural Gas Pipeline, which is still under preparation, is to take its place in the Mediterranean as the fourth project (Hamouchene and Pérez, 2016: 10).

The global oil crises of the 1970s were as effective as the declining reserves in shifting production from oil to natural gas. The crisis that started with the increase in oil prices affected not only consumer countries but also producer countries such as Algeria. During the 1973 Arab-Israeli War (Yom Kippur), OPEC members used oil as a political weapon against the states that supported Israel. They announced on October 16, 1973 that they would increase the price of oil by 70% from USD 3.09 per barrel. Meanwhile, members of the Organization of Arab Petroleum Exporting Countries (OAPEC), acting with the same objectives, announced that they would cut oil production by no less than 5% each month based on September 1973 production (Yılmaz and Kalkan, 2017: 185). With these decisions, oil barrel prices rose to 9.35 USD in 1974 and 12.21 USD in 1975 (InflationData, 2020).

Algeria (along with Saudi Arabia) played a key role in the embargo decisions and their implementation. In the 1967 Arab-Israeli War, Algeria closed its hydrocarbon industry to Anglo-American investments, and as an experienced actor, its influence and role in the OPEC decisions is predictable. Its Third Worldist foreign policy orientation during those years was an important factor as well. Under Boumédiène, ideology-based foreign policy objectives and the national oil industry were harmonized. Algeria, on the one hand, adopted a Third Worldist foreign policy and developed an active diplomacy within the Non-Aligned Movement, and on the other hand, nationalized the oil industry and made energy a part of this diplomacy. OPEC membership was a common outcome of these two policies. Sonatrach acted both as a tool of diplomacy and a source of finance for political objectives. In fact, the costs of meetings with representatives of non-aligned countries, travel of delegations, and scholarships to young people from those countries were covered by Sonatrach's revenues (Malti, 2013: 12).

The Non-Aligned Movement (NAM), which convened under the leadership of Algeria about a month before the Yom Kippur war (September 1973), foreshadowed the sanctions to be taken very soon with its decisions. Convened with the aim of establishing international cooperation among Third World countries and changing the terms of trade in favor of the South, the most striking decision taken at the NAM was to continue the struggle against economic neo-colonialism by nationalizing strategic industries and demanding fair regulation of raw material prices (Garavini, 2015: 86). Ultimately, the NAM meeting and the OPEC embargo, with similar political objectives, provide important clues about Algeria's influence and hydrocarbon policy, as Algeria was a participant or decision-maker in both.

In 1974, although the Arab countries withdrew the embargo, Algeria's hardline stance did not change significantly. However, it was not possible to develop and implement an effective discourse due to disagreements within the OPEC. While members such as Saudi Arabia and Kuwait, which developed political relations with consumer countries, avoided weakening the world economy and trade relations by raising oil prices, members such as Iran, Algeria and Iraq wanted to keep prices as high as possible in order to sustain their industrial growth programs (Addi, 1995: 94). This divergence ended up in favor of the first group, which had larger reserves and produced more on a global scale.

In 1986, a new oil crisis became inevitable when Saudi Arabia increased its daily production from 3.8 million barrels to 10 million barrels. With this move, the price per barrel, which was 26.92 USD in 1985, dropped to 14.44 USD in 1986 (InflationData, 2020). Algeria was one of the states most affected by this period of plummeting oil prices. Within a year, total export revenues fell by 55% and the share of hydrocarbon revenues in total GDP by 20% (Lowi, 2009: 3). Export revenues dropped from 13.2 billion USD in 1980 to 4.5 billion USD in 1986 (Shabafrouz, 2010: 13). Thus, from the early 1980s onwards, Algeria entered a difficult phase in economic and political terms with the addition of oil crisis to increasing external dependence, declining oil reserves and prices, foreign debts and high levels of unemployment. Growing popular uprisings induced new energy and economic policies (Gaillard and Lebois, 2015: 21; Abderrezak, 2007: 108).

Under Chadli Bendjedid, who succeeded Boumédiène, international crises and domestic political-economic troubles further squeezed the hydrocarbon industry. Declining investments and international cooperation, weakened state mechanisms and insufficient economic resources forced Algeria to draw a more liberal road map by making concessions from its nationalist and statist policies in order to attract more foreign capital, especially due to its increasing foreign debt. The Hydrocarbons Law (1986) included the strategies necessary to attract foreign investors, whose powers and assets in oil and gas production had been restricted since 1971 (Addi, 1995: 89). Although the law relaxed legal restrictions on foreign capital, Sonatrach's authority over exploration, production and transportation activities remained unchanged (Laframboise, 1998: 72). Foreign oil companies were prevented from engaging in hydrocarbon exploration and production activities without establishing a partnership with Sonatrach (Krotoff & Bonnefoy, 2007: 57). Foreign companies were granted a shareholding of no more than 49%, whereas the government retained the right to acquire a majority stake in any joint venture, (Naylor, 2000: 158). Thus, in the first phase, the industry was opened up to the outside world under state control and to a limited extent.

The 1986 legislation had a modest but positive impact on the hydrocarbon industry. 11 oil exploration contracts were signed with foreign companies within the four years following the Law. However, foreign companies did not find these investment opportunities attractive. Restrictions on foreign companies were

Table 5. Hydrocarbon revenue and export data (2000-2004)

	2000	2002	2004
Ratio of Hydrocarbon Revenues to Total Revenues (%)	76.9	62.9	70.9
Ratio of Hydrocarbon Exports to All Exports (%)	97.3	96.8	97.9

Source: Werenfels, 2007.

related to their shareholding in the projects, and they were excluded from natural gas concessions and not involved in the production of previously discovered reserves. In addition, Sonatrach's monopoly on pipeline transportation remained in place. Under these circumstances, the state's, and therefore Sonatrach's, monopolistic hold on the industry was more seriously questioned as the desired objectives were not achieved. New regulations became inevitable (Ainas et al., 2012: 14). The hydrocarbon sector was made more open to foreign investors with another regulation in 1991. In this framework, foreign companies were allowed to participate in natural gas and pipeline projects and to acquire capital in production. This broke Sonatrach's monopoly in many activities. Several oil companies (mostly based in the US) turned back to Algeria to invest in oil and gas industry (Shabafrouz, 2010: 17).

The 1991 changes and decisions were interpreted as a rejection of the ideological attitude that culminated in nationalization of the sector in 1971 (Naylor, 2000: 175). At the beginning of the 2000s, Algeria entered a period of relative stability, both politically and economically, and set new goals and strategies to rebuild its economy and international prestige. Developments at the national and international level, such as the increase in oil prices, the intense interest of investors in the industry, the construction of a more stable political order, and the development of relations with Europe, provided a favorable ground for the realization of these goals (Ainas et al., 2012: 15).

In parallel with the new objectives and global changes, the legal framework governing the Algerian hydrocarbon sector has been redefined. The new Hydrocarbon Law adopted in 2005 redrew the boundaries of the sector and the institutions involved. In particular, Sonatrach's monopolistic presence in the entire sector was stretched through the division of labor (Senator, 2015: 6). Thus, the areas of responsibility of state institutions involved in the hydrocarbon sector (i.e. the Ministry of Energy and Mines, *Agence nationale pour la valorisation des ressources en hydrocarbures* (ALNAFT), *Autorité de régulation des hydrocarbures* (ARH), and Sonatrach) were reorganized (Sahbani, 2020). According to the redistributed tasks, the Ministry of Energy and Mines would manage strategic decision-making on energy policy, but would not be the decision-maker on technical issues. ARH and ALNAFT, which were established with this law, assumed some of Sonatrach's duties. In addition to technical regulations, ARH is responsible for the implementation of tariffs and arrangements for third party access to pipeline transportation and storage facilities. ALNAFT, responsible for exploration and operational investments, was also tasked with managing and updating technical information on hydrocarbon exploration and exploitation (Krotoff & Bonnefoy, 2007: 58; Ainas et al., 2012: 15-16). In addition, ALNAFT was charged with the task of regulating agreements between Sonatrach and foreign companies for exploration and production activities, inspecting the performance of exploration and/or production contracts as a party, and approving development programs (Gaillard & Lebois, 2015: 23). The tasks assigned to Sonatrach in this new division of labor are purely technical: the exploration, production, transportation, processing and sale of hydrocarbons. Sonatrach, which had regulatory powers and could act almost like the energy ministry, was now asked to act only as a "company" (Senator, 2015). The 2005 Hydrocarbon Law remains in force despite various amendments in 2006, 2013, 2014 and 2015.

THE BACKSIDE OF INDUSTRIAL DEVELOPMENT: CHALLENGES OF RENTIER ECONOMY

In addressing the problems that a rent-centered economy can face, Alvarez (2010) draws attention to the development of a "petro-mania culture". The concept refers to the strong orientation of economic and political representatives/elites involved in oil activities towards predatory behaviors. This culture can be found in Algeria's experience as a producer and exporter state. In the case of Algeria, national taxation turns foreign income from oil exports into rent. The future of Algeria as a gas rentier economy is unclear, but a major restructuring of international gas trade may lead to its petrolization as well (Mañé-Estrada & Albinyana, 2023).

Since the early years of its independence, Algeria has faced economic problems - notwithstanding or because of its rich natural resources - and has never been able to overcome them, despite occasional improvements. Instead of seeing hydrocarbon as a savior of the economy, some researchers place it at the center of the problems (Mohammed, Mohamed, & Abderrahim, 2017: 11). They point out to the failure of industrialization and nationalization initiated by the government in the early 1970s. These policies brought with them a series of problems defined as the "Dutch Disease". Investments in other sectors came to a standstill as a result of the shift of investments to the nationalized natural gas sector. In other words, the rent from hydrocarbon exports resulted in the neglect of agriculture and other industries. Especially during periods of high oil prices, financial resources and labor shifted from food crops and manufactured goods to Sonatrach. These developments resulted in weaker agriculture and industry, greater dependence on imports of food and consumer goods, and a collapse of non-hydrocarbon exports. It has essentially made Algeria vulnerable to oil crises at the national and international level (Shabafrouz, 2010, pp. 14-5).

The rent economy has a political dimension. According to Ross (2001: 334), oil revenues can be used by a government to prevent the formation of social groups that might be inclined to claim political rights. Citing a number of cases, including Algeria, Ross argues that oil-rich states prevent the formation of independent social groups, a necessary precondition for democracy. Almost all revenues from oil and gas sectors, for which Sonatrach is responsible, are controlled by the ruling power (patrimonial and military elites). The FLN party, as the sole actor of the one-party system, has used this rent to strengthen its autocratic rule and to maintain it through high security expenditures (Shabafrouz, 2010: 16). Sonatrach built networks of loyal supporters through the selective distribution of rent. As hydrocarbon revenues increased, the military regime became increasingly reliant and dependent on the rents and power it obtained through Sonatrach (Lowi, 2009: 91).

The decrease in oil prices in the early 1980s, coupled with the mismanagement of Algeria's highly centralized economy, brought to light social and economic problems that had been covered up since the early days of independence. The decline in oil revenues exacerbated the already existing problems in the Algerian economy. Furthermore, the economic liberalization initiated by Bendjedid in the mid-1980s remained a futile attempt to solve the oil and gas-driven economy without interfering with Sonatrach (Entelis, 1992: 16). The privatization of Sonatrach was considered tantamount to transferring one's own blood circulation in his heart into the hands of foreigners (Martinez, 2010: 14). Those who oppose the privatization of hydrocarbons, more specifically Sonatrach, include members of the military and bureaucrats at different points of the rent stream. They had the most to lose in any change in the status quo. Control over rent allowed the regime of military, bureaucrats and elites - through corruption and repression - to maintain power by granting them privileges. Entelis (2012: 564) argues that the regime's survival in power, with limited support from the population, was entirely dependent on the rent from oil and gas.

Werenfels (2002), in her analysis of why elites were reluctant to privatize Sonatrach, lists three reasons that help us better understand the state-corporate rent relationship: First, the lack of a unified bureaucracy with a coherent economic strategy due to competing factions in the administration has been an obstacle to privatization and has delayed overall economic development. Second, privatization of state-owned industrial enterprises is closely related to rent distribution and patronage relations. Trade liberalization poses a threat to the classes that derive rent from state-owned enterprises. Hence, any change in the status quo through the redistribution of rent and power can lead to resistance from these groups and the outbreak of conflicts. The third reason relates to the strong residue of the nationalist, statist and ideological foundations on which post-independence Algeria was built. This residue, surrounded by a strong distrust of the private sector and foreign investment, remains a powerful tool in the discourse of groups fighting privatization.

Sonatrach as a symbol of power for members of the ruling class has been exempt from state control since its early years. It meant that Sonatrach was not subject to financial controls applied to other companies. This not only hindered the creation of economic order and infrastructure, but also caused widespread corruption (Werenfels, 2002: 15). The scale of corruption has grown so much over time that Sonatrach is now referred to as the main source of embezzlement and elite enrichment (Werenfels, 2007: 50). Sonatrach's name has been synonymous with corruption cases. In 2010, Sonatrach CEO Mohame Meziane and three of his deputies were subjected to a judicial investigation into corruption allegations and dismissed from their positions. The court released Mr. Meziane, while Belkacem Boumediene, the company's deputy in charge of the upstream department, and Benamar Zenasni, the deputy in charge of the oil and gas transportation department, were sentenced to imprisonment (Entelis, 2012: 576-7). Following this case, Sonatrach was ordered to freeze 275 contracts it signed or awarded between December 2009 and February 2010 due to suspicion of fraud (Achy, 2013: 5). Chekib Khelil, who at different times served as the Minister of Energy as well as a director of Sonatrach, was involved in a number of corruption cases. In 2013, an arrest warrant was issued against him. In 2019, Khelil was once again prosecuted for corruption charges (Anadolu Agency, 2019). Abdelaziz Bouteflika, who served as President between 1999 and 2019, was also accused of benefiting from hydrocarbon rents to finance his election campaign. The veracity of the accusations, which have not yet been brought to trial, is still a matter of debate (Werenfels, 2007: 140).

CONCLUSION

There is an intertwined relationship between industry and politics. The fact that hydrocarbons are a strategic energy source generating high revenue plays an important role in the formation of this relationship. However, it is necessary to consider the reasons specific to Algeria, namely the political developments since the discovery of hydrocarbons. France's discovery of oil reserves in the Sahara and its domination there for many years despite the formal independence of Algeria is the first specific reason.

Algeria's nationalist policies against the French hegemony reinforced the industry-politics relationship. The gradual elimination of concessions to France, the nationalization of the industry, and the establishment of a national oil company with regulatory powers are reflections of the relationship in question. Another reason that shaped the relationship was the state-centered order guided by the protectionism caused by the occupation experience and the nationalist development goals pursued by the founding power. Sonatrach, which was established to put an end to the strong influence of foreign elements, particularly France, on the hydrocarbon industry, continued to be an indispensable tool of nationalist policies in the following years. This process was reflected in resource nationalism discourses and statist economic policies. The rights and duties given to Sonatrach help us understand why the hydrocarbon industry was never privatized and why the relevant reforms were ineffective.

The building of Algerian economy on the hydrocarbon industry has caused serious problems. Power relations influence the distribution of rents from hydrocarbon industry within the country. The remarkably low level of investment in other sectors has made the country vulnerable to oil crises and led to the growth of domestic unrest because of employment, access to consumer goods and the cost of living. Moreover, Algeria's interference in hydrocarbon sector as a reaction and defense against France's post-colonial policy has been a permanent theme later and strengthened Algeria's autocratic identity. The increasing hegemony of the military elite over Sonatrach is linked to that trend of autocracy.

REFERENCES

Abderrezak, A. (2002). Hydrocarbon price shocks and uncertainty: Implications for Algeria's economic growth. *Journal of North African Studies*, *7*(2), 86–98. doi:10.1080/13629380208718467

Addi, L. (1995). Algeria's new oil strategy. In G. Kate & C. M. Henry (Eds.), *Oil in the New World Order*. University Press of Florida.

Adjel-Debbich, S. (2018). La crise de l'oléoduc Edjeleh-Gabès: Au coeur des enjeux de souveraineté du Maghreb (1954-1962). *L'Année du Maghreb*, *18*(18), 129–148. doi:10.4000/anneemaghreb.3647

Agreements Relating to Algerian Independence. (1962). Agreements Relating to Algerian Independence. *International Legal Materials*, *1*(2), 214–230. doi:10.1017/S0020782900061234

Ainas, Y., Nacer, O., & Saïd, S. (2012). Hydrocarbons: An asset or an impediment to Algerian development? *Revue Tiers Monde*, *210*(2), 69–88. doi:10.3917/rtm.210.0069

Aissaoui, A. (2001). *Algeria: The political economy of oil and gas*. Oxford University Press.

Belhoul, H. (1984). *The performance of public industrial enterprises in Algeria: An empirical study*. University of Keele.

Bendib, R. (1988). *Hydrocarbons,rent and the Algerian growth strategy: A critical appraisal of the process of building an independent and national economy*. University of Glasgow.

BP. (2021). *Statistical Review of World Energy*. https://www.bp.com/content/dam/bp/business-sites/en/global/corporate/pdfs/energy-economics/statistical-review/bp-stats-review-2021-full-report.pdf#page13

Byrne, J. J. (2016). *Mecca of Revolution: Algeria, decolonization, and the Third World order*. Oxford University Press. doi:10.1093/acprof:oso/9780199899142.001.0001

Calouste Gulbenkian Foundation. (n.d.). *Mr. Five Percent.* https://gulbenkian.pt/en/the-foundation/calouste-sarkis-gulbenkian/mr-five-percent/

Cantoni, R., & Leucha, V. (2014). Underground and underwater: Oil security in France and Britain during the Cold War. In The Surveillance Imperative: Geosciences During the Cold War and Beyond (pp. 45-66). New York: Palgrave.

CIA Intelligence Memorandum. (1970). *Algeria: The Impotrance of the Oil Industry*. CIA.

CIA. (2021). *The World Factbook-Algeria.* https://www.cia.gov/the-world-factbook/countries/algeria/#economy

Cornat, H. (1965). *Senat: Première session ordinaire de 1965-1966.* https://www.senat.fr/rap/1965-1966/i1965_1966_0022.pdf

EIA. (2021). *Algeria.* https://www.eia.gov/international/content/analysis/countries_long/Algeria/archive/pdf/algeria_2013.pdf

El-Katiri, M. (2010). Sonatrach: An International giant in the making. *Defence Academy of the United Kingdom Special Series*, *10*(5), 1–19.

Entelis, J. P. (1981). Elite political culture and socialization in Algeria: Tensions and discontinuities. *The Middle East Journal*, *35*(2), 191–208.

Entelis, J. P. (2012). Sonatrach: The political economy of an Algerian state institution. In D. G. Victor (Ed.), *Oil and governance state-owned enterprises and the world energy supply*. Cambridge University Press.

Entelis, J. P., & Arone, L. J. (1992). Algeria in turmoil: Islam, democracy and the state. *Middle East Policy*, *1*(2), 23–35. doi:10.1111/j.1475-4967.1992.tb00031.x

Gaillard, E., & Maude, L. (2015). Algeria. In G. Pereira, Eduardo & K. Patrik Talus (Eds.), African Upstream Oil and Gas: A Practical Guide to the Law and Regulation (pp. 17-47). Globe Business Publishing Ltd.

Garavini, G. (2015). From Boumedienomis to Reaganomics: Algeria, OPEC, and the international struggle for economic equality. *Humanity*, *6*(1), 79–92. doi:10.1353/hum.2015.0004

Grimaud, N. (1972). Le conflit pétrolier Franco-Algérien. *Revue Française de Science Politique*, *22*(6), 1276–1307. doi:10.3406/rfsp.1972.418929

Guidelines for Petroleum Policy in O.P.E.C. Member Countries. (1968). Guidelines for Petroleum Policy in O.P.E.C. Member Countries. *International Legal Materials*, *7*(5), 1183–1186. doi:10.1017/S002078290005172X

Hamouchene, H., & Alfons, P. (2016). *Energy colonialism: The EU's gas grab in Algeria*. Observatory on Debt and Globalisation.

Hayes, M. H. (2004). *Algerian Gas to Europe: The Transmed pipeline and early Spanish gas import projects*. James A. Baker Institute.

Högselius. (2013). *The European natural gas industry and the oil crisis of 1973/74.* https://networks.h-net.org/system/files/contributed-files/henergy-p-hogselius-natural-gas-and-oil-crisis-1973.pdf

Hughes, L. (2014). *Globalizing Oil: Firms and oil market governance in France, Japan, and the United States.* Cambridge University Press. doi:10.1017/CBO9781107323643

InflationData. (n.d.). *Historical crude oil prices.* https://inflationdata.com/articles/inflation-adjusted-prices/historical-crude-oil-prices-table/

Iratni, B. (1986). *Foreign policy and nation-state building in Algeria, 1962-1985.* University of Warwick.

Laframboise, N., Feler, A. Bazzoni, S. Nashashibi, K., Horvitz, S. P. (1998). Algeria: Stabilization and transition to the market. Washington, DC: International Monetary Fund.

Les éditions de l'Asymétrie. (1964). *Charte d'Alger.* https://www.axl.cefan.ulaval.ca/afrique/algerie-charte_d%27alger1964.htm

Lowi, M. R. (2009). *Oil wealth and the poverty of politics.* Cambridge University Press. doi:10.1017/CBO9780511691621

Malti, H. (2010). *Histoire secrète du pétrole algérien.* La Découverte.

Malti, H. (2020). Algeria and OPEC. In D. Harald Claes & G. Garavini (Eds.), *Handbook of OPEC and the global energy order past, present and future challenges.* Routledge. doi:10.4324/9780429203190-6

Mañé-Estrada, A. & Albinyana, R. (2023). Revisiting rentierism through the lens of Algerian gas. *Revue internationale des études du développement, 251*, 35-62.

Marcel, V. (2006). *Oil Titans: National oil companies in the Middle East.* Brookings Institution Press.

Martinez, L. (2010). Algérie: Les illusions de la richesse pétrolière. *Les Etudes du CERI, 168*, 1–36.

McDougall, J. (2017). *A history of Algeria.* Cambridge University Press. doi:10.1017/9781139029230

Mohammed, C. D., Mohamed, B., & Abderrahim, C. (2017). Oil rents and institutional quality: Empirical evidence from Algeria. *Topics in Middle Eastern and African Economies, 19*(2), 2–31.

Musso, M. (2017). Oil will set us free: The hydrocarbon industry and the Algerian decolonization process. In Britain, France and the Decolonization of Africa (pp. 62-84). UCL Press.

Naylor, C. (2000). *France and Algeria: A History of decolonization and transformation.* University Press of Florida.

OEC. (2021). *Algeria.* https://oec.world/en/profile/country/dza

Oirere, S. (2020). Sonatrach to expand pipeline network in new contracts. *Pipeline & Gas Journal, 24*(11), 47–50.

OPEC. (2019). *Annual Statistical Bulletin.* https://www.opec.org/opec_web/static_files_project/media/downloads/publications/ASB_2019.pdf

OPEC. (2020). *Annual Statistical Bulletin.* https://www.opec.org/opec_web/static_files_project/media/downloads/publications/ASB_2020.pdf

Öztürk, S., & Saygın S. (2017). 1973 petrol krizinin ekonomiye etkileri ve stagflasyon olgusu. *Balkan Sosyal Bilimler Dergisi, 6*(12), 1-12.

Prasad, R. (2019). *Larsen & Toubro's hydrocarbon arm get order worth over rs 7,000 crore in Algeria.* https://economictimes.indiatimes.com/industry/indl-goods/svs/engineering/larsen-toubros-hydrocarbon-arm-get-order-worth-over-rs-7000-crore-in-algeria/articleshow/67955504.cms?from=mdr

Ross, M. L. (2001). Does oil hinder democracy? *World Politics, 53*(3), 325–361. doi:10.1353/wp.2001.0011

Sahbani, L. (2020). *The main developments introduced by the Algerian new hydrocarbon law.* https://pwcalgerie.pwc.fr/fr/files/pdf/2020/01/en-algeria-pwc-hdyrocarbon-law-2020.pdf

Salut, S. (2006). Politique nationale du pétrole, sociétés nationales et pétrole franc. *Revue Historique (Paris, France), 2*(638), 355–388. doi:10.3917/rhis.062.0355

Sassi, M. (2003). *The emergence of the French oil industry between the two wars.* https://thebhc.org/sites/default/files/sassi.pdf

Sèbe, B. (2010). In the shadow of the Algerian war: The United States and the Common Organisation of Saharan Regions (OCRS), 1957–62. *The Journal of Imperial and Commonwealth History, 38*(2), 303–322. doi:10.1080/03086531003743999

Senator, K. (2015). *The new legal framework of the hydrocarbons and its impact on investments in the sector. Conference of use of energetic resources policies: between the national development requirements and securing the international needs.* Université Sétif.

Shabafrouz, M. (2010). Oil and the eruption of the algerian civil war: A context-sensitive analysis of the ambivalent impact of resource abundance. *SSRN, 118*, 1–45. doi:10.2139srn.1541906

Skeet, I. (1989). *OPEC: Twenty-five years of prices and politics.* Cambridge University Press.

Sönmez, Ş. (2007). *Cezayir bağimsizlik hareketi ve Türk kamuoyu (1954–1962)* [PhD Dissertation]. Hacettepe Üniversitesi, Ankara.

Soustelle, J. (1959). *The Wealth of the Sahara.* https://www.foreignaffairs.com/articles/north-africa/1959-07-01/wealth-sahara

Stein, S. A. (2014). *Saharan Jews and the fate of French Algeria.* The University of Chicago Press. doi:10.7208/chicago/9780226123882.001.0001

Tordo, S., Brandon, S. T., & Noora, A. (2011). *National oil companies and value creation.* World Bank Working Paper, No. 218.

Werenfels, I. (2002). Obstacles to privatisation of state-owned industries in Algeria: The Political Economy of a Distributive Conflict. *Journal of North African Studies, 7*(1), 1–28. doi:10.1080/13629380208718455

Werenfels, I. (2007). *Managing instability in Algeria elites and political change since 1995.* Routledge. doi:10.4324/9780203964682

World Bank. (1982). *Algeria the five-year development plan and the medium-term prospects for 1980-84.* Report No. 3668-AL.

Chapter 12
Parameters of Poverty Alleviation Through Efficient Modern Energy Utilization in Nigeria

Yusuf Wara Abubakar
https://orcid.org/0000-0003-3410-6113
Kastamonu University, Turkey

ABSTRACT

Efficient energy utilization should contribute to poverty alleviation in developing countries. A society that successfully shifted from non-modern sources of energy consumption to modern ones is said to witness more significant development. In developing countries such as Nigeria, inefficient modern energy use is connected with the high poverty level among the populace. Targeting assistance to improve modern energy utilization in society that directly affects people experiencing poverty might enhance a healthy society, improve the physical environment, and increase production in society. This research tends to establish the nexus between three parameters: modern energy efficiency health improvement wealth, modern energy efficiency environmental protection wealth, and the modern energy efficiency increased production wealth, relationships. The research will test the hypothesis that the higher the modern energy utilization, the lower the poverty in society. It will also respond to the question of how efficient modern energy utilization can alleviate poverty in society.

INTRODUCTION

Modern energy utilization against the traditional one is ultimately one of the ways that would alleviate poverty in modern-world developing countries. Due to a lack of the required education and limited technological know-how folks in developing countries mostly rely on traditional sources of energy which are demanded for use and are accompanied by numerous environmental consequences that increase global warming which contributes to poor agricultural yield in a given society. Relying on traditional sources of

DOI: 10.4018/979-8-3693-0440-2.ch012

energy not only promote delay and retard progress, but it has also proven to be endangering agricultural activities which are the mainstay of the majority of low-income countries.

Energy poverty contributes to the worsening situation of the already battling vicious circle of poverty in the developing world. There is a strong connection between energy poverty, which is the situation in which a household lacks a socially and materially necessitated level of energy services in the home (Bouzarovski, 2014, p. 277), and absolute poverty in a given society. A society where the majority of people rely on traditional sources of energy tends to distance itself from modern innovations and human creativity that would aid production that would generate more individual, family, group, and state incomes.

To fight poverty- situational, generational, absolute, relative, urban or rural poverty there is a dire need for developing countries especially in Asia and Africa to drastically shift their economy from consumptive to productive. Adopting a productive economy means enhancing gross production via the use of modern energy and equipment. In other words, for the less developed world to effectively fight poverty, they need to carry out an 'energy revolution' by abandoning crude traditional energy and significantly promoting new energy utilization in all the segments of their society.

The majority of the households in Nigeria and generally in third-world countries depend on biomass (firewood) energy at home, and endosomatic energy at work and business environment. Relying on the traditional sources of energy in Nigeria's haphazard energy crisis increases the level of poverty and retard production and a progressive economy. The Nigerian energy crisis is caused by inadequate power sector financing, non-payment of electricity bills, corruption, and the shutdown of key power facilities owing to infrastructure degradation and non-performance. These have resulted in increasing poverty, slowed economic activity, a subpar healthcare system, environmental deterioration, and significant development setbacks (Onyejelam, 2015). A society that relies on traditional sources of energy is a distance far away from large-scale production of all kinds, it will depend on crude equipment that requires only physical human and animal energy to operate. In other words, society will be lacking in modern productive capacity and capability because as classified by Adam Smith out of the four distinct stages which mankind passes through: -1st, the Age of Hunters, 2dly, the Age of Shepherds; 3dly, the Age of Agriculture; and 4thly, the Age of Commerce" to develop, the society will be in either the first or the second (Paganelli, 2022, p. 98).

The majority of the local dwellers in Nigeria solemnly depend on traditional sources of energy for daily personal and business needs. The reliance on traditional sources of energy pinpoints that the people are at the primitive stage of development where crude instruments and biomass are utilized to execute the work that would aid human existence (Rostow, 1991, p. 4). In the contemporary global village for a society to develop, there is a strong need to shift to a modern production style via the utilization of modern energy sources. To fight poverty in developing countries such as Nigeria the government, policymakers, and thinktanks have to draw a roadmap that would redirect the society to the absolute utilization of modern energy through tripartite synergy that includes modern energy efficiency⇒-health improvement⇒wealth, modern energy efficiency⇒environmental protection⇒wealth and modern energy efficiency⇒increased production⇒wealth.

The main purpose of this research work is to justify how modern energy utilization reduces poverty and creates wealth as opposed to traditional energy usage which does the opposite. The research adopts secondary sources that include books, articles, facts, and figures from the websites of relevant organizations to descriptively explain that modern energy utilization instead of traditional energy utilization drastically reduces poverty in the contemporary global village. Considering the significance of the utilization of modern energy, the higher the utilization of modern energy; the lower the poverty in a society shall be the prime hypothesis of this chapter, it will also respond to an important question of how can pursuit modern energy create wealth and attenuate poverty in a given community?

TRADITIONAL ENERGY UTILIZATION

In the third-world countries or the lower-middle-income economies in which Nigeria falls, and also in low-income economies as classified by the World Bank (Bank, 2023), the major source of energy is conventional. Reliance on this kind of platitudinous energy retards the countries under the above categories from remarkable progress and development. In lower-middle income and low-income countries where traditional energy sources are the most consumed energy sources in the world, including mainly three types of fossil fuels, coal, natural gas, and oil technological advancement boosts massive production that would create numerous jobs for the teeming population is lacking (Huang & Wang, 2021, p. 1100).

The main reason why most nations rely on traditional energy is the fact that conventionally sourced energy has a lower initial cost than non-traditional energy sources such as solar or geothermal (İTÜ, 2023). Most developing countries choose to opt for the lowest initial cost of traditional energy possible because they lack sufficient funds for the higher initial cost of modern energy, but in the long run, this choice will always appear to be unprofitable and detrimental to health and environment thereby making every idea of sustainable development cumbersome in those countries maintaining the vicious cycle of poverty already battling the countries.

MODERN ENERGY UTILIZATION

It is widely recognized in the modern world that technology created for the use of replenishable energy sources, such as solar energy, wind power, and geothermal energy, is significant to the growth and development of advanced countries. In the modern world, new, faster, and more efficient equipment and machines are produced that run on modern energy, non-attainment of renewable energy means non-utilization of such more beneficial machines, therefore losing all the benefits they may present.

In the contemporary global environment, modern society utilizes modern energy the most which is significant for their current development and advancement. It is clear that in the modern world modern economies and modern energy have coevolved, leading to "synergistic development"—a method of fostering growth between energy and economy-which is now ingrained in both (John, Noah, & Young-Doo, 2006, p. viii). It is obvious that countries that greatly pursue modern energy are far more developed and have a high level of cheap energy and technological know-how compared to those that depend on traditional energy.

MODERN ENERGY-MODERN ECONOMY SYNERGY

Modern energy and modern economy work in a symbiotic relationship- whether mutualistic or parasitic, the relationship aids the growth of individual, group, and the state's ability and capacity to produce via enhancing efficiency in all the sectors of production in a community. It is no doubt that in the modern world, the coevolution of energy and economy has resulted in "'synergistic development'—a process of reinforcing growth between energy and economy"; this synergism is now incorporated in both (Byrne, Noah, & Young-Doo, 2006, p. viii). Without modern energy, it would not be possible for the modern economy to come to the limelight and prosper. Global modern main sources of energy such as oil (about 34 percent), coal (about 25 percent), and gas (24 percent) are being utilized in different homes, organizations, and industries that create millions of jobs thereby increasing individuals and group income as well as state revenues.

The adoption of the utilization of modern sources of energy: hydrocarbon fuels—oil, coal, and natural gas—that powered the Industrial Revolution has led to the massive replacement of a largely subsistence-based economy with the modern surplus economy. In developing countries where modern energy is scarcely utilized, subsistence agricultural activity dominates economic activity shielding the way for modern economic practices (Clem & Tisdell, 1982, p. 2). In Nigeria, despite massive efforts of the youth in the establishment of small-scale enterprises due to high levels of corruption, inequality, suffocating economic environment, insecurity, and ethno-religious crises; modern energy utilization and technology exploration that would increase efficiency and fight poverty significantly remain obsolete (Igwe, 2018, p. 1). To boost individual, group, and state economies, there is a need to explore modern technological devices that run on modern energy. Reliance on traditional energy retard progress and closes every opportunity for economic growth and development.

TRADITIONAL ENERGY-TRADITIONAL ECONOMY SYNERGY

In some societies, biomass for food and fuel (firewood) continues to be an important source of energy for humans. In such kind of society, there is hardly a massive production that would further propel the engine of economic growth. Due to the reliance on traditional energy households, small and medium-scale industries' mode of production is characterized by primitive instruments of production. In the scenarios of a traditional economy, the usage of energy is largely endosomatic instead of exosomatic which makes Energy Return on Investment (EROI)- which measures the amount of energy invested to get a certain amount of energy back, higher than usual (Hali, Sylvia, & Beatriz, 2012).

It is important to note that the process of conversion of biomass into carbohydrates to energize work by humans and animals has since been abandoned by the developed world because the energy, the process produces is very slow and inefficient to meet the needs of contemporary demands that aided gross development in production to reduce poverty significantly (John, Noah, & Young-Doo, 2006, p. viii).

MODERN ENERGY UTILIZATION VERSUS TRADITIONAL ENERGY UTILIZATION

It has been argued that in contemporary times, no country has been able to significantly reduce poverty without increasing energy use. Modern energy has the greatest impact on poverty since it increases impoverished people's productivity and hence their income traditional biomass energy does the direct opposite (Saghir, 2005, p. 1). Modern machines and equipment that aid production and ensure efficient and massive output do no longer rely on traditional energy. For this reason, you cannot run large, medium, or even small-scale industries without the acquisition of modern machines that use modern energy. As Saghir projected by 2030 more than 2.6 billion people around the world will still rely on traditional biomass fuels, a source of energy that no modern equipment uses. From kitchen appliances to factories' equipment modern energy from electricity to gas are inevitable for effective, efficient, and mass production. The use of modern energy increases jobs in society and also saves the environment without which the masses will be compelled to cut down trees exposing the arable land to flood thereby destroying agriculture which is the major job provider in the most less developed countries. For this reason, reliance on traditional biomass creates joblessness, an act that increases poverty and insecurity. In Nigeria for example, where the majority relies on traditional biomass as a source of energy, the population is tied to poverty it has become very difficult to fight poverty

MERITS OF MODERN ENERGY UTILIZATION

To highlight the bundle of advantages associated with modern energy we have to pose a question-how efficient modern energy utilization could have direct environmental and socio-economic gain for the common man? Modern energy utilization does not only increase efficiency in the production of goods and services, but it also ensures a habitable and healthy environment that could support a happy life. Solar for example is a modern energy source that has numerous advantages both for the environment and for mankind. In addition to its silent nature and low maintenance, it is also available worldwide and is highly environmentally friendly. Another high point associated with modern energy can be found in bioenergy which can contribute to a more secure, sustainable, and economically sound future by supplying clean energy, generating jobs, and fortifying rural economy, especially in less developed countries.

Modern energy that includes renewable energy is essential in tackling global warming and other climate crises on our planet. The key to resolving climate crises is to end reliance on energy generated from fossil fuels - the main cause of climate change (UN, 2021). The drastic shift from traditional biomass as a source of energy at home and factories to modern sources of energy increases efficiency, curbs global warming, and ensures a healthy atmospheric environment. Health is wealth and a dirty environment is hazardous; a haphazard environment maintains and sustains poverty.

DEMERITS OF MODERN ENERGY UTILIZATION

In as much as there are numerous advantages associated with modern energy, it is not free from certain loopholes. For example, renewable geothermal energy despite its reliability, is proven to be an earthquake causer, especially in extreme cases, has a high upfront cost and its reservoir must be properly managed to remain sustainable (Vieira, 2023). One of the best forms of modern energy is tidal even though has a high energy density and environmentally friendly futures, its plant construction cost is very high and has negative effects on marine life. Another shortcoming of the tidal source of energy is the fact that it cannot be constructed in every location, it has location limitations which make it very unlikely in some countries especially landlocked.

Despite the numerous advantages possessed by bioenergy, it is strongly lacking in some respects. In countries where arable agricultural land is not abundant, there will be shortages of crops to produce bioenergy, and if excessive diversion of food crops to produce biomass energy continues, there will be negative consequences that might lead to food shortages for human consumption in the society (Sparrow, 2023).

The unpredictability and uncertainty of winds make its energy unreliable sources of non-conventional energy type. Another drawback of wind energy is that it can only be used in places with strong enough winds and weather that is windy for most of the year. In addition to the aforementioned drawbacks, another issue with wind power is that the best wind sites are frequently found in distant places, making it difficult to deliver electricity from wind farms to metropolitan areas, where it is required to satisfy demand (Energy.gov, 2023).

MERITS OF TRADITIONAL ENERGY UTILIZATION

Traditional energy sources or conventional energy or non-renewable energy as it is also been referred to, despite their shortcomings have some certain advantages for the economy and mankind. Coal, oil, natural gas, and nuclear energy are some of the most widely used conventional energy sources in existence today. Most of the conventional energy sources' production cost is low compared to non-conventional energy sources. Non-renewable energy does not require a specific place for installation compared to tidal energy where access to sea is required; wind energy that needs a strong windy area; hydro energy that river is needed and solar energy that cannot be established in areas with limited solar lights.

One significant advantage of traditional energy is that the materials needed are easily accessible in abundant. A typical example is coal and firewood which can easily be found in different parts of most societies, and these sources are inexpensive. It is also a reliable source of energy because of the huge global reserve of coal which is a plentiful fuel source that may be produced at a low cost and converted into usable energy (EIA, 2022).

DEMERITS OF TRADITIONAL ENERGY UTILIZATION

One of the major shortcomings of traditional energy is that it is very cumbersome and burdensome to produce. As I indicated elsewhere, the amount of human energy required to produce traditional energy is much more than the energy obtained. For this reason, traditional energy wastes a lot of time, resources, and human energy that it could not reciprocate.

Secondly, conventional energy sources can emit a variety of pollutants. Air pollution, acid rain, and greenhouse gases are some of the most frequent. Chemicals and particles are discharged into the atmosphere as a result of the burning of fossil fuels. Carbon monoxide, carbon dioxide, hydrocarbons, nitrogen oxide, and sulfur dioxide are common examples (Salameh, 2014, p. 1). Pollution of all kinds destroys arable land and causes an outbreak of diseases in society. A polluted environment is vulnerable to diseases that would render the physical, psychological, and mental energy of mankind obsolete. An unhealthy environment produces unhealthy individuals who will remain moribund to come up with innovative ideas that would develop the community.

One another disastrous effect of traditional energy is that it makes a lot of animals endangered and even causes extinction. Logging for biomass to obtain a pellet of wood led to the destruction of forests which are the main habitats for most animals on Earth (Davis, 2022). Due to the massive cutting down of trees as a source of energy and other uses the global natural forests are shrinking in size and health. Homes for animals are now limited and unhealthy which causes several diseases and deaths.

A serious negative effect of dependence on traditional energy especially in the third world countries is poverty increment. Without clean energy, energy costs will be so high that customers' income will be largely consumed by their energy expenses. In such a scenario, small-income earners will be forced to cut back on energy use to an extent that is detrimental to their health and well-being (EC, 2023). Nigeria and other developing countries must provide clean energy which is cheaper which would make the people stop using generators for electricity which emit dioxides that add to air pollution besides it is a very expensive way of obtaining energy because people have to buy the generator itself, fuel, and oil it. Dependence on generators as a source of energy for small and medium-scale industries makes production very expensive, and the consequences of this are tax aversion and shying away from recruiting workers by the entrepreneurs. In the long run, the governmental tax is affected and a large number of unemployed youths will be realized because, in all parts of the world, most jobs are provided by small and medium-scale industries, not by the government. Therefore, to fight poverty significantly the government must provide the community with clean and cheap energy.

THE NEXUS OF TRADITIONAL ENERGY UTILIZATION AND INCREMENT OF POVERTY IN NIGERIA

It is regrettable that in Nigeria today, the ongoing production and use of conventional energy sources like oil and natural gas have a detrimental influence on the adoption of renewable energy sources. The country so much relies on traditional energy sources which is making it very lethargic in shifting to replenishable energy sources which are cheaper and healthier to use. Too much reliance on traditional energy sources by individuals, households, and businesses across the country is seen as one of the main causes of the country's continued lagging in industrialization and productive economic phase. For small and medium-scale industries to prosper and provide jobs for the teeming population of the most populous country in Africa, there is a strong need to shift to modern energy sources considering their numerous advantages compared to their counterparts. Unfortunately, in Nigeria, most companies including small-scale industries are run on traditional energy that is more expensive and detrimental to health and the environment.

MODERN ENERGY UTILIZATION AN AVENUE OF POVERTY ALLEVIATION IN NIGERIA

Effective modern energy utilization can be an avenue to eradicate poverty in Nigeria. Because Nigeria is a coastal country it has the potential and opportunity to construct a tidal energy plant. It has been observed that tidal energy can be constructed in four sites along Nigeria's coastal belt, such as - Akassa, Bayelsa State (Lat. 4.3167° N, Long. 6.0667° E); Bonny, Rivers State (Lat. 4.4500° N, Long. 7.1667° E); Calabar, Cross River State (Lat. 4.9667°N, Long. 8.3167° E) and Lagos Bar Beach, Lagos State (Lat. 6.400°N, Long. 3.400°E) (Nwaokocha, Mufutau, & Abayomi, 2015, p. 163). We can therefore infer that Nigeria has the high potential of establishing a tidal energy plant and benefit from all its advantages while offsetting whatever disadvantages that traditional energy sources present. By so doing, factories and other productive sectors will have easy and stable access to power to increase their productive capacity and be able to compete with standard companies around the world.

Because Nigeria is a country that has a wide range of biomass sources that include but are not limited to agricultural residues, woody biomass, forest residues, human and animal wastes, aquatic biomass, and energy crops; if properly harnessed, could be suitable for development in the country (Jekayinfa, Joseph, & Ralf, 2020, p. 6). Agricultural residues alone can boost Nigerian energy supply which would enhance industrial efficiency via increased production capacity. This industrial development through efficient bioenergy in Nigeria is feasible because the country has 34 million hectares of arable land, of which 6.5 million hectares are used for perennial crops and 28.6 million hectares are used for meadows and pastures, in fact about 23% of Nigeria's GDP is derived from agriculture (Sasu, 2023). In Nigeria large amounts of cassava which is a source of ethanol; cocoa whose shell is the source of ethanol and pyrolysis; coconut from which bioethanol is produced; coffee from which biogas is generated; cowpea for ethanol production; groundnut from whose shell bioethanol is produce; millet from which bioethanol is derived; and other crops that are good sources of biomass energy such as sorghum, sugarcane, wheat, and potato produce. Properly harnessing the aforementioned crops towards producing bioenergy will increase the energy supply and strengthen economic activities in the country, this will raise economic activities that would reduce joblessness and alleviate poverty in the society (Jekayinfa, Joseph, & Ralf, 2020, pp. 7-17).

One other source of modern energy that can be an avenue for poverty reduction in Nigeria is wind energy. Nigeria is a country that is estimated to have high wind power prospects that can generate clean energy and produce sufficient and clean electricity in the country (Felix, Akinbulire, & Awosope, 2012, p. 595). The wind energy reserve in Nigeria, according to a report cited by Felix et al. (2012, p.596), is at a height of 10 m (or 40 m), based on data evaluated for ten wind stations that span the North West, North East, North Central, South East, and South West geopolitical zones. Nigeria comes under a moderate wind regime, as evidenced by the report's findings that certain sites have wind regimes between 1.0 and 5.1 m/s (1.0 and 6.3 m/s) depending on the specific stations. We can therefore deduce that Nigeria has the potential to establish wind turbines and generate a lot of power that would aid human and capital development. From the establishment of wind turbines to connecting and distributing the produced power in the urban areas jobs can be created for thousands of Nigerians aside stable supply of power to the targeted industries.

Solar energy can be a very effective source of energy in Nigeria, this is because the country has a tropical climate with variable rainy and dry seasons which makes it potential for the production of energy via sunlight (Britannica, 2023). It has been highlighted that Nigeria has a solar energy potential of around 6,500 Terawatt hours (TWh) annually, which is more than the nation's current power output of 3,570 megawatts per day on average (Ayanfeoluwa, 2023). Nigeria's wind and solar potentials indicate that the country can harness renewable energy to boost economic development while protecting the environment. The kind of economic development will be tremendous as the industries, small and medium scale industries as well as the households can have access to clean, stable, and cheap energy that would enhance their daily activities and increase their production which in the long run can provide jobs for the teeming Nigeria's population. Developing the renewable energy sectors can also empower companies to the extent that their products can compete with most companies around the world, this can increase exports of Nigerian-made products to other parts of the world thereby generating more revenues for the government and for the companies that can be invested in educational, social, agricultural, scientific, health and economic development- at this stage poverty will be at minimal stage.

POVERTY ALLEVIATION STRATEGIES WITH A FOCUS ON MODERN ENERGY

One of the strongest ways to fight poverty in a given society is to promote self-reliance and self-sustenance among the youth of the given community. To promote self-reliance, the policy architectures must adopt modern techniques that would ensure superfluous production that would supersede personal consumption level and reach the commercial level. Production in large quantities requires the acquisition of sophisticated machines and equipment that can only be run by modern energy. Traditional utilization of energy retard progress and is associated with some setbacks that create poverty in a society.

To eradicate poverty significantly modern energy, need to be utilized effectively from household to industries. Individuals, groups, organizations, society, and the state have to indispensably utilize the use of clean modern energy to enhance mass production. Modern energy utilization plays a significant role in improving the living standard of individuals, strengthening organizations, and improving the economic cum political power of a state (Asghar, 2022, pp. 1-3). Today, the utilization of clean, modern, and sustainable energy resources instead of traditional energy sources ensures the economic advancement of the individual, group, and the entire community, for it is efficient, effective, and sustainable.

Take for instance, a community that relies on biomass energy instead of electricity will need to waste a lot of human energy to provide firewood. In addition to wasting human energy, it takes unnecessary time and it can be very cumbersome and tiresome to obtain. On the other hand, electric energy ensures the acquisition of modern sophisticated machines that would render functions quickly and efficiently.

PARAMETERS OF POVERTY ALLEVIATION THROUGH MODERN ENERGY UTILIZATION

It has been observed that the level of poverty is alarming around the world. According to research, across 111 countries, 1.2 billion people—19.1 percent —live in acute multidimensional poverty (Alkire & et al, 2022, p. 2). The government, policymakers, international organizations, and civil society organizations must take drastic necessary action to eradicate poverty around the world. In so far as there are several ways to reduce poverty in a society, the adoption of the utilization of modern energy is of utmost importance. Through the utilization of modern energy instead of traditional energy poverty could be eradicated through the following parameters.

MODERN ENERGY EFFICIENCY ⇒ HEALTH IMPROVEMENT ⇒ WEALTH

It goes without saying "Health is Wealth and Dirty Environment is Hazardous," according to Davis (2022), biomass production generates a lot of air pollution, which can harm human health. None of the chemicals produced by the manufacturing of wood pellets should be breathed. Biomass energy is one of the dirtiest energy sources available. It is also needless to say that, a healthy environment habitats healthy individuals that are capable of being productive in a society.

Modern wealth is directly connected with modern energy, and a healthy community is a wealthy community. A society whose atmospheric condition is intoxicated by air pollution, climate change, water pollution, thermal pollution, and solid waste disposal caused by burning fossil fuels will be susceptible to water and airborne diseases (EEA, 2004). When a society is ruptured by diseases, it will be insecure health-wise and, in such an environment, foreign investors will be lacking; instead of innovation and creativity the populace will be rather battling with the nagging diseases caused by the offshoot of traditional energy sources. Modern energy, on the other hand, assures a healthy environment and, as a result, a healthy and inventive populace; and has launched various aspects of our lives to new heights, revealing new avenues for our civilizations to grow (SEE, 2023).

Utilization of traditional energy in Africa and majorly in developing countries has resulted in polluting the environment which consequently led to an increase in airborne and waterborne diseases. For instance, after HIV/AIDS, air pollution is already Africa's second leading cause of mortality (Sowah, 2023). Most communities in Nigeria are in besmirched and dirty situations polluted by smoke from firewood, carbon monoxide from homes carbon dioxides from industrial processes, and exhaust gasses emitted by cars, tricycles, and motorcycles. It has been observed that residential pollution is mostly caused by cooking and heating with biomass, as well as generating power from fossil fuels for our houses and transportation. Windblown dust is also a significant source in arid areas of Africa and West Asia (UNEP, 2022).

Developing countries, such as Nigeria, must pursue an alternative energy scenario in which cities install clean air measures as they expand, such as improved public transportation, cleaner cookstoves, and greener industrial technologies and energy. Adherence to the use and utilization of modern energy will ensure a cleaner environment that will bring about a healthy environment and healthy environment habitats and healthy people who will be capable of learning and innovation to develop the society without difficulties. However, a dirty environment contaminated by traditional biomass will be ridden by diseases that will make society very unhealthy and such society will rather be battling on how to cure itself instead of being educative and innovative to foster development.

To fight poverty, we must shift away from traditional to modern energy utilization, because this will ensure a healthy innovative, and productive society. We should remember that health is wealth and a dirty environment is hazardous, impoverished, and disconsolate.

MODERN ENERGY EFFICIENCY ⇒ ENVIRONMENTAL PROTECTION ⇒ WEALTH

Anthropogenic pollution is the major cause of environmental pollutants in most less-developed countries around the world. In Nigeria for example, oil spillage has destroyed arable agricultural land and grossly affected aquatic animals which makes fishing occupation unlucrative (Fagorite, Anifowose, & Chiokwe, 2021, p. 16). We can deduce from the aforementioned point that traditional energy-based industrial processes pollute the environment and such pollution negatively affects the agricultural activities of the people in such society. Take for instance, combustion from industrial boilers, leaking pipelines, and other sources such as propylene, carbon monoxide, acetylene, and ethylene that cause plant injury and greatly affect a variety of cash and food crops, and livestock production (Lawal, 2014, p. 12). In such a situation local farmers, who are majorly the poor will be greatly affected because such combustion effects will reduce their annual agricultural yields.

Renewables such as solar and wind must be prioritized by governments, community groups, and people. Solar and wind power provide significant emissions reductions at a tenth of the cost of burning wood for energy. Whereas traditional energy systems can harm the climate, air, water, land, and urban environment; posing occupational and public health concerns, solar energy technologies are virtually completely pure and safe. Their applications offer major socioeconomic benefits- including energy supply security and employment creation (Chow, 2016, p. 525).

The big question is: How is the utilization of modern energy connected with wealth? Of course, it does. People who live in a clean environment with abundant oxygen, and free from carbon monoxide are no doubt healthier compared to their counterparts who live in dirty environments. Furthermore, a clean environment is arable-producing more crops and preparing grazing land for animals compared to a polluted environment. It is easier to innovate and be productive in a clean environment than in a polluted one. It is based on the premise that wealth, security, and innovation go hand in hand. A society that relies on modern energy will have stable electricity that would aid production through the use of modern equipment. Stable electricity will also increase the security situation in the community because most modern gadgets and security apparatus use electricity to function.

Developing societies such as Nigeria have to take drastic actions to ensure that their environment is protected from all sorts of contaminations. An environment that should be devoid of pollution must adhere to the use of modern energy, for it is the traditional energy sources that make the environment unsuitable for agricultural purposes and inhabitable.

MODERN ENERGY EFFICIENCY ⇒ INCREASED PRODUCTION ⇒ WEALTH

Undoubtedly, modern energy utilization instead of dependence on long-term traditional energy increases production and ensures a healthy, arable, and habitable environment in our community. A community that relies on traditional energy will be using old model machines and crude equipment that are not fast and produce carbon monoxide that contaminates the environment. In a polluted environment outbreak of different kinds of diseases is imminent; sterilization of land would be augmented and production of goods and services will remain very low. The idea is that, for a society to increase its production it must have a healthy environment that entails healthy and capable individuals who can innovate to increase their production capacity and capability by adopting the use of modern, simple, easy, and fast instruments and machines that are run on the utilization of modern energy sources.

The argument is that modern energy has given us the ability to enhance our lives by improving our health- thanks to access to electric lights, operating equipment, pharmaceuticals, antiseptics, and new technologies. A healthy population is better equipped to work and contribute to society, increasing the overall wealth of the community. This cycle is reproduced in how we produce food, make commodities, design ways of transportation, and so on (Watt, 2022). In other words, utilization of modern energy means the use of modern machines that are fast in production and emit limited amounts of all forms of dioxides that create a lot of diseases in a community, society, country, or even region or the world at large. Resorting the use of machines that use modern energy sources means spending less energy to produce more. This will maximize profit and create wealth thereby reducing poverty naturally.

There is no doubt that the utilization of modern energy reduces environmental pollution thereby reducing the dangers of contracting diseases; an action which increases the wealth of individual and tackle poverty as well as increasing revenue to the government. Nigeria can resort to producing electricity by uranium through the construction of nuclear energy. Due to its great stability and capability for multiplication, nuclear energy has a very favorable Energy Return by the Energy Invested (EROEI). It is feasible to produce a significant quantity of thermal energy in the form of steam from a very small mass of enriched uranium, which powers the turbines that produce electricity compared to other sources of energy (Jônatas, Amir, & Rieder, 2017). Nigeria can establish a nuclear plant and obtain uranium from its sister neighboring country Republic of Niger which is the seventh largest producer of Uranium in the world. Considering the geographical alikeness between some parts of Nigeria and Niger it is more likely that uranium could be found in Nigeria which will be an advantage to greater energy production in the country.

SUGGESTION AND RECOMMENDATION

It is obvious reliance on traditional energy sources has been causing a mirage of problems that are hindering the development of economic, social, agricultural, industrial, health, and educational sectors in Nigeria. The policymakers can do a lot to redefine and modernize energy production in the country to have more sufficient, easily accessible, universally stable, and generally affordable energy across the country. Nigeria has to undergo a significant energy revolution to use energy more efficiently to achieve social progress, economic development, poverty reduction, and sustainability. For the country to achieve abundant energy sources that would alleviate poverty, this chapter recommends the following:

Nigeria has the potential to massively invest in solar, wind, and tidal energies, especially when considering the tropical nature, the availability of winds, and the maritime nature of the country. To grossly enhance modern energy in Nigeria there is a strong need for the establishment of a Ministry of Renewable/Modern Energy that would oversee the process and procedures as well as diligent coordination for the enhancement of modern energy across the country. The establishment of the Ministry for Renewable Energy could not be enough for the country to achieve a high level of modern energy. Therefore, there is a strong need for the ministry to partner with modern energy-developed countries to ensure the transfer of technology and expertise through necessary energy bilateral agreements and cooperation.

The establishment of the National Energy Training Institute (NETI) would be saddled with the responsibility of training Nigerian youths on different sectors of renewable/ modern energy within the country and abroad and would be an avenue that would clear the ground for having indigenous energy experts that would form a team of national energy experts and come out with a roadmap for developing and maintaining nuclear energy plants, windmills and solar power plants in the country.

To establish sound modern energy units that would be successful and be able to serve as an avenue for development there is a strong need for Nigeria to eradicate serious corruption, poor macroeconomic management, and bad governance. Modern energy plants such as windmills, geothermal power stations, tidal power stations, and biomass plants need diligent, dedicated, and transparent management to prosper. The Nigerian policymakers should know that the continued corrupted and unaccountable mindset applied in the management of the country's traditional energy sources such as petroleum sectors cannot be allowed in the modern energy they need proper and competent management. Every modern energy plant needs proper maintenance and continuous monitoring, so, administrative, economic, and technological disciplines are highly required in the administration of modern energy power stations.

CONCLUSION

We have analyzed how the utilization of modern energy can be an avenue to eradicate poverty not only in Nigeria, but also in most developing countries in the Middle East, some parts of Asia, and Africa. We should realize that a community that has access to contemporary energy is more likely to have access to education, healthcare, and other liberties that can improve their overall quality of life. Unfortunately, obtaining energy is not always simple. Geographic constraints, corruption, and conflict may make exploiting a country's natural resources and employing modern energy extremely challenging. The inability to eliminate the constraints serving as stumbling blocks to utilizing modern energy increases the level of poverty in less developed world communities.

In Nigeria inability to remove all forms of constraints to modern energy utilization is part of the reason why the nation lacks enough electricity that would negate the patronize of traditional biomass that would save the environment provide clean energy and aid massive production in the community.

The Nigerian government and its policymakers should bear in mind that commercially traded energy sources (such as coal, oil, gas, or grid electricity) contaminate the environment and endanger not only the life of animals both on land and in waters but also lead to breaking out of numerous diseases that would make mankind unhealthy and unhealthy population is unproductive population and vice versa. Nigeria and developing countries' policymakers should also know that the utilization of modern biofuels, solar, wind, hydropower, nuclear, and natural gas protects and enriches the environment, in addition, they supply cheaper and cleaner energy that makes a healthy productive environment. In a healthy environment, people remain in healthy condition and energetic to sustain a productive society, so there is a significant relationship between a healthy society and a productive society. Nigeria as well as developing countries must abide by the global standard environmental protection policies so that they can have a clean, fresh, and healthy society free from dirtiness and diseases that emanate from environmental pollution.

The developing world should take necessary measures to shift from traditional biomass – crop residues, wood, and other organic matter to modern energy. Over-reliance on traditional energy results in environmental contamination which will kill the aquatic animals in the sea, rivers, and lakes thereby making fishing occupation disadvantageous and unprofitable. In addition to dangers caused by piscary occupation, environmental pollution also renders agricultural activities toilsome and unfavorable.

A large amount of energy is expanded to produce a small amount of energy via traditional sources. To have sufficient, cheap, and reliable clean energy Nigeria and other advancing countries must resort to the development of modern energy units that would provide cheaper energy to households, small and medium-scale industries as well as large corporations. The provision of sufficient energy through modern sources will make the environment cleaner and production cheaper. When companies do not need to spend a colossal amount of money on their production processes, they will be able to pay taxes to the government and hire more youths. Paying of taxes and employment generations by companies will help government functions and reduce joblessness and poverty in a given society, to achieve this positive scenario, it is believed that the government must play a significant part in Nigeria's future green energy development process. The government may expand the use of renewable energy sources, enact new laws, and encourage technical advancements.

REFERENCES

Alkire, S. (2022). *Unpacking deprivation bundles to reduce multidimensional poverty.* United Nations Development Programme and Oxford Poverty and Human Development Initiative.

Asghar, N., Amjad, M. A., Rehman, H., Munir, M., & Alhajj, R. (2022, November 20). Achieving sustainable development resilience: Poverty reduction through affordable access to electricity in developing economies. *Journal of Cleaner Production, 376*, 1–3. doi:10.1016/j.jclepro.2022.134040

Ayanfeoluwa, P. (2023, August 31). *Nigeria's Solar Energy Potential Higher than Current Consumption — Ikeja Electric*. vanguardngr: https://shorturl.at/oOQW9

Bank, W. (2023). *World Bank Country and Lending Groups*. datahelpdesk.worldbank.org: https://datahelpdesk.worldbank.org/knowledgebase/articles/906519-world-bank-country-and-lending-groups

Bouzarovski, S. (2014). Energy poverty in the European Union: Landscapes of vulnerability. *Wiley Interdisciplinary Reviews. Energy and Environment, 3*(3), 277. doi:10.1002/wene.89

Britannica. (2023). *Climate of Nigeria*. https://www.britannica.com/place/Nigeria/Settlement-patterns

Byrne, J., Noah, T., & Young-Doo, W. (2006). Modern Energy and Modern Society. In Transforming Power: Energy, Environment, and Society in Conflict (p. viii). Routledge.

Chow, T. (2016). Combined photovoltaic/thermal technology for building applications. In Advances in Solar Heating and Cooling (p. 525). Woodhead Publishing.

Clem, F., & Tisdell, T. I. (1982). *Subsistence Economies and Unsustainable Development and Trade: Some Simple Theory.* Working Paper No. 77, University of Newcastle.

Davis, S. (2022, March 15). *Why is Biomass Bad? 5 Reasons to Stop Importing Bioenergy*. Dogwood Alliance: https://rb.gy/qal2q

EC. (2023). *Energy poverty in the EU*. European Commission: https://rb.gy/0uolq

EEA. (2004). *Environmental Impact of Energy*. European Environment Agency: https://rb.gy/jlujy

EIA. (2022, November 16). *U.S. Energy Information Administration*. Coal explained Coal and the Environment: https://shorturl.at/dKY58

Energy.gov. (2023). *Advantages and Challenges of Wind Energy*. Energy.gov: https://www.energy.gov/eere/wind/advantages-and-challenges-wind-energy

Fagorite, V. I., Anifowose, F. A., & Chiokwe, V. N. (2021, January). Air Pollution; Causes, Effects and Remediation in Nigeria. *International Journal of Advanced Academic Research (Sciences, Technology and Engineering), 7*(1), 16.

Felix, A. A., Akinbulire, T. A., & Awosope, C. (2012). Wind Energy Potential in Nigeria. *International Electrical Engineering Journal, 3*(1), 595.

Hali, H., Sylvia, L., & Beatriz, R.-L. (2012, 12). *EROI (Energy Return on Energy Input/Invested).* Environmental Justice Organization Liabilities and Trade: http://www.ejolt.org/2012/12/eroi-energy-return-on-energy-inputinvested/

Huang, G., & Wang, H. (2021). Traditional Energy and Renewable Energy: The Differences and Transitions. *Advances in Social Science, Education and Humanities Research, 638,* 1100.

Igwe, P. A. (2018). Enhancing Productivity in Nigeria: From Subsistence to Transformational Entrepreneurship. Position paper presented to the Transformational Entrepreneurship Think Tank.

İTÜ. (2023). *Non-Renewable Conventional Energy Division.* Energy İTÜ: https://enerji.itu.edu.tr/en/education/divisions/conventional-energy-division

Jekayinfa, S. O., Joseph, I. O., & Ralf, P. (2020). An Assessment of Potential Resources for Biomass Energy in Nigeria. *MDPI Resources,* 6.

John, B., Noah, T., & Young-Doo, W. (2006). Modern Energy and Modern Society. In Transforming Power, Energy, Environment and Society in Conflict (p. viii). Routledge.

John, B., Noah, T., & Young-Doo, W. (2006). *Transforming Power, Energy, Environment, and Society in Conflict.* Routledge.

Jônatas, F. C., Amir, Z. M., & Rieder, O. N. (2017). Comparison of the Performance, Advantages and Disadvantages of Nuclear Power Generation Compared to other Clean Sources of Electricity. In *2017 International Nuclear Atlantic Conference - INAC.* Belo Horizonte: International Nuclear Atlantic Conference - INAC.

Lawal, T. E. (2014). Agriculture and Environmental Pollution: Causes, Consequences and Control. In Agric Ecology and Environment (p. 12). Discovery Publishing House.

Nwaokocha, C. N., Mufutau, A. W., & Abayomi, T. L. (2015). Estimation of Tidal Power Potential of Nigeria Coastal Area. In Renewable Energy and Sustainable Development (p. 163). Nova Science Publishers, Inc.

OnyejelamE. (2015, October 11). *The Energy Crisis in Nigeria and the Role of Law in Promoting Renewable Energy Development.* doi:10.2139/ssrn.2672625

Paganelli, M. P. (2022, March 1). Adam Smith and Economic Development in Theory and Practice: A Rejection of the Stadial Model? *Journal of the History of Economic Thought, 44*(1), 98. doi:10.1017/S1053837220000309

Rostow, W. W. (1991). *The Stages of Economic Growth: A Non-Communist Manifesto.* Cambridge University Press. doi:10.1017/CBO9780511625824

Saghir, J. (2005). *Energy and Poverty: Myths, Links, and Policy Issues.* International Energy Forum in Amsterdam. Amsterdam: Energy & Mining Sector Board of World Bank.

Salameh, Z. (2014). Factors Promoting Renewable Energy Applications. In *Ziyad Salameh* (p. 1). Academic Press.

Sasu, D. D. (2023, Sep 20). *Agriculture in Nigeria - statistics and facts*. Statista: https://www.statista.com/topics/6729/agriculture-in-nigeria/#topicOverview

SEE. (2023). *Smart Energy Education*. Retrieved from How Is Wealth Connected To Energy?: https://rb.gy/feqza

Sowah, M. A. (2023). *Clean Air*. From Pollution to Solutions In Africa's Major Cities: https://rb.gy/in2tw

Sparrow, P. (2023). *Biomass Energy: Advantages and Disadvantages*. ianswer4u: https://www.ianswer4u.com/2012/02/biomass-energy-advantages-and.html#axzz3Qs5RV0Sb

UN. (2021). *Five ways to jump-start the renewable energy transition now*. July 03, 2023, from United Nation: https://rb.gy/f9733

UNEP. (2022, 08 30). *Pollution Action Note – Data you need to know*. United Nations Environment Program: https://rb.gy/kabwe

Vieira, S. (2023). *Pros and Cons of 10 Types of Energy*. AJE Springer Nature: https://www.aje.com/arc/energy-types-pros-cons/

Watt, W. (2022, August 4). *How is wealth connected to energy?* Watt Watchers: https://www.watt-watchers.com/how-is-wealth-connected-to-energy/

Chapter 13
Economic Rise With LNG Model:
A Case Study of Qatar

Lütfi Tutuş
https://orcid.org/0000-0002-4920-0092
Ankara Hacı Bayram Veli Üniversitesi, Turkey

ABSTRACT

The transformation of natural gas that marked the 21st century was realised by transforming it into liquefied natural gas (LNG). Starting in 1971 with the discovery of the Northern Gas Field, Qatar's rise in LNG has heralded an important industrial and economic transformation with the first LNG transfer to Japan in 1997. The Doha administration, which stands out as a reliable partner with its infrastructure investments in the LNG sector, has managed to get the economic return of the cooperation network it has established. In this way, the revenues obtained have been transformed into investments in many areas from infrastructure to industry, health, culture, and education. Modern education cities, a global company in the aviation sector, communication and media investments have formed the basis of the partnership process with important industrial organisations. Moreover, the country has become one of the leading welfare countries in the world with its per capita income. From this point of view, it is the subject of the study that LNG trade is the main dynamo of Qatar's economic rise.

INTRODUCTION

There exists a strong relationship between natural resources and human beings, encompassing processes as simple as harnessing a river's flow to those as complex as extracting and refining minerals from beneath the Earth's surface. The position that civilizations have attained today reflects triumph in the struggle against nature, and within this struggle, natural resources play a significant role. Human beings and natural resources have intertwined like partners in the development of civilizations. Just as human beings have managed to harness nature to meet its needs, resources have also become elements that work for the welfare of human beings. In this context, throughout human beings' historical journey, no natural resource has served the advancement of civilizations as profoundly as petroleum, coal, and natural gas.

DOI: 10.4018/979-8-3693-0440-2.ch013

Natural resources can, on a smaller scale, serve as a source of identity for nations, much like they do for human beings as a whole. This perspective is particularly evident when examining energy resources. Indeed, there are countries across the world that hold resources as if they hold a sacred treasure, and there are also countries that emerge with these resources. Just like in the case of Qatar, a country with rich natural gas resources in the Persian Gulf.

Exploring Qatar's history also provides an opportunity to observe the dominant powers, in global and regional power struggles. Throughout history, the region has been influenced and governed by forces such as the Portuguese, Abbasids, Ottoman Empire, British, and The United States. The ruptures that shaped Qatar's history are explained by these political powers.

The decolonization process, which was expedited in the latter half of the 20th century, marked the independence of Qatar. The natural gas reserves upon which Qatar has laid on have seemingly blessed the country with the gift of independence. The Middle East possesses the world's third-largest natural gas reserves, making it a region blessed with rich resources. It is the effective and efficient utilization of these resources that has transformed Qatar into a nation of energy marvels. The process of managing energy resources initially manifested through a profound understanding of the Liquefied Natural Gas (LNG) model. Subsequently, infrastructure, technology, and a diversified network of bilateral relationships became crucial elements of success. Qatar demonstrates the ability to simultaneously export its energy resources to different continents, and geographies including Germany, Japan, China, India, UK, and Pakistan. While this might initially appear as a simple trade network, it is essential to recognize that in a geography fraught with geopolitical risks and an international system marked by ideological divisions, steering LNG trade requires delicately maintaining a balance. At this point, we see the fact that Qatar is conducting good energy diplomacy. In other words, the LNG trade for Qatar has been supported not only by material elements but also by effective diplomacy.

It is a fact that the world today has an unshakable connection with energy. However, this reality cannot overlook the necessity for the proper management of each energy source. Energy trade evolves within a realm encompassing political power dynamics, geopolitical risks, wars, conflicts, international sensitivities, and numerous diverse contexts. In addition, a civilization trying to get rid of hydrocarbons is on the horizon in the transformation of the world. In this regard, Qatar's ascent through energy resources depends on various elements to ensure its sustainability. Thus far, it is possible to say that Qatar has shown an example of good governance. Moving beyond the successful continuation of energy trade, Qatar is converting resource revenues into investments in various sectors. The aim here is to create a multi-faceted income base from a single-based economy.

At this point, it is valuable to focus on a context in which energy geopolitics is established for Qatar. The tension created by regional geopolitics makes it inevitable for the energy equation to be built on delicate balances. At the same time, this tension reveals the necessity of addressing the LNG issue with multilateral diplomacy. In this study, the power of the LNG model in energy geopolitics and its contribution to Qatar's transformation are discussed.

HISTORICAL AND POLITICAL STRUCTURE OF THE COUNTRY

The region in which the State of Qatar is located dates back to the 5th century BC. Due to the strategic geographical positioning of the region, the Canaan Tribes with a seafaring lifestyle became the first inhabitants. In the past, an important port in the Arabian boundaries, Zubara, was known as "Qatra".

As we delve further into the region's history, we find evidence of a historical struggle within Qatar's borders. In the 13th century, governance of the region passed from the Abbasids to the Portuguese, but in the 16th century, the Ottoman Empire took control of the region (MOFA, 2022a). Bahrain's struggle for dominance over the Qatari territories failed with the Ottoman Empire coming to the fore. With the onset of the 20th century, the United Kingdom entered the scene as the final actor in the region's power struggles. Through a treaty signed in 1913 between the Ottoman Empire and the UK, Qatar's protector and sovereign power changed hands. Hence, the UK became the region's protector and ruler (Boyce, 2013, p. 365).

This historical process can be broadly interpreted as a regional reflection of the rise and fall of great powers. As the Ottoman Empire's power eroded, authority in the region shifted to another power. At the outset of the 20th century, while Qatar distanced itself from Ottoman rule, it came under British sovereignty, becoming a new member of the British system. Now the UK is the center depending on security and foreign policy (Roberts, 2012, p. 234). As the world witnessed decolonization, Qatar took part in this transformation. In 1971, it declared independence from the UK, establishing the modern State of Qatar (MOFA, 2022a).

The disappearance of British influence with independence has created space for the shadow of another power to emerge over Qatar. Riyadh began to feel like an important axis in Qatar's foreign policy framework and security relations (Roberts, 2012, p. 234). Foreign policy and security relations centered on Saudi Arabia have emerged as an element of pressure over time. The Doha administration has replicated its historical power struggle over the region, this time against Riyadh. At the same time, the US emerged as a new actor in this balancing act. Built in 1996, the Al-Udeyd airbase has become one of the most important US military bases in the region. It was further used as an important power projection center to manage the Afghanistan front (Cooper & Momani, 2011, p. 123). Hence, Qatar has remained a small state continually subjected to the political and military dictation of significant powers – including Portugal, the Ottoman Empire, the UK, Saudi Arabia, and ultimately the US.

In Qatar, where the absolute monarchy is maintained in terms of governance, the Al-Thani family holds this power and continues to rule in the country. Although coups have an important role in the change of governance, the transition process in 2013 was different from other Gulf monarchies. In 2013, Emir Hamad, who had held authority since 1995, passed on leadership to Sheikh Tamim(Henderson, 2014). While Emir Hamad has managed an important transition process, this also means the transfer to another generation of a management profile in which the channels of dialogue with the international system are maintained, a moderate foreign policy axis is maintained, and a development process that is open to information is operated (Roberts, 2012, p. 235). Indeed, Hamad had used his tenure to steer the state toward innovative diplomacy, facilitate a smooth transition from the Saudi axis to the international community, and adopt a political and economically liberal stance (Cooper & Momani, 2011, p. 117).

NATURAL RESOURCES AND ECONOMY

In the early days, the region relied on fishing as a significant economic activity until the discovery of pearl beds ushered in its first natural resource-based economy. Especially in the 19th century, driven by strong demand from the US and Europe, the region experienced an influx of those interested in pearl hunting and trade (Kurşun, 2004, p. 39). The outbreak of World War I dealt the initial blow to the demand from the US and Europe, and the second blow came from the production of cheap cultured pearls initiated in

Japan. In 1929, with the Great Depression that almost engulfed the world, the economy of the region experienced the end of growth based on natural resources (Krane, 2009, p. 32).

From the late half of the 20th century, another commodity began to shape Qatar's economy. Qatar would experience a renaissance as a blessed nation with petroleum and natural gas resources (Cooper & Momani, 2011, p. 127). Starting from the mid-20th century, with the discovery of oil in the country, Qatar's economy embarked on a new era of natural resource-based growth. This transformation impacted diverse sectors, including education, healthcare, sports, culture, infrastructure, technology, and media, as an outcome of these resources (Bölükbaşı, 2019, p. 328). As a result, Qatar effectively used its natural resources as both a collaborative tool among regional nations and a counterforce against policies that diverged from those of neighboring countries. This shift also signaled a departure from mainstream Arab policies led by Riyadh (Cooper & Momani, 2011, p. 118).

THE IMPORTANCE OF OIL IN QATAR'S ECONOMY

The inception of Qatar's oil industry was marked by the discoveries in Dukhan in 1939. However, the outbreak of World War II necessitated a pause in exploration activities. After the war, exploration activities gained momentum, leading to the successful extraction of the first oil reserves in 1949. By 1960, significant discoveries were made in two important fields: Idd Al-Shargi and Maydan Mahzam. In 1970, the largest offshore area, Bul Hanine, yielded oil. These discoveries also gave rise to Qatar Petroleum, the national oil company, established in 1974 (Qatar Energy, 2022).

The traces of Qatar's rise through hydrocarbon resources became evident from these years onwards. Indeed, the growth of Qatar's economy was measured through energy export revenues. In 1960, export revenues stood at around $55 million. The oil shocks of 1974 significantly boosted these revenues, generating a colossal income of around $1.6 billion after the oil crises. Qatar's substantial earnings from oil revenues allowed it to capitalize on global economic fluctuations and leverage a significant opportunity through natural resources (Hassan, 1978, p. 147-148). Qatar's total oil reserves are estimated at 25 billion barrels (EIA, 2023a). Presently, the country produces an average of over 1.6 million barrels of oil per day (Worldometer, n. d.).

After gaining independence in 1971, Qatar's development accelerated through its petroleum industry. The initial effects of growth through natural resources translated into investments in infrastructure, education, health, and urbanization, leading to a transformative process (Turan, 2002). Thanks to oil revenues, substantial shifts occurred in real estate investments and capital market expansion. However, the impacts of being a typical resource-dependent nation were particularly felt between 2014 and 2020 due to the low oil prices (Refai et al., 2021, p. 2).

THE IMPORTANCE OF NATURAL GAS IN QATAR'S ECONOMY

We can assert that natural gas holds a greater significance for Qatar's economy than oil. This supremacy is primarily substantiated by Qatar's reserves. Furthermore, the context surrounding the global natural gas sector highlights the relevance of natural gas's dependence on a conjunctural environment.

Looking at a more expansive perspective, the world's proven natural gas reserves are 207 trillion m^3. The distribution of reserves is mainly concentrated in the Middle East, Russia, and the Caspian region.

While the Middle East holds about 40% of the natural gas reserves, Iran and Qatar lead the way in this resourceful geography (EIA, 2023b). Qatar's natural gas reserves are estimated at approximately 25 billion m^3. This reserve amount has made Qatar the third-largest reserve country in the world after Russia and Iran (Statista, 2023). In particular, the North Gas Field, which was discovered in 1971 in the Persian Gulf about 75 kilometers off the coast, stands out as the world's largest single proven natural gas field. This field also borders Iran's South Pars Field (Qatargas, 2023).

The trade of natural gas, a transformational force for Qatar's economy, has also found support in the global context. This context is nourished by a range of factors that favor Qatar. Firstly, concerns about global warming and climate change have led to efforts like the Paris Agreement, which aims to mitigate global warming and maintain temperature increases within the goal of 1.5°C (UNFCCC, 2017). Achieving the world's climate goals hinges on transitioning to renewable resources, but the world's ongoing reliance on hydrocarbons signals the challenge of affecting this shift. Natural gas, as the most environmentally friendly among hydrocarbon fuels, assumes a pivotal role in this transition. It aids in reducing carbon emissions compared to oil and coal, offering both affordability and a dependable supply (Meza et al., 2022, p. 2). The increasing incidents of fires, floods, and rising global temperatures in various regions underscore the irrevocable nature of this reality. Nonetheless, the world is grappling with the dilemma of overcoming hydrocarbon dependency while being compelled to consume them. In this struggle, natural gas remains a robust player as the most environmentally friendly hydrocarbon.

The convergence of energy and conflicts on the global agenda underscores the significant role that energy holds in international discussions. Throughout history, energy resources have found their place either as causes or consequences of conflicts, emphasizing their crucial status (Sevim, 2012, p. 4379). In the midst of the Russia-Ukraine conflict, the far-reaching effects of war are evident across various domains. The imposition of mutual embargoes has revived the historical process in which energy was used as a weapon in the power struggle. The imposition of sanctions on Russian energy resources by the US and the EU to deter the devastating effects of the war, and Russia's response to supply disruptions, remain a reality. It is not difficult to conclude that Russia, the power with the world's largest natural gas reserves, is being sidelined by embargoes and that Iran's problems in extracting and exploiting its resources for a long time in the shadow of sanctions have created a prime opportunity for Qatar. As a matter of fact, the natural gas deficit created by the European Union after the Russia-Ukraine war was intended to be replaced by Qatari resources. In this context, Qatar has increased its weight in the natural gas markets with the agreements made by the EU, especially Germany (EIA, 2023c, p. 12-13).

The most significant development supporting Qatar's strong position is its LNG model. Possessing energy resources doesn't guarantee the creation of commercial value. This is because a crucial aspect of energy trade involves transporting these resources to the regions where they are consumed. The presence of geopolitical risks has revealed a challenge against Qatar's natural gas trade. The structural characteristics of natural gas have also added an important dimension to this challenge. It was the LNG model that minimized the impact of these challenges and transformed Qatar into an unimpeded alternative. Natural gas is an important energy source in the world's energy consumption as it is more environmentally friendly than oil and an alternative to oil. Qatar has also stood out with its more reliable position against Iran and Russia, which control the two largest natural gas reserves (Koçgündüz, 2011, p. 75).

Figure 1. Qatar's LNG and natural gas trade worldwide (2023)
Source: EIA, 2023c

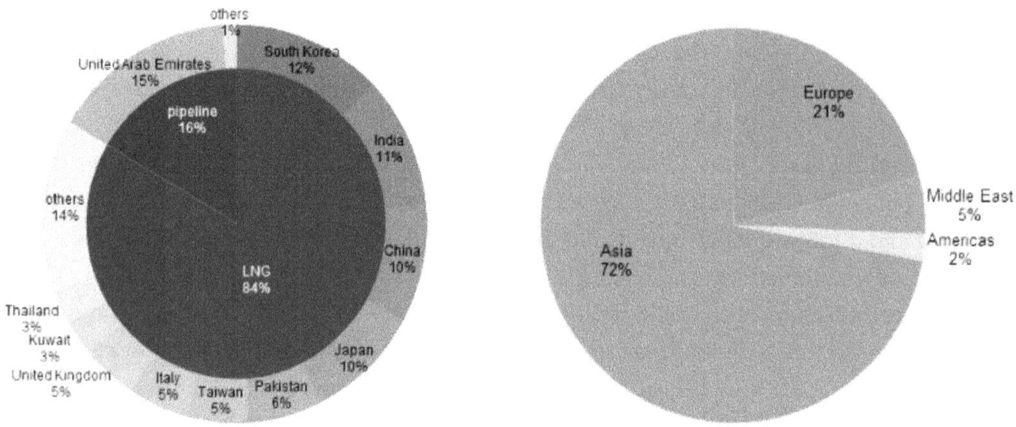

LNG MODEL AND QATAR'S TRANSFORMATION

The 21st century has witnessed breathtaking advancements across technology, economy, infrastructure, and numerous other domains worldwide. This era, marked by concerns about global warming, has heralded the acceleration of transitioning to renewable sources, such as wind, solar, and biofuels (Ashkanani & Kerbache, 2023, p. 1063). As an extension of this progression, the LNG technology stands as a remarkable milestone in the efficient utilization of the world's energy resources. Dry natural gas is cooled to -162 degrees under atmospheric pressure to convert it into LNG. Approximately shrinking its volume by 650 times, dry natural gas is transformed into LNG (Avcı et al., 1995, p. 138). Once loaded onto tankers, LNG is transported to its demand destinations, where it is re-gasified and integrated into national networks. Notably, tanker transportation offers significant flexibility in route selection based on demand points. This flexibility overcomes the disadvantages of pipeline constraints concerning commercial limitations, geopolitical risks, and the adaptability to supply-demand imbalances. It enables both importers and exporters to swiftly determine supply-demand directions, discover new suppliers, and explore market areas (Meza et al., 2022, p. 6).

The 2023 report by the Energy Information Administration (EIA) sheds light on Qatar's natural gas trade, allowing us to draw important insights into the flexibility of LNG trade. In the first figure, it is observed that 84% of natural gas is exported as LNG, while the remaining portion is distributed only to the UAE through pipelines. The second figure highlights the dominance of the Asian market in the distribution of LNG to countries and regions. Notably, exports to Europe and the Americas are also noteworthy. From this distribution, it can be inferred that Qatar has overcome the limitations of pipelines through LNG and has successfully balanced regional and global risks.

The transformation in the natural gas industry, brought about by the LNG model, can be viewed as a result of efforts to overcome certain challenges. These challenges stem from the unique structural characteristics of natural gas. At this point, we can observe that the transportation of natural gas presents specific difficulties, compared to oil and coal, due to higher costs and complexities (Nagayama & Horita, 2014, p. 89). The primary transportation option for natural gas is through pipelines. The extensive length of cross-border pipelines, coupled with the need to maintain pressure along these pipelines, results in significant costs during construction and transfer (Meza et al., 2022, p. 2). Transnational pipelines, which interconnect regions, also carry a geopolitical cost, encompassing the risks of the regions they traverse. This risk factor becomes pronounced in crisis-prone regions such as the Middle East. The blowing up of the Iraq-Haifa pipeline during the Second Arab-Israeli War exemplifies how pipelines turn into magnets for risks during crisis periods (Issawi, 1979, p. 4). A more contemporary instance involves the detonations within the Nord Stream Pipeline, responsible for transporting natural gas from Russia to Germany. These explosions brought to light indications of deliberate sabotage, highlighting the susceptibility of pipelines to risks in various circumstances. (Nichols, 2023). Therefore, pipelines can be characterized by their vulnerability (Burrows & Treverton, 2007, p. 81; Kruyt et al., 2009, p. 2170). It is at this juncture that LNG, delivered to consumption areas in its LNG format, gains maneuverability devoid of dependency on any central hub (Meza et al., 2022, p. 2). This aspect is considered very important in terms of its position in energy geopolitics.

The concept of energy geopolitics took its place on the world agenda after the oil shock in 1973. At this point, it is seen that it is in a close relationship with energy security. For actors, access to energy constitutes an important goal of foreign policy (Conant ve Gold, 1978). In general terms, energy geopolitics encompasses a series of processes extending from resource areas to consumption geographies. The processes involving the sharing, extraction, and delivery of resources to the demand geography are completed by actors in an environment where competition is inevitable. One aspect of the competition is centered on market areas (Correlje ve Linde, 2006, s. 532). It can be said that the LNG transformation allows for a reinterpretation of energy geopolitics. The establishment of transfer routes constitutes an important dimension in energy geopolitics. When LNG is transported by tankers over sea areas, it eliminates the limiting effect of pipelines. The long and almost unchangeable routes of pipelines eliminate flexibility between source and market. In this context, competition over market areas has also accelerated thanks to LNG. Especially the impact of the Russia-Ukraine war can be considered at this point. The disruption of energy flows between Russia and the EU is the most recent example of the limitations of pipelines. On the other hand, LNG trade outperforms the competition with its flexibility to be delivered to regions with sudden supply interruptions. As a matter of fact, the transformation experienced by Qatar has shown itself and solutions have been developed in a short time for the natural gas demand of EU partners (EİA, 2023c, p. 12). This is important in terms of demonstrating Qatar's power in energy geopolitics and its competitive advantage over Russia in market areas.

Foremost, states are closely tied to energy resources for both sustainable economic growth and the continuity of people's daily needs. While developed countries expect this supply to remain vibrant for the continuity of their economies, resource-rich countries want demand to remain uninterrupted for sustainable incomes. At the same time, they desire to diversify the geography of demand and distribute both price fluctuations and possible risks as much as possible. Within this equation, it can be contended that LNG makes the most substantial contribution to the overall benefit, resulting in a mutually advantageous win-win situation. Thanks to the advantages offered by the LNG model, energy trade has reached a substantial magnitude today. The volume of LNG trade, which was 168 billion m^3 in 2003, reached 393 billion m^3 in 2017 (Magnier & Jrad, 2019, p. 1221). Even recent growth in trade volume signifies the vast potential within the sector. However, the growth of LNG trade by about 176 times from 1970 to 2021 underscores the striking potential of the sector (Statista, 2023).

Aware of the expanding LNG sector, the Doha administration initiated a breakthrough. The first LNG shipment to Japan in 1997 marked an entry into the Far East market. Qatar intensified infrastructure investments, transforming the Ras Laffan Port into a global LNG terminal. The development of

Figure 2. Annual liquefied natural gas export from exporting countries (2018-2022)
Source: EIA, 2023a

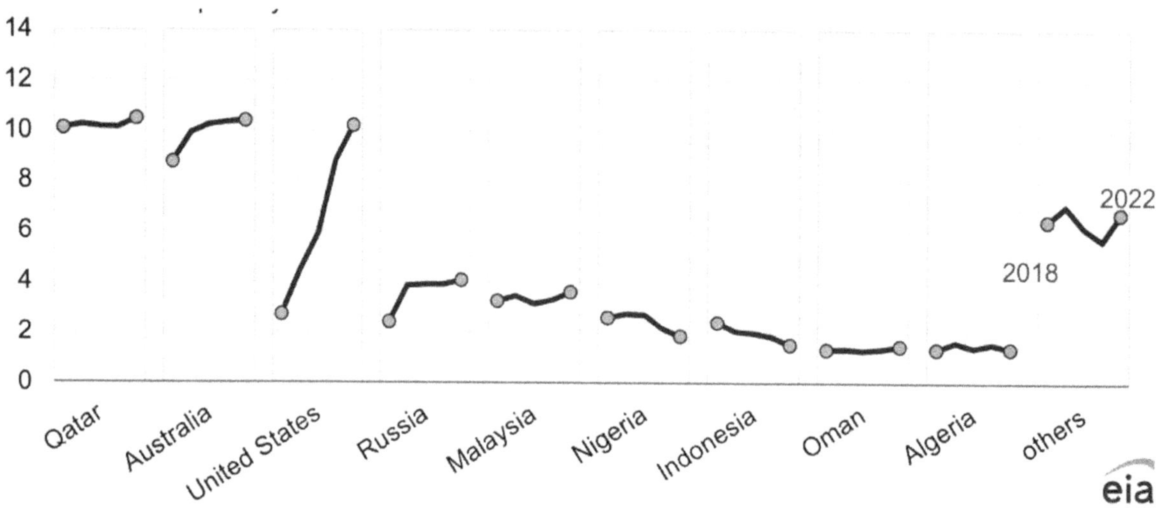

an advanced fleet of LNG tankers aimed at minimizing losses during transportation was implemented (Ghoble, 2013, p. 110). Additionally, the Qatargas Company, with 14 LNG terminals, has secured its position among the world's largest LNG producers. Through collaborations with international companies like ExxonMobil, ConocoPhillips, Shell, Total, and Japanese firms such as Marubeni Corporation and Mitsui, significant project partnerships have been forged (Qatargas, 2023). By maintaining dominant shares in these partnerships, Qatar has preserved its role as a market-maker. Moreover, through collaboration with international companies, it has achieved considerable progress in technology and infrastructure transfer. In return, these investments paid off, with Qatar accounting for 25% of the world's LNG trade in 2018 (Ashkanani & Kerbache, 2023, p. 1065). The application of advanced technology has maximized efficiency through modern infrastructure. This aspect, coupled with a strengthened transportation fleet of large LNG tankers, has opened the way for customers to access energy at lower costs. In a fiercely competitive international environment, especially against the likes of the US, Russia, Iran, and Australia, Qatar has positioned itself as a formidable contender (Meza et al., 2022, p. 5).

Qatar's transformation and investments in the LNG sector, coupled with clean energy transitions in global energy policies and conjunctural factors, have found resonance in the global market. Predictions suggest that the sector will maintain this position and peak by 2035 (McKinsey, 2022, p. 15-16). In 2022, the industry's outlook further emphasizes Qatar's position as a global LNG player, as evidenced by a 5% increase in LNG exports from 2021 to 2022. Among the three countries shaping global LNG trade - the US, Australia, and Qatar - Qatar has secured a prominent position (EIA, 2023a).

In 2021, Qatar was the world's third largest LNG exporter, and by 2022, it became the first exporter, meeting 21% of global LNG demand. By signing long-term LNG contracts with Germany for 15 years and China for 26 years, it has both strengthened its dominant position in global trade and guaranteed its demand side for a long time (EIA, 2023c, p. 12-13). It shows that for Qatar, LNG policies are at the center of sustainable economic growth and this position will continue in the future. Upon closer examination, Qatar's vision appears to have translated historical insights into energy resources into action. This is because states with natural resources can sometimes be dragged into a failed model where resource revenues are not well managed through wrong policies. In particular, what the literature characterizes as the "Dutch Disease" is a typical example of this (Eğilmez, 2019). In another dimension, although country policies show good governance characteristics, they are affected by the geography or the processes the world is going through. Centered on the Middle East geography, the conceptualization of the "Energy Vortex" offers a crucial lens through which to examine energy resources, shedding light on their regional and global implications. Resource-rich governments are the first to be affected by crises and to be thrown into an unstable environment. This drift is fueled by the mobilization of regional geopolitical risks or global crises such as the COVID-19 pandemic that the world has recently experienced (Özel Özcan & Öten, 2022, p. 200-201). In the context of both the "Dutch Disease" and the "Energy Vortex", one can argue that Qatar has managed to both get rid of its previous examples of bad governance and protect itself against regional and global risks. With its implemented policies, Qatar stands as the most robust player in resource utilization among Middle Eastern nations.

RESOURCE UTILIZATION AND ECONOMIC GOVERNANCE

According to data released by the World Bank, Qatar generated a Gross Domestic Product (GDP) of $237 billion in 2022, with a per capita GDP of $88,000. With these numerical values, Qatar has entered the top five countries with the highest per capita income (The World Bank, 2023). It's evident that Qatar's GDP heavily relies on energy resources, outlining a basic economic model. Moreover, this situation exposes Qatar's vulnerability to energy price fluctuations, which can easily impact its economy (Al-Mohannadi & Al-Mohannadi, 2023, p. 110). A closer look at World Bank data reveals a vertical growth trajectory for Qatar's GDP since the early 2000s. In 2000, it was $17.76 billion, reaching $237.3 billion in 2022. Notable declines in GDP during 2008 and 2014-2020 are remarkable within this high-growth trend. The effects of the 2008 crisis and the downward energy price trend during 2014-2020 are noteworthy trends amidst this substantial growth (The World Bank, 2023). These fluctuations demonstrate Qatar's economic growth vulnerability tied to energy prices.

The rentier state model used to characterize resource-dependent countries offers an important assessment. This economic framework characterizes state budgets that fluctuate with oil prices, production dependent on foreign workers, unfair income distribution, rapid population growth, and unemployment. In particular, the general framework of the situation in the Persian Gulf countries is characterized as a rentier state model (Mohammadzadeh, 2017, p. 23). The Doha administration has endeavored to move away from the singular growth based on hydrocarbons from which the economy has spread. In this context, Qatar is an example of a departure from the resource base, replacing vulnerability with a resilient economy. This resilient, strong economic rise has initiated a process of branding, advanced infrastructure investments, efforts to develop a skilled workforce, and entrepreneurial individuals, and building an innovation-driven, high-value-added, knowledge society (Cooper & Momani, 2011, p. 117). The Doha administration is aware that economic growth based on hydrocarbon reserves will be replaced by alternative methods of wealth creation. Hence, it also started to make breakthroughs in the field of education by establishing the Qatar Foundation in 1994 to pave the way for educational and scientific development. Education City, which was established in 1998 after the Qatar Foundation, is home to important universities with proven international success, as well as offering high-tech facilities and enabling scientific research. With an educational capacity in a wide range of fields from medical sciences to engineering technologies and from art studies to information technologies, Education City is a distinctive area where Qatar reflects its economic and social development (Ibrahim & Harrigan, 2012, p. 3). This also serves as a tool to adapt to the information age and foster a skilled workforce. The presence of major US universities like Georgetown, Cornell, and Texas A&M underscores Qatar's commitment to education and the information age (Cooper & Momani, 2011, p. 117).

Furthermore, Qatar has recognized the power of media and communication, evident in developed industries. Media and communication play a vital role in attracting foreign investors and introducing Qatar to the world. Qatar's prominent tool for global recognition and a significant instrument in steering its foreign policy is the establishment of Al Jazeera. This media entity sets Qatar apart from neighboring countries and functions as a unique soft power tool. Acknowledging the power of media, the Doha government successfully transformed Al Jazeera, founded in 1996, into a global media network within a short span (Devran & Özcan, 2018). It has generated the "Al Jazeera Effect," similar to the "CNN Effect," offering critical perspectives on regional policies. While opening Qatar and the Arab region to the outside world, this media giant influences society, despite facing pressures. Managed by the private sector, it overcame financial challenges thanks to Qatar's economic strength (Cooper & Momani, 2011, p. 118).

Established as a modest airline in 1997, Qatar Airways is now at the forefront of the country's brand values. Awarded the Airline of the Year title by international aviation rating agency Skytrax in 2011, 2012, 2015, 2017, and 2019, Qatar Airways has become the flagship carrier operating flights to over 150 destinations across six continents (Qatar Airways, 2023). As an essential institution in brand creation, the airline reveals another aspect of Qatar's engagement with the world. Notably, Qatar Airways' branding is visible on the jerseys of prominent football clubs like Paris Saint-Germain and Barcelona. Through sports, Qatar's brands are showcased to the world.

Another crucial aspect, equally vital to acquiring capital, is the effective and efficient utilization of that capital. With a visionary perspective and a systematic approach, success can be achieved. In this regard, the Doha government introduced the "2030 National Vision" in 2008 to guide its capital accumulation toward efficient utilization (GCO, 2023). This also involves the transformation of energy-based growth into diverse sectors for a sustainable future. Managing a portfolio larger than the budgets of many countries, the Qatar Investment Authority acquires high-profile companies or establishes partnerships to broaden its portfolio. Leading European companies like Porsche, Volkswagen, and Deutsche Bank are part of this portfolio (Boyce, 2013, p. 376). Qatar showcases different brands, investments in various sectors, and endeavors to construct a modern nation. The world is moving towards a transition where hydrocarbon consumption will eventually cease or decrease in strength. This implies that the current demand might disappear in the future. Under this future projection, Qatar is on its way to sustaining the current level of its economy by distributing its current revenues to different sectors and areas as much as possible.

CONCLUSION

In the historical progression of Qatar's economy, natural resources have held a significant place from its early periods to the present day. Fishing and pearl hunting were the foundational natural resources of this economy's primitive stages. However, this resource-based economy of the initial period faced setbacks influenced by global developments. Particularly, events like World War II and the 1929 Economic Crisis marked the decline of pearl hunting. As the world entered the era of oil, the Middle East's abundant resources took center stage on the global agenda, as energy became paramount. Qatar, founded upon these rich resources, developed an economic system centered on hydrocarbon resources. Notably, its natural gas reserves hold immense economic value.

For Qatar, the main dynamo for generating economic value has been the transition to the LNG model. This model has been the best alternative to overcome the region's political conflicts and minimize geopolitical risks. Indeed, the LNG model provides extraordinary flexibility to act according to changing demand and to create new routes in a short time. In this way, Qatar responds to any demand with maritime transportation. This transformation has ultimately paid off and turned Qatar into an energy miracle country. In fact, Qatar's national income has increased exponentially, and it ranks high in the per capita income rankings.

Beyond its wealth of resources, the Doha government has taken the first step in effectively utilizing energy revenues through established funds. Early on, the country's infrastructure was developed, aligning with civilized standards in areas such as healthcare, arts, sports, and education. Furthermore, with the established fund, investments with high brand value have been initiated. Resources have been managed successfully through acquisitions and partnerships across various global regions. Leveraging the Qatar LNG model, wealth has been reinvested in diverse areas. The transition from energy dependence, which constituted the most robust part of the country's income, has led Qatar toward generating multidimensional economic strength.

REFERENCES

Al-Mohannadi, S. A., Dhabia, M., & Al-Mohannadi, D. M. (2022). Qatar in the Energy Transition: Low Carbon Economy Challenges and Opportunities. In Sustainable Qatar (109–126). Gulf Studies.

Ashkanani, S. H., & Kerbache, L. (2023). Enhanced megaproject management systems in the LNG industry: A case study from Qatar. *Energy Reports*, *9*, 1062–1076. doi:10.1016/j.egyr.2022.12.030

Avcı, A., & Can, M. ve Kılıç, M. (1995). Doğal gaz sıvılaştırma yöntemleri, sıvılaştırılmış doğal gazın (LNG) nakli ve depolanması üzerine bir inceleme. *Pamukkale Üniversitesi Mühendislik Bilimleri Dergisi*, *1*(3), 137–144.

Bölükbaşı, M. (2019). Tarihsel süreçte Katar devletinin ekonomik gelişimi ve uygulanan ambargo. *Uluslararası Sosyal Araştırmalar Dergisi*, *12*(68), 323–331.

Boyce, S. G. (2013). Qatar's foreign policy. *Asian Affairs*, *44*(3), 365–377. doi:10.1080/03068374.2013.826003

Burrows, M., & Treverton, G. F. (2007). A strategic view of energy futures, Survival. *Survival*, *49*(3), 79–90. doi:10.1080/00396330701564703

Conant, M., & Gold, F. (1978). *The Geopolitics of Energy*. Westview Press.

Cooper, A. F., & Momani, B. (2011). Qatar and expanded contours of small state diplomacy. *The International Spectator*, *46*(3), 113–128. doi:10.1080/03932729.2011.576181

Correlje, A., & Linde, C. (2006). Energy supply security and geopolitics: A European perspective. *Energy Policy*, *34*(5), 532–543. doi:10.1016/j.enpol.2005.11.008

Devran, Y. (2018). Katar krizi ve El Cezire: Ortadoğu'da özgür yayıncılığın geleceği. *Gümüşhane Üniversitesi İletişim Fakültesi Dergisi*, *6*(1), 305–325. doi:10.19145/e-gifder.340128

EİA. (2023a). *Today in Energy*. Retrieved May 25, 2023 from https://www.eia.gov/todayinenergy/detail.php?id=57000

EİA. (2023b). *What is the volume of world natural gas reserves?* Retrieved June 1, 2023 from https://www.eia.gov/tools/faqs/faq.php?id=52&t=8#:~:text=As%20of%20January%201%2C%202020,proved%20reserves%20of%20natural%20gas

EİA. (2023c). *Country Analysis Brief: Qatar*. Retrieved June 5, 2023 https://www.eia.gov/international/content/analysis/countries_long/Qatar/qatar.pdf

GCO. (2023). *Qatar National Vision 2030*. Retrieved July 22, 2023 https://www.gco.gov.qa/en/about-qatar/national-vision2030/

Ghoble, V. T. (2013). The economics of natural gas its geopolitical implications. *World Affairs*, *17*(2), 108–123.

Hassan, M. F. (1978). Agricultural development in a petroleum-based economy. Qatar. *Economic Development and Cultural Change*, *27*(1), 145–167. doi:10.1086/451078

Henderson, S. (2014). *Regime Change in Qatar*. Foreign Policy. Retrieved May 15, 2023 from https://foreignpolicy.com/2013/06/14/regime-change-in-qatar/

Ibrahim, I., & Harrigan, F. (2012). Qatar's economy: Past, Present and Future. *QScience Connect*, (1), 2–24.

Issawi, C. (1978-1979). The 1973 oil crisis and after. *Journal of Post Keynesian Economics*, *1*(2), 3–26. doi:10.1080/01603477.1978.11489099

Koçgündüz, L. M. (2011). Basra Körfezi'nin parlayan incisi: Katar. *ORSAM*, *3*(26), 71–81.

Krane, J. (2009). *City of Gold Dubai and the Dream of Capitalism*. St. Martin's Press.

Kruyt, B., Vuuren, D. P., Vries, H. J. M., & Groenenberg, H. (2009). Indicators for energy security. *Energy Policy*, *37*(6), 2166–2181. doi:10.1016/j.enpol.2009.02.006

Kurşun, Z. (2004). *Basra Körfezi'nde Osmanlı İngiliz Çekişmesi, Katar'da Osmanlılar (1871-1916)*. Türk Tarih Kurumu Yayınları.

Magnier, H. J., & Jrad, A. (2019). A minimal simplified model for assessing and devising global LNG equilibrium trade portfolios while maximizing energy security. *Energy*, *173*, 1221–1233. doi:10.1016/j.energy.2019.02.134

McKinsey. (2022). *Global Energy Perspective 2022*. Retrieved July 22, 2023 https://www.mckinsey.com/~/media/McKinsey/Industries/Oil%20and%20Gas/Our%20Insights/Global%20Energy%20Perspective%202022/Global-Energy-Perspective-2022-Executive-Summary.pdf

Meza, A., Ari, I., Al Sada, M. A., & Koç, M. (2022). Disruption of maritime trade chokepoints and the global LNG trade: An agent-based modeling approach. *Maritime Transport Research*, *3*, 1–17. doi:10.1016/j.martra.2022.100071

MOFA. (2022a). *Historical Overview*. Retrieved May 2, 2023 from https://mofa.gov.qa/en/qatar/history-of-qatar/historical-overview

Mohammadzadeh, B. (2017). Status and foreign policy change in small States: Qatar's emergence in perspective. *The International Spectator*, *52*(2), 19–36. doi:10.1080/03932729.2017.1298886

Nagayama, D., & Horita, M. (2014). A network game analysis of strategic interactions in the international trade of Russian natural gas through Ukraine and Belarus. *Energy Economics*, *43*, 89–101. doi:10.1016/j.eneco.2014.02.010

Nichols, M. (2023). *Germany tells UN: Nord Stream inquiry found subsea explosive traces on yacht*. Reuters. Retrieved July 18, 2023 https://www.reuters.com/world/europe/germany-tells-un-nord-stream-inquiry-found-subsea-explosive-traces-yacht-2023-07-11/

Özel Özcan, M. S., & Öten, C. (2022). Enerji kriz girdabı kavramsallaştırması bağlamında Orta Doğu'da petrol krizleri. *Bölgesel Araştırmalar Dergisi*, *6*(1), 174–208.

Qatar Airways. (2023). *About Qatar Airways*. Retrieved July 20, 2023 https://www.qatarairways.com/press-releases/en-WW/about/

QatarEnergy. (2022). *Our History*. Retrieved May 20, 2023 from https://www.qatarenergy.qa/en/WhoWeAre/Pages/OurHistory.aspx

Qatargas. (2023). *North Field*. Retrieved June 3, 2023 from https://www.qatargas.com/english/aboutus/north-field

Refai, H. A., Eissa, M. A., & Zeitun, R. (2021). The dynamics of the relationship between real estate and stock markets in an energy-based economy: The case of Qatar. *Journal of Economic Asymmetries*, *23*, 1–15. doi:10.1016/j.jeca.2021.e00200

Roberts, D. (2012). Understanding Qatar's foreign policy objectives. *Mediterranean Politics*, *17*(2), 233–239. doi:10.1080/13629395.2012.695123

Sevim, C. (2012). Küresel enerji jeopolitiği ve enerji güvenliği. *Yaşar Üniversitesi E-Dergisi*, *7*(26), 4378–4391.

Statista. (2023). *Natural gas production in Qatar from 1989 to 2022*. Retrieved June 1, 2023 from https://www.statista.com/statistics/265336/natural-gas-production-in-qatar/

The World Bank. (2023). *GDP Growth Qatar*. Retrieved June 5, 2023 https://data.worldbank.org/indicator/NY.GDP.MKTP.KD.ZG?locations=QA

UNFCC. (2017). *The Paris Agreement*. Retrieved June 5, 2023 http://unfccc.int/paris_agreement/items/9485.php

Worldometer. (n.d.). *Qatar Oil*. https://www.worldometers.info/oil/qatar-oil/

Compilation of References

Abderrezak, A. (2002). Hydrocarbon price shocks and uncertainty: Implications for Algeria's economic growth. *Journal of North African Studies*, *7*(2), 86–98. doi:10.1080/13629380208718467

Abylkasymova, A. (2019). *Hydropower Potential of the Central Asian Countries*. Central Asia Data-Gathering and Analysis Team. https://www.researchgate.net/publication/331716216_Hydropower_Potential_of_the_Central_Asian_Countries

Addi, L. (1995). Algeria's new oil strategy. In G. Kate & C. M. Henry (Eds.), *Oil in the New World Order*. University Press of Florida.

Adjel-Debbich, S. (2018). La crise de l'oléoduc Edjeleh-Gabès: Au coeur des enjeux de souveraineté du Maghreb (1954-1962). *L'Année du Maghreb*, *18*(18), 129–148. doi:10.4000/anneemaghreb.3647

Ağpak, F., & Özçiçek, Ö. (2018). Bir istihdam politikası aracı olarak yenilenebilir enerji. *Ömer Halisdemir Üniversitesi İktisadi ve İdari Bilimler Fakültesi Dergisi, 11*(2), 112-128.

Agreements Relating to Algerian Independence. (1962). Agreements Relating to Algerian Independence. *International Legal Materials*, *1*(2), 214–230. doi:10.1017/S0020782900061234

Ahlborg, H. (2017). Towards a conceptualization of power in energy transitions. *Environmental Innovation and Societal Transitions*, *25*, 122–141. doi:10.1016/j.eist.2017.01.004

Aidarkhanova, A., Larionova, N., Tleukanova, Z., Mamyrbaeva, A., Ermakova, R., Svetacheva, Y., Aktayev, M., & Panitskiy, A. (2022). The character of radionuclide contamination of natural lakes at the territory of the Semipalatinsk test site. *Journal of Environmental Radioactivity*, *255*, 107041. Advance online publication. doi:10.1016/j.jenvrad.2022.107041 PMID:36265400

Ainas, Y., Nacer, O., & Saïd, S. (2012). Hydrocarbons: An asset or an impediment to Algerian development? *Revue Tiers Monde*, *210*(2), 69–88. doi:10.3917/rtm.210.0069

Aissaoui, A. (2001). *Algeria: The political economy of oil and gas*. Oxford University Press.

Akhmet Yassavi University. (2023). *Kırgızistan'ın Yenilenebilir Enerji Sektöründeki Gelişmeler*. Eurasian Research Institute: www.eurasian-research.org/publication/kirgizistanin-yenilenebilir-enerji-sektorundeki-gelismeler/?lang=tr#wpcf7-f20009

Akhtar, M. Z., Khan, H. U. R., Sriyanto, S., Jabor, M. K., Rashid, A., & Zaman, K. (2022). How do industrial ecology, energy efficiency, and waste recycling technology (circular economy) fit into China's plan to protect the environment? Up to speed. *Recycling*, *7*(6), 83. doi:10.3390/recycling7060083

Aktan, S. (2022, 25 August). Avrupa ülkeleri enerji krizinden nasıl etkileniyor; hangi önlemleri aldılar? *Euronews*. Retrieved from https://tr.euronews.com/2022/08/25/avrupa-ulkeleri-enerji-krizinden-nasil-etkileniyor-hangi-onlemleri-aldilar

Al Shaher, S., & Zreik, M. (2022b). Sino-Iranian Relations: More Cooperation Despite Sanctions. *Resmilitaris, 12*(2), 637-649.

Al Shaher, S., & Zreik, M. (2022a). The Belt and Road Initiative in Lebanon: A Promising Initiative in a Complex Society. *The Journal of Asian Finance Economics and Business, 9*(2), 151–158.

Alaloul, W. S., Musarat, M. A., Rabbani, M. B. A., Altaf, M., Alzubi, K. M., & Al Salaheen, M. (2022). Assessment of Economic Sustainability in the Construction Sector: Evidence from Three Developed Countries (the USA, China, and the UK). *Sustainability (Basel), 14*(10), 6326. doi:10.3390u14106326

Aleluia, J., Tharakan, P., Chikkatur, A. P., Shrimali, G., & Chen, X. (2022). Accelerating a clean energy transition in Southeast Asia: Role of governments and public policy. *Renewable & Sustainable Energy Reviews, 159*, 112226. doi:10.1016/j.rser.2022.112226

Alkire, S. (2022). *Unpacking deprivation bundles to reduce multidimensional poverty.* United Nations Development Programme and Oxford Poverty and Human Development Initiative.

Al-Mohannadi, S. A., Dhabia, M., & Al-Mohannadi, D. M. (2022). Qatar in the Energy Transition: Low Carbon Economy Challenges and Opportunities. In Sustainable Qatar (109–126). Gulf Studies.

Alonso, F., Ayuso, J., & Martínez-Pagés, J. (2000). The informational content of inflation for Spanish interest rates. *Investigacion Economica, 24*, 455–471.

Alpanda, S., & Peralta-Alva, A. (2010). Oil crisis, energy-saving technological change and the stock market crash of 1973–74. *Review of Economic Dynamics, 13*(4), 824–842. doi:10.1016/j.red.2010.04.003

Álvarez, L., Hurtado, S., Sánchez, I., & Thomas, C. (2011). The impact of oil price changes on Spanish and euro area consumer price inflation. *Economic Modelling, 28*(1-2), 422–431. doi:10.1016/j.econmod.2010.08.006

Anadolu Ajansı. (2023, June 28). *İlham Aliyev: Azerbaycan'ın şimdiki hedefi yenilenebilir enerji.* AA: https://www.aa.com.tr/tr/dunya/ilham-aliyev-azerbaycanin-simdiki-hedefi-yenilenebilir-enerji/2788986

Ang, B. W., Choong, W. L., & Ng, T. S. (2015). Energy security: Definitions, dimensions and indexes. *Renewable & Sustainable Energy Reviews, 42*, 1077–1093. doi:10.1016/j.rser.2014.10.064

ANKASAM. (2023a). *Orta Asya'nın Artan Enerji İhtiyacı ve Alternatif Yöntemler.* https://www.ankasam.org/orta-asyanin-artan-enerji-ihtiyaci-ve-alternatif-yontemler/

ANKASAM. (2023b). *Rusya-Kazakistan Arasında İvme Kazanan Enerji İlişkileri.* https://www.ankasam.org/rusya-kazakistan-arasinda-ivme-kazanan-enerji-iliskileri/

Apak, S., Atay, E., & Tuncer, G. (2011). Financial risk management in the renewable energy sector: Comparative analysis between the European Union and Turkey. *Procedia: Social and Behavioral Sciences, 24*, 935–945. doi:10.1016/j.sbspro.2011.09.013

Arbitration Journal. (2021, February 11). *The Naftogaz - Gazprom Saga, Debunking Myths about the Arbitration Awards.* Retrieved from https://journal.arbitration.ru/analytics/the-naftogaz-gazprom-saga-debunking-myths-about-the-arbitration-awards/

Asghar, N., Amjad, M. A., Rehman, H., Munir, M., & Alhajj, R. (2022, November 20). Achieving sustainable development resilience: Poverty reduction through affordable access to electricity in developing economies. *Journal of Cleaner Production, 376*, 1–3. doi:10.1016/j.jclepro.2022.134040

Ashkanani, S. H., & Kerbache, L. (2023). Enhanced megaproject management systems in the LNG industry: A case study from Qatar. *Energy Reports, 9*, 1062–1076. doi:10.1016/j.egyr.2022.12.030

Asia Wind Energy Association. (2022). *Turkmenistan.* https://www.asiawind.org/research-data/market-overview/turkmenistan/

Atavatan Türkmenistan. (2023). *Türkmenistan ile BAE arasında yenilenebilir enerji alanındaki ortaklık yeni bir aşamaya giriyor.* https://www.atavatan-turkmenistan.com/tr/turkmenistan-ile-bae-arasinda-yenilenebilir-enerji-alanindaki-ortaklik-yeni-bir-asamaya-giriyor/

Atlantic Council. (n.d.). *Russia Sanctions Database*. Retrieved from https://www.atlanticcouncil.org/blogs/econographics/russia-sanctions-database/

Avcı, A., & Can, M. ve Kılıç, M. (1995). Doğal gaz sıvılaştırma yöntemleri, sıvılaştırılmış doğal gazın (LNG) nakli ve depolanması üzerine bir inceleme. *Pamukkale Üniversitesi Mühendislik Bilimleri Dergisi, 1*(3), 137–144.

Ayanfeoluwa, P. (2023, August 31). *Nigeria's Solar Energy Potential Higher than Current Consumption — Ikeja Electric.* vanguardngr: https://shorturl.at/oOQW9

Ayuso, J., & Escrivá, J. (1998). Trends in the monetary policy strategy in Spain. In Monetary policy and inflation in Spain. St. Martin's Press.

Azam, W., Khan, I., & Ali, S. A. (2023). Alternative energy and natural resources in determining environmental sustainability: A look at the role of government final consumption expenditures in France. *Environmental Science and Pollution Research International, 30*(1), 1949–1965. doi:10.100711356-022-22334-z PMID:35925458

Baccani, L. (2013). Global energy governance: Trade, infrastructure, and the diffusion of international organization. *International Interactions, 39*(2), 192–216. doi:10.1080/03050629.2013.768512

Backlund, S., Thollander, P., Palm, J., & Ottosson, M. (2012). Extending the energy efficiency gap. *Energy Policy, 51*, 392–396. doi:10.1016/j.enpol.2012.08.042

Bagher, A. M., Vahid, M., Mohsen, M., & Parvin, D. (2015). Hydroelectric energy advantages and disadvantages. *American Journal of Energy Science, 2*(2), 17–20.

Bank, W. (2023). *World Bank Country and Lending Groups.* datahelpdesk.worldbank.org: https://datahelpdesk.worldbank.org/knowledgebase/articles/906519-world-bank-country-and-lending-groups

Barrell, R., & Pomerantz, O. (2004). *Oil prices and the world economy.* NIESR Discussion Paper No. 242.

Başol, F. (2021). *Yenilenebilir Enerji Kaynaklarının Avantaj, Risk ve Tehlikeleri. Çankaya Üniversitesi Fen Bilimleri Enstitüsü.* Yayımlanmamış Yüksek Lisans Tezi.

Battır, O., & Yiğittepe, L. (2023). Rusya-Ukrayna Savaşında Yaptırımlar ve Enerji Güvenliği; Karşılıklı Ekonomik Bağımlılıklar Perspektifinden Bir Değerlendirme. *Yönetim ve Ekonomi Dergisi, 30*(3), 549–573. doi:10.18657/yonveek.1222200

Bayraç, H. N., & Çildir, M. (2017). AB Yenilenebilir Enerji Politikalarının Ekonomik Büyüme Üzerindeki Etkisi. *Uluslararası Yönetim İktisat ve İşletme Dergisi, 13*(13), 201–212.

BBC. (2022, March 1). *Ukraine Conflict: EU and US Impose Sanctions over Invasion.* Retrieved from https://www.bbc.com/news/world-europe-60506681

BBC. (2023, January 26). *Russia Sanctions: What Impact Have They Had on its Oil and Gas Exports?* Retrieved from https://www.bbc.com/news/58888451

Bekar, N. (2020). Yenilenebilir Enerji Kaynakları Açısından Türkiye'nin Enerji Jeopolitiği. *Türkiye Siyaset Bilimi Dergisi*, *3*(1), 37–54.

Belhoul, H. (1984). *The performance of public industrial enterprises in Algeria: An empirical study*. University of Keele.

Bendib, R. (1988). *Hydrocarbons,rent and the Algerian growth strategy: A critical appraisal of the process of building an independent and national economy*. University of Glasgow.

Bernanke, B., Gertler, M., Watson, M., Sims, C. A., & Friedman, B. M. (1997). Systematic monetary policy and the effects of oil price shocks. *Brookings Papers on Economic Activity*, *1*(1), 91–158. doi:10.2307/2534702

Bertoldi, P. (2022). Policies for energy conservation and sufficiency: Review of existing policies and recommendations for new and effective policies in OECD countries. *Energy and Building*, *264*, 112075. doi:10.1016/j.enbuild.2022.112075

Bharti, M. S. (2023a). The European Union's Economic Development Strategy and Cooperation with the Countries of Central Asia. *Nowa Polityka Wschodnia*, *36*(1), 220–244. doi:10.15804/npw20233611

Bharti, M. S. (2023b). The Sustainable Development and Economic Impact of China's Belt and Road Initiative in Ethiopia. *East Asia (Piscataway, N.J.)*, *40*(2), 175–194. doi:10.100712140-023-09402-y PMID:37065271

Bharti, M. S., & Bharti, S. S. (2022). The EU Public Diplomacy in the Time of Virtual Reality: Political, Social and Economic Implications. In B. Olbrych (Ed.), *Life in Virtual Reality, Chances and dangers* (Vol. 2, pp. 13–25). Akademia Handlowa Nauk Stosowanych w Radomiu.

Bharti, M. S., & Goswami, A. (2023). Geopolitical Perspective of the EU's Post-Pandemic Public Diplomacy: Prospects and Challenges. In S. Kavoğlu & E. Köksoy (Eds.), *Global Perspectives on the Emerging Trends in Public Diplomacy* (pp. 24–49). IGI Global. doi:10.4018/978-1-6684-9161-4.ch002

Bharti, M. S., & Singh, A. (2023). India and France bilateral partnership for advancing strategic autonomy in the Indo-Pacific region: Special reference to the Indo-French strategic partnership. *Cogent Social Sciences*, *9*(1), 2215561. doi: 10.1080/23311886.2023.2215561

Bhattacharyya, S. S., Leite, F. F. G. D., Adeyemi, M. A., Sarker, A. J., Cambareri, G. S., Faverin, C., Tieri, M. P., Castillo-Zacarías, C., Melchor-Martínez, E. M., Iqbal, H. M. N., & Parra-Saldívar, R. (2021). A paradigm shift to CO2 sequestration to manage global warming–With the emphasis on developing countries. *The Science of the Total Environment*, *790*, 148169. doi:10.1016/j.scitotenv.2021.148169 PMID:34380249

Blanco, M. I. (2009). The economics of wind energy. *Renewable & Sustainable Energy Reviews*, *13*(6-7), 1372–1382. doi:10.1016/j.rser.2008.09.004

Bloomberg, H. T. (2023, April 4). *Petrol fiyatları OPEC+ kararı sonrası rallide*. https://www.bloomberght.com/petrol-fiyatlari-opec-karari-sonrasi-rallide-2329305

Bloomberg. (2022, March 1). *Brent Oil Gains, US Crude Falls amid Market Volatility*. Retrieved from https://www.bloomberg.com/news/articles/2022-03-03/oil-extends-gain-as-investors-weigh-strain-of-ukraine-conflict

Bloomberg. (2022, March 3). *Europe's Gas Prices Head for Highest since 2018 with Russia Sidelined*. Retrieved from https://www.bloomberg.com/news/articles/2022-03-04/europe-s-gas-prices-head-for-highest-since-2018-with-russia-sidelined

Bloomberg. (2022, March 4). *Russia Gas Output Down 13% in First Half after EU Exports Cut*. Retrieved from https://www.bloomberg.com/news/articles/2023-07-26/russia-gas-output-down-13-in-first-half-after-eu-exports-cut#xj4y7vzkg

Blumstein, C., Krieg, B., Schipper, L., & York, C. (1980). Overcoming social and institutional barriers to energy conservation. *Energy*, *5*(4), 355–371. doi:10.1016/0360-5442(80)90036-5

Bluszcz, A. (2017). European economies in terms of energy dependence. *Quality & Quantity*, *51*(4), 1531–1548. doi:10.100711135-016-0350-1 PMID:28725090

Bollen, J., Hers, S., & van der Zwaan, B. (2010). An integrated assessment of climate change, air pollution, and energy security policy. *Energy Policy*, *38*(8), 4021–4030. doi:10.1016/j.enpol.2010.03.026

Bolsen, T. (2011). The Construction of News: Energy Crises, Advocacy Messages, and Frames toward Conservation. *The International Journal of Press/Politics*, *16*(2), 143–162. doi:10.1177/1940161210392782

Bölükbaşı, M. (2019). Tarihsel süreçte Katar devletinin ekonomik gelişimi ve uygulanan ambargo. *Uluslararası Sosyal Araştırmalar Dergisi*, *12*(68), 323–331.

Bosetti, V., Carraro, C., Duval, R., & Tavoni, M. (2011). What should we expect from innovation? A model-based assessment of the environmental and mitigation cost implications of climate-related R&D. *Energy Economics*, *33*(6), 1313–1320. doi:10.1016/j.eneco.2011.02.010

Bostan, A., Yilmaz, A., & Ravanoğlu, G. A. (2015). Kırgızistan Enerji Tüketiminin Ayrıştırma Yöntemiyle Analizi (2002-2011). *Ege Academic Review*, *15*(1), 39. doi:10.21121/eab.2015117998

Bouzarovski, S. (2014). Energy poverty in the European Union: Landscapes of vulnerability. *Wiley Interdisciplinary Reviews. Energy and Environment*, *3*(3), 277. doi:10.1002/wene.89

Bown, C. P. (2021). The US–China trade war and Phase One agreement. *Journal of Policy Modeling*, *43*(4), 805–843. doi:10.1016/j.jpolmod.2021.02.009

Boyce, S. G. (2013). Qatar's foreign policy. *Asian Affairs*, *44*(3), 365–377. doi:10.1080/03068374.2013.826003

Boyd, R., & Ufimtseva, A. (2021). Facilitating peaceful rise: The increasing role of geopolitics and domestic legitimacy in China's energy policy. *Energy Policy*, *158*, 112532. doi:10.1016/j.enpol.2021.112532

BP. (2021). *Statistical Review of World Energy*. https://www.bp.com/content/dam/bp/business-sites/en/global/corporate/pdfs/energy-economics/statistical-review/bp-stats-review-2021-full-report.pdf#page13

Bradshaw, M. (2013). Sustainability, climate change, and transition in global energy. In A. Goldthau (Ed.), *The handbook of global energy policy* (pp. 48–64). Wiley-Blackwell. doi:10.1002/9781118326275.ch3

Britannica. (2023). *Climate of Nigeria*. https://www.britannica.com/place/Nigeria/Settlement-patterns

British Petroleum. (2022). *BP Statistical Review of World Energy*. 71 st. Edition. Author.

Brown, S. P. A., & Huntington, H. G. (2017). OPEC and world oil security. *Energy Policy*, *108*, 512–523. doi:10.1016/j.enpol.2017.06.034

Burrows, M., & Treverton, G. F. (2007). A strategic view of energy futures, Survival. *Survival*, *49*(3), 79–90. doi:10.1080/00396330701564703

Byrne, J., Noah, T., & Young-Doo, W. (2006). Modern Energy and Modern Society. In Transforming Power: Energy, Environment, and Society in Conflict (p. viii). Routledge.

Byrne, J. J. (2016). *Mecca of Revolution: Algeria, decolonization, and the Third World order*. Oxford University Press. doi:10.1093/acprof:oso/9780199899142.001.0001

Cabbarov, F. R. (2018). *Ekonomik Büyüme ve Enerji Tüketimi İlişkisi. G. Üniversitesi içinde, 1.* Uluslararası Ekonomi ve İşletme Sempozyumu.

Caffentzis, G. (1980). The Work/Energy Crisis and the Apocalypse. In In Letters of Blood and Fire: Work, Machines, and the Crisis of Capitalism. PM Press.

Caineng, Z. O. U., Songqi, P. A. N., & Qun, H. A. O. (2020). On the connotation, challenge and significance of China's "energy independence" strategy. *Petroleum Exploration and Development, 47*(2), 449–462. doi:10.1016/S1876-3804(20)60062-3

Calouste Gulbenkian Foundation. (n.d.). *Mr. Five Percent.* https://gulbenkian.pt/en/the-foundation/calouste-sarkis-gulbenkian/mr-five-percent/

Camacho Ballesta, J. A., da Silva Almeida, L., & Rodríguez, M. (2022). An analysis of the main driving factors of renewable energy consumption in the European Union. *Environmental Science and Pollution Research International, 29*(23), 35110–35123. doi:10.100711356-022-18715-z PMID:35044609

Camarero, M., Ordóñez, J., & Tamarit, J. (2002). Monetary transmission in Spain: A structural cointegrated VAR approach. *Applied Economics, 34*(17), 2201–2212. doi:10.1080/00036840210138419

Camarero, M., & Tamarit, J. (2002a). Oil prices and Spanish competitiveness: A cointegrated panel analysis. *Journal of Policy Modeling, 24*(6), 591–605. doi:10.1016/S0161-8938(02)00128-X

Camarero, M., & Tamarit, J. (2002b). A panel cointegration approach to the estimation of the peseta real exchange rate. *Journal of Macroeconomics, 24*(3), 371–393. doi:10.1016/S0164-0704(02)00043-5

Camu, N. (2023, June 13). *CIA Warned Ukraine Not to Blow Up Nord Stream, Reports Say.* Retrieved from https://www.politico.eu/article/cia-warned-ukraine-not-to-blow-up-nord-stream-reports-pipeline/

Cantoni, R., & Leucha, V. (2014). Underground and underwater: Oil security in France and Britain during the Cold War. In The Surveillance Imperative: Geosciences During the Cold War and Beyond (pp. 45-66). New York: Palgrave.

Carlisle, J. E. (2017). *The politics of energy crises.* Oxford University Press.

Casper, J. K. (2007). *Natural resources-energy: Powering the past, present, and future.* Chelsea House Publishers.

Çetinkaya, B. (2019). *Erken Cumhuriyet Dönemi Enerji Politikaları. Karabük Üniversitesi Sosyal Bilimler Enstitüsü.* Yayımlanmamış Yüksek Lisans Tezi.

Chandler, W. (2018). *Energy and environment in the transition economies: between cold war and global warming.* Routledge. doi:10.4324/9780429500817

Chatuverdi, A. K. (2017). Geopolitics of energy. In A. Shukla & A. Sharma (Eds.), *Energy security and sustainability* (pp. 363–398). CRC Press.

Cheba, K., Bąk, I., & Pietrzak, M. B. (2023). Conditions of the green transformation. The case of the European Union. *Technological and Economic Development of Economy, 29*(2), 438–467. doi:10.3846/tede.2022.17993

Cheba, K., Bąk, I., Szopik-Depczyńska, K., & Ioppolo, G. (2022). Directions of green transformation of the European Union countries. *Ecological Indicators, 136*, 108601. doi:10.1016/j.ecolind.2022.108601

Chen, D., & Galkin, P. (2023). China's energy investment through the lens of the Belt and Road Initiative. In *A Research Agenda for Energy Politics* (pp. 93–126). Edward Elgar Publishing. doi:10.4337/9781789901764.00015

Cheng, D., Shi, X., & Yu, J. (2021). The impact of green energy infrastructure on firm productivity: Evidence from the Three Gorges Project in China. *International Review of Economics & Finance*, *71*, 385–406. doi:10.1016/j.iref.2020.09.022

Cherlet, M., Hutchinson, C., Reynolds, J., Hill, J., Sommer, S., & von Maltitz, G. (2018). *World Atlas of Desertification*. Publication Office of the European Union.

Cherp, A., Jewell, J., & Goldthau, A. (2011). Governing global energy: Systems, transitions, complexity. *Global Policy*, *2*(1), 75–88. doi:10.1111/j.1758-5899.2010.00059.x

Chester, L. (2010). Conceptualising energy security and making explicit its polysemic nature. *Energy Policy*, *38*(2), 887–895. doi:10.1016/j.enpol.2009.10.039

Chow, T. (2016). Combined photovoltaic/thermal technology for building applications. In Advances in Solar Heating and Cooling (p. 525). Woodhead Publishing.

CIA Intelligence Memorandum. (1970). *Algeria: The Impotrance of the Oil Industry*. CIA.

CIA. (2021). *The World Factbook-Algeria*. https://www.cia.gov/the-world-factbook/countries/algeria/#economy

Claes, D. H. (2013). Cooperation and conflict in oil and gas markets. In A. Goldthau (Ed.), *The handbook of global energy policy* (pp. 176–189). Wiley-Blackwell. doi:10.1002/9781118326275.ch11

Clark, A., & Zhang, W. (2022). Estimating the employment and fiscal consequences of thermal coal phase-out in china. *Energies*, *15*(3), 800. doi:10.3390/en15030800

Clem, F., & Tisdell, T. I. (1982). *Subsistence Economies and Unsustainable Development and Trade: Some Simple Theory*. Working Paper No. 77, University of Newcastle.

Cleveland, C., & Morris, C. G. (2006). *Dictionary of energy*. Elsevier.

Coenen, J., Bager, S., Meyfroidt, P., Newig, J., & Challies, E. (2021). Environmental governance of China's belt and road initiative. *Environmental Policy and Governance*, *31*(1), 3–17. doi:10.1002/eet.1901

Conant, M., & Gold, F. (1978). *The Geopolitics of Energy*. Westview Press.

Cooper, A. F., & Momani, B. (2011). Qatar and expanded contours of small state diplomacy. *The International Spectator*, *46*(3), 113–128. doi:10.1080/03932729.2011.576181

Cornat, H. (1965). *Senat: Première session ordinaire de 1965-1966*. https://www.senat.fr/rap/1965-1966/i1965_1966_0022.pdf

Correlje, A., & Linde, C. (2006). Energy supply security and geopolitics: A European perspective. *Energy Policy*, *34*(5), 532–543. doi:10.1016/j.enpol.2005.11.008

Costantini, V., Gracceva, F., Markandya, A., & Vicini, G. (2007). Security of energy supply: Comparing scenarios from a European perspective. *Energy Policy*, *35*(1), 210–226. doi:10.1016/j.enpol.2005.11.002

Cui, L. B., Peng, P., & Zhu, L. (2015). Embodied energy, export policy adjustment and China's sustainable development: A multi-regional input-output analysis. *Energy*, *82*, 457–467. doi:10.1016/j.energy.2015.01.056

Cuñado, J., & Pérez de Gracia, F. (2003). Do oil price shocks matter? Evidence from some European countries. *Energy Economics*, *25*(2), 137–154. doi:10.1016/S0140-9883(02)00099-3

Cushman, D., & Zha, T. (1997). Identifying monetary policy in a small open economy under flexible exchange rates. *Journal of Monetary Economics*, *39*(3), 433–448. doi:10.1016/S0304-3932(97)00029-9

Da Graça Carvalho, M. (2012). EU energy and climate change strategy. *Energy*, *40*(1), 19–22. doi:10.1016/j.energy.2012.01.012

DailyU. Z. (2023, June 20). *внедрение ВЭИ в Ташкенте планируется направить $1 млрд*. https://www.uzdaily.uz/ru/post/75414

Damar, N. B. (2022). Elektrik Enerjisinde Uygulanan Politikalar Elektrik Hizmetinde Krizi Kapıya Getirmektedir. *Makine Mühendisleri Odası*, *731*, 89–104.

Dark, M. (2014). Taking emerging renewable technologies to market. In E. D. Coyle & R. A. Simmons (Eds.), *Understanding the global energy crisis* (pp. 193–213). Purdue University Press.

Dave, B. (2018). Silk Road Economic Belt: Effects of China's Soft Power Diplomacy in Kazakhstan. In M. Laruelle (Ed.), *China's Belt and Road Initiative and its Impact in Central Asia* (pp. 97–108). The George Washington University. https://www.fpri.org/wp-content/uploads/2022/01/louthan-1.pdf

Davis, S. (2022, March 15). *Why is Biomass Bad? 5 Reasons to Stop Importing Bioenergy*. Dogwood Alliance: https://rb.gy/qal2q

De la Cruz-Lovera, C., Perea-Moreno, A.-J., De la Cruz-Fernández, J.-L., Alvarez-Bermejo, J. A., & Manzano-Agugliaro, F. (2017). Worldwide research on energy efficiency and sustainability in public buildings. *Sustainability (Basel)*, *9*(8), 1294. doi:10.3390u9081294

De Miguel, C., Manzano, B., & Martín-Moreno, J. (2003). Oil price shocks and aggregate fluctuations. *The Energy Journal (Cambridge, Mass.)*, *24*(2), 47–61. doi:10.5547/ISSN0195-6574-EJ-Vol24-No2-2

De Miguel, C., Manzano, B., & Martín-Moreno, J. (2006). Oil shocks and the business cycle in Europe. In C. De Miguel, X. Labandeira, & B. Manzano (Eds.), *Economic modelling of climate change and energy policies*. Edward Elgar Publishing. doi:10.4337/9781781958957.00021

De Paepe, M., T'Joen, C., Huisseune, H., Van Belleghem, M., & Kessen, V. (2013). Comparison of different testing methods for gas fired domestic boiler efficiency determination. *Applied Thermal Engineering*, *50*(1), 275–281. https://doi.org/https://doi.org/10.1016/j.applthermaleng.2012.06.027

Decree of the President of the Republic of Kazakhstan. (2013). *On the Concept of transition of the Republic of Kazakhstan to 'green economy'. No 577*. https://gbpp.org/wp-content/uploads/2014/04/Green_Concept_En.pdf

Demirel, Y. (2012). *Energy: Production, conversion, storage, conservation, and coupling*. Springer. doi:10.1007/978-1-4471-2372-9

Devran, Y. (2018). Katar krizi ve El Cezire: Ortadoğu'da özgür yayıncılığın geleceği. *Gümüşhane Üniversitesi İletişim Fakültesi Dergisi*, *6*(1), 305–325. doi:10.19145/e-gifder.340128

Dikambayev, Ş. (2019). *Kırgız Cumhuriyeti Ulusal Sürdürülebilir Enerji Eylem*. https://unece.org/fileadmin/DAM/project-monitoring/unda/16_17X/E2_A2.3/NSEAP_Kyrgyzstan_RUS.pdf

Dışişleri Bakanlığı, T. C. (2023). *No: 56, 12 Şubat 2015, Ukrayna Krizi'ne Çözüm Bulunmasına Yönelik 12 Şubat Tarihli Minsk Anlaşması Hk*. https://www.mfa.gov.tr/no_-56_-12-subat-2015_-ukrayna-krizi_ne-cozum-bulunmasina-yonelik-12-subat-tarihli-minsk-anlasmasi-hk_.tr.mfa

Dışişleri Bakanlığı, T. C. (2023). *Türkiye'nin Uluslararası Enerji Stratejisi*. https://www.mfa.gov.tr/turkiye_nin-enerji-stratejisi.tr.mfa

Doaemo, W., Dhiman, S., Borovskis, A., Zhang, W., Bhat, S., Jaipuria, S., & Betasolo, M. (2021). Assessment of municipal solid waste management system in Lae City, Papua New Guinea in the context of sustainable development. *Environment, Development and Sustainability*, *23*(12), 18509–18539. doi:10.100710668-021-01465-2 PMID:33942012

Downie, C. (2020). Strategies for Survival: The International Energy Agency's response to a new world. *Energy Policy*, *141*, 111452. doi:10.1016/j.enpol.2020.111452

Duffie, J. A., & Beckman, W. A. (2013). *Solar engineering of thermal processes*. John Wiley & Sons. doi:10.1002/9781118671603

Dursun, S. (2011). Avrupa Birliği'nin Enerji Politikası ve Türkiye. *Ankara Üniversitesi Avrupa Toplulukları Araştırma ve Uygulama Merkezi Araştırma Dizisi*, 36.

Durukan, A., & Yilmaz, M. (2021). Yenilenebilir Enerjinin Önemi Ve Latin Amerika Coğrafyasindaki Yeri: Brezilya Örneği. *Ankara Üniversitesi Dil ve Tarih-Coğrafya Fakültesi Dergisi*, *61*(1), 339–358. doi:10.33171/dtcfjournal.2021.61.1.13

Dutta, A. (2022a, June 13). *Europe's Energy Security in the Aftermath of Ukrainian Crisis*. Indian Council of World Affairs. Retrieved from https://www.icwa.in/show_content.php?lang=1&level=3&ls_id=7471&lid=5009#:~:text=The%20plans%20put%20forward%20by,and%20transitioning%20to%20green%20alternatives

Dutta, A. (2022b, September 28). *Assessing Europe's spiralling energy crisis*. Observer Research Foundation. Retrieved from https://www.orfonline.org/expert-speak/assessing-europes-spiralling-energy-crisis/

EC. (2023). *Energy poverty in the EU*. European Commission: https://rb.gy/0uolq

Economidou, M., Todeschi, V., Bertoldi, P., D'Agostino, D., Zangheri, P., & Castellazzi, L. (2020). Review of 50 years of EU energy efficiency policies for buildings. *Energy and Building*, *225*, 110322. doi:10.1016/j.enbuild.2020.110322

EEA. (2004). *Environmental Impact of Energy*. European Environment Agency: https://rb.gy/jlujy

Egli, F., Steffen, B., & Schmidt, T. (2018). A dynamic analysis of financing conditions for renewable energy technologies. *Nature Energy*, *3*(12), 1084–1092. doi:10.103841560-018-0277-y

Eguchi, S. (2022). CO2 Reduction potential from efficiency improvements in China's coal-fired thermal power generation: A combined approach of metafrontier DEA and LMDI. *Energies*, *15*(7), 2430. doi:10.3390/en15072430

EIA (US Energy Information Administration). (2022). *Short-Term Energy Outlook*. Retrieved from https://www.eia.gov/outlooks/steo/

EIA (US Energy Information Administration). (2023, July 5). *Global Liquefied Natural Gas Trade Volumes Set A New Record in 2022*. Retrieved from https://www.eia.gov/todayinenergy/detail.php?id=57000

EIA. (2021). *Algeria*. https://www.eia.gov/international/content/analysis/countries_long/Algeria/archive/pdf/algeria_2013.pdf

EIA. (2022, November 16). *U.S. Energy Information Administration*. Coal explained Coal and the Environment: https://shorturl.at/dKY58

EİA. (2023a). *Today in Energy*. Retrieved May 25, 2023 from https://www.eia.gov/todayinenergy/detail.php?id=57000

EİA. (2023b). *What is the volume of world natural gas reserves?* Retrieved June 1, 2023 from https://www.eia.gov/tools/faqs/faq.php?id=52&t=8#:~:text=As%20of%20January%201%2C%202020,proved%20reserves%20of%20natural%20gas

EİA. (2023c). *Country Analysis Brief: Qatar*. Retrieved June 5, 2023 https://www.eia.gov/international/content/analysis/countries_long/Qatar/qatar.pdf

Elagöz, A. (1992). Energy savings training in the member states of the EC. *Proceedings*, *2*, 2140–2145.

Elagöz, A. (1994). Legal and administrative measures for energy savings in non-industrial buildings in the member states of the EC. *Renewable Energy*, *4*(1), 109–112. doi:10.1016/0960-1481(94)90071-X

El-Katiri, M. (2010). Sonatrach: An International giant in the making. *Defence Academy of the United Kingdom Special Series*, *10*(5), 1–19.

Elkind, J. (2009). Energy security: Call for a broader agenda. In C. Pascual & J. Elkind (Eds.), *Energy security: Economics, politics, strategies and implications* (pp. 119–148). Brookings Institution Press.

Elliott, G. (1999). Efficient tests for a unit root when the initial observation is drawn from its unconditional distribution. *International Economic Review*, *40*(3), 767–783. doi:10.1111/1468-2354.00039

Elliott, G., Rothenberg, T., & Stock, J. (1996). Efficient tests for an autoregressive unit root. *Econometrica*, *64*(4), 813–836. doi:10.2307/2171846

Ember Climate. (n.d.). https://ember-climate.org/countries-and-regions/countries/egypt/

Energifaktonorge. (2023). Retrieved from: https://energifaktanorge.no/en/norsk-energiforsyning/kraftproduksjon

Energy Brainpool. (n.d.). https://blog.energybrainpool.com/en/chinas-energy-system-in-2020-record-expansion-of-renewables-despite-corona-pandemic/

Energy Information Administration (EIA). (2022, December 22). *What is Energy?* Retrieved from https://www.eia.gov/energyexplained/what-is-energy/

Energy Information Administration (EIA). (2022, June 28). *What is Energy? Sources of Energy*. Retrieved from https://www.eia.gov/energyexplained/what-is-energy/sources-of-energy.php

Energy.gov. (2023). *Advantages and Challenges of Wind Energy*. Energy.gov: https://www.energy.gov/eere/wind/advantages-and-challenges-wind-energy

Entelis, J. P. (1981). Elite political culture and socialization in Algeria: Tensions and discontinuities. *The Middle East Journal*, *35*(2), 191–208.

Entelis, J. P. (2012). Sonatrach: The political economy of an Algerian state institution. In D. G. Victor (Ed.), *Oil and governance state-owned enterprises and the world energy supply*. Cambridge University Press.

Entelis, J. P., & Arone, L. J. (1992). Algeria in turmoil: Islam, democracy and the state. *Middle East Policy*, *1*(2), 23–35. doi:10.1111/j.1475-4967.1992.tb00031.x

Environmental and Energy Study Institute. (2021). *Fossil Fuels*. Environmental and Energy Study Institute: https://www.eesi.org/topics/fossil-fuels/description#:~:text=Fossil%20fuels%E2%80%94including%20coal%2C%20oil,percent%20of%20the%20world's%20energy

Erfle, S., & McMillan, H. (1990). Media, political pressure, and the firm: The case of petroleum pricing in the late 1970s. *The Quarterly Journal of Economics*, *105*(1), 115–134. doi:10.2307/2937821

Erfle, S., McMillan, H., & Grofman, B. (1989). Testing the regulatory threat hypothesis: Media coverage of the energy crisis and petroleum pricing in the late 1970s. *American Politics Quarterly*, *17*(2), 132–152. doi:10.1177/1532673X8901700202

Erias, A. F., & Iglesias, E. M. (2022). The daily price and income elasticity of natural gas demand in Europe. *Energy Reports*, *8*, 14595–14605. doi:10.1016/j.egyr.2022.10.404

Eshchanov, B. (2019). *Renewable energy policies of the Central Asian countries*. Norwegian Institute of International Affairs (NUPI).

Eshchanov, B.R. (2013). Prospects of renewable energy penetration in Uzbekistan—Perception of the Khorezmian people. *Renewable and Sustainable Energy Reviews*, *21*, 789–797. doi:10.1016/j.rser.2013.01.023

Euronews. (2023, June 10). *Kazakistan yeşil enerjiye geçişte rüzgar ve güneş enerjisi potansiyeline güveniyor*. https://tr.euronews.com/next/2022/12/02/kazakistan-yesil-enerjiye-geciste-ruzgar-ve-gunes-enerjisi-potansiyeline-guveniyor

European Bank for Reconstruction and Development. (2012). *Turkmenistan Country Profile*. Author.

European Commission. (2021). *European Energy Security Strategy*. Retrieved from https://www.europarl.europa.eu/factsheets/en/sheet/142/european-energy-security-strategy

European Commission. (2022). *European Green Deal*. Retrieved from https://ec.europa.eu/info/strategy/priorities-2019-2024/european-green-deal_en

European Commission. (2022, May 5). *Inauguration of Gas Interconnection between Poland and Lithuania*. Retrieved from https://commission.europa.eu/news/inauguration-gas-interconnection-between-poland-and-lithuania-2022-05-05_en

European Commission. (2022a). *RePowereu Plan, COM(2022)230*. Retrieved from https://eur-lex.europa.eu/legal-content/EN/TXT/?uri=COM%3A2022%3A230%3AFIN&qid=1653033742483

European Commission. (2022b, March 8). *REPowerEU: Joint European action for more affordable, secure and sustainable energy*. Retrieved from https://ec.europa.eu/commission/presscorner/detail/en/ip_22_1511

European Commission. (2023). *Secure Gas Supplies*. Retrieved from https://energy.ec.europa.eu/topics/energy-security/secure-gas-supplies_en

European Council. (2023, June 26). *EU Sanctions against Russia Explained*. Retrieved from https://www.consilium.europa.eu/en/policies/sanctions/restrictive-measures-against-russia-over-ukraine/sanctions-against-russia-explained/

European Parliament. (2021). *Security of Gas Supply in the EU*. Retrieved from https://www.europarl.europa.eu/factsheets/en/sheet/66/security-of-gas-supply-in-the-eu

European Parliament. (2023, February 9). *Energy policy: general principles*. Retrieved from https://www.europarl.europa.eu/ftu/pdf/en/FTU_2.4.7.pdf

European Wind Energy Association. (2009). *The economics of wind energy*. EWEA.

Eurostat. (2022). *Imports of Natural Gas by Partner Country*. Retrieved from https://appsso.eurostat.ec.europa.eu/nui/submitViewTableAction.do

Fagorite, V. I., Anifowose, F. A., & Chiokwe, V. N. (2021, January). Air Pollution; Causes, Effects and Remediation in Nigeria. *International Journal of Advanced Academic Research (Sciences, Technology and Engineering)*, *7*(1), 16.

Fan, M., He, G., & Zhou, M. (2020). The winter choke: Coal-Fired heating, air pollution, and mortality in China. *Journal of Health Economics*, *71*, 102316. doi:10.1016/j.jhealeco.2020.102316 PMID:32179329

Fan, Y., & Xu, J. H. (2011). What has driven oil prices since 2000? A structural change perspective. *Energy Economics*, *33*(6), 1082–1094. doi:10.1016/j.eneco.2011.05.017

Fawcett, T., Rosenow, J., & Bertoldi, P. (2019). Energy efficiency obligation schemes: Their future in the EU. *Energy Efficiency*, *12*(1), 57–71. doi:10.100712053-018-9657-1

Fay, J. A., & Golomb, D. S. (2002). *Energy and the environment*. Oxford University Press.

Felix, A. A., Akinbulire, T. A., & Awosope, C. (2012). Wind Energy Potential in Nigeria. *International Electrical Engineering Journal*, *3*(1), 595.

Fesharaki, F., Isaak, D., & Yamaguchi, N. (1991, May). The Asia-Pacific petroleum market: Critical issues for the 1990s. *Natural Resources Forum*, *15*(2), 140–153. doi:10.1111/j.1477-8947.1991.tb00125.x

Financial Times. (2023, August 10). *Gas Price Spike Underscores Europe's Vulnerability to Global Energy Shocks.* https://www.ft.com/content/452f2664-fd70-4f91-b8a2-1a208f72c4e4

Flaherty, C., & Filho, W. L. (2013). Energy security as a subset of national security. In W. L. Filho & V. Voudouris (Eds.), *Global energy policy and security* (pp. 11–26). Springer. doi:10.1007/978-1-4471-5286-6_2

Florini, A. (2009). Global governance and energy. In C. Pascual & J. Elkind (Eds.), *Energy security: Economics, politics, strategies and implications* (pp. 149–181). Brookings Institution Press.

Florini, A., & Sovacool, B. J. (2009). Who governs energy? The challenges facing global energy governance. *Energy Policy*, *37*(12), 5239–5248. doi:10.1016/j.enpol.2009.07.039

Foster, R., Ghassemi, M., & Cota, A. (2009). *Solar energy: renewable energy and the environment.* CRC press. doi:10.1201/9781420075670

Gaillard, E., & Maude, L. (2015). Algeria. In G. Pereira, Eduardo & K. Patrik Talus (Eds.), African Upstream Oil and Gas: A Practical Guide to the Law and Regulation (pp. 17-47). Globe Business Publishing Ltd.

Garavini, G. (2015). From Boumedienomis to Reaganomics: Algeria, OPEC, and the international struggle for economic equality. *Humanity*, *6*(1), 79–92. doi:10.1353/hum.2015.0004

Gavin, G. (2023, July 12). *Ukraine Warns Key Russian Gas Supply to Europe Will Be Cut*. Politico. Retrieved from https://www.politico.eu/article/ukraine-warns-it-wont-negotiate-new-russian-gas-transit-deal/

GCO. (2023). *Qatar National Vision 2030.* Retrieved July 22, 2023 https://www.gco.gov.qa/en/about-qatar/national-vision2030/

Geller, H., Harrington, P., Rosenfeld, A. H., Tanishima, S., & Unander, F. (2006). Polices for increasing energy efficiency: Thirty years of experience in OECD countries. *Energy Policy*, *34*(5), 556–573. doi:10.1016/j.enpol.2005.11.010

German, B. (2023, January 23). *Ukraine War Upended Energy Markets Forever*. Axios. https://www.axios.com/2023/01/23/ukraine-war-russia-energy-markets

Ghoble, V. T. (2013). The economics of natural gas its geopolitical implications. *World Affairs*, *17*(2), 108–123.

Gielen, D., Boshell, F., Saygin, D., Bazilian, M. D., Wagner, N., & Gorini, R. (2019). The role of renewable energy in the global energy transformation. *Energy Strategy Reviews, 24*, 38-50.

Gilbert, A., Bazilian, M. D., Gross, S. (2022). *The Emerging Global Natural Gas Market and the Energy Crisis of 2021–2022.* Brookings Report.

Gitelman, L., Kozhevnikov, M., & Visotskaya, Y. (2023). Diversification as a Method of Ensuring the Sustainability of Energy Supply within the Energy Transition. *Resources*, *12*(2), 19. doi:10.3390/resources12020019

Giuli, M., & Oberthür, S. (2023). Third time lucky? Reconciling EU climate and external energy policy during energy security crises. *Journal of European Integration*, *45*(3), 395–412. doi:10.1080/07036337.2023.2190588

Global Wind Atlas. (2023, July 10). *Welcome to the Global Wind Atlas*. Global Wind Atlas: https://globalwindatlas.info/en

Godfrey, S., & Tunhuma, F. A. (2020). İklim krizi: Sahra Altı Afrika'daki çocukların iklim değişikliği etkileri, eğilimleri ve savunmasızlıkları. Nairobi: Birleşmiş Milletler Çocuklara Yardım Fonu Doğu ve Güney Afrika Bölge Ofisi.

Goldemberg, J. (2012). *Energy: What everyone needs to know*. Oxford University Press. doi:10.1093/wentk/9780199812905.001.0001

Goldstein, E. (2022). What does China want in Kazakhstan? *Harvard International Review*. https://hir.harvard.edu/chinas-kazakhstan-gambit/

Goldthau, A. (2010). Energy diplomacy in trade and investment of oil and gas. In A. Goldthau & J. M. Witte (Eds.), *Global energy governance: The new rules of the game* (pp. 25–48). Brookings Institution Press.

Goldthau, A. (2013). Introduction: Key dimensions of global energy policy. In A. Goldthau (Ed.), *The handbook of global energy policy* (pp. 1–11). Wiley-Blackwell. doi:10.1002/9781118326275.ch0

Goldthau, A., Hoxtell, W., & Witte, J. M. (2010). Global energy governance: The way forward. In A. Goldthau & J. M. Witte (Eds.), *Global energy governance: The new rules of the game* (pp. 341–356). Brookings Institution Press.

Gómez-Loscos, A., Montañés, A., & Gadea, M. D. (2011). The impact of oil shocks on the Spanish economy. *Energy Economics*, *33*(6), 1070–1081. doi:10.1016/j.eneco.2011.05.016

Grimaud, N. (1972). Le conflit pétrolier Franco-Algérien. *Revue Française de Science Politique*, *22*(6), 1276–1307. doi:10.3406/rfsp.1972.418929

Guidelines for Petroleum Policy in O.P.E.C. Member Countries. (1968). Guidelines for Petroleum Policy in O.P.E.C. Member Countries. *International Legal Materials*, *7*(5), 1183–1186. doi:10.1017/S002078290005172X

Gulagi, A., Ram, M., Bogdanov, D., Sarin, S., Mensah, T. N. O., & Breyer, C. (2022). The role of renewables for rapid transitioning of the power sector across states in India. *Nature Communications*, *13*(1), 5499. doi:10.103841467-022-33048-8 PMID:36130937

Gürbüz, Ö. (2014). *ABD ve Çin'in iklim hamlesi Türkiye'yi masaya çağırıyor*. BBC Türkçe: https://www.bbc.com/turkce/ekonomi/2014/11/141113_iklim_turkiye

Guzman, L. P., & Majkut, J. (2023, January 17). *U.S. LNG remapping energy security*. Retrieved from https://features.csis.org/us-lng-remapping-energy-security/

Gyamfi, B. A., Bein, M. A., & Bekun, F. V. (2020). Investigating the nexus between hydroelectricity energy, renewable energy, nonrenewable energy consumption on output: Evidence from E7 countries. *Environmental Science and Pollution Research International*, *27*(20), 25327–25339. doi:10.100711356-020-08909-8 PMID:32347487

Hali, H., Sylvia, L., & Beatriz, R.-L. (2012, 12). *EROI (Energy Return on Energy Input/Invested)*. Environmental Justice Organization Liabilities and Trade: http://www.ejolt.org/2012/12/eroi-energy-return-on-energy-inputinvested/

Hamilton, J. D. (2011). Historical Oil Shocks. In R. Parker & R. Whaples (Eds.), Routledge Handbook of Major Events in Economic History. Routledge.

Hamilton, J. (1983). Oil and macroeconomy since World War II. *Journal of Political Economy*, *91*(2), 228–248. doi:10.1086/261140

Hamilton, J. (1996). This is what happened to the oil price-macroeconomy relationship. *Journal of Monetary Economics*, *38*(2), 215–220. doi:10.1016/S0304-3932(96)01282-2

Hamilton, J., & Herrera, A. (2004). Oil shocks and aggregate macroeconomic behavior: The role of monetary policy. *Journal of Money, Credit and Banking*, *36*(2), 265–286. doi:10.1353/mcb.2004.0012

Hamouchene, H., & Alfons, P. (2016). *Energy colonialism: The EU's gas grab in Algeria.* Observatory on Debt and Globalisation.

Hanks, R. R. (2021). "Louder than Words": A Profile of the Destruction of the Aral Sea and Its Consequences. *Association of Asian Studies, 26*(1). https://www.asianstudies.org/publications/eaa/archives/louder-than-words-a-profile-of-the-destruction-of-the-aral-sea-and-its-consequences/

Hariciye. (2020). *1973 Petrol Krizi: Etkileri ve Sonuçları.* Retrieved from https://medium.com/hariciye/1973-petrol-krizi-etkileri-ve-sonu%C3%A7lar%C4%B1-7ec1d90ad4a1

Hassan, M. F. (1978). Agricultural development in a petroleum-based economy. Qatar. *Economic Development and Cultural Change, 27*(1), 145–167. doi:10.1086/451078

Hayes, M. H. (2004). *Algerian Gas to Europe: The Transmed pipeline and early Spanish gas import projects.* James A. Baker Institute.

Heinberg, R., & Fridley, D. (2016). *Our renewable future: Laying the path for one hundred percent clean energy.* Island Press. doi:10.5822/978-1-61091-780-3

Henderson, S. (2014). *Regime Change in Qatar.* Foreign Policy. Retrieved May 15, 2023 from https://foreignpolicy.com/2013/06/14/regime-change-in-qatar/

Hepbasli, A. (2008). A key review on exergetic analysis and assessment of renewable energy resources for a sustainable future. *Renewable & Sustainable Energy Reviews, 12*(3), 593–661. doi:10.1016/j.rser.2006.10.001

Hernandez, J. (2023, June 4). *Saudi Arabia Cuts Oil Production again to Shore Up Prices — This Time on its Own.* NPR. https://www.npr.org/2023/06/04/1180056198/saudi-arabia-oil-opec

Herrera, A. M., Karaki, M. B., & Rangaraju, S. K. (2019). Oil price shocks and U.S. economic activity. *Energy Policy, 129*, 89–99. doi:10.1016/j.enpol.2019.02.011

Heshmati, A., & Abolhosseini, S. (2017). European Energy Security: Challenges and Green Opportunities. In The Political Economy of Clean Energy Transitions (pp. 292–310). doi:10.1093/oso/9780198802242.003.0015

Hodgson, P. E. (2010). *Energy, environment and climate change.* Imperial Collage Press. doi:10.1142/p651

Hoffmann, S. (1966). Obstinate or obsolete? The fate of the nation-state and the case of Western Europe. *Daedalus, 95*(3), 862–916.

Högselius. (2013). *The European natural gas industry and the oil crisis of 1973/74.* https://networks.h-net.org/system/files/contributed-files/henergy-p-hogselius-natural-gas-and-oil-crisis-1973.pdf

Holzman, S. L. (2006). *A Need for Change: The Looming Energy Crisis.* Army War College. Retrieved from http://www.dtic.mil/dtic/tr/fulltext/u2/a461433.pdf

Hooker, M. (1996). What happened to the oil price-macroeconomy relationship? *Journal of Monetary Economics, 38*(2), 195–213. doi:10.1016/S0304-3932(96)01281-0

Horton, J., Palumbo, D., & Bowler, T. (2022). *Russia sanctions: Can the world cope without its oil and gas.* BBC News.

Hou, L. (2020). *Building for oil: Daqing and the formation of the Chinese socialist state.* BRILL.

Huang, G., & Wang, H. (2021). Traditional Energy and Renewable Energy: The Differences and Transitions. *Advances in Social Science, Education and Humanities Research, 638*, 1100.

Hughes, L. (2014). *Globalizing Oil: Firms and oil market governance in France, Japan, and the United States*. Cambridge University Press. doi:10.1017/CBO9781107323643

Hughes, L., & Lipscy, P. Y. (2013). The politics of energy. *Annual Review of Political Science*, *16*(1), 449–469. doi:10.1146/annurev-polisci-072211-143240

Hu, J., Wang, K. H., Su, C. W., & Umar, M. (2022). Oil price, green innovation and institutional pressure: A China's perspective. *Resources Policy*, *78*, 102788. doi:10.1016/j.resourpol.2022.102788

Huo, T., Ma, Y., Xu, L., Feng, W., & Cai, W. (2022). Carbon emissions in China's urban residential building sector through 2060: A dynamic scenario simulation. *Energy*, *254*, 124395. doi:10.1016/j.energy.2022.124395

Hu, Y., Han, Y., & Zhang, Y. (2020). Land desertification and its influencing factors in Kazakhstan. *Journal of Arid Environments*, *180*, 104203. Advance online publication. doi:10.1016/j.jaridenv.2020.104203

Ibrahim, I., & Harrigan, F. (2012). Qatar's economy: Past, Present and Future. *QScience Connect*, (1), 2–24.

IDBT Energy Outlook. (2022). https://www.tskb.com.tr/uploads/file/enerji-gorunumu-final.pdf

IEA. (2020). *Uzbekistan energy profile*. IEA. https://www.iea.org/reports/uzbekistan-energy-profile

IEA. (2022, December 12). *How the European Union can avoid natural gas shortages in 2023*. Retrieved from https://www.iea.org/news/how-the-european-union-can-avoid-natural-gas-shortages-in-2023

IEA. (2023) Retrieved from: https://www.iea.org/reports/renewable-energy-essentials-geothermal

IEEFA. (2023, March 21). *Over Half of Europe's LNG Infrastructure Assets Could Be Left Unused By 2030*. Retrieved from https://ieefa.org/articles/over-half-europes-lng-infrastructure-assets-could-be-left-unused-2030#:~:text=Europe's%20LNG%20terminal%20capacity%20could,at%20the%20end%20of%202022

Igwe, P. A. (2018). Enhancing Productivity in Nigeria: From Subsistence to Transformational Entrepreneurship. Position paper presented to the Transformational Entrepreneurship Think Tank.

İklim Haber. (2023, April 28). *Almanya 2035'e Kadar %100 Yenilenebilir Enerjiye Geçmesini Sağlayacak Yasayı Hazırladı*. İklim Haber: https://www.iklimhaber.org/almanya-2035e-kadar-0-yenilenebilir-enerjiye-gecmesini-saglayacak-yasayi-hazirladi/

Imagambetova, A. (2022). Problems of sharing transboundary water resources in Central Asia. *Journal of Academic Approaches*, *13*(2). https://dergipark.org.tr/tr/pub/ayd

İnat, K. (2022). Rusya-Ukrayna Savaşı'nın Avrupa Enerji Politikalarına Etkisi. *Kriter*, *7*(73). Retrieved from https://www.iea.org/data-and-statistics/charts/evolution-of-key-regional-natural-gas-prices-june-2021-october-2022

InflationData. (n.d.). *Historical crude oil prices*. https://inflationdata.com/articles/inflation-adjusted-prices/historical-crude-oil-prices-table/

International Energy Agency (IEA). (2022 November 16). *Frequently Asked Questions on Energy Security*. Retrieved from https://www.iea.org/articles/frequently-asked-questions-on-energy-security

International Energy Agency (IEA). (2022). *Oil Market and Russian Supply*. Retrieved from https://www.iea.org/reports/russian-supplies-to-global-energy-markets/oil-market-and-russian-supply-2

International Energy Agency (IEA). (n.d.). *Global Energy Crisis*. IEA. Retrieved from https://www.iea.org/topics/global-energy-crisis

International Energy Agency. (2023). https://www.iea.org/countries

International Energy Agency. (2023, July 13). *Electricity consumption.* https://www.iea.org/reports/electricity-information-overview/electricity-consumption2023

International Energy Agency. (2023, July 15). *Azerbaijan Energy Profile.* IEA: https://www.iea.org/reports/azerbaijan-energy-profile

International Energy Agency. (2023, July 15). *Context of renewable energy in Uzbekistan* IEA: https://www.iea.org/reports/solar-energy-policy-in-uzbekistan-a-roadmap/context-of-renewable-energy-in-uzbekistan

International Energy Agency. (2023a, July 15). *Solar PV.* IEA: https://www.iea.org/energy-system/renewables/solar-pv

International Energy Agency. (2023b, July 15). *Wind.* IEA: https://www.iea.org/energy-system/renewables/wind

International Hydropower Association. (2023, August 1). *Hydropower and the pathway to net zero.* IHA: https://www.hydropower.org/net-zero

International Renewable Energy Agency. (2023). https://www.irena.org/Data

Iratni, B. (1986). *Foreign policy and nation-state building in Algeria, 1962-1985.* University of Warwick.

IRENA. (2021) Retrieved from: https://www.irena.org/publications/2021/Aug/Renewable-energy-statistics-2021

IRENA. (2023a, April 28). *Finance & investment.* International Renewable Energy Agency: https://www.irena.org/Energy-Transition/Finance-and-investment

IRENA. (2023b, April 28). *Use of renewable energy for transport in Europe.* International Renewable Energy Agency: https://www.eea.europa.eu/ims/use-of-renewable-energy-for

IRENASTAT. (2022). https://pxweb.irena.org/pxweb/en/IRENASTAT/IRENASTAT__Power%20Capacity%20and%20Generation/RESHARE_2023_cycle1.px/table/tableViewLayout1/

Irina, S. (2023, April 24). *Top 10 Countries With Largest Oil Reserves.* Retrieved from https://oilprice.com/Energy/Crude-Oil/Top-10-Countries-With-Largest-Oil-Reserves.html

Isaev, R. E., & Tolomushev, A. E. (2016). The potential and resources of renewable energy sources in the Kyrgyz Republic and the problems of their development. *Proceedings of the Kyrgyz State Technical University named after I. Razzakov*, 112–119.

Islam, M. S. (2017). Alternative Energy Sources for Energy Crisis: Rethinking the Global and Bangladesh Perspectives. *Journal of Technology Innovations in Renewable Energy*, *6*(1), 18–31. doi:10.6000/1929-6002.2017.06.01.3

Issawi, C. (1978-1979). The 1973 oil crisis and after. *Journal of Post Keynesian Economics*, *1*(2), 3–26. doi:10.1080/01603477.1978.11489099

İTÜ. (2023). *Non-Renewable Conventional Energy Division.* Energy İTÜ: https://enerji.itu.edu.tr/en/education/divisions/conventional-energy-division

İzmir Kalkınma Ajansı. (2023, April 28). *Yenilenebilir Enerjinin Yarattığı İstihdam Potansiyeli.* İzmir Kalkınma Ajansı: https://kalkinmaguncesi.izka.org.tr/index.php/2021/08/05/yenilenebilir-enerjinin-yarattigi-istihdam-potansiyeli/

Jefferson, M. (2013). Challenges to global energy policy and supply security. In W. L. Filho & V. Voudouris (Eds.), *Global energy policy and security* (pp. 27–44). Springer. doi:10.1007/978-1-4471-5286-6_3

Jekayinfa, S. O., Joseph, I. O., & Ralf, P. (2020). An Assessment of Potential Resources for Biomass Energy in Nigeria. *MDPI Resources*, 6.

Jenkins, R. (2022). *How China is reshaping the global economy: Development impacts in Africa and Latin America*. Oxford University Press. doi:10.1093/oso/9780192866356.001.0001

Jewell, J., Cherp, A., & Riahi, K. (2014). Energy security under de-carbonization scenarios: An assessment framework and evaluation under different technology and policy choices. *Energy Policy, 65*, 743–760. doi:10.1016/j.enpol.2013.10.051

Jia, Q. (2023). The impact of green finance on the level of decarbonization of the economies: An analysis of the United States', China's, and Russia's current agenda. *Business Strategy and the Environment, 32*(1), 110–119. doi:10.1002/bse.3120

Jiménez-Rodríguez, R., & Sánchez, M. (2005). Oil price shocks and real GDP growth: Empirical evidence for some OECD countries. *Applied Economics, 37*(2), 201–228. doi:10.1080/0003684042000281561

Johansson, B. (2013). Security aspect of future renewable energy systems- A short overview. *Energy, 61*, 598–605. doi:10.1016/j.energy.2013.09.023

John, B., Noah, T., & Young-Doo, W. (2006). Modern Energy and Modern Society. In Transforming Power, Energy, Environment and Society in Conflict (p. viii). Routledge.

John, B., Noah, T., & Young-Doo, W. (2006). *Transforming Power, Energy, Environment, and Society in Conflict*. Routledge.

Jônatas, F. C., Amir, Z. M., & Rieder, O. N. (2017). Comparison of the Performance, Advantages and Disadvantages of Nuclear Power Generation Compared to other Clean Sources of Electricity. In *2017 International Nuclear Atlantic Conference - INAC*. Belo Horizonte: International Nuclear Atlantic Conference - INAC.

Jones, T. C. (2012). America, Oil, and War in the Middle East. *The Journal of American History, 99*(1), 208–218. doi:10.1093/jahist/jas045

Juliet, E. C., Jessica, T. F., Kristy, E. H. M., & Eric, R. A. N. S. (2017). *The Politics of Energy Crises*. Oxford University Press.

Kabir, E., Kumar, P., Kumar, S., Adelodun, A. A., & Kim, K. H. (2018). Solar energy: Potential and future prospects. *Renewable & Sustainable Energy Reviews, 82*, 894–900. doi:10.1016/j.rser.2017.09.094

Kakışım, C. (2019). Enerji Krizlerinin Etkisiyle Şekillenen Avrupa Birliği'nin Enerji Politikası. *Gümüşhane Üniversitesi Sosyal Bilimler Enstitüsü Elektronik Dergisi, 10*(2), 460–472.

Kaltschmitt, M., Streicher, W., & Wiese, A. (Eds.). (2007). *Renewable energy: technology, economics and environment*. Springer Science & Business Media.

Kanwal, S., Mehran, M. T., Hassan, M., Anwar, M., Naqvi, S. R., & Khoja, A. H. (2022). An integrated future approach for the energy security of Pakistan: Replacement of fossil fuels with syngas for better environment and socio-economic development. *Renewable & Sustainable Energy Reviews, 156*, 111978. doi:10.1016/j.rser.2021.111978

Karachaganak Petroleum Operating. (2021). *Business and Human Rights Resource Centre*. https://www.business-humanrights.org/documents/36055/Karachaganak_Petroleum_Operating.pdf

Karatayev, M., Hall, S., Kalyuzhnova, Y., & Clarke, M. L. (2016). Renewable energy technology uptake in Kazakhstan: Policy drivers and barriers in a transitional economy. *Renewable & Sustainable Energy Reviews, 66*, 120–136. doi:10.1016/j.rser.2016.07.057

Kardaś, S. (2023, May 4). *Keeping the Lights On: The EU's Energy Relationships since Russia's Invasion of Ukraine*. European Council on Foreign Relations. Retrieved from https://ecfr.eu/publication/keeping-the-lights-on-the-eus-energy-relationships-since-russias-invasion-of-ukraine/

Karsh, E. (2014). The Iran–Iraq War 1980–1988. Bloomsbury Publishing.

Kavaz, İ. (2018). Küresel Piyasalar Kapsamında AB'nin Son Dönem Enerji Politikaları. *SETA Perspektif, 185*, 1–8.

Kaya, İ. S. (2012). Uluslararası Enerji Politikalarına Bir Bakış:Türkiye Örneği. *TBB Dergisi, 102*, 269–288.

Kayişoğlu, B., & Diken, B. (2019). Türkiye'de yenilenebilir enerji kullanımının mevcut durumu ve sorunları. *Tarım Makinaları Bilimi Dergisi, 15*(2), 61–65.

Kazakhstan, P. W. C. (2021). *Renewable Energy Market in Kazakhstan: Potential, Challenges, and Prospects*. PWC Eurasia Deals.

Kerr, J. (2017). *Introduction to Energy and Climate: Developing a Sustainable Environment*. CRC Press. doi:10.1201/9781315151885

Kesici, G. E. (2022). Rusya-Ukrayna Savaşı'nın AB'nin Enerji Politikalarına Yansıması. *EURO Politika, 15*, 46–54.

Kester, J. (2018). *The politics of energy security: Critical security studies, new materialism and governmentality*. Routledge. doi:10.4324/9781315177892

Kestner, M. (1991). First energy efficiency directives under SAVE programme. *Energy in Europe, 1*(7), 25.

Khan, S. A. R., Godil, D. I., Yu, Z., Abbas, F., & Shamim, M. A. (2022). Adoption of renewable energy sources, low-carbon initiatives, and advanced logistical infrastructure—An step toward integrated global progress. *Sustainable Development (Bradford), 30*(1), 275–288. doi:10.1002d.2243

Khatiwada, D., Vasudevan, R. A., & Santos, B. H. (2022). Decarbonization of natural gas systems in the EU–costs, barriers, and constraints of hydrogen production with a case study in Portugal. *Renewable & Sustainable Energy Reviews, 168*, 112775. doi:10.1016/j.rser.2022.112775

Kilian, L. (2008). A comparison of the effects of exogenous oil supply shocks on output and inflation in the G7 countries. *Journal of the European Economic Association, 6*(1), 78–121. doi:10.1162/JEEA.2008.6.1.78

Kiliç, A. M. (2006). Turkey's Main Energy Sources and Importance of Usage in Energy Sector. *Energy Exploration & Exploitation, 24*(1-2), 1–17. doi:10.1260/014459806779388001

Kim, S., & Roubini, N. (2000). Exchange rate anomalies in the industrial countries: A solution with a structural VAR approach. *Journal of Monetary Economics, 45*(3), 561–586. doi:10.1016/S0304-3932(00)00010-6

Kingdon, J. W., & Stano, E. (1984). *Agendas, alternatives, and public policies* (Vol. 45). Little, Brown.

Kirkegaard, J. K., Rudolph, D., Nyborg, S., & Cronin, T. (2023). The landrush of wind energy, its socio-material workings, and its political consequences: On the entanglement of land and wind assemblages in Denmark. Environment and Planning C. *Politics and Space, 41*(3), 548–566. doi:10.1177/23996544221143657

Klare, M. T. (2009). Petroleum anxiety and the militarization of energy security. In D. Moran & J. A. Russell (Eds.), *Energy security and global politics: The militarization of resource management* (pp. 39–61). Routledge.

Klare, M. T. (2009). There will be blood: Political violanece, regional warfare, and the risk of great-power conflict over contested energy resources. In G. Luft & A. Korin (Eds.), *Energy security challenges for the 21st century: A reference handbook* (pp. 44–65). Praeger Security International.

Knodt, M., & Kemmerzell, J. (2022). *Handbook of Energy Governance in Europe*. Springer Nature. doi:10.1007/978-3-030-43250-8

Koçgündüz, L. M. (2011). Basra Körfezi'nin parlayan incisi: Katar. *ORSAM, 3*(26), 71–81.

Kopnina, H. (2016). Energy Policy in the European Union: Renewable Energy and the Risks of Subversion. In J. de Zwaan, M. Lak, A. Makinwa, & P. Willems (Eds.), Governance and Security Issues of the European Union: Challenges Ahead (pp. 167–184). T.M.C. Asser Press. doi:10.1007/978-94-6265-144-9_10

Kottari, M. (2016). A new era for global energy governance? The environmental imperatives and the EU perspective. *Politikon: IAPSS Political Science Journal, 29*, 124–139. doi:10.22151/politikon.29.7

Koulouri, A., & Mouraviev, N. (2019). Energy security through the lens of renewable energy resources and resource efficiency. In N. Mouraviev & A. Koulouri (Eds.), *Energy security: Policy challenges and solutions for resource efficiency* (pp. 9–36). Palgrave Macmillan. doi:10.1007/978-3-030-01033-1_2

Krane, J. (2009). *City of Gold Dubai and the Dream of Capitalism*. St. Martin's Press.

Krischer, K., & Schönleber, K. (2015). *Physics of energy conversion*. De Grutyer. doi:10.1515/9781501510632

Kul, C., Zhang, L., & Solangi, Y. A. (2020). Assessing the renewable energy investment risk factors for sustainable development in Turkey. *Journal of Cleaner Production, 276*, 124164. doi:10.1016/j.jclepro.2020.124164

Kurşun, Z. (2004). *Basra Körfezi'nde Osmanlı İngiliz Çekişmesi, Katar'da Osmanlılar (1871-1916)*. Türk Tarih Kurumu Yayınları.

Kuyt, B. (2009). Indicators for energy security. *Energy Policy, 37*(6), 2166–2181. doi:10.1016/j.enpol.2009.02.006

Kuzio, T. (2002). Ukraine: State and Nation Building. Routledge.

Laframboise, N., Feler, A. Bazzoni, S. Nashashibi, K., Horvitz, S. P. (1998). Algeria: Stabilization and transition to the market. Washington, DC: International Monetary Fund.

Laldjebaev, M. (2021). *Renewable energy in Central Asia: An overview of potentials, deployment, outlook, and barriers. Energy Reports*. doi:10.1016/j.egyr.2021.05.014

Lapillonne, B. (2020). *Definition of energy efficiency index ODEX in ODYSSEE database*. Energy efficiency index. Retrieved from: https://www.odyssee-mure.eu/publications/other/odex-indicators-database-definition.html

Laruelle, M. (2018). *China's Belt and Road Initiative and its Impact in Central Asia*. The George Washington University.

Lawal, T. E. (2014). Agriculture and Environmental Pollution: Causes, Consequences and Control. In Agric Ecology and Environment (p. 12). Discovery Publishing House.

Lazaro, L. L. B., Soares, R. S., Bermann, C., Collaço, F. M. A., Giatti, L. L., & Abram, S. (2022). Energy transition in Brazil: Is there a role for multilevel governance in a centralized energy regime? *Energy Research & Social Science, 85*, 102404. doi:10.1016/j.erss.2021.102404

Lee, K., Ni, S., & Ratti, R. (1995). Oil shocks and the macroeconomy: The role of price variability. *The Energy Journal (Cambridge, Mass.), 16*(4), 39–56. doi:10.5547/ISSN0195-6574-EJ-Vol16-No4-2

Leimbach, M., Bauer, N., Baumstark, L., & Edenhofer, O. (2010). Mitigation Costs in a Globalized World: Climate Policy Analysis with REMIND-R. *Environmental Modeling and Assessment, 15*(3), 155–173. doi:10.100710666-009-9204-8

Les éditions de l'Asymétrie. (1964). *Charte d'Alger*. https://www.axl.cefan.ulaval.ca/afrique/algerie-charte_d%27alger1964.htm

Li, Q. (2023). The impact of energy transition on economy and health and its fairness. *Journal of Cleaner Production, 425*. doi:10.1016/j.jclepro.2023.138953

Liadze, I., Macchiarelli, C., Mortimer-Lee, P., & Sanchez Juanino, P. (2023). Economic costs of the Russia-Ukraine war. *World Economy*, *46*(4), 874–886. doi:10.1111/twec.13336

Lin, B., & Guan, C. (2023). Evaluation and determinants of total unified efficiency of China's manufacturing sector under the carbon neutrality target. *Energy Economics*, *119*, 106539. doi:10.1016/j.eneco.2023.106539

Liu, J. (2019). China's renewable energy law and policy: A critical review. *Renewable & Sustainable Energy Reviews*, *99*, 212–219. doi:10.1016/j.rser.2018.10.007

Liu, S. Q., Huang, X., Li, X., Masoud, M., Chung, S. H., & Yin, Y. (2021). How is China's energy security affected by exogenous shocks? Evidence of China–US trade dispute and COVID-19 pandemic. *Discover Energy*, *1*(1), 1–23. doi:10.100743937-021-00002-6

Liu, Z., Deng, Z., He, G., Wang, H., Zhang, X., Lin, J., Qi, Y., & Liang, X. (2022). Challenges and opportunities for carbon neutrality in China. *Nature Reviews. Earth & Environment*, *3*(2), 141–155. doi:10.103843017-021-00244-x

Li, W., & Han, M. (2023). Mapping renewable energy transition worldwide: Gravity trajectory, contribution decomposition and income levels. *Renewable Energy*, *206*, 1265–1274. doi:10.1016/j.renene.2023.02.119

Lockwood, M., & Devenish, A. (2022, April 28). *Dutch and British Responses to the Gas Crisis*. Retrieved from https://ukerc.ac.uk/news/dutch-and-british-responses-to-the-gas-crisis/

Lo, K. (2021). Authoritarian environmentalism, just transition, and the tension between environmental protection and social justice in China's forestry reform. *Forest Policy and Economics*, *131*, 102574. doi:10.1016/j.forpol.2021.102574

López, V. (2002). Has Banco de España followed a Taylor rule using real-time information? *Investigaciones económicas*, *26*, 475-496.

Lovaas, D. (2009). Balancing energy security and the environment. In G. Luft & A. Korin (Eds.), *Energy security challenges for the 21st century: A reference handbook* (pp. 318–334). Praeger Security International.

Lowi, M. R. (2009). *Oil wealth and the poverty of politics*. Cambridge University Press. doi:10.1017/CBO9780511691621

Luciani, G. (2022). Macroeconomics of the Energy Transition. In M. Hafner & G. Luciani (Eds.), *The Palgrave Handbook of international energy economics*. Palgrave Macmillan. doi:10.1007/978-3-030-86884-0_25

Luft, G., & Korin, A. (2009). Energy security: In the eyes of the beholder. In G. Luft & A. Korin (Eds.), *Energy security challenges for the 21st century: A reference handbook* (pp. 1–17). Praeger Security International.

Lukashenko, S., Kabdyrakova, A., Lind, O. C., Gorlachev, I., Kunduzbayeva, A., Kvochkina, T., Janssens, K., De Nolf, W., Yakovenko, Y., & Salbu, B. (2020). Radioactive particles released from different sources in the Semipalatinsk Test Site. *Journal of Environmental Radioactivity*, *216*, 106160. Advance online publication. doi:10.1016/j.jenvrad.2020.106160 PMID:32217195

Lynch, M. (2018). New energy and the geopolitics of the future. In J. I. Considine & K.-W. Paik (Eds.), *Handbook of energy politics* (pp. 276–287). Edward Elgar. doi:10.4337/9781784712303.00022

Mæhle, N., & King, D. (2022). Transitioning Operational Targets: From Reserve Money to Interest Rates. In Technical Assistance Handbook. Monetary and Capital Markets Department, International Monetary Fund.

Magnier, H. J., & Jrad, A. (2019). A minimal simplified model for assessing and devising global LNG equilibrium trade portfolios while maximizing energy security. *Energy*, *173*, 1221–1233. doi:10.1016/j.energy.2019.02.134

Majone, G. (2002). The European Commission: The Limits of Centralization and the Perils of Parliamentarization. *Governance: An International Journal of Policy, Administration and Institutions*, *15*(3), 375–392. doi:10.1111/0952-1895.00193

Makine Mühendisleri Odası. (2022). Türkiye'nin Enerji Görünümü. *MMO Yayınları*, 731.

Makinen, G. (2002). The economic effects of 9/11: A retrospective assessment. Congressional Research Service (CRS).

Mallon, K. (2006). Myhts, pitfalls and oversights. In K. Mallon (Ed.), *Renewable energy policy and politics: A handbook for decision-making* (pp. 5–34). Earthscan.

Maltby, T. (2013). European Union energy policy integration: A case of European Commission policy entrepreneurship and increasing supranationalism. *Energy Policy*, *55*, 435–444. doi:10.1016/j.enpol.2012.12.031 PMID:24926115

Malti, H. (2010). *Histoire secrète du pétrole algérien*. La Découverte.

Malti, H. (2020). Algeria and OPEC. In D. Harald Claes & G. Garavini (Eds.), *Handbook of OPEC and the global energy order past, present and future challenges*. Routledge. doi:10.4324/9780429203190-6

Mambra, S. (2022). Aral Sea Disaster: Why One of the Biggest Inland Seas Dried Up? *Marine Insight*. https://www.marineinsight.com/environment/aral-sea-disaster-why-one-of-the-biggest-inland-seas-dried-up/

Mañé-Estrada, A. & Albinyana, R. (2023). Revisiting rentierism through the lens of Algerian gas. *Revue internationale des études du développement, 251*, 35-62.

Månsson, A., Johansson, B., & Nilsson, L. J. (2014). Assessing energy security: An overview of commonly used methodologies. *Energy*, *73*, 1–14. doi:10.1016/j.energy.2014.06.073

Maqbool, R. (2018). Efficiency and effectiveness of factors affecting renewable energy projects; an empirical perspective. *Energy*, *158*, 944–956. doi:10.1016/j.energy.2018.06.015

Marcel, V. (2006). *Oil Titans: National oil companies in the Middle East*. Brookings Institution Press.

Martinez, L. (2010). Algérie: Les illusions de la richesse pétrolière. *Les Etudes du CERI*, *168*, 1–36.

Mastoi, M. S., Munir, H. M., Zhuang, S., Hassan, M., Usman, M., Alahmadi, A., & Alamri, B. (2022). A comprehensive analysis of the power demand–supply situation, electricity usage patterns, and the recent development of renewable energy in China. *Sustainability (Basel)*, *14*(6), 3391. doi:10.3390u14063391

Mayer, S. (2008). Path dependence and Commission activism in the evolution of the European Union's external energy policy. *Journal of International Relations and Development*, *11*(3), 251–278. doi:10.1057/jird.2008.12

McBride, J. (2022, February 22). R*ussia's Energy Role in Europe: What's at Stake With the Ukraine Crisis | Council on Foreign Relations*. Retrieved from https://www.cfr.org/in-brief/russias-energy-role-europe-whats-stake-ukraine-crisis

McCollum, D. L., Krey, V., & Riahi, K. (2011). An integrated approach to energy sustainability. *Nature Climate Change*, *1*(9), 428–429. doi:10.1038/nclimate1297

McCollum, D. L., Krey, V., Riahi, K., Kolp, P., Grubler, A., Makowski, M., & Nakicenovic, N. (2013). Climate policies can help resolve energy security and air pollution challenges. *Climatic Change*, *119*(2), 479–494. doi:10.100710584-013-0710-y

McDougall, J. (2017). *A history of Algeria*. Cambridge University Press. doi:10.1017/9781139029230

McElroy, M. B. (2010). *Energy: Perspectives*. Oxford University Press.

McKinsey. (2022). *Global Energy Perspective 2022*. Retrieved July 22, 2023 https://www.mckinsey.com/~/media/McKinsey/Industries/Oil%20and%20Gas/Our%20Insights/Global%20Energy%20Perspective%202022/Global-Energy-Perspective-2022-Executive-Summary.pdf

Mehmet, O., & Yorucu, V. (2020). *Modern geopolitics of Eastern Mediterranean hydrocarbons in an age of energy transformation* (Vol. 78). Springer Nature. doi:10.1007/978-3-030-43585-1

Mercom India Solar Project Tracker. (n.d.). https://www.mercomindia.com/solar-share-india-power-mix-q4-2021

Meza, A., Ari, I., Al Sada, M. A., & Koç, M. (2022). Disruption of maritime trade chokepoints and the global LNG trade: An agent-based modeling approach. *Maritime Transport Research, 3*, 1–17. doi:10.1016/j.martra.2022.100071

Ministry of Energy of the Republic of Kazakhstan. (2022). *Razvitiye vozobnovlyayemykh istochnikov energii* [Development of renewable energy sources]. https://www.gov.kz/memleket/entities/energo/activities/4910?lang=ru

Ministry of Foreign Affairs of the Republic of Türkiye. (2023). *Türkiye'nin uluslararası Stratejisi.* https://www.mfa.gov.tr/turkiye_nin-enerji-stratejisi.tr.mfa#:~:text=%C3%96te%20yandan%2C%20T%C3%BCrkiye%20enerji%20talebini,alanda%20uluslararas%C4%B1%20ili%C5%9Fkilerin%20%C3%B6nemini%20art%C4%B1rmaktad%C4%B1r

Mišík, M. (2022). The EU needs to improve its external energy security. *Energy Policy, 165*, 112930. doi:10.1016/j.enpol.2022.112930

MOFA. (2022a). *Historical Overview.* Retrieved May 2, 2023 from https://mofa.gov.qa/en/qatar/history-of-qatar/historical-overview

Mohammadzadeh, B. (2017). Status and foreign policy change in small States: Qatar's emergence in perspective. *The International Spectator, 52*(2), 19–36. doi:10.1080/03932729.2017.1298886

Mohammed, C. D., Mohamed, B., & Abderrahim, C. (2017). Oil rents and institutional quality: Empirical evidence from Algeria. *Topics in Middle Eastern and African Economies, 19*(2), 2–31.

Mohtasham, J. (2015). Renewable energies. *Energy Procedia, 74*, 1289–1297. doi:10.1016/j.egypro.2015.07.774

Mojon, B., & Peersman, G. (2003). A VAR description of the effects of monetary policy in the individual countries of the euro area. In I. Angeloni, A. Kashyap, & B. Mojon (Eds.), *Monetary transmission in the euro area* (pp. 56–74). Cambridge University Press. doi:10.1017/CBO9780511492372.005

Moloney, N. (2023). *EU securities and financial markets regulation.* Oxford University Press.

Moran, D., & Russell, J. A. (2009). Introduction: The militarization of energy security. In D. Moran & J. A. Russell (Eds.), *Energy security and global politics: The militarization of resource management* (pp. 1–18). Routledge.

Mordor İntelligence. (2023). *Hungary Geothermal Energy Market Sıze & Share Analysıs - Growth Trends & Forecasts (2023 - 2028).* https://www.mordorintelligence.com/industry-reports/hungary-geothermal-energy-market#:~:text=According%20to%20preliminary%20statistics%20by,a%20Y-o-Y%20increase%20of%2054.3%25

Mork, K. (1989). Oil and macroeconomy when prices go up and down: An extension of Hamilton's results. *Journal of Political Economy, 97*(3), 740–744. doi:10.1086/261625

Mork, K., Olsen, O., & Mysen, H. (1994). Macroeconomic responses to oil price increases and decreases in seven OECD countries. *Energy Journal, 15*, 19–35.

Mouraviev, N., & Koulouri, A. (2019). Renewable energy and resource efficiency: Governance is key. In N. Mouraviev & A. Koulouri (Eds.), *Energy security: Policy challenges and solutions for resource efficiency* (pp. 255–262). Palgrave Macmillan. doi:10.1007/978-3-030-01033-1_10

Moussa, R. R., & Gurguis, M. N. (2023). Integrating renewable energy devices with streetscape elements to electrify the Egyptian roads. *Scientific Reports, 13*(1), 6720. doi:10.103841598-023-32773-4 PMID:37185786

Murshed, M. (2021). Can regional trade integration facilitate renewable energy transition to ensure energy sustainability in South Asia? *Energy Reports*, *7*, 808–821. doi:10.1016/j.egyr.2021.01.038

Musiał, W., Zioło, M., Luty, L., & Musiał, K. (2021). Energy policy of European Union member states in the context of renewable energy sources development. *Energies*, *14*(10), 28–64. doi:10.3390/en14102864

Musso, M. (2017). Oil will set us free: The hydrocarbon industry and the Algerian decolonization process. In Britain, France and the Decolonization of Africa (pp. 62-84). UCL Press.

Mylroie, L. (2019). Saddam Hussein's invasion of Kuwait: A premeditated act. In *The Iraqi Aggression Against Kuwait* (pp. 39–50). Routledge. doi:10.4324/9780429312007-3

Nabiyeva, K. (2015). *Renewable Energy and Energy Efficiency in Central Asia: Prospects for German Engagement*. Michael Succow Foundation.

Nagayama, D., & Horita, M. (2014). A network game analysis of strategic interactions in the international trade of Russian natural gas through Ukraine and Belarus. *Energy Economics*, *43*, 89–101. doi:10.1016/j.eneco.2014.02.010

Narayan, D. (2018). *Kyrgyz Republic-Energy sector review*. Academic Press.

Narayan, R. (2006). Rationale, drivers, standards, and technology or biobased materials. In P. Fornasiero & M. Graziani (Eds.), *Renewable resources and renewable energy: A global challange* (pp. 3–18). CRC Press. doi:10.1201/9781420020861.pt1

Naylor, C. (2000). *France and Algeria: A History of decolonization and transformation*. University Press of Florida.

Ngo, C., & Natowitz, J. (2009). *Our energy future: Resources, alternatives, and the environment*. Wiley. doi:10.1002/9780470473795

Nichols, M. (2023). *Germany tells UN: Nord Stream inquiry found subsea explosive traces on yacht*. Reuters. Retrieved July 18, 2023 https://www.reuters.com/world/europe/germany-tells-un-nord-stream-inquiry-found-subsea-explosive-traces-yacht-2023-07-11/

Niemann, A. (2021). Neofunctionalism. In M. Riddervold, J. Trondal, & A. Newsome (Eds.), *The Palgrave Handbook of EU Crises* (pp. 115–133). Springer International Publishing. doi:10.1007/978-3-030-51791-5_6

Nieto, J., Carpintero, Ó., Miguel, L. J., & de Blas, I. (2020). Macroeconomic modeling under energy constraints: Global low carbon transition scenarios. *Energy Policy*, *137*, 111090. doi:10.1016/j.enpol.2019.111090

Normatov, I. (2010). Geothermal water resources of the Republic of Tajikistan and a perspective on their use. *Proceedings World Geothermal Congress*, 25-29.

Nurdavletova, S., & Akatayeva, A. (2018). The renewable energy in the regional development of Central Asia. *Society and Security Insights*, 162–185. https://cyberleninka.ru/article/n/the-renewable-energy-in-the-regional-development-of-centralasia/viewer

Nwaokocha, C. N., Mufutau, A. W., & Abayomi, T. L. (2015). Estimation of Tidal Power Potential of Nigeria Coastal Area. In Renewable Energy and Sustainable Development (p. 163). Nova Science Publishers, Inc.

Nye, J. (2004). *Soft Power: The means to success in world politics*. Public Affairs.

O'Sullivan, M. L. (2013). The entanglement of energy, grand strategy, and international security. In A. Goldthau (Ed.), *The handbook of global energy policy* (pp. 30–47). Wiley-Blackwell. doi:10.1002/9781118326275.ch2

OEC. (2021). *Algeria*. https://oec.world/en/profile/country/dza

Oirere, S. (2020). Sonatrach to expand pipeline network in new contracts. *Pipeline & Gas Journal*, *24*(11), 47–50.

OnyejelamE. (2015, October 11). *The Energy Crisis in Nigeria and the Role of Law in Promoting Renewable Energy Development*. doi:10.2139/ssrn.2672625

OPEC. (2019). *Annual Statistical Bulletin*. https://www.opec.org/opec_web/static_files_project/media/downloads/publications/ASB_2019.pdf

OPEC. (2020). *Annual Statistical Bulletin*. https://www.opec.org/opec_web/static_files_project/media/downloads/publications/ASB_2020.pdf

Our World in Data. (2023). *Energy Consumption by Source, World*. Retrieved from https://ourworldindata.org/grapher/energy-consumption-by-source-and-country?stackMode=absolute

Our World in Data. (n.d.). https://ourworldindata.org/grapher/modern-renewable-prod?facet=metric&country=EGY~IND~TUR~BRA~CHN

Our World in Data. (n.d.). https://ourworldindata.org/grapher/sugar-cane-production?tab=chart

Overland, I., Juraev, J., & Vakulchuk, R. (2022). Are renewable energy sources more evenly distributed than fossil fuels? *Renewable Energy*, *200*, 379–386. doi:10.1016/j.renene.2022.09.046

Oxford Analytica. (2022). *Germany may struggle to fill new LNG import capacity*. Emerald Expert Briefings.

Özel Özcan, M. S., & Öten, C. (2022). Enerji kriz girdabı kavramsallaştırması bağlamında Orta Doğu'da petrol krizleri. *Bölgesel Araştırmalar Dergisi*, *6*(1), 174–208.

Özel Özcan, M. S., & Öten, C. (2022). Enerji Kriz Girdabı Kavramsallaştırması Bağlamında Orta Doğu'da Petrol Krizleri. *Bölgesel Araştırmalar Dergisi*, *6*(1), 174–208.

Öziç, E. A. (2018). *Türkiye'nin Yenilenebilir Enerji Potansiyeli ve Gelecek Hedefleri*. Ordu Üniversitesi Sosyal Bilimler Araştırmaları Dergisi.

Öztürk, S., & Saygın S. (2017). 1973 petrol krizinin ekonomiye etkileri ve stagflasyon olgusu. *Balkan Sosyal Bilimler Dergisi, 6*(12), 1-12.

Özturk, S., Sözdemir, A., & Ülger, O. (2013). The Real Crisis Waiting for the World: Oil Problem and Energy Security. *International Journal of Energy Economics and Policy*, *3*(4), 74–79.

Paganelli, M. P. (2022, March 1). Adam Smith and Economic Development in Theory and Practice: A Rejection of the Stadial Model? *Journal of the History of Economic Thought*, *44*(1), 98. doi:10.1017/S1053837220000309

Painuly, J. P. (2001). Barriers to renewable energy penetration; a framework for analysis. *Renewable Energy*, *24*(1), 73–89. doi:10.1016/S0960-1481(00)00186-5

Pan, J., Li, Y., Zhang, Y., & Ji, Z. (2023). China's Revolutionary Transition towards Carbon Neutrality and Prevention of Relevant Risks. *Chinese Journal of Urban and Environmental Studies*, 2350003.

Pandey, B., & Karki, A. (2016). *Hydroelectric energy: renewable energy and the environment*. CRC Press. doi:10.1201/9781315374840

Papadis, E., & Tsatsaronis, G. (2020). Challenges in the decarbonization of the energy sector. *Energy*, *205*, 118025. doi:10.1016/j.energy.2020.118025

Papadopoulos, A. M. (2016). Forty years of regulations on the thermal performance of the building envelope in Europe: Achievements, perspectives and challenges. *Energy and Building*, *127*, 942–952. doi:10.1016/j.enbuild.2016.06.051

Pascual, C., & Elkind, J. (2009). Introduction. In C. Pascual & J. Elkind (Eds.), *Energy security: Economics, politics, strategies and implications* (pp. 1–8). Brookings Institution Press.

Pascual, C., & Zambetakis, E. (2009). The geopolitics of energy: From security to survival. In C. Pascual & J. Elkind (Eds.), *Energy security: Economics, politics, strategies and implications* (pp. 9–35). Brookings Institution Press.

Pastukhova, M., Pepe, J., & Westphal, K. (2020, June 31). *Beyond the Green Deal: Upgrading the EU's Energy Diplomacy for a New Era.* SWP Comment. Retrieved from https://www.energiewende-global.com/fileadmin/user_upload/giz-website/Media_Library/Erneuerbare_Energien/Beyond_the_Green_Deal_Upgrading_the_EUs_Energy_Diplomacy_for_a_New_Era.pdf

Pekmezci, Z. (2020). *Nükleer Santrallere Karşı Yerel Halkın Bakışı: Sinop İli Örneği. Ondokuz Mayıs Üniversitesi Lisansüstü Eğitim Enstitüsü.* Yayımlanmamış Yüksek Lisans Tezi.

Peña-Ramos, J.A. (2021). Water Conflicts in Central Asia: Some Recommendations on the Non-Conflictual Use of Water. *Sustainability*, *13*(6), 3479. doi:10.3390/su13063479

Peñasco, C., & Díaz Anadón, L. (2023). Assessing the effectiveness of energy efficiency measures in the residential sector gas consumption through dynamic treatment effects: Evidence from England and Wales. *Energy Economics*, *117*, 106435. doi:10.1016/j.eneco.2022.106435

Pepe, J. M. (2020). The "Eastern Polygon" of the Trans-Siberian rail line: A critical factor for assessing Russia's strategy toward Eurasia and the Asia-Pacific. *Asia Europe Journal*, *18*(3), 305–324. doi:10.100710308-019-00543-5

Peter Dizikes. (2022, December 13). *Energy, War, and the Crisis in Ukraine.* Retrieved from https://news.mit.edu/2022/energy-war-and-crisis-ukraine-1213

Popkostova, Y. (2022, January). *Europe's Energy Crisis Conundrum.* The EUISS Is an Agency of the European Union. Retrieved from https://www.iss.europa.eu/sites/default/files/EUISSFiles/Brief_2_Energy%20Crisis.pdf

Prasad, R. (2019). *Larsen & Toubro's hydrocarbon arm get order worth over rs 7,000 crore in Algeria.* https://economictimes.indiatimes.com/industry/indl-goods/svs/engineering/larsen-toubros-hydrocarbon-arm-get-order-worth-over-rs-7000-crore-in-algeria/articleshow/67955504.cms?from=mdr

Priest, J. (2004). Mechanical energy. In C. Cleveland (Ed.), *Encyclopedia of energy* (Vol. 4, pp. 1–9). Elsevier. doi:10.1016/B0-12-176480-X/00078-4

Prontera, A. (2017). *The New Politics of Energy Security in the European Union and Beyond: States, Markets, Institutions.* Taylor & Francis. doi:10.4324/9781315555126

Qatar Airways. (2023). *About Qatar Airways.* Retrieved July 20, 2023 https://www.qatarairways.com/press-releases/en-WW/about/

QatarEnergy. (2022). *Our History.* Retrieved May 20, 2023 from https://www.qatarenergy.qa/en/WhoWeAre/Pages/OurHistory.aspx

Qatargas. (2023). *North Field.* Retrieved June 3, 2023 from https://www.qatargas.com/english/aboutus/north-field

Qinhua, X. U., & Chung, W. (2016). *China's Energy Policy from National and International Perspectives: The Energy Revolution and One Belt One Road Initiative*. City University of HK Press.

Qi, T., Winchester, N., Karplus, V. J., Zhang, D., & Zhang, X. (2016). An analysis of China's climate policy using the China-in-Global Energy Model. *Economic Modelling*, *52*, 650–660. doi:10.1016/j.econmod.2015.09.036

Qu, Z., & Perron, P. (2007). Estimating and testing structural changes in multivariate regressions. *Econometrica*, *75*(2), 459–502. doi:10.1111/j.1468-0262.2006.00754.x

Rabbi, M. F., Popp, J., Máté, D., & Kovács, S. (2022). Energy security and energy transition to achieve carbon neutrality. *Energies*, *15*(21), 8126. doi:10.3390/en15218126

Radovanovic, M., Filipović, S., & Andrejević Panić, A. (2021). Sustainable energy transition in Central Asia: Status and challenges. *Energy, Sustainability and Society*, *11*(1), 49. doi:10.118613705-021-00324-2

Rao, S., & Riahi, K. (2006). The role of non-CO2 greenhouse gases in climate change mitigation: Long-term scenarios for the 21st century. *The Energy Journal (Cambridge, Mass.)*, *27*(3), 177–200. doi:10.5547/ISSN0195-6574-EJ-VolSI2006-NoSI3-9

Rathore, N. S., & Panwar, N. L. (2022). *Fundamentals of renewable energy*. CRC Press.

Refai, H. A., Eissa, M. A., & Zeitun, R. (2021). The dynamics of the relationship between real estate and stock markets in an energy-based economy: The case of Qatar. *Journal of Economic Asymmetries*, *23*, 1–15. doi:10.1016/j.jeca.2021.e00200

Renewables Now 21. (2023, August 2). *Renewables 2019 Global Status Report*. REN21: https://www.ren21.net/gsr-2019

Report of the Ministry of Energy and Industry of the Kyrgyz Republic. (2013). *Development of Renewable Resources*. https://www.unescap.org/sites/default/files/C_Kyrgyz_Orozaliev_R.pdf

ReportW. S. (2020). Retrieved from: https://desapublications.un.org/file/558/download

Republic of Türkiye Ministry of Energy and Natural Resources. (2023, August 1). *Hidrolik*. https://enerji.gov.tr/bilgi-merkezi-enerji-hidrolik

Republic of Türkiye Ministry of Trade. (2022a). *Macaristan'da Güneş Enerjisi Kapasitesi 3.000 MW'ın Üzerine Çıktı*. https://dtybs.ticaret.gov.tr/blog/post/12260/

Republic of Türkiye Ministry of Trade. (2022b). *Özbekistan 8 GW Kapasiteli Yenilenebilir Enerji Üretmeyi Planlıyor*. https://dtybs.ticaret.gov.tr/blog/post/13477/#

Reuters. (2018, February 28). *Ukraine's Naftogaz Claims $2.56 Billion Victory in Gazprom Legal Battle*. Retrieved from https://www.reuters.com/article/us-ukraine-crisis-russia-gazprom-idUSKCN1GC2Z8

Reuters. (2022a, March 1). *Russia Says No Need for Western Banks, but Will Adjust*. Retrieved from https://www.reuters.com/markets/europe/russias-lukoil-says-oil-and-gas-sector-targeted-by-sanctions-2022-03-10/

Reuters. (2022b, March 10). *European Gas, Coal and Power Prices Hit Record Highs*. Retrieved from https://www.reuters.com/business/european-gas-coal-power-prices-hit-record-highs-2022-03-10/

Reuters. (2023, March 22). *Explainer: Does China need more Russian gas via the Power-of-Siberia 2 pipeline?* Retrieved from https://www.reuters.com/business/energy/does-china-need-more-russian-gas-via-power-of-siberia-2-pipeline-2023-03-22/

Roberts, D. (2012). Understanding Qatar's foreign policy objectives. *Mediterranean Politics*, *17*(2), 233–239. doi:10.1080/13629395.2012.695123

Ross, M. L. (2001). Does oil hinder democracy? *World Politics*, *53*(3), 325–361. doi:10.1353/wp.2001.0011

Rostow, W. W. (1991). *The Stages of Economic Growth: A Non-Communist Manifesto*. Cambridge University Press. doi:10.1017/CBO9780511625824

Roy, J. (2013). Energy efficiency: Technology, behavior, and development. In A. Goldthau (Ed.), *The handbook of global energy policy* (pp. 282–301). Wiley-Blackwell. doi:10.1002/9781118326275.ch17

Rozenberg, J., Hallegatte, S., Vogt-Schilb, A., Sassi, O., Guivarch, C., Waisman, H., & Hourcade, J.-C. (2010). Climate policies as a hedge against the uncertainty on future oil supply. *Climatic Change*, *101*(3), 663–668. doi:10.100710584-010-9868-8

Russian Crude Oil Tracker. (2023, July 27). *Bruegel | The Brussels-based Economic Think Tank*. Retrieved from https://www.bruegel.org/dataset/russian-crude-oil-tracker#:~:text=In%202021%2C%20Russia%20produced%20540,comprising%2013%25%20of%20global%20exports

Rusya-UkraynaS. K. E. N. E. (2023, March 14). Retrieved from https://www.trthaber.com/haber/dunya/rusya-ukrayna-savasi-kuresel-ekonomiyi-nasil-etkiledi-752972.html

Sachs, J. D. (2015). *The age of sustainable development*. Columbia University Press. doi:10.7312ach17314

Sadovskaya, Y., & Utyasheva, L. (2017). Human Silk Road. In M. Laruelle (Ed.), *The People-to-People Aspect of the Belt and Road Initiative in China's Belt and Road Initiative and its Impact in Central Asia* (pp. 109–125). The George Washington University Press.

Saghir, J. (2005). *Energy and Poverty: Myths, Links, and Policy Issues*. International Energy Forum in Amsterdam. Amsterdam: Energy & Mining Sector Board of World Bank.

Sahbani, L. (2020). *The main developments introduced by the Algerian new hydrocarbon law*. https://pwcalgerie.pwc.fr/fr/files/pdf/2020/01/en-algeria-pwc-hdyrocarbon-law-2020.pdf

Salameh, M. G. (2018). Will there ever be a post-oil era? In J. I. Considine & K.-W. Paik (Eds.), *Handbook of energy politics* (pp. 235–247). Edward Elgar. doi:10.4337/9781784712303.00020

Salameh, Z. (2014). Factors Promoting Renewable Energy Applications. In *Ziyad Salameh* (p. 1). Academic Press.

Saltybayev, Y. (2018). BRI and Kazakhstan. *Journal for International Relations and Sustainable Development*, *10*, 76–85.

Salut, S. (2006). Politique nationale du pétrole, sociétés nationales et pétrole franc. *Revue Historique (Paris, France)*, *2*(638), 355–388. doi:10.3917/rhis.062.0355

Samimi, A. J. (2011). Environmental Performance and HDI: Evidence from Countries Around the World. *Middle East Journal of Scientific Research*, *10*(3), 249–301. https://idosi.org/mejsr/mejsr10(3)11/3.pdf

Sánchez, M. (2011). Modelling anti-inflationary monetary targeting in Romania. *International Economic Journal*, *25*(1), 125–145. doi:10.1080/10168737.2010.487541

Saraswat, R., Sharma, S., & Saraswat, D. (2022). Effect of air pollution on climate. *International Journal of Research in Engineering and Scienc*, *10*(5), 22–25.

Sassi, M. (2003). *The emergence of the French oil industry between the two wars*. https://thebhc.org/sites/default/files/sassi.pdf

Sasu, D. D. (2023, Sep 20). *Agriculture in Nigeria - statistics and facts*. Statista: https://www.statista.com/topics/6729/agriculture-in-nigeria/#topicOverview

Satymov, R., Bogdanov, D., & Breyer, C. (2021). The value of fast transitioning to a fully sustainable energy system: The case of Turkmenistan. *IEEE Access : Practical Innovations, Open Solutions*, *9*, 13590–13611. doi:10.1109/ACCESS.2021.3050817

Saygın, H. (2006). Küresel Enerji Politikaları ve Türkiye. *Türk Harb-İş Dergisi*, (219), 26–31.

Schlachter, A. (2010). Worldwide Energy Crisis: Energy Trends in Brazil. *Revista Mexicana de Física*, *56*(2), 34–39.

Schmitter, P. C. (2002, July). *Neo-Functionalism*. European University Institute. Retrieved from https://www.eui.eu/Documents/DepartmentsCentres/SPS/Profiles/Schmitter/NeoNeoFunctionalismRev.pdf

Schneider, S. A. (1975). The Tiger Starts to Roar: The Origins of The Energy Crisis. *Berkeley Journal of Sociology*, *20*, 13–54.

Schramm, L., Krotz, U., & De Witte, B. (2022). Building 'Next Generation'after the pandemic: The implementation and implications of the EU Covid Recovery Plan. *Journal of Common Market Studies*, *60*(S1), 114–124. doi:10.1111/jcms.13375

Sciorati, G. (2021). *Time to Talk Climate Change in the Post-Soviet Region.* Italian Institute for International Political Studies. https://www.ispionline.it/en/publication/time-talk-climate-change-post-soviet-region-30008

Scoones, I., Leach, M., & Newell, P. (2015). *The politics of green transformations*. Taylor & Francis. doi:10.4324/9781315747378-1

Sèbe, B. (2010). In the shadow of the Algerian war: The United States and the Common Organisation of Saharan Regions (OCRS), 1957–62. *The Journal of Imperial and Commonwealth History*, *38*(2), 303–322. doi:10.1080/03086531003743999

Secretariat, E. C. (2013). *Investment climate and market structure review in the energy sector of Kazakhstan.* Brussels: Energy Charter Secretariat. www. energy charter. org/fileadmin/DocumentsMedia/ICMS/ICMS-Kazakhstan_2013_en.

SEE. (2023). *Smart Energy Education*. Retrieved from How Is Wealth Connected To Energy?: https://rb.gy/feqza

Selivanova, Y. (2010). Managing the patchwork of agreements in trade and investment. In A. Goldthau & J. M. Witte (Eds.), *Global energy governance: The new rules of the game* (pp. 49–72). Brookings Institution Press.

Senator, K. (2015). *The new legal framework of the hydrocarbons and its impact on investments in the sector. Conference of use of energetic resources policies: between the national development requirements and securing the international needs*. Université Sétif.

Sevim, C. (2012). Küresel enerji jeopolitiği ve enerji güvenliği. *Yaşar Üniversitesi E-Dergisi*, *7*(26), 4378–4391.

Shabafrouz, M. (2010). Oil and the eruption of the algerian civil war: A context-sensitive analysis of the ambivalent impact of resource abundance. *SSRN*, *118*, 1–45. doi:10.2139srn.1541906

Shadrina, E. (2019). *Renewable energy in Central Asian economies: role in reducing regional energy insecurity* (No. 993). ADBI Working Paper Series.

Shadrina, E. (2020). Non-hydropower renewable energy in central Asia: Assessment of deployment status and analysis of underlying factors. *Energies*, *13*(11), 2963. doi:10.3390/en13112963

Shaffer, B. (2009). *Energy politics*. University of Pennsylvania Press. doi:10.9783/9780812204520

Sharma, A., Rajpurohit, B. S., & Singh, S. N. (2018). A review on economics of power quality: Impact, assessment and mitigation. *Renewable & Sustainable Energy Reviews*, *88*, 363–372. doi:10.1016/j.rser.2018.02.011

Shen, X., & Lin, B. (2021). Does industrial structure distortion impact the energy intensity in China? *Sustainable Production and Consumption*, *25*, 551–562. doi:10.1016/j.spc.2020.12.012

Simmons, R. A., Coyle, E. D., & Chapman, B. (2014). Global energy policy perspectives. In E. D. Coyle & R. A. Simmons (Eds.), *Understanding the Global Energy Crisis* (pp. 27–72). Purdue University Press.

Simmons, R. A., Coyle, E. D., & Chapman, B. (2014). Global Energy Policy Perspectives. In R. A. Simmons & E. D. Coyle (Eds.), *Understanding the Global Energy Crisis* (pp. 27–72). Purdue University Press.

Simonov, E. (2020). Environmental Aspects of Belt and Road Projects in Central Asia. *Crude Accountability Environmental Justice*. https://crudeaccountability.org/environmental-aspects-of-belt-and-road-projects-incentral-asia/

Simpson, J., & McNamara, K. (2011). *Elements of energy Policy*. International Energy Agency.

Sims, G. P. (1991). Hydroelectric energy. *Energy Policy*, *19*(8), 776–786. doi:10.1016/0301-4215(91)90047-R

Skeet, I. (1989). *OPEC: Twenty-five years of prices and politics*. Cambridge University Press.

Smets, F. (1997). Measuring monetary policy shocks in France, Germany and Italy: The role of exchange rate. *SSRN*, *133*, 597–616. doi:10.2139srn.860664

Smets, F., & Wouters, R. (1999). The exchange rate and the monetary transmission mechanism in Germany. *De Economist*, *147*(4), 489–521. doi:10.1023/A:1003803228309

Smil, V. (1994). *Energy in world history*. Westview Press.

Smith, E. R., Carlisle, J., & Michaud, K. (2003). *Trust During an Energy Crisis*. UC Berkeley: University of California Energy Institute. Retrieved from https://escholarship.org/uc/item/3v30p0wh

Soeiro, S., & Dias, M. F. (2020). Energy cooperatives in Southern European countries: Are they relevant for sustainability targets? *Energy Reports*, *6*, 448–453. doi:10.1016/j.egyr.2019.09.006

Solangi, K. H., Islam, M. R., Saidur, R., Rahim, N. A., & Fayaz, H. (2011). A review on global solar energy policy. *Renewable & Sustainable Energy Reviews*, *15*(4), 2149–2163. doi:10.1016/j.rser.2011.01.007

Solar, C. (2023). *Causes, Effects and Solutions to the Global Energy Crisis*. Retrieved from https://coldwellsolar.com/commercial-solar-blog/causes-effects-and-solutions-to-the-global-energy-crisis/

Sönmez, Ş. (2007). *Cezayir bağimsizlik hareketi ve Türk kamuoyu (1954–1962)* [PhD Dissertation]. Hacettepe Üniversitesi, Ankara.

Sonone, S. S., Jadhav, S., Sankhla, M. S., & Kumar, R. (2020). Water contamination by heavy metals and their toxic effect on aquaculture and human health through food Chain. *Lett. Appl. NanoBioScience*, *10*(2), 2148–2166.

Sorbello, P. (2015). *The Role of Energy in Russian Foreign Policy towards Kazakhstan*. Energy Brains.

SoukissianT.O'HaganA. M.AzzellinoA.BoeroF.Brito e MeloA.ComiskeyP.GaoZ.HowellD.Le BoulluecM.MaisondieuC.ScottB.TedeschiE.MaheriA.PennockS. (2023). European Offshore Renewable Energy: Towards a Sustainable Future. Zenodo. https://doi.org/ doi:10.5281/ZENODO.7561906

Soustelle, J. (1959). *The Wealth of the Sahara*. https://www.foreignaffairs.com/articles/north-africa/1959-07-01/wealth-sahara

Sovacool, B. K., & Mukherjee, I. (2011). Conceptualizing and measuring energy security: A synthesized approach. *Energy*, *36*(8), 5343–5355. doi:10.1016/j.energy.2011.06.043

Sovacool, B. K., & Saunders, H. (2014). Competing policy packages and the complexity of energy security. *Energy*, *67*, 641–651. doi:10.1016/j.energy.2014.01.039

Sovacool, B. K., Sidortsov, R. V., & Jones, B. R. (2014). *Energy security, equality and justice*. Routledge.

Sowah, M. A. (2023). *Clean Air*. From Pollution to Solutions In Africa's Major Cities: https://rb.gy/in2tw

Sparrow, P. (2023). *Biomass Energy: Advantages and Disadvantages*. ianswer4u: https://www.ianswer4u.com/2012/02/biomass-energy-advantages-and.html#axzz3Qs5RV0Sb

State Committee for Industry, Energy and Subsoil Utilisation of the Kyrgyz Republic. (2018). http://ptfcar.org/wp-content/uploads/2018/06/5-Kyrgyzstan-State-Committee-on-Energy-Industry-and-Subsoil-Use-Marat-Chalponkulov-EN.pdf

Statista. (2022, November 21). *Coal Mining in Russia – Statistics and Facts.* Retrieved from https://www.statista.com/topics/7049/coal-mining-in-russia/#topicOverview

Statista. (2023). *Natural gas production in Qatar from 1989 to 2022.* Retrieved June 1, 2023 from https://www.statista.com/statistics/265336/natural-gas-production-in-qatar/

Statista. (2023, March 2). *Gas Inflow for Transit from Russia to Europe in Ukraine from February 1, 2022 to February 28, 2023, By Entry Point.* Retrieved from https://www.statista.com/statistics/1308480/ukraine-russian-gas-transit-volume-by-route/

Statistical, B. P. Review of World Energy. (2022). https://www.bp.com/content/dam/bp/business-sites/en/global/corporate/pdfs/energy-economics/statistical-review/bp-stats-review-2022-full-report.pdf

Stein, S. A. (2014). *Saharan Jews and the fate of French Algeria.* The University of Chicago Press. doi:10.7208/chicago/9780226123882.001.0001

Stern, J. (2007). The 2006 Russian–Ukrainian Gas Crisis: Implications for Europe. *Oxford Review of Economic Policy, 23*(2), 226–240.

Stern, J., & Zafirakis, D. (2010). The 2009 Russia–Ukraine Gas Dispute: Implications for EU-Russia Gas Relations. *International Affairs, 86*(4), 887–909.

Stern, N., & Xie, C. (2023). China's new growth story: Linking the 14th Five-Year Plan with the 2060 carbon neutrality pledge. *Journal of Chinese Economic and Business Studies, 21*(1), 5–25. doi:10.1080/14765284.2022.2073172

Stern, R. (2007). The Iranian petroleum crisis and United States national security. *Proceedings of the National Academy of Sciences of the United States of America, 104*(1), 377–382. doi:10.1073/pnas.0603903104 PMID:17190820

Stiglitz, J. E. (2011). A new agenda for global warming. In *The Economists' Voice: Top Economists Take On Today's Problems* (pp. 22–27). Columbia University Press. doi:10.7312/columbia/9780231143653.003.0003

Strikeleva, E. (2018). Influence of Land and Water Rights on Land Degradation in Central Asia. *Hydrological Impacts of Climate Change and Land Use/Land Cover Change, 10*(9), 1242. doi:10.3390/w10091242

Sulich, A., & Zema, T. (2023, June). The green energy transition in Germany: a bibliometric study. In Forum Scientiae Oeconomia (Vol. 11, No. 2). Academic Press.

Suna, M., Ozcan, O., & Öten, C. (2022). *Turkish Energy Policy and Energy Security.* IJOPEC Publication Limited.

Sun, Y. (2020). The achievement, significance and future prospect of China's renewable energy initiative. *International Journal of Energy Research, 44*(15), 12209–12244. doi:10.1002/er.5243

Swisher, J. N. (1996). Regulatory and Mixed Policy Options for Reducing Energy Use and Carbon Emissions. *Mitigation and Adaptation Strategies for Global Change, 1*(1), 23–49. doi:10.1007/BF00625614

Syzdykova, A. (2020). Kazakistan'ın Yenilenebilir Enerji Potansiyeli. *Ekonomi İşletme ve Maliye Araştırmaları Dergisi, 2*(1), 79–88. doi:10.38009/ekimad.699911

T.C. Dışişleri Bakanlığı AB Başkanlığı. (2023). *Fasıl 15: Enerji.* https://www.ab.gov.tr/fasil-15-enerji_80.html

T.C. Enerji ve Tabi Kaynaklar Bakanlığı. (2023). *Yenilenebilir Enerji Çalışmaları.* https://enerji.gov.tr/enerji-isleri-genel-mudurlugu-yenilenebilir-enerji

Taghizadeh-Hesary, F., & Yoshino, N. (2020). Sustainable Solutions for Green Financing and Investment in Renewable Energy Projects. *Energies*, *13*(4), 788. doi:10.3390/en13040788

Tan, H. (2022, June 21). *Europe is Drawing Up Emergency Plans to Switch Back to Coal after Russia Cuts Natural-Gas Supplies*. Business Insider. Retrieved from https://www.businessinsider.com/europe-energy-emergency-plans-coal-power-russia-cuts-gas-supply-2022-6

Tass. (2021, November 21). *Ukrainian Government Claims it is at 'Energy War' with Russia*. Retrieved from https://tass.com/world/1360437

Tass. (2023, July 27). *Russia, Algeria Agree on Extension of Russian Companies' Participation in Gas Projects*. Retrieved from https://tass.com/economy/1653073

Taylor, M. (2021). China's evolving energy security strategy. *Asian Affairs*, *52*(4), 890–913. doi:10.1080/03068374.2021.2004031

Teodoro, R. (2023). Eni Inks Deal to Build Hybrid Renewables-Gas Plant in Kazakhstan. *Rigzone*. https://www.rigzone.com/news/eni_inks_deal_to_build_hybrid_renewablesgas_plant_in_kazakhstan-09-jun-2023-173013-article/

The Kazakhstan energy politics: is oil diversification a geopolitical conundrum? (2022). *Special Eurasia*.

The White House. (2023, April 3). *Joint Statement on U.S.-EU Task Force on Energy Security*. Retrieved from https://www.whitehouse.gov/briefing-room/statements-releases/2023/04/03/joint-statement-on-u-s-eu-task-force-on-energy-security/

The World Bank. (2023). *GDP Growth Qatar*. Retrieved June 5, 2023 https://data.worldbank.org/indicator/NY.GDP.MKTP.KD.ZG?locations=QA

Tian, C., Li, X., Xiao, L., & Zhu, B. (2022). Exploring the impact of green credit policy on green transformation of heavy polluting industries. *Journal of Cleaner Production*, *335*, 130257. doi:10.1016/j.jclepro.2021.130257

Tong, Zh., Xunpeng, Sh., Dayong, Zh., & Junji, X. (2019). Socio-economic development and electricity access in developing economies: A long-run model averaging approach. *Energy Policy*, *132*, 223–23. doi:10.1016/j.enpol.2019.05.031

Tordo, S., Brandon, S. T., & Noora, A. (2011). *National oil companies and value creation*. World Bank Working Paper, No. 218.

Türk Devletleri Teşkilatı. (2021). *Türk Dünyası 2040 Vizyonu*. https://turkicstates.org/assets/pdf/haberler/turk-dunyasi-2040-vizyonu-2396-98.pdf

Türkçe, B. B. C. (2023, April 28). *Avrupa'da enerji krizi: Rusya Kuzey Akımı'nı kesti, AB ne yapacak?* BBC News Türkçe: https://www.bbc.com/turkce/haberler-dunya-62971871

Tursumbayeva, M., Muratuly, A., Baimatova, N., Karaca, F., & Kerimray, A. (2022). Cities of Central Asia: New Hotspots of Air Pollution in the World. SSRN *Electronic Journal*. doi:10.2139/ssrn.4208086

Turton, H., & Barreto, L. (2006). Long-term security of energy supply and climate change. *Energy Policy*, *34*(15), 2232–2250. doi:10.1016/j.enpol.2005.03.016

U.S Energy Information Administration. (2023, July 19). *Electricity*. EIA: https://www.eia.gov/international/data/world/electricity/electricity-consumption?pd=2&p=0000002&u=0&f=A&v=mapbubble&a=-&i=none&vo=value&t=C&g=00000000000000000000000000000000000000000000001&l=249-ruvvvvvfvtvnvv1vrvvvvfvvvvvvfvvvou20evvvvvvvvvvnvvvs0008&s=315532800000&e=1609459200000&

U.S. Energy Information Administration. (n.d.). https://www.eia.gov/todayinenergy/detail.php?id=49436

UN. (2021). *Five ways to jump-start the renewable energy transition now*. July 03, 2023, from United Nation: https://rb.gy/f9733

UNEP. (2022, 08 30). *Pollution Action Note – Data you need to know*. United Nations Environment Program: https://rb.gy/kabwe

UNFCC. (2017). *The Paris Agreement*. Retrieved June 5, 2023 http://unfccc.int/paris_agreement/items/9485.php

Uribe, J. M., Mosquera-López, S., & Arenas, O. J. (2022). Assessing the relationship between electricity and natural gas prices in European markets in times of distress. *Energy Policy*, *166*, 113018. doi:10.1016/j.enpol.2022.113018

US Energy Information Administration (EIA). (2021, February 12). *Top World Oil Producers, Exporters, and Consumers*. Retrieved from https://www.eia.gov/todayinenergy/detail.php?id=47776

US Energy Information Administration (EIA). (2023, July 2). *Europe is A Key Destination for Russia's Energy Exports*. Retrieved from https://www.eia.gov/todayinenergy/detail.php?id=51618

US Energy Information Administration (EIA). (2023, June 16). *Russia*. Retrieved from https://www.eia.gov/international/analysis/country/RUS

Uzun, Y. (2023). Yenilenebilir Enerji-Sürdürülebilir Kalkınma: Rusya Örneği. *Ekonomik Büyüme ve Verimlilik Politikaları*, 46-67.

Vakulchuk, R., Øverland, I., Aminjonov, F., Abylkasymova, A., Eshchanov, B., & Moldokanov, D. (2019). *BRI in central Asia: Overview of Chinese projects. Central Asia Data-Gathering and Analysis Team*. CADGAT.

Vakulenko, S. (2023, April 18). *What Russia's First Gas Pipeline to China Reveals About a Planned Second One*. Carnegie Endowment for International Peace. Retrieved from https://carnegieendowment.org/politika/89552

Valentine, S. C. (2011). Emerging symbiosis: Renewable energy and energy security. *Renewable & Sustainable Energy Reviews*, *15*(9), 4572–4578. doi:10.1016/j.rser.2011.07.095

Van de Graff, T., & Colgan, J. (2016). Global energy governance: A review and research agenda. *Palgrave Communications*, *2*(1), 1–12. doi:10.1057/palcomms.2015.47

van Vuuren, D. P., Stehfest, E., den Elzen, M. G. J., Kram, T., van Vliet, J., Deetman, S., Isaac, M., Klein Goldewijk, K., Hof, A., Mendoza Beltran, A., Oostenrijk, R., & van Ruijven, B. (2011). RCP2.6: Exploring the possibility to keep global mean temperature increase below 2°C. *Climatic Change*, *109*(1), 95–116. doi:10.100710584-011-0152-3

van Wees, M. T., Uyterlinde, M. A., & Maly, M. (2002). Energy efficiency and renewable energy policy in the Czech Republic within the framework of accession to the European Union. *Energy*, *27*(11), 1057–1067. doi:10.1016/S0360-5442(02)00068-3

Venn, F. (2016). *The oil crisis*. Routledge. doi:10.4324/9781315840819

Veum, K., & Bauknecht, D. (2019). How to reach the EU renewables target by 2030? An analysis of the governance framework. *Energy Policy*, *127*, 299–307. doi:10.1016/j.enpol.2018.12.013

Vieira, S. (2023). *Pros and Cons of 10 Types of Energy*. AJE Springer Nature: https://www.aje.com/arc/energy-types-pros-cons/

Vivoda, V. (2009). Diversification of oil import sources and energy security: A key strategy or an elusive objective? *Energy Policy*, *37*(11), 4615–4623. doi:10.1016/j.enpol.2009.06.007

Walker, M. (1996). *Chapter II: Concept of Energy*. Centre Daily Times.

Wang, C., Raza, S. A., Adebayo, T. S., Yi, S., & Shah, M. I. (2023). The roles of hydro, nuclear and biomass energy towards carbon neutrality target in China: A policy-based analysis. *Energy*, *262*, 125303. doi:10.1016/j.energy.2022.125303

Wang, H., & Zhang, R. (2022). Effects of environmental regulation on CO2 emissions: An empirical analysis of 282 cities in China. *Sustainable Production and Consumption*, *29*, 259–272. doi:10.1016/j.spc.2021.10.016

Wang, K., Zhang, Y., Lei, L., & Qiu, S. (2021). Evaluation on the efficiency of LED energy enterprises in China by employing the DEA model. *Mathematics*, *9*(19), 2356. doi:10.3390/math9192356

Wang, S., Sun, L., & Iqbal, S. (2022). Green financing role on renewable energy dependence and energy transition in E7 economies. *Renewable Energy*, *200*, 1561–1572. doi:10.1016/j.renene.2022.10.067

Wang, X. C., Klemeš, J. J., Wang, Y., Dong, X., Wei, H., Xu, Z., & Varbanov, P. S. (2020). Water-Energy-Carbon Emissions nexus analysis of China: An environmental input-output model-based approach. *Applied Energy*, *261*, 114431. doi:10.1016/j.apenergy.2019.114431

Wang, Z., Kong, Y., & Li, W. (2022). Review on the development of China's natural gas industry in the background of "carbon neutrality. *Natural Gas Industry B*, *9*(2), 132–140. doi:10.1016/j.ngib.2021.08.021

Wariavwalla, B. (1975). The Energy Crisis, the Developing World and Strategy. *Adelphi Papers*, *115*(115), 32–37. doi:10.1080/05679327508448397

Watt, W. (2022, August 4). *How is wealth connected to energy?* Watt Watchers: https://www.watt-watchers.com/how-is-wealth-connected-to-energy/

Weinthal, E., & Watters, K. (2010). Transnational environmental activism in Central Asia: The coupling of domestic law and international conventions. *Environmental Politics*, *19*(5), 782–807. doi:10.1080/09644016.2010.508311

Werenfels, I. (2002). Obstacles to privatisation of state-owned industries in Algeria: The Political Economy of a Distributive Conflict. *Journal of North African Studies*, *7*(1), 1–28. doi:10.1080/13629380208718455

Werenfels, I. (2007). *Managing instability in Algeria elites and political change since 1995*. Routledge. doi:10.4324/9780203964682

Wiel, S., Martin, N., Levine, M., Price, L., & Sathaye, J. (1998). The role of building energy efficiency in managing atmospheric carbon dioxide. *Environmental Science & Policy, 1*(1), 27–38. https://doi.org/https://doi.org/10.1016/S1462-9011(98)00004-5

Williams, S. (2013). Turkmenistan Natural Gas Reserves Estimates. *The Wall Street Journal, 12*.

Wilson, T. (2022, October 25). Saudi Arabia Willing to Pump More Oil if Global Energy Crisis Worsens. *Financial Times*. Retrieved from https://www.ft.com/content/8598d326-2989-4468-9bcd-a9a905ca4f67

Wiser, W. H. (2000). *Energy resources: Occurrence, production, conversion, use*. Springer. doi:10.1007/978-1-4612-1226-3

Wisevoter. (2022). https://wisevoter.com/country-rankings/renewable-energy-by-country/#map

Wolff, P. (2016). *China's 'Belt and Road' Initiative- Challenges and Opportunities*. German Development Institute.

Wołowiec, T., Kolosok, S., Vasylieva, T., Artyukhov, A., Skowron, Ł., Dluhopolskyi, O., & Sergiienko, L. (2022). Sustainable governance, energy security, and energy losses of Europe in turbulent times. *Energies*, *15*(23), 8857. doi:10.3390/en15238857

World Bank. (1982). *Algeria the five-year development plan and the medium-term prospects for 1980-84*. Report No. 3668-AL.

World Energy Outlook. (2022). *International Energy Agency.* Retrieved from https://iea.blob.core.windows.net/assets/830fe099-5530-48f2-a7c1-11f35d510983/WorldEnergyOutlook2022.pdf

Worldometer. (n.d.). *Qatar Oil.* https://www.worldometers.info/oil/qatar-oil/

Wu, H., Carroll, J., & Denny, E. (2022). Harnessing citizen investment in community-based energy initiatives: A discrete choice experiment across ten European countries. *Energy Research & Social Science, 89*, 102552. doi:10.1016/j.erss.2022.102552

WWF. (2011). *2050 Yılında %100 Yenilenebilir Enerji.* https://www.wwf.org.tr/?1410/2050deyuzde100yenilebilirenerji

Xiang, N., Wang, L., Zhong, S., Zheng, C., Wang, B., & Qu, Q. (2021). How does the world view China's carbon policy? A sentiment analysis on Twitter data. *Energies, 14*(22), 7782. doi:10.3390/en14227782

Xu, B., Luo, Y., Xu, R., & Chen, J. (2021). Exploring the driving forces of distributed energy resources in China: Using a semiparametric regression model. *Energy, 236*, 121452. doi:10.1016/j.energy.2021.121452

Yang, T., & Liu, W. (2019). Health effects of energy intensive sectors and the potential health co-benefits of a low carbon industrial transition in China. *International Journal of Environmental Research and Public Health, 16*(17), 3022. doi:10.3390/ijerph16173022 PMID:31438537

Yang, Y., Wang, H., Löschel, A., & Zhou, P. (2022). Energy transition toward carbon-neutrality in China: Pathways, implications and uncertainties. *Front. Eng. Manag., 9*(3), 358–372. doi:10.100742524-022-0202-8

Yao, L. (2022). Domestic dynamics and china's engagement in global renewable energy governance. *The Chinese Journal of International Politics, 15*(1), 69–86. doi:10.1093/cjip/poac004

Yazdani, M., Torkayesh, A. E., Santibanez-Gonzalez, D. R., & Otaghsara, S. K. (2020). Evaluation of renewable energy resources using integrated Shannon Entropy—EDAS model. *Sustainable Operations and Computers, 1*, 35–42. doi:10.1016/j.susoc.2020.12.002

Yergin, D. (2006). Ensuring energy security. *Foreign Affairs, 85*(2), 69–82. doi:10.2307/20031912

Yıldızoğlu, E. (2022, 16 August). Enerji Krizinin Bu Sefer Küresel Olması Dünyayı Nasıl Değiştiriyor? *BBC News.* Retrieved from https://www.bbc.com/turkce/articles/cp6kpy4g4r6o

Yilmaz, E. A., & Hatice, C. A. N. (2018). Türkiye'nin yenilenebilir enerji potansiyeli ve gelecek hedefleri. *Ordu Üniversitesi Sosyal Bilimler Enstitüsü Sosyal Bilimler Araştırmaları Dergisi, 8*(3), 525–535.

York, R. (2012). Do alternative energy sources displace fossil fuels? *Nature Climate Change, 2*(6), 441–443. doi:10.1038/nclimate1451

Yorucu, V., & Mehmet, O. (2018). *The Southern Energy Corridor: Turkey's Role in European Energy Security* (Vol. 60). Springer International Publishing. doi:10.1007/978-3-319-63636-8

Yu, K. (2023). *China's Energy Security in the Twenty-First Century: The Role of Global Governance and Climate Change* (Vol. 2). Hong Kong University Press. doi:10.2307/jj.4303780

Yu, Z., Ridwan, I. L., Tanveer, M., & Khan, S. A. R. (2023). Investigating the nexuses between transportation Infrastructure, renewable energy Sources, and economic Growth: Striving towards sustainable development. *Ain Shams Engineering Journal, 14*(2), 101843. doi:10.1016/j.asej.2022.101843

Zabanova, Y. (2023). Towards a Geoeconomics of Energy Transition in Central Asia's Hydrocarbon-Producing Countries. In R. Sabyrbekov, I. Overland, & R. Vakulchuk (Eds.), *Climate Change in Central Asia. SpringerBriefs in Climate Studies*. Springer. doi:10.1007/978-3-031-29831-8_8

Zachmann, G., Sgaravatti, G., & McWilliams, B. (2023, July 27). *European natural gas imports*. Bruegel. Retrieved from https://www.bruegel.org/dataset/european-natural-gas-imports

Zettelmeyer, J., Tagliapietra, S., Zachmann, G., & Heussaff, C. (2022, December). *Beating the European Energy Crisis*. International Monetary Fund. Retrieved from https://www.imf.org/en/Publications/fandd/issues/2022/12/beating-the-european-energy-crisis-Zettelmeyer

Zgajewski, T. (2014, June). *Energy Efficiency: The Ever-Neglected Priority of The European Energy Strategy*. Egmont Paper 66: The Royal Institute for International Relations. Retrieved from https://www.egmontinstitute.be/app/uploads/2014/05/ep66.pdf?type=pdf+2014

Zhang, D., Wang, J., Lin, Y., Si, Y., Huang, C., Yang, J., Huang, B., & Li, W. (2017). Present situation and future prospect of renewable energy in China. *Renewable & Sustainable Energy Reviews*, *76*, 865–871. doi:10.1016/j.rser.2017.03.023

Zhang, H., Xiong, P., Yang, S., & Yu, J. (2023). Renewable energy utilization, green finance and agricultural land expansion in China. *Resources Policy*, *80*, 103163. doi:10.1016/j.resourpol.2022.103163

Zhang, S., Andrews-Speed, P., & Perera, P. (2015). The evolving policy regime for pumped storage hydroelectricity in China: A key support for low-carbon energy. *Applied Energy*, *150*, 15–24. doi:10.1016/j.apenergy.2015.03.103

Zhao, C., Ju, S., Xue, Y., Ren, T., Ji, Y., & Chen, X. (2022). China's energy transitions for carbon neutrality: Challenges and opportunities. *Carbon Neutrality*, *1*(1), 7. doi:10.100743979-022-00010-y

Zhao, P., Lu, Z., Fang, J., Paramati, S. R., & Jiang, K. (2020). Determinants of renewable and non-renewable energy demand in China. *Structural Change and Economic Dynamics*, *54*, 202–209. doi:10.1016/j.strueco.2020.05.002

Zou, C., Zhao, Q., Zhang, G., & Xiong, B. (2016). Energy revolution: From a fossil energy era to a new energy era. *Natural Gas Industry B*, *3*(1), 1–11. doi:10.1016/j.ngib.2016.02.001

Zreik, M. (2021). China and Europe in Africa: Competition or Cooperation? *Malaysian Journal of International Relations, 9*(1), 51-67.

Zreik, M. (2022). US-China Relations in The Era of Multi-Polarism: Trade War Between the Two Economic Giants. *Eurasian Research Journal*, *4*(2), 43–65. doi:10.53277/2519-2442-2022.2-03

Zreik, M. (2023). Analytical study on Foreign Direct Investment Divestment Inflows and Outflows in Developing Economies: Evidence of China. *Chinese Economy*, *56*(6), 1–16. doi:10.1080/10971475.2023.2193118

Zreik, M. (2023b). The Integration of China's Belt and Road Initiative into Global Supply Chains: New Pathways for Social and Environmental Responsibility. In A. Taghipour (Ed.), *Government Impact on Sustainable and Responsible Supply Chain Management* (pp. 74–94). IGI Global. doi:10.4018/978-1-6684-9062-4.ch005

About the Contributors

Merve Suna Ozel Ozcan is an Associate Professor of International Relations at Kirikkale University in Turkey. She majored in history and graduated from Gazi University's Department of International Relations in 2011. In 2013, she joined Kirikkale University as a research assistant. In 2014, she earned her Master's degree in the Department of Political and Social Science from Gazi University and subsequently started her doctoral studies in International Relations at Kirikkale University. She completed her PhD in International Relations in 2019 and was appointed Associate Professor at Kirikkale University in 2020. "Additionally, she holds the position of Vice Chair in the IR department." She is pursuing a second PhD in Political and Social Sciences at Gazi University. Her research interests include Russian Studies, the role of great powers, energy, and international relations of Eurasia. Her work has been published in numerous book chapters and papers. She has also participated in several meetings and conferences related to her field of work in various countries, such as Europe, Central Asia, and the Balkans.

* * *

Ejazul Haq Ateed is an accomplished researcher with a profound academic background. He holds a Master's Degree in International Relations from Kirikkale University in Türkiye. Prior to this, he earned his Bachelor's Degree in International Relations from the distinguished International Islamic University in Islamabad, Pakistan. Notably, he was formerly affiliated with the Center for Research and Security Studies (CRSS) based in Islamabad, Pakistan. Presently, he serves as a contributing researcher at the esteemed International Institute for Global Strategic Analysis (IIGSA). His scholarly pursuits encompass an array of vital subjects, including International Security, Central Asia, South Asia, and the Middle East. Noteworthy is his affiliation with Afghanistan.

Aslan Azimzadeh received a bachelor's degree in World Economy at Azerbaijan State University of Economics (UNEC). In 2019-2021, he graduated with honors from Azerbaijan State University of Economics (UNEC) with a master's degree in "International Finance and Currency Credit Relations" majoring in "World Economy". The topic of the master's thesis was "The main directions contributing the sustainable development of the financial system of the People's Republic of China." In 2021, he was admitted to the postgraduate study in "World Economy" at Azerbaijan State University of Economics (UNEC).He is a member of the Chinese Economists Society. He is a researcher at UNEC "One Belt One Road" research center. Since 2021, he has been a lecturer of the Department of International Economics of the Azerbaijan State University of Economics. Since 2022, he is a lecturer of the Department of Economics of the Azerbaijan State University of Economics.At the same time, since 2021, he is senior lecturer of the Department of Economics and Economic Relations of Odlar Yurdu University. Field of research: Chinese economy, Macroeconomics, International Finance, Development Economics, Advanced mechanisms of economic management in modern conditions.

Mürsel Bayram received his bachelor's, master's, and doctoral degrees from Selçuk University, Ahi Evran University, and Kırıkkale University, respectively. He is currently the Head of the Department of African Studies at the Institute for Area Studies, Social Sciences University of Ankara. He is the author of Une histoire diplomatique des États ouest-africains (Diplomatic History of West African States) and Çin-Afrika İş Birliği (China-Africa Cooperation). Bayram is also the editor of the books titled Mağrib Diplomasisi (Maghreb Diplomacy), Afrika Yıllığı 2021 (Africa Yearbook 2021), and Doğu Afrika'da Siyaset ve Diplomasi (Politics and Diplomacy in East Africa).

Mukesh Shankar Bharti is a research scholar with a research background in foreign policy analysis and social science research. The author holds a PhD degree in International Relations with a specialization in East and Central Europe. His research area includes democracy, political institutions, European Union and South Asia.

Emine Erden Kaya is an Assistant Professor and currently a member of the Political Science and Public Administration department at Amasya University. She graduated from the Department of Political Science and Public Administration at Girne American University in 2009. She got her master's degree in Political and Social Science at Gazi University in 2014. Also, she completed her PhD in Politics and Social Sciences program at Gazi University in 2021. Her research interests are comparative politics and ideologies. She has published about Racism, Islamophobia, Ethnic Conflicts and the West and Rest Dichotomy.

Şeyma Eşki Çaylak graduated from the Department of Public Administration at Selçuk University Faculty of Economics and Administrative Sciences in 2009. In 2011, she was appointed as a research assistant in the Department of Public Administration at Muş Alparslan University Faculty of Economics and Administrative Sciences. She completed her master's degree in 2014 with a thesis on Public Administration Ethics in the Department of Administrative Sciences at Ankara University Faculty of Political Sciences. In 2022, she successfully completed her doctoral studies with a thesis titled "Implementation and Transformation of Performance Audit in the Government: 1996-2010 Court of Accounts Experience." PhD Eşki Çaylak currently works as a Research Assistant at Muş Alparslan University. Her research interests are public administration reform, ethics, public financial management and auditing. She has published about Local Governments, Public personnel system, European Union, Türkiye-France Relations, SAI audit, Ethical practices, Accountability.

Aida Guliyeva is an Associate Professor, PHD of economic science, dean of the faculty "SABAH QROUPS" Azerbaijan State University of Economics, UNEC She was born on August, 28 1959. She graduated from Baku State University, mechanic-mathematical faculty and aspirantura ASUE (UNEC). She had postdoctoral research in Oxford University, UK and MBA courses certificates in GSU, Atlanta, USA. She published more than 75 scientific researches (both in Azerbaijan and abroad) including 4 monographs and 1 manual The spheres of her scientific activity are: economic theory, macroeconomics, economic development, new economy and technologies. She was awarded by the medal of honor of Azerbaijan "TARAGGI."

Rajoli Siddharth Jayaprakash is a Ph.D scholar at the Center for Russian and Central Asian Studies JNU. He is working on the political economy of Sanctions. His area of interests includes: Russian politics and energy studies

Rebeca Jiménez-Rodríguez received her bachelor degree in Economics from the University of Salamanca, Spain, in 1998. This was followed by her master degree in Quantitative Economics in 2000 and her Ph.D. in Economics from the University of Alicante, Spain, in 2003. She is currently Full Professor at the University of Salamanca, Spain. She has previously taught at the University of Alicante, University of Málaga and University Autónoma de Barcelona, and she has been a post-doctoral Marie Curie fellow at the University of Salerno, Italy. She has also worked at European Central Bank and Bank of Spain. Her fields of interest include econometrics, applied macroeconomics and international economics. She has over 30 academic articles in Energy Economics, International Journal of Central Banking, The Energy Journal, Review of Development Economics, Journal of Policy Modeling, among others.

Selçuk Efe Kuçukkambak completed his undergraduate education at Istanbul University, Faculty of Business Administration, Department of Business Administration as an "Honor Student." Then, he completed the Marketing Management Master's Program at Istanbul University, Faculty of Business Administration, Institute of Business Economics, "International Marketing Strategies and the L'oreal Turkey Example" between 2011 and 2014—the researcher who completed the MSc. Program as a "High Honor Student," graduated from the Aydın Adnan Menderes University Social Sciences Institute Business Administration Doctorate Program between 2015 and 2020 with the doctoral thesis, "Measuring Consumer-Based Brand Equity in Touristic Destinations: A Research in Fethiye." After completing his specialization in marketing, the researcher has published many publications in highly prestigious academic publishing organizations at home and abroad. In addition to his marketing expertise, the researcher has been involved in multidisciplinary research by conducting joint studies in different disciplines in the field of social sciences. The researcher, who gave many seminars on quantitative research methods in the country, especially in the social sciences field, also participated in various research projects financed by the European Union. Currently, the researcher continues to conduct academic studies on numerous subheadings in the marketing discipline, such as consumer behavior, tourism marketing, neuromarketing, and marketing research.

Mustafa Yasir Kurt received his Master degree from the Department of International Relations at Istanbul Medeniyet University, Türkiye, with his thesis titled "An examination on the effect of national oil companies on domestic and foreign policy: The case of Algeria-Sonatrach". Kurt joined Social Sciences University of Ankara Institute for Area Studies as a research assistant in 2019.

Ulviyya Rzayeva is the post-doctoral Researcher at the Department of Digital Technologies and Applied Informatics, Azerbaijan State University of Economics, Baku Azerbaijan. Her research interests include mathematical modelling, fuzzy systems, econometrics, and international finance.

Ayushi Saini is a Junior Research Fellow and a Ph.D. candidate in the Centre for Russian and Central Asian Studies at Jawaharlal Nehru University, New Delhi. Her area of interest resides at the intersection of environment and international relations. Currently, she is working on the Belt and Road Initiative and its impact on Kazakhstan's ecology and human security.

Marcelo Sánchez is a Staff member at the European Central Bank. He has received a Ph.D. degree from the University of California at Berkeley. His areas of specialization are Macroeconomics, Economic Growth and International Finance.

Yusuf Abubakar Wara is an Assistant Professor at the Kastamonu University, Turkiye. He was born in 1982 at Wara district in Kebbi state of Nigeria. He was educated at Federal Government College Ilorin between 1988-1993. He graduated from Ahmadu Bello University, Department of Political Science, in 2010. He completed his master's degree in Gazi University Department of International Relations in 2015 and his Ph.D. in Political and Social Sciences in 2021. He is an analyst in Political Science, Good Governance and Diplomacy.

Mohamad Zreik, a Postdoctoral Fellow at Sun Yat-sen University, is a recognized scholar in International Relations, specializing in China's Arab-region foreign policy. His recent work in soft power diplomacy compares China's methods in the Middle East and East Asia. His extensive knowledge spans Middle Eastern Studies, China-Arab relations, East Asian and Asian Affairs, Eurasian geopolitics, and Political Economy, providing him a unique viewpoint in his field. Dr. Zreik is a proud recipient of a PhD from Central China Normal University (Wuhan). He's written numerous acclaimed papers, many focusing on China's Belt and Road Initiative and its Arab-region impact. His groundbreaking research has established him as a leading expert in his field. Presently, he furthers his research on China's soft power diplomacy tactics at Sun Yat-sen University. His significant contributions make him a crucial figure in understanding contemporary international relations.

Index

F

G

H

I

K

L

N

O

P

Q

R

S

T

U

W

www.ingramcontent.com/pod-product-compliance
Lightning Source LLC
LaVergne TN
LVHW062153300926
849161LV00010B/2653
* 9 7 9 8 3 6 9 3 0 4 4 0 2 *